AID IN PLACE OF MIGRATION?

AID IN PLACE OF MIGRATION?

Selected contributions to an ILO-UNHCR meeting

Edited by
W. R. Böhning and M.-L. Schloeter-Paredes

A WEP study

INTERNATIONAL LABOUR OFFICE   GENEVA

Copyright © International Labour Organization 1994
First published 1994

Publications of the International Labour Office enjoy copyright under Protocol 2 of the Universal Copyright Convention. Nevertheless, short excerpts from them may be reproduced without authorization, on condition that the source is indicated. For rights of reproduction or translation, application should be made to the Publications Branch (Rights and Permissions), International Labour Office, CH-1211 Geneva 22, Switzerland. The International Labour Office welcomes such applications.

Böhning, W. R.; Schloeter-Paredes, M.-L.
Aid in place of migration? Selected contributions to an ILO-UNHCR meeting
Geneva, International Labour Office, 1994

/International migration/, /Emigration/, /Development aid/, /Economic and social development/, /Role of OECD countries/, /Central America/, /East Africa/, /Eastern Europe/.
14.09.2
ISBN 92-2-108749-2

ILO Cataloguing in Publication Data

The designations employed in ILO publications, which are in conformity with United Nations practice, and the presentation of material therein do not imply the expression of any opinion whatsoever on the part of the International Labour Office concerning the legal status of any country, area or territory or of its authorities, or concerning the delimitation of its frontiers.
The responsibility for opinions expressed in signed articles, studies and other contributions rests solely with their authors, and publication does not constitute an endorsement by the International Labour Office of the opinions expressed in them.
Reference to names of firms and commercial products and processes does not imply their endorsement by the International Labour Office, and any failure to mention a particular firm, commercial product or process is not a sign of disapproval.

ILO publications can be obtained through major booksellers or ILO local offices in many countries, or direct from ILO Publications, International Labour Office, CH-1211 Geneva 22, Switzerland. A catalogue or list of new publications will be sent free of charge from the above address.

Contents

Introduction 1
by W. R. Böhning and M.-L. Schloeter-Paredes
    1. Background 1
    2. Why focus on international aid? 4
    3. Quo vadis UNHCR and ILO? 7

1. Towards a comprehensive refugee policy: 13
Conflict and refugees in the post-Cold War world
by A. Suhrke
    1. From World War to Cold War 14
    2. Peacemaking and the crisis of reconstruction 18
    3. State v. People 25
    4. New challenges for a comprehensive refugee policy 29
    5. Conclusions and policy implications 33

2. Can foreign aid reduce East-West migration in Europe, ... 39
with particular reference to Poland?
by W. T. M. Molle, J. de Koning and C.Th. Zandvliet
    1. Introduction 39
    2. Aid and development 40
    3. Analysis of migration 46
    4. Policy issues 60
    5. Conclusions 68

3. East-West migration in Europe and the role of international aid 73
in reducing the need for emigration
by J. Blaschke
    1. The evolution of East-West migration 75
    2. Systems of migration 76
    3. Migration policy and development policy 77
    4. Development policy and migration systems in Eastern Europe 80
    5. Summary 96

4.	**Displacement-generating conflicts and international assistance in the Horn of Africa** by A. Zolberg and A. Callamard	**101**
	1. Introduction	101
	2. International assistance: Trends and implications	102
	3. Conclusion: The future role of international assistance in the Horn of Africa	111
5.	**The use of foreign aid for reducing incentives to emigrate from Central America** by S. Weintraub and S. Díaz-Briquets	**119**
	1. Introduction	119
	2. Demographic overview of Central America, 1990 and 2025	122
	3. Emigration from Central America	124
	4. Post-Second World War developments in Central America	126
	5. Past foreign aid	129
	6. Evaluation of past foreign aid and optimizing future assistance	132
	7. Needed future foreign aid to staunch emigration pressures	137
	8. Final comments	146
6.	**International aid to reduce the need for emigration: The Tunisian case** by M. Bel Hadj Amor	**151**
	1. Introduction	151
	2. Tunisian economic strategy: Growth and development	152
	3. The employment problem	160
	4. International cooperation as a factor in reducing migration pressure	165
	5. Conclusion	176
7.	**International migration and foreign assistance: The case of the Philippines** by G. Ranis	**177**
	1. Introduction	177
	2. The Philippines: Past development patterns, migration and the role of ODA	179
	3. Potential for change in the role of ODA, the development pattern and the size of the excess demand for migration	190
	4. Conclusions	199
8.	**Reducing emigration pressure in Turkey: Analysis and suggestions for external aid** by G. Schiller	**203**
	1. Introduction	203
	2. The economic framework of migration between Turkey and Germany	205
	3. Economic cooperation and assistance	215
	4. Sectoral focus of measures	221
	5. Selected fields of cooperation	232
	6. Concluding remarks	236

Epilogue
Reducing emigration pressure: What role can foreign aid play?   **241**
by P.L. Martin

List of tables

2.1	GNP and GNP per capita in Europe, 1989 (based on purchasing power parities)	41
2.2	Catch-up rates of growth for East Group countries in relation to the EC, 1990-2020	42
2.3	Migration from Eastern to Western Europe: (Estimated) numbers for some major countries, 1980-89	48
2.4	Hard-to-fill vacancies by occupational class, the Netherlands, 1990	57
2.5	Vacancies (1987 and 1990) and vacancy rate (1987) by occupational class, Federal Republic of Germany	58
4.1	Total recorded net flow of resources from OECD Development Assistance Committee (DAC) countries and from international agencies, 1970-77 (US$ million)	104
4.2	Total net ODA from DAC countries, multilateral agencies and OPEC, 1980-83 (US$ million)	104
4.3	Total net ODA from DAC countries, multilateral agencies and OPEC, 1985-89 (US$ million)	104
4.4	Gross receipts of ODA by donor, annual average, 1969-72 (US$ million)	104
4.5	ODA by donor, annual average, 1981-82 (percentage of total allocated ODA)	104
4.6	Bilateral foreign aid to Somalia by source (US$ million)	106
4.7	Soviet economic aid, 1959 to 1983 (converted to millions of constant 1987 US dollars)	106
4.8	Percentage of total ODA per country	106
4.9	ODA as a percentage of GNP	106
5.1	Central America: Basic demographic data, 1990 and 2025	123
5.2	Growth of the economically active population, 1990-2025 (thousands)	124
5.3	Central Americans apprehended, fiscal years 1986-91	126
5.4	Gross domestic product: Average annual growth rates, 1961-70 to 1981-90 (per cent)	127
5.5	Total net resource flows: Central American countries, 1980-89 (millions of US dollars)	129
5.6	Total debt stocks, Central America, 1980 and 1982-90 (millions of US dollars)	132
6.1	Tunisia: Economic and demographic statistics, actual and forecast, 1961-96	158
6.2	Tunisians legally resident in EC countries, 1988	163
6.3	Number of Tunisian return migrants, 1984-89	164
6.4	Composition of external aid (per cent)	172
7.1	Average real per capita GDP growth rates, selected countries or areas (per cent)	183
7.2	Income distribution (Gini coefficients) selected countries or areas	183
7.3	Annual growth of employment in manufacturing, selected countries or areas	183
7.4	Public and publicly guaranteed disbursements to the Philippines (millions of US dollars)	185
7.5	Sectoral allocation of United States aid disbursements to the Philippines (percentage distribution)	185
7.6	Processed land-based Philippine contract workers by major occupation group, 1975-86	189
7.7	Processed land-based Philippine contract workers by major destination, 1975-86	189
8.1	Performance of the Turkish economy, 1961-89	209

8.2	Labour supply and employment in Turkey, 1990	213
8.3	Labour surplus in the Turkish economy, 1975-87	213
8.4	Development assistance from Germany to Turkey, 1961-90 (million DM)	216
8.5	Financial assistance of the World Bank, 1980-84 (million US$)	217
8.6	Performance of enterprises according to size, 1985	223
8.7	Employment in selected branches, 1985	224
8.8	Wages and labour productivity in small and large enterprises, 1970-85	225
8.9	Growth of employment in small and large enterprises, 1970-85	226

List of figures

2.1	Trends in emigration from Eastern Europe, 1980-89	47
2.2	Employment and unemployment by education, Poland, 1991 (first quarter)	53
2.3	Percentage unemployment by age group, Poland, 1991 (second quarter)	54
2.4	Unemployment-to-vacancy ratio by gender, 1990-91	54
2.5	Structure of employment, Poland, 1989	63
5.1	United States aid to Central America, 1962-90	131
7.1a	Non-participatory growth path: The Philippine case	188
7.1b	Participatory growth path: The East Asian case	188
8.1	Growth rate of GNP and investment, Turkey, 1964-88	210
8.2	Growth rate of employment and investment in manufacturing, Turkey, 1964-88	210

Introduction

W.R. Böhning and M. Schloeter-Paredes

1. Background

International migration is increasing. There are several reasons for this trend, including the growing internationalization of nation states' economies, the interpenetration of the world's communications and media systems, the seemingly unbridgeable gap between poor and rich countries, armed conflicts or serious internal disturbances, and the existence of widespread oppression. They have led many people from poor countries to look for income-earning opportunities or a safe haven in richer countries. Since the 1970s there have been more people seeking to migrate or to find refuge in richer countries than the latter have been willing to admit, either temporarily or permanently.

Even though immigration quotas have tended to increase in North America, the queues of people seeking entry have lengthened. In Western Europe there has been a rising number of *de facto* immigrants, in spite of declared policies emphasizing that further immigration was not desired. Asylum applications rose from 30,000 in the 1970s to well over half a million in 1992. Although these figures represent only a small percentage of the global refugee population, this wave of asylum applicants pushed the refugee system that had worked reasonably well for four decades dangerously close to breakdown. Unwanted immigration also appeared in Asia during the 1970s and 1980s. In Japan, the newly industrialized countries of the Far East, the Arab countries of the Middle East, even in Malaysia, more foreigners want to partake in their rapid development than these countries are willing or able to accommodate. The number of emigrating nationalities goes up – almost all nations are involved today – and the formation of bridgeheads or social networks sustains migration flows once they have been set in motion. In other parts of the world, regional or internal conflicts fuelled by political repression, poverty, human rights violations, recurrent famine and environmental degradation had by the end of the 1980s produced displacement on an unprecedented scale that prompted emigration from Mozambique, Ethiopia, Sudan, Somalia, Liberia, Angola, Indo-China, Central America and Afghanistan. The worldwide refugee population, which was around eight million at the end of 1970, came close to 20 million in 1991. The conflict in the former Yugoslavia displaced an additional two million people within a year.

One needs little foresight to state that henceforth there will be ever more people desirous of entering, legally or illegally, the rich countries, far more than these countries are prepared to absorb. The migration pressure from poor to rich countries is demonstrably increasing rather than declining,[1] notwithstanding a few "success stories" where former emigration countries – such as Italy or Malaysia – have managed to develop sufficiently to see their status change to that of immigration countries. Other traditional emigration countries, including comparatively developed ones, today send more migrants to rich immigration countries with whom they have been linked than they did in the past – Mexicans in the United States are an illustration – or they have more migration candidates now than they had in the past – as in the case of Turks aspiring to move to Germany.[2]

As regards refugees, recent changes in the international political environment have not by themselves brought solutions to refugee problems. In some ways, these changes have led to an intensification of them. Nationalistic, ethnic and religious violence, previously suppressed by authoritarian regimes, have sometimes been revived, leading to violent internal conflicts, contributing to the estimated 20 million internationally displaced persons.

Foreign havens or opportunities to start anew are often not available to refugees and displaced persons. In many cases, the economies of the host countries are overstrained; there is a negative public perception of abuse of asylum procedures as a way of circumventing immigration control; racism and xenophobia challenge humanitarian principles; and many refugees have to return to devastated areas in their countries of origin. The question of international peace and security cannot be considered in isolation from economic and social matters.

The return of refugees, made possible by the opportunities resulting from the end of the Cold War, can help to reverse former displacement. But repatriation requires additional efforts to rehabilitate and develop returnee areas. Given the number of countries and people involved, and the fact that their successful reintegration is critical to the national reconciliation and reconstruction process, a special type of development assistance is required that anchors returnees and stabilizes their communities.

Just after the Second World War, first the ILO, then the OECD and finally the European Community (EC) embraced a philosophy that economic growth should not be held up in one country for lack of labour so long as there was suitable labour available elsewhere.[3] The 1976 ILO World Employment Conference was the first major international occasion where a different perspective was aired, putting emphasis on providing alternatives to emigration.[4] In the mid-1980s the new philosophy found normative international expression in the ILO Employment Policy (Supplementary Provisions) Recommendation, 1984 (No. 169), in the following words:

---

[1] See ILO, 1992, especially pp. 52-55.

[2] Martin, 1991, p. 94; and Straubhaar, 1991, especially pp. 53-58.

[3] See The ILO Migration for Employment Recommendation (Revised), 1949 (no. 86), paragraphs 4(1) and (4); the OEEC Decision of the Council of October 1953, C(53) 251 (Final); and articles 48 and 49 of the Treaty of Rome of 1957.

[4] See the Declaration of Principles and Programme of Action adopted by the Tripartite World Conference on Employment, Income Distribution and Social Progress and the International Division of Labour, Geneva, 4-17 June 1976, paragraphs 36-37.

[Member States] should, where international migration takes place, adopt policies designed

(a) to create more employment opportunities and better conditions of work in countries of emigration so as to reduce the need to migrate to find employment; and

(b) to ensure that international migration takes place under conditions designed to promote full, productive and freely chosen employment.

> Members which habitually or repeatedly admit significant numbers of foreign workers with a view to employment should, when such workers come from developing countries, endeavour to cooperate more fully in the development of such countries, by appropriate intensified capital movements, the expansion of trade, the transfer of technical knowledge and assistance in the vocational training of local workers, in order to establish an effective alternative to migration for employment and to assist the countries in question in improving their economic and employment situation (paragraphs 39 and 40).

Since then, more and more insistent pronouncements have been made along these lines at the multilateral level,[5] as well as by leading migrant or refugee-receiving countries,[6] especially in Europe.[7]

Besides the protection of refugees, the Statutes of UNHCR, adopted by the General Assembly in December 1950, set out criteria for voluntary repatriation, local settlement in the country of asylum, and resettlement in third countries. Repatriation, settlement, and resettlement were considered the durable solutions that the international community should pursue.

In the four decades that followed, solutions were tailored to the nature of the outflow. While UNHCR actively attempted to promote voluntary repatriation as the optimal solution, it recently took the lead to formulate and implement comprehensive plans that also attempted to address the root causes of refugee outflows. The 1989 International Conference on Central American Refugees (CIREFCA), the Comprehensive Plan of Action (CPA) adopted by the 1989 International Conference on Indo-Chinese Refugees (ICIR), and the 1991 Dar-es-Salaam Summit Declaration on the Rwandese refugee question are significant examples of this new trend. These regional initiatives succeeded earlier international ones, most notably the Canadian initiative within the United Nations General Assembly and the Human Rights Commission to examine Human Rights and Mass Exodus, and the German initiative within the General Assembly for a code of conduct and practical measures to avert further mass flows of refugees. Both these initiatives remain on

---

[5] See the 1991 "Strategy Platform" agreed upon by 16 Governments forming part of the Intergovernmental Consultations on Asylum, Refugee and Migration Policies in Europe, North America and Australia; and the Conclusions reached by the Fourth Conference of European Ministers Responsible for Migration Affairs in Luxembourg, 1991, in Council of Europe document MMG-4 (91)9, final.

[6] See the US Commission for the Study of International Migration and Cooperative Economic Development, especially its summary report *Unauthorized migration: An economic development response* (Washington, DC, July 1990).

[7] See Groupe de réflexion interdépartemental DFJP, DFAE, DFEP, 1989; Swedish Ministry of Labour, 1990, pp. 48-49; and Bundesminister des Innern, 1990.

the agenda of the General Assembly and the Human Rights Commission under the item on Human Rights and Mass Exodus.

In recent years, UNHCR and its Executive Committee have frequently invoked the responsibilities of States towards their nationals[8] and have called for the strengthening of joint international efforts to deal with the causes of flows of asylum-seekers and refugees so as to avert further such flows.[9] Innovative approaches are being developed by the international community in the former Yugoslavia, Kenya and Somalia.

In view of the rising interest in the question of enabling people to achieve at home what they seek to achieve abroad, whether economic advancement or freedom from persecution and insecurity, the Director-General of the ILO, Mr. M. Hansenne, and the High Commissioner for Refugees, Mrs. S. Ogata, decided to give the fledgling discussion a decisive push by commissioning a range of case studies and holding a joint meeting on "International aid as a means to reduce the need for emigration". The meeting took place in Geneva in May 1992, and a report on it exists in the form of an Informal Summary Record.[10] This book contains a selection of the case studies.

2. Why focus on international aid ?

Why did the ILO and UNHCR concentrate on international aid in general and Official Development Assistance (ODA for short)[11] in particular as a means of dealing with emigration pressures? The reason is simple: aid or ODA are the only international instruments whose impact on the propensity to emigrate had never been explored before in any detail or used for the purpose of reducing the need of people in poor countries to expatriate themselves on political, economic or social grounds. Yet the recent discussions seemed to look to ODA as a promising, perhaps the only remaining, means of changing the circumstances in poor emigration countries to enable their citizens to choose freely whether to stay or to leave, whether to work in their own or in another country. In other words, there was a knowledge gap; and the ILO and UNHCR decided to make a joint contribution to filling it.

There are, of course, other international measures – such as foreign direct investment (FDI) and trade liberalization – that could be called upon to achieve the same objective, i.e. to make it possible for people to stay in their own country. In the case of either of these measures, there is already literature of their impact on development in poor emigration countries. FDI will usually result in faster economic growth and thus more jobs and higher incomes. Such developments directly impinge on the desire of economic migrants to leave or to stay, even though they may in the first instance increase their ability to move abroad. Economic growth also impacts on

---

[8] UNHCR Executive Committee Conclusion No. 40 (XLI) of 1985.

[9] UNHCR Executive Committee Conclusion No. 54 (LIV) of 1989.

[10] See ILO, 1992.

[11] ODA differs from aid in that loans extended as ODA must have a subsidy element of at least 25 per cent. ODA can take the form of bilateral grants, loans, technical cooperation, food aid and support to international organizations which, like the World Bank, extend loans or, like the UNDP, engage in technical cooperation activities.

poverty-based social and ethnic tensions that give rise to dictatorial regimes, which in turn give rise to asylum-seekers and, finally, to slower growth, less employment and a less equal income distribution.

The most striking example of FDI that accelerated growth and democratization are Japan's investments in the Republic of Korea, Hong Kong, Malaysia, Singapore, Thailand and Taiwan (China). With the exception of Hong Kong, these were emigration countries or areas, which had often been losing their brightest and best through emigration. Today they are all immigration countries, with in-movements on a large scale (except, as yet, in Thailand). Some of their citizens continue to move abroad for economic reasons: Thais to the Middle East, Malaysians to Singapore, Koreans to the United States, etc. However, it is not surprising that a farmer from northern Thailand wishes to emigrate, while an industrial worker remains in Bangkok. Nor is it undesirable; on the contrary, development and geographical mobility of labour are two sides of the same coin. What is important is that circumstances do not force people to move abroad, and this is the case today for the worker from Thailand as much as for the worker from Malaysia or from the Republic of Korea.

FDI, however, has not saved Japan from immigration pressures; immigrants whose origins are as varied as Bangladesh, the Islamic Republic of Iran and the Philippines are arriving. Nor is FDI a tool over which governments have control in terms of directing it to certain countries rather than others. The decisions of private investors, even the investment decisions of state enterprises, are determined by return-on-investment criteria, which tend not to favour poor emigration or refugee-producing countries because of their lack of economic attractiveness or lack of political stability. Investors from rich countries invest mainly in other rich countries, and governments cannot penalize them for doing so. Providing subsidies for investments elsewhere has at best a marginal impact. Poor countries have been receiving a shrinking share of global international capital investment – down from 31 per cent in 1968 to 17 per cent twenty years later – suggesting that its effects on emigration pressures can only be limited.

As regards *trade liberalization*, the picture is similarly gloomy. While it is probably true, as the U.S. Commission for the Study of International Migration and Cooperative Economic Development emphasized, that trade expansion "is the single most important long-term remedy" to emigration pressures,[12] the trends here too point in the wrong direction – in the direction of protectionism.[13] The problem with trade is not that rich governments lack means of influencing it, but that their trade policies often reduce employment prospects in poor countries. For example, much of the trade in goods that would be most directly beneficial to migrant-sending countries involves labour-intensive products. Rich countries protect most strongly the sectors that produce competing labour-intensive goods. Electoral pressures favour protectionism, irrespective of whether the goods are imported from poor countries or from other rich countries, as occurs when Spanish lorries full of fruit and vegetables are turned over by French farmers. There are many other examples of trade policies that

---

[12] US Commission for the Study of International Migration and Cooperative Economic Development, 1990, p. xv. See also the numerous working papers prepared for the Commission and an older ILO study by Hiemenz and Schatz, 1979.

[13] For a brief summary with supporting statistics, see Ghosh, 1992.

stimulate rather than reduce migration. Towards the end of 1991, the EC negotiated an association agreement with Poland. Poland sought, among other things, easier market access for its agricultural produce, which its predominantly private agricultural sector previously exported to communist countries. In the end, the Polish farmers did not gain greater access to the EC's markets for their beef and pork. In this case, it appears that the EC was signalling that Polish workers were preferred to Polish goods. The EC's common agricultural policy may be the most important trade policy stimulating emigration – not by design, but in its effects.

The trade option as a means to reducing the need for emigration is promising in theory. However, trade in place of migration is at best a long-term tool for reducing emigration pressures, and for two reasons. First, it appears that it is most difficult to reduce the trade barriers that would benefit poor migrant-producing countries most. Second, the basic principle underlying exchanges between countries is the most-favoured nation status. When all countries receive the same trade preferences, emigration countries cannot be singled out for treatment that would benefit their citizens most.

Therefore, neither FDI nor trade liberalization, on their past track record, constitutes a compelling measure to reduce unemployment, to raise incomes, or to achieve political stability rapidly, in countries characterized by strong emigration or refugee movements. There are of course, many exceptions to this somewhat pessimistic picture. These two options do work in theory, and they should be tried more vigorously in practice. Nevertheless, governments should explore the possibilities of using ODA to reduce emigration pressures.

Unfortunately, ODA has something of a bad reputation in several donor countries. Taxpayers are less and less inclined to see their money used for something intangible. Even experts wonder whether ODA has really helped poor countries to grow more rapidly. Most ODA consists of loans, which have to be repaid, and many of these loans are used to buy armaments.

As a child of the Cold War, aid was sprinkled across the world. Employment was actually at the most a minor element in the assessment of the appropriateness of aid. Targeting aid to reduce emigration pressure was simply not attempted in any serious way.

So there are good reasons for governments and researchers to look to ODA as a possible, potentially promising, means of accelerating the generation of employment and incomes in poor countries and thereby decreasing the need for emigration. Aid is, moreover, the only international measure over which governments have complete control.

The research that the ILO and UNHCR commissioned, and of which this book contains a selection, was inspired by the question of what international aid could be expected to achieve if it was targeted and structured for the purpose of reducing the need for economic migrants and refugees to leave their own country.[14]

The focus of the researchers engaged by the ILO was oriented to economic and long-term criteria, while the focus of the researchers engaged by UNHCR was

---

[14] For the full list of documents prepared for the Joint ILO-UNHCR meeting of May 1992, see *Informal Summary Record, op.cit.*, Appendix VII, ILO, 1992.

naturally on human rights issues, humanitarian assistance, the protection of displaced persons and refugees, asylum, safe return and support for the reintegration of returnees. The contributions are complementary and, therefore, have been assembled in one publication. This book arranges chapters by decreasing degree of generality – from the global approaches to the country case studies, from the macro-analyses via typological treatment to sectoral focus – rather than by ILO or UNHCR origin. The book is rounded off with a review of the issues by Philip L. Martin.

3. Quo vadis UNHCR and ILO ?

UNHCR

During the past decade, population movements have increasingly been motivated by a combination of political, conflict-related, structural and economic causes. As a consequence, drawing a distinction between who is in need of international protection and who is not has become more complex. This is made worse by the fact that, in some regions, refugees and returnee groups live side by side with internally displaced persons – victims of man-made or natural disasters – whose plight may often be just as tragic and their need for protection and basic assistance just as compelling. In these situations, UNHCR has had to reappraise its traditional approaches to the search for durable solutions for refugees, recognizing that a comprehensive response adequately mobilizing international cooperation is essential if such solutions are to be truly durable. UNHCR's capacity to respond and seek innovative approaches is dependent in large measure on the international community's ability to refocus the various elements of international aid.

On the bilateral side, it is apparent that those sectors dealing with asylum, migration, human rights and economic development are intimately interrelated. Their linkage needs to be reinforced. On the multilateral side, there is also a need to implement coherent strategies for the prevention of refugee flows. This cannot be achieved without a strengthened partnership among countries of origin and asylum, donor countries, financial institutions, UNHCR and other agencies of the UN system, as well as international governmental and non-governmental organizations (NGOs).

Such preventive and curative strategies are essential in view of the increasingly complex emergency situations and repatriation movements which are occurring or likely to occur. Such strategies, however, must also continue to recognize basic international protection principles, such as the right to seek asylum, and take into account the measures and resources required and accepted in countries of origin, the complementarity of mandates and expertise of relevant organizations, and the need to coordinate approaches.

With the support of the international community and in coordination with other agencies of the UN system and NGOs, UNHCR has already begun to adopt some innovative approaches to face the complex challenges posed in today's world, conscious that humanitarian action is today an integral part of a broader process aimed at restoring peace and stability in a world in transition. One of the basic premises of such approaches is that humanitarian aid alone cannot be effective without concomitant political initiatives aimed at resolving conflicts. Peace, conflict mediation and conflict resolution are crucial to make possible the return of refugees and to prevent further or new outflows. Humanitarian actions must therefore be linked to other measures. Preventing violations of human rights before they occur is of primary importance. The promotion of democratic forms of government, the strengthening of human rights monitoring mechanisms, institution-building, and support for legal reforms, are all important components of preventive strategies.

An increased focus on "preventive" protection and assistance in countries of origin is a promising but limited strategy, however, and should not be viewed as a substitute for asylum. The situation arising from the conflict in the former Yugoslavia has made it clear that preventive protection and assistance measures do not obviate the need to provide protection abroad, even if temporarily, for victims of conflict.

Another new approach has been developed as a result of the very scale of some emergencies and the mix of populations involved. Faced with a grave humanitarian crisis caused by a combination of armed conflict, drought and famine in the Horn of Africa, UNHCR has also designed a new, flexible approach to discourage mass movements into Kenya by providing multisectoral assistance to groups inside Ethiopia and Sudan. This "cross-mandate/cross-border" operation, mobilizing the efforts of the international community, UN agencies and NGOs, assists populations in targeted areas, irrespective of whether they are refugees, returnees, internally displaced people or drought-stricken groups. This approach is based on the conviction that only by stabilizing the areas of origin can large mass movements be avoided.

While population movements caused by poverty alone do not breed refugees, extensive social unrest resulting from extreme poverty, associated with human rights violations in a context of limited development prospects, may lead to violent internal conflicts and spur flows. Better targeted development assistance with an emphasis on satisfying human needs in countries of origin is another strategy which can clearly play a role in reducing or preventing refugee flows.

The amount, nature, and uses of development aid have to be assessed to ensure that it furthers effective national and regional development. Until now, this has not been done in the context of reducing emigration pressures.

As regards the growing momentum of voluntary repatriation movements, it has also become apparent that the success of returnee programmes depends not only on the removal of immediate obstacles to return, but also on the availability of rehabilitation and reconstruction assistance in the country of origin. UNHCR has identified the existence of a gap between the limited form of returnee aid currently being provided by the international community, and traditional development assistance which does not focus on returnee areas in a way that encourages returnees to stay home.

In countries where repatriation is likely to be massive in scale and reintegration prospects are uncertain because of massive destruction – such as Afghanistan, Angola and Mozambique – this gap needs to be bridged by measures such as the implementation of quick impact projects in areas of return. Basic services must also be established quickly in returnee areas, perhaps with targeted development aid. Stable and durable reintegration, and indeed national reconciliation, hinge on such communities being given a chance to rebuild the fabric of social and economic links torn by conflict and widespread destruction. The mobilization of additional resources is as important as ensuring that investments are targeted more effectively.

Preventing and solving refugee problems, particularly where refugee flows are only one component of large-scale population movements, cannot be achieved without the commitment of the international community to providing development aid better adapted to today's needs. This aid should be given in the context of a comprehensive plan that addresses the interests and needs of all concerned. Some initiatives can be taken by UNHCR itself; others require the diversified cooperation of governments, UN agencies and NGOs.

Better targeted ODA which complements humanitarian assistance is a necessary component of any comprehensive response to refugee problems. Some signs of a trend in this direction may be found in certain aspects of the Comprehensive Plan of Action for Indo-Chinese Refugees (CPA), bilateral and multilateral agreements in the context of the International Conference on Central American Refugees (CIREFCA), the comprehensive political settlement in Nicaragua and El Salvador, and the peace agreement in Cambodia.

ILO

As a follow-up to the research and the Joint ILO-UNHCR Meeting, the ILO has launched an innovative initiative concerning the emigration countries of the Maghreb region. It is based on the belief that several features of international aid procedures will have to change before ODA can effectively reduce the *need* for people to leave their own country.

The first thing that will have to change is the tendency to scatter ODA. If bilateral and multilateral donors want to reduce emigration pressure, they will have to *concentrate* their aid not only on countries of most interest to them but, inside countries, on employment creation and income generation in regions and for population groups with high emigration rates.

This may require an increase in financial and other resources. Whatever the volume of aid that can be earmarked, one should not expect miracles immediately. It will take many years, possibly several decades, for aid to help poor countries to develop faster.

The end of "ODA scattering" has another dimension. Bilateral and multilateral donors will have to *cooperate*. They will have to cooperate in order to concentrate their scarce resources; to ensure that counter-productive aid measures are not implemented; and to arrive at a division of labour between them over a long period of time that helps the aid-receiving countries in a manner that leads to reduced emigration pressures.

ODA can be counter-productive. For example, it is very fashionable to help poor countries with training courses in a variety of fields, frequently in occupations with which donor countries' experts are most familiar. Sometimes, these courses are set up without considering where the trained young people will find jobs to use their skills. If enough such jobs are not available in a country with a dense network of human relationships with major immigration countries, these young people will feel tempted to head for the rich countries whose trainers came to teach them. Training assistance in such a country makes sense only if there are jobs available for those who are to be trained.

Bilateral and multilateral donors will have to work together. They will have to come to an understanding of what should be done, what should not be done, and who should support which measures to achieve the common goal.

The most important condition that will have to be fulfilled is to ensure the voluntary, wholehearted, effective and lasting *collaboration of the emigration country* one wishes to help. Nobody can oblige a poor country to accept international aid for aims that it does not share. If, for example, Algeria is intent on taking a laissez-faire attitude towards emigration pressure, it will not be easy for French aid or EC assistance to reduce Algerian emigration pressures. ODA may well be accepted in pursuit of other objectives, and such aid may, as a side-effect, contribute to the reduction of emigration pressure. But this effect would be incidental and marginal.

It is, therefore, of crucial importance to gain the confidence and commitment of the aid-receiving countries in the battle against emigration pressure. This will not be realized if one wields the threat of conditionality or of withholding ODA unless it is used exactly along the lines envisaged by the donor country or multilateral institution. Confidence and commitment are born of solidarity, mutual understanding, discussion and respect of the other side.

This is the framework within which the ILO has launched the Maghreb programme, as it is called, with the financial support of the Italian Government. It is an attempt to bring together the major national and multilateral donors with key aid officials from Algeria, Morocco and Tunisia in an interactive process whose aim is to agree on an integrated programme designed to reduce emigration pressure.[15]

If the bilateral and multilateral aid agencies are willing to cooperate, the ILO would like to extend the same kind of approach to other parts of the world where immigration and emigration countries have a common interest in reducing the need for people to go abroad for employment.

---

[15] A first meeting in this process took place in Turin, Italy, April 1993. See ILO, 1993.

Bibliography

Bundesminister des Innern. 1990. *Flüchtlingskonzeption* (Bonn), 25 Sep.
Ghosh, G. 1992. *Migration, trade and international economic cooperation. Do the linkages work?*, Tenth IOM Seminar on Migration, 15-17 September (Geneva).
Groupe de réflexion interdépartemental DFJP, DFAE, DFEP. 1989. *Stratégie pour la politique des années 90 en matière d'asile et de réfugiés* (Bern), January.
Hiemenz, U.; K.W. Schatz. 1979. *Trade in place of migration: An employment-oriented study with special reference to the Federal Republic of Germany, Spain and Turkey* (Geneva).
ILO. 1993. *Atelier régional sur un programme d'actions visant à la réduction de la pression migratoire dans les pays du Maghreb: Algérie, Maroc, Tunisie. Résumés, conclusions, suites*. Working document (Geneva).
—. 1992. "ODA as a means to reduce economic and social emigration pressure", paper for *Joint ILO-UNHCR meeting on international aid as a means to reduce the need for emigration: Informal summary record* (Geneva, ILO and UNHCR, 1992), esp. pp. 52-55.
Martin, P.L. 1991. *The unfinished story: Turkish labour migration to Western Europe, with special reference to the Federal Republic of Germany* (Geneva, ILO), p. 94.
Straubhaar, Th. 1991. "Migration pressure", in W.R. Böhning, P.V. Schaeffer and Th. Straubhaar: *Migration pressure: What is it? What can one do about it?* (Geneva, ILO, WEP working paper), October, esp. pp. 53-58.
Swedish Ministry of Labour. 1990. *A comprehensive refugee and immigration policy: An outline from an inter-departmental study group* (Stockholm), pp. 48-49.
United States Commission for the Study of International Migration and Cooperative Economic Development. 1990. *Unauthorized migration: An economic development response* (Washington, DC, July).

1

Towards a comprehensive refugee policy: Conflict and refugees in the post-Cold War world

A. Suhrke

Conventional wisdom deems that violence is the cause of refugees. Strategies to modify the outflow of refugees, therefore, must be informed by an understanding of social conflict. Following a brief analysis of refugee flows during the Cold War years, this chapter will look at the emerging structure of refugee-producing conflicts in the post-Cold War era and discuss relevant policy strategies. The starting-point is the conclusion of the UN debate on root causes in the 1980s: to be effective, refugee policy has to address the causes of conflict as well as provide relief to its victims. The result can be called a *comprehensive* refugee policy.

Violence is neither random nor unstructured. Social violence appears in patterns of conflict between or within states, and these patterns in turn are shaped by world-historical processes. Particularly significant is the tendency for external and internal forces to combine to produce extreme or protracted violence. In the second half of the twentieth century, the principal forces which generated refugee-producing conflicts came together in precisely this way.

The legacy of the Second World War was the division of Europe and decolonization of Africa and Asia. For the next 40 years, the Cold War became the overarching, defining principle of world politics. Starting out in Europe but rapidly enveloping the entire world, the Cold War set the framework for the reconstruction of Europe and the advancement of developing countries. Millions of people were uprooted in the course of both processes.

As the 1990s began, Soviet socialism suddenly disappeared and the Cold War ended. A new post-Cold War era was taking shape, in the process unleashing forces of conflict that the emerging structures of international order were unable to contain. The very speed of historical transition tended to overwhelm both UN mechanisms and regional organizations such as the Conference on Security and Cooperation in Europe (CSCE); on both levels, leaders were groping to adjust to the new realities. The result was a variety of military conflicts and massive refugee flows. Some developed close to the centre of the now vanished Cold War (e.g. the disintegration of Yugoslavia); others occurred at the periphery (Iraq's invasion of Kuwait).

The magnitude of refugee crises arising in the new era focused renewed attention on how to modify the sources of outflow. It was clear, however, that conventional aid strategies could have little impact in the conflicts that generated the largest refugee flows. In the most troubled areas, moreover, mechanisms for restoring peace were weak, and the very principles on which a post-Cold War order should be based were in dispute.

1. From World War to Cold War

Three crises

The creation of the UNHCR and its immediate predecessor, the International Refugee Organisation (IRO), was designed to resolve a European refugee problem, arising initially from the displacements of people in the Second World War and subsequently from the westward flight of Eastern European and Soviet citizens. Rebellion and repression in the Warsaw Pact countries (Hungary 1956, Czechoslovakia 1968) led to massive outflows that again absorbed the funds and energies of UNHCR. Simultaneous flows in Asia and the Middle East were largely ignored by the international refugee regime, or dealt with by way of ad hoc institutional arrangements (Vernant, 1953; Holborn, 1975; Marrus, 1985; Loescher and Monahan, 1988).

The narrow European orientation of the international refugee regime was not seriously challenged until the early 1960s, when Africa moved to the fore with nearly simultaneous flows resulting from the decolonization struggles in Algeria (1959), Zaire (1960), Rwanda (1963) and Portuguese Africa (c.1961), as well as the increasingly violent confrontation between north and south in Sudan (c.1963). The decade culminated in an even larger outpouring – variously estimated at 5 million to 9 million refugees – when the Bengali war of secession engulfed the north-eastern corner of the Indian subcontinent in violence.

Although the populations uprooted by wars of decolonization and secession had a homeland to which they eventually could – and mostly did – return, the interim demand for asylum and relief was considerable. An emerging sense of crisis gripped the international refugee community. The number of those in need steadily increased, and UNHCR formally undertook to aid them by expanding its mandate to care for populations displaced by liberation wars under a "good offices" doctrine.

In the mid- to late 1970s, a third crisis developed, related to the internationalization of revolutionary or ethnic liberation struggles in the developing world. Complex and protracted struggles unfolded in southern Africa and the Horn. The end of the Viet Nam war and renewed war in Cambodia produced massive flight from Indo-China. For the first time, large bodies of refugees also appeared in Central and South America, followed by dramatic new outflows from Cuba and Haiti. The refugee decade peaked with the USSR's invasion of Afghanistan, causing the beginning of an outflow that eventually reached about 5 million people.

This third crisis posed distinct, new problems for the international community. A growing number of the refugees appeared destined to remain indefinitely in camp or legal limbo. Conditions in the homeland rarely permitted repatriation, either because the new regime or social order became entrenched, or because war continued. The strain on first asylum countries mounted, leading to large-scale denial of protection in south-east Asia. In the affluent, industrialized countries, economic recession and popular fears of being flooded by developing country refugees – added to already large numbers of migrants – resulted in greater restriction on asylum (Kritz, 1983; Martin, 1987). Only select groups such as the Indo-Chinese benefited from an extensive resettlement programme. Soon, however, the programmes became controversial because of their economic costs and preferential treatment when there were millions of equally needy refugees elsewhere. There was only one exit from the crisis: to deal with the root causes of the outflows.

The first root-cause debate [1]

The debate was initiated in the UN system in 1980 as the United States and the Federal Republic of Germany sought to censure the communist regimes of Viet Nam and Cuba. Overwhelmed by refugees from the two countries in 1979-80, the United States and its Western allies used the opportunity to call for international cooperation to "avert" mass outflows. The ensuing debate in the UN's Special Political Committee rapidly divided along an internal/external axis (UN, 1980). Some blamed internal abuse perpetrated by the regimes of the sending countries, others looked to global structures of inequality and oppression. The United States, Western Europe and their anti-communist allies in particular linked mass exodus to the violation of human rights in the sending countries. Socialist and many developing countries responded by calling attention to colonialism, global economic inequality and apartheid as the underlying causes of social conflict, and hence mass outflows. Economic issues prominent in the debate over the new international economic order at the time were cited, especially deteriorating terms of trade and balance of payments problems in the South.

The internal/external division was also reflected in the UN documents which followed. Called upon to explore means of "averting" refugee flows, the findings of a Group of Governmental Experts emphasized global structures of inequality. The conclusions, which took five years to reach, reflected the group's large developing country representation (UN, 1985). A second report from a special rapporteur appointed by the Secretary-General received wide attention. Prepared under Sadruddin Aga Khan, a former High Commissioner for Refugees, this report was more balanced: an adequate assessment of root causes must take into account national conditions as well as global economic structures (UN, 1981). Both necessarily shape the political upheavals and violence which figure as proximate causes of refugee flows.

Specifically, the Sadruddin report identified certain political processes that lead to major human rights violations and consequent refugee outflows. The growth of nationalism accompanying the transition from a feudal-tribal society to the modern nation state often generates ethnic strife, repression and persecution of minorities.

---

[1] Actually, it was not the first. Those with longer historical memories will recall the letter of resignation of James G. McDonald, the High Commissioner for German Refugees, in 1938: "In the present economic conditions of the world, the European States, and even those overseas, have only a limited power of absorption of refugees. The problem must be tackled at its source if disaster is to be avoided." Cited in Loescher and Monahan, 1988, p. 409.

The ready availability of firearms makes it likely that civil strife will turn violent. But the entire process of state formation in large parts of the developing world, above all in Africa, is saddled by the heavy legacy of colonialism which left structural imbalances, fragmented societies, artificial borders and weak states. Prolonged liberation struggles exacerbated destruction and tension. On the socioeconomic side, problems associated with high population growth, massive unemployment, large rural-to-urban migrations, and – for parts of Africa especially – desertification – add up to "a lack of economic opportunity for all too many people". The "unavoidable corollary is political disruption which triggers the uprooting of sections of the population" (p. 37). The result is "the inability of many governments to create conditions in which the population as a whole can expect to enjoy – quite apart from civil and political rights – the economic, social and cultural rights set out in the Declaration of Human Rights…" (p. 38).

A more systematic analysis would reveal that social conflict in the period under discussion generally fell into two categories: conflicts of state formation and conflicts over the social order. As we have discussed elsewhere (Zolberg, Suhrke and Aguayo, 1989) such conflicts were responsible for all the major refugee flows in the post-colonial world.

Conflicts over state formation typically involved opposing ethnic groups or targeting of a particular minority. In extreme forms, violence took the form of pogroms, expulsions or autonomy/secessionist struggles. The result was large outflows of people seeking to escape violence that was directed along ascribable ethnic or religious boundaries. By the nature of the conflict, however, some people had the equivalent of an ethnic "homeland" where they could seek safety. The classic contemporary case was the partition of the Indian subcontinent in 1947 when large numbers of Hindus fled from Pakistan to India, while many Indian Muslims went to Pakistan. Only minorities that had no "homeland", nor prospects of truce or a new social contract which would permit return, became the long-term wards of the international refugee regime.

In a different category, conflicts over social order produced, in extreme form, full revolutionary struggles. While historically rare, they typically led to massive and irreversible outflows. A first wave of people fleeing the generalized violence of war was sometimes reversed when the fighting subsided. Depending upon the outcome, new waves subsequently developed. Successful revolutions initially displaced the old élite. As the revolutionary forces sought to consolidate the new order – typically in the face of hostility from established, international forces – the resulting hardship alienated broader segments of the populace whom the revolution had intended to serve. At that point, a large secondary outflow of people materialized.

The breakdown of democratic regimes – another form of social order conflict – displaced especially large numbers of people when civil society had been highly developed and the authoritarian successor regime particularly ruthless (as in South America in the 1970s). Those who were not killed or gaoled as opponents of the new regime had to seek safety beyond the reach of state power, i.e. they became international refugees. Under other conditions, authoritarian rule produced only a trickle of exiles (e.g. during periods of martial law in the Philippines, Thailand and the Republic of Korea).

As the "root cause" debate correctly assumed, it is possible to delineate the nature of refugee flows according to types of social conflict. The pattern of violence, moreover, is embedded in the historical context of state formation and social ordering. The central point which engaged the root cause debate in the early 1980s was the significance of the international context. Freed from distortions of the political debate, the main conclusion stands out clearly: the processes of state formation and social ordering which produced refugees during the Cold War period were familiar to earlier periods in European history, but the international context had changed dramatically. In the new states of Africa, Asia and Latin America, nation state formation proceeded under conditions of extreme international inequality, intense population pressure on national resources, and a Cold War that tended to internationalize domestic conflict. The typical result was frequent and intense conflict, and massive refugee flows.

Durable solutions to refugee problems consequently had to be sought at the international level. That meant not only international aid for long-term economic development and a stronger refugee regime: a breakthrough was required at the level of the international strategic system.

The Cold War and its legacy

For 40 years, the Cold War had provided ordering principles for a tumultuous world. While the battlefront changed, the main issues and rules were "etched with remarkable clarity", as a former American secretary of defence later observed (Schlesinger, 1991, p. 3). The Cold War provided a *sancta simplicitas*, first for Europe and subsequently for the developing world when large power competition moved outwards from the centre. In Asia, Africa and Latin America, the superpowers competed to build up local allies. On both sides of the East-West divide, regimes with thin structures of legitimacy could count on economic aid, diplomatic support, and a full range of conventional weapons. Well-armed military institutions emerged; assorted liberation movements were also equipped.

Some rules of intervention prevailed. After Viet Nam, the United States preferred to intervene by proxy, while the USSR until the very end relied on its own or allied troops. Given the ideological element in superpower rivalry, struggles involving fundamental social order conflicts engaged them most directly. In ethnic conflicts or those more muddled ideologically, the superpowers showed less interest, although regional powers frequently did (de Silva and May, 1991). Military-strategic considerations helped to define areas of intervention, but it is noticeable that the centres of turbulence which the superpowers defined as their "regional" conflicts all had a revolutionary element. The refugee consequences were graphically depicted in a UNHCR map of the mid-1980s. Five explosive areas or countries were marked: Indo-China, Afghanistan, the Horn of Africa, southern Africa and Central America. In all cases, a revolutionary struggle was part of the original conflict; this element was also the principal mechanism which linked the local conflict to the Cold War and transformed it into a protracted war with huge refugee flows.

As the Cold War wound down, so did all the regional conflicts – a striking testimony to the importance of the global divisions in generating them in the first place. The collapse of Soviet socialism undermined the revolutionary left everywhere. As Jorge Castaneda observed with respect to Latin America, revolutionary struggle appeared to have no future (Castaneda, 1990). This created incentives for compromise at the local level, and simultaneously offered the United States an exit from foreign commitments that were inconclusive, controversial or of declining strategic value. The process initiated by Mikhail Gorbachev's "new thinking" thus set in motion a decisive de-escalation. When this harmonized with local conditions, the process was steady, and led to the next phase: monitoring the peace process and permitting reconstruction along with repatriation of refugees.

Elsewhere the negative legacy of the Cold War dominated. Decades of violence and intrusive large power rivalry had transformed states and societies. Where competitive intervention had been the rule, local divisions grew into well-armed, institutionalized, semi-autonomous entities. Military and paramilitary institutions built to suppress identifiable enemies during the Cold War were turned loose on rival factions or civilians. The challenge of national reconciliation and demilitarization was most formidable in areas where social fragmentation was already pronounced, as in Africa's regional conflicts and Afghanistan. In Africa, the Cold War legacy came on top of a debilitating colonial legacy, thereby creating a double burden.

2. Peacemaking and the crisis of reconstruction

The defused but still smouldering regional conflicts of the Cold War mark the transition from the old era to a new international order. In these areas, sustained peacemaking and reconstruction are prerequisites for dealing with the remaining refugee problem. The process requires an active and supportive international environment, both regionally and in the UN. While not a substitute for local efforts, nor in itself sufficient, external support is necessary: just as the competitive rivalry of the Cold War inflated local conflicts, international cooperation can now deflate them. An international neutral, indeed neutralizing, effort is especially important when advanced national fragmentation is exacerbated by regional rivalries. The cases of El Salvador and Afghanistan illustrate two different paths, each having clear policy implications for external parties.

El Salvador

The waning of Soviet power removed the ideological underpinnings for United States involvement in the Salvadorian civil war, an involvement already strongly questioned at home (Montgomery, 1982; Berryman, 1984; LeoGrande, 1990). By that time, the costs of a long and inconclusive struggle had created deep war weariness within El Salvador, and victory appeared an elusive goal for both sides. The FMLN offensive in 1989 did not have the expected impact, and the fate of the Sandinistas in Nicaragua showed that even a military victory could, with United

States assistance, be turned into electoral defeat. On the government side, sharp cuts in United States military aid, and warnings of more to come, signalled the need to settle before it was too late. The compromise nature of the peace agreement – signed on 31 December 1991 after prolonged negotiations – reflected the stand-off. Both parties were to be demilitarized and reintegrated into the body politic. The eventual governmental configuration was to be decided through national elections. The major issue of the war – land distribution – was to be addressed through the legislative process, while agrarian reforms carried out in rebel areas would remain. "Truth commissions" would investigate past human rights violations to establish accountability, but there was little expectation of large-scale punishment. The UN, which had played a critical role in promoting the peace negotiations, would maintain its presence by active and extensive in-country monitoring of the peace process.

A regional consensus on the principles of democratization and demilitarization strengthened the peace process in El Salvador. Outlined by President Arias of Costa Rica and affirmed by the heads of government of the Central American states, the Esquipulas Agreement of 1987 had established a common basis for political reconstruction in the region. The agreement pledged support for democratization, a system of free elections, respect for human rights and progress towards regional arms reductions. Regional unity would, if sustainable, render critical support to the process of national reconciliation, just as a divided region would have the opposite effect.

Afghanistan

Afghanistan remained more of a problem, although the turning-point had already occurred in May 1988 when the USSR started to withdraw troops in accordance with the Geneva Accords (Saikal, 1989). Soviet withdrawal changed the nature of the Afghan war from a holy war against foreign aggression to a factional power struggle, at one level driven by clan-based alignments, at another touching fundamental ideological questions of national development (Roy, 1986; Rupert, 1989; Rubin, 1989/90; Suhrke, 1990). The rate of violence decreased and informal, partial cease-fires developed at the local level. But a political settlement was elusive. As long as the warring Afghan factions continued to receive political and material support from their foreign patrons, they had little incentive to enter into a compromise. The complete and mutual non-interference stipulated by the Accords was not implemented. Instead, so-called "positive symmetry" prevailed. The United States, Pakistan and Saudi Arabia continued to provide the rebel forces with most of their weapons; the USSR supplied the Kabul Government. Not until the further thawing of the Cold War did Moscow and Washington agree to change from "positive symmetry" of mutual arms aid to "negative symmetry" of a mutual cut-off.

The importance of the external environment was underlined when shortly after the agreement went into effect in January 1992, major pieces of a settlement fell into place. Most significantly, Pakistan agreed to end its arms supplies for the rebels, thus depriving them of their critical rear base. Soon after, key Afghan factions announced their support for a UN peace plan which called for national reconciliation, brokered by the UN, and national elections.

Violence soon resumed, demonstrating that the frail peace process could be undermined by problems that had long historical roots. For centuries, the Afghan state had been weak and society fragmented; the last war further accentuated social divisions as factions became institutionalized and well armed. An enduring peace agreement would require greater consensus on the nature of Afghan society than was evident by the early 1990s. Disagreement on fundamental issues was aggravated by external factors, as Pakistan, the Islamic Republic of Iran and Saudi Arabia vied for influence in the area. Simultaneously, substantial caches of arms accumulated during the 13-year-old war had given the rival Afghan parties considerable capacity for independent military action.

By comparison, the Salvadorians had fought an essentially class-based war to a standstill, and were less subject to distorting North American intervention in the post-Cold War era; in addition, the regional context reinforced the peace process.

While the UN was active in both conflicts, the weakness of the Afghan peace process suggested a commensurately greater role for the organization here. The UN could offer the Afghan factions a neutral ground to work out a political settlement and dampen the effects of divisive regional interference. As appropriate, the UN could also link the peace process to the next phase of reconstruction and refugee repatriation.

The conflicts in the Horn of Africa and parts of southern Africa resembled that in Afghanistan. Indeed, Angola, Somalia and Ethiopia were probably more extreme cases of national fragmentation exacerbated by an intrusive and competitive external environment. The Horn as a whole was characterized by national deconstruction and uncertain terms of reconstruction, including the nature of coexistence between the two former constituent parts of larger Ethiopia. Under these conditions, peacemaking was necessarily slow and hesitant, constantly delaying reconstruction and repatriation. The issue, as the study team led by Anthony Lake concluded, was "really one of *construction* rather than *reconstruction*, of building rather than rebuilding – politically as well as economically" (Lake, 1990, p. 16).

Repatriation, reconstruction and peacemaking: An integrated process

With an estimated 15 million people displaced, repatriation in the regional conflicts of the Cold War represented an enormous administrative and social task. As the processes typically run parallel and are mutually interdependent, a careful integration between reconstruction, repatriation and continued peacemaking was required. In particular, it was imperative to ensure the safety of returnees and that *refoulement* disguised as repatriation did not occur. The memory of disastrous repatriations after the Second World War, carried out by the International Refugee Organization, remained a warning.

As a presumed neutral actor with multiple functions, the UN had a central role in the combined tasks of repatriation, reconstruction and peacemaking. The ability of the UN system to fulfil its potential in this respect, however, was circumscribed by financial constraints. The point was demonstrated in the Cambodian case.

Peacemaking in Cambodia did not require a definition of the nature of the Khmer nation. The country has a long-established tradition of statehood and is culturally distinct. Yet two decades of war had left Cambodia with a divided polity, a massive refugee problem, and a devastated economy (Chandler, 1991). Under the terms of the UN peace plan, the warring parties – including prominently the Khmer Rouge – were to be largely disarmed. Refugees were to return from Thailand to participate in UN-supervised national elections, which in turn would constitute the transition to a postwar order. Yet the refugees were reluctant to return unless they were given minimal security guarantees and resources for repatriation and reconstruction. While the process moved reasonably well during 1991-92, the accumulating costs created weariness in the UN system and worries about continued financing. At one point it was feared that delays in the implementation schedule would jeopardize the elections and possibly the peace agreement as a whole.

A buffer state which lacks internal harmony becomes an easy target for rival, external forces. The point has been made with respect to peacemaking in southeast Asia in an earlier era, and is equally valid today (Black et al., 1968). An uncertain UN presence in Cambodia would undoubtedly encourage traditionally divisive, regional forces to intrude once again. Historically squeezed by its two larger neighbours, contemporary Cambodia has suffered from the aggressive rivalry between Thailand and Viet Nam, as well as unsettled relations between China and Viet Nam. Rising hostility between the latter was a major factor that precipitated and sustained the last war in Cambodia (1978-89). In general, reconstruction and repatriation can be linked to the peacemaking process in two ways – positively to support the process of reconciliation, or negatively to feed a continued conflict. Which tendency prevails depends heavily on the modalities of reconstruction and repatriation.

Both tendencies were at work in Afghanistan as the war wound down. Across-the-border projects from Pakistan involved foreign assistance to rebel forces, mainly through bilateral donor programmes for reconstruction and repatriation. These were partisan in nature, formally illegal, and highly problematic (Baitenmann, 1990). They had the effect, if not the intent, of strengthening the rebel factions in whose jurisdiction the programmes were placed. As such, aid became a move in the continuing war rather than a spur to compromise. By contrast, the UN-supported special programme for Afghanistan, Operation Salam, worked on the explicit premise that all parties involved must consent to a particular programme. Consent could be obtained by spreading the programmes wide. In practice, this took the form of shipping in aid from both Pakistan and the northern, former Soviet border, and distributing it in both government and rebel areas. Aid was used as building blocks to promote national reconciliation, starting with aid incentives to induce local cease-fires. The approach had some success in building "zones of tranquillity" in the countryside, but the limitations were evident. Until greater progress towards national political agreement was achieved, reconstruction and repatriation could move only slowly ahead (UNOCA, 1988, 1989; Harrison, 1990).[2]

If a full and formal peace agreement has been concluded, repatriation is unproblematic in a political sense. But even under the best of circumstances, two dif-

---

[2] This section also draws on the author's meetings with UNOCA staff in Kabul, August 1990.

ficulties typically recur. One concerns the terms of repatriation. If land was an issue in the original conflict and owners have been away for a long time, repatriation is likely to generate new conflicts of ownership, as Beatriz Manz observed with reference to Guatemala (1988). The other concerns the timing. If refugees abroad are engaged in productive pursuits rather than living a dependent camp-life, immediate repatriation will place a double burden on the home country. It will increase the demands on a war-damaged infrastructure, and deprive the economy of foreign exchange from refugee remittances. Both concerns surfaced in El Salvador and Eritrea, leading to legitimate requests for delayed repatriation.

The reconstruction phase

From a refugee perspective, the reconstruction phase has special significance. It represents a critical transition period which tends to set the direction for future population movements, at least in the short run. If reconstruction becomes an austerity period with no end in sight, and hopes for normality fade, refugees abroad will have few incentives to return. At home, pressures for renewed out-migration will mount, facilitated by the existence of migratory networks established during the war years. If renewed conflict occurs, large-scale out-migration can easily develop. A decisive commitment to reconstruction, by contrast, will induce refugees to return. The lessons from reconstruction efforts in Nicaragua and Viet Nam are unambiguous. The hardships of reconstruction – partly self-induced but much worsened by an international embargo – inflicted severe economic pain, sharpened political divisions, and contributed to a population outflow ranging from significant to massive. Renewed war in both cases aggravated the situation.

A different challenge of reconstruction arose in the regional conflicts of the Cold War. There were no revolutionary victors to be isolated and embargoed, but isolation and its consequences might occur by default. The end of the Cold War, which made de-escalation of these conflicts possible, also removed incentives for donor funding. The strategic rationale for Western aid had eroded, other priorities had emerged as economic crisis spread throughout the former Warsaw Pact countries, and the major donor of the past – the United States – was mired in an economic recession.[3]

By any measure, the reconstruction tasks were enormous. Wars in the afflicted regions had lasted for at least one decade, sometimes nearly two. In El Salvador, recovery from the greatest conflict in its history was estimated to require an initial investment of close to US$ 3 billion. The monetary value of damage to economic and social infrastructure was about US$ 1 billion; the cost of replacing or repairing damaged goods was set at almost US$ 1.8 billion. An estimated one million persons were displaced (Ministry of Planning, 1992, p. 1). Yet, the stringent international aid climate made the Government propose a modest US$ 1.1 billion reconstruction plan over five years.

---

[3] It is indicative that the United States in early 1992 held up plans to expand IMF funding facilities from US$ 120 billion to US$ 180 billion, an expansion at any rate designed to accommodate the needs of the former USSR and Eastern Europe rather than the developing countries.

Elsewhere the total bill had yet to be reckoned, but its size was clear. In Afghanistan, one-third of all villages were destroyed, two-thirds of all paved roads were unusable, and at least 26 types of mine were strewn all over the countryside (Harrison, 1990). In Cambodia the destruction, started in the early 1970s with systematic American bombing, worsened as the Khmer Rouge razed the social infrastructure, and was completed in a ten-year war following the Vietnamese invasion in 1978. With massive refugee outflows and mass killings of the educated and skilled, even elementary technical skills were in short supply (Chanda, 1990). In the Horn, the compounded impacts of war, drought and massive refugee flows had inflicted serious, in part irreversible, damage on a fragile, semi-arid environment. Desertification and other forms of land degradation were widespread (Hjort and Salih, 1989; GLASOD, 1991). In southern Africa, protracted warfare had devastated already poor Mozambique and blocked national development plans in Angola. About one million people were internal or external refugees (Chona and Herbst, 1990).

All arguments favoured a concerted international aid effort; the extensive damage required a major commitment. A moral obligation flowed from the role played by external powers as agents of destruction in the first place, and failure to deal with the reconstruction issue would have encouraged renewed conflict and worsened the refugee problem. In this scenario, the regional conflicts of the Cold War would not only have survived the Cold War, but would have acquired new life and a potentially devastating impact on security and development in their respective areas.

Recognizing the need, Japan and the United States called for international aid consortia for Cambodia and Central America. A regionalization of reconstruction solutions is, of course, a double-edged sword. Regional leaders may be expected to play a prominent role in their area, yet the collective interest in reconstruction should be emphasized by appropriate institutional links to the UN and its agencies. Since the UN has played an active peacemaking role in these conflicts, a major UN presence in the reconstruction phase seems a natural extension.

Where possible, reconstruction should harmonize with regional efforts at greater economic cooperation. As in Europe after 1945, the devastation of war might open up new opportunities for integrative reconstruction. In some areas, such as the Horn of Africa, the truly regional extent of the damage favours regional planning for reconstruction. In south-east Asia, a strong regional organization already exists (Association of South East Asian Nations [ASEAN]) that could aid Cambodia's reconstruction.

In addition, three important recommendations from the Lake study concern the conditions of reconstruction and hence repatriation (Lake, 1990). First, reconstruction should enhance the absorptive capacity of the receiving country through appropriate training programmes. This is especially important for Cambodia, where the social infrastructure has been destroyed. Second, as all the countries in question have largely agricultural economies, rural reconstruction must receive high priority. Third, to integrate reconstruction with the peace process, thought should be given to imposing conditionality by tying aid to local compliance with the peace agreement. Donors too would need to accept restraints. In the aftermath of war, donors should not strain the fragile political consensus by making demands that may be economically sensible but politically self-defeating.

Reconstruction delayed: The case of Viet Nam

As several countries in Africa, Latin America and Asia enter a phase of reconstruction and repatriation, it is appropriate to consider the lessons from Viet Nam. This was a case of delayed reconstruction and international isolation. As signs of postwar normality failed to appear, a large-scale population outflow developed to present the international refugee regime with its most vexing challenge and costly burden in recent history.

The Viet Nam war ended with a settlement denied recognition. The United States continued its economic embargo of the country, and a United States-led international coalition also blocked aid from the principal financial institutions (the World Bank, the International Monetary Fund and the Asian Development Bank). Viet Nam was pushed into greater dependence on the Soviet economic bloc (CMEA), a move which reinforced the rigidities in its own planning system. The result was economic stagnation, diplomatic isolation and a climate of continued confrontation. Hopes for reconstruction, normality and peace were replaced by austerity, repression and a renewed regional war, this time in Cambodia. Combined with the socioeconomic transformation of southern Viet Nam and repression of the Chinese minority, the result was a massive refugee flow. Out-migration reached a high point in 1979, but continued at lower though still substantial levels for over a decade to reach approximately one million people (Sutter, 1990; Chan, 1990; Suhrke, 1991).

The troubled legacy outlasted the Cold War. By early 1992, Viet Nam was still embargoed by all the principal multilateral lending institutions and cut off from major bilateral sources of trade and investment. Only the UNDP and a few Western countries had modest programmes in the country. At the same time, the entire economic support structure linked to the former Soviet bloc collapsed. Under these conditions, the promises of Viet Nam's economic reform policy (*doi moi*), instituted in 1986 to move the command economy towards a market-oriented system, generated only modest growth (Williams, 1992; UNDP, 1992).

For a long time, the confrontational climate between Viet Nam and the West also prevented any consideration of repatriation. Only recently did the international community put aside political considerations to return Vietnamese not found to be refugees. As authorities in 1989 started to screen and return Vietnamese "boatpeople" from Hong Kong, the EC and some smaller bilateral donors sought to sweeten the pill with reconstruction aid, planned for provinces where the returnees would settle. Economic revival in Viet Nam would help to broadly encourage repatriation and reduce out-migration pressures. For this purpose, an end to the embargo and concerted aid for reconstruction were essential.

3. State v. People

Among social order conflicts, revolutionary struggles have historically generated numerous refugees, typically forming large and irreversible outflows. This was also the case during the Cold War period, but may not be repeated. One of the most astute students of modern revolutions, Barrington Moore, wondered back in 1966 "whether the great wave of peasant revolutions, so far one of the most distinctive features of the twentieth century, may ... have spent its force" (Moore, 1966, p. 483). Since then, classical peasant revolutions have failed in Ethiopia and Afghanistan, as well as in the more likely environment of the Central American oligarchies. As the twentieth century draws to a close and classical Marxism is widely discredited as ideological inspiration, there seem to be few, if any, candidates left (Zolberg, 1989).

Nevertheless, this does not mean that mass outflows from civil strife will cease. Fundamental struggles over the social order are not unique to class-based agrarian societies. Students of revolution are now reinterpreting the dynamics of even the classical revolutions. They find that demographic pressures, which produced rapid urbanization but falling real incomes, generated discontent. The urban population, not the peasantry of classical revolutions, provided critical manpower that was mobilized for political rivalries and riots, and – if the state itself was weakened – that culminated in social upheaval of a total kind (Goldstone, 1991; Goldstone, Gurr and Moshiri, 1991).

The profile fits a good many states in the developing world today. A striking feature is indeed the rapidly growing pressure on resources in Africa, Asia and Latin America. International mechanisms to provide aid are grossly inadequate, while domestic institutions are often weak and societies fragmented. As the development process becomes strained, it may erupt in recurring violence or, more rarely, lead to a fundamental transformation of society. Revolutionary ideologies need not be rooted in Marxism, as the rising consciousness of radical Islam demonstrates. When a struggle of this kind succeeds, refugee flows tend to be large and irreversible, consisting of entire social segments that were linked to the old order. The refugee flows from the revolution in the Islamic Republic of Iran fit this classic mould. The other main type of refugee-producing conflict – that associated with state formation – actually increased in the post-Cold War world. As the political structures of the past crumbled, ethnic conflicts and nationality problems multiplied in the former USSR and the Balkans. Parts of Africa and Asia also showed signs of a resurgence – or at least a continuity – of old ethnic conflicts. India was shaken by sustained violence in the Punjab, Kashmir and various parts of its north-eastern area. The refugee profile from ethnic conflicts of this kind is distinct: in the first instance, a people delineated by ethnic boundaries seeks safety across a state border or, where possible, among ethnic kin elsewhere.

In so far as conflict is inherent in social change, a range of confrontations between state and society will continue to produce refugees. The question is what forms such conflicts will take in the new international context, and how the international refugee regime can respond. It will be recalled that the very large refugee flows of the past 40 years were linked to the Cold War mainly in two ways: superpower intervention increased the violence (e.g. in Afghanistan); while support for refugees, which enabled them to move on a large scale, was an element in the superpower rivalry itself (e.g. Western aid to refugees from communist states).

The post-Cold War era is likely to differ on both accounts. Intervention will no doubt continue, but is likely to proceed on two levels – by regional actors, and collectively through the UN. The political significance of refugee aid, likewise, will be reshaped to fit the regional context of international politics which is replacing the overarching bipolar structure of the Cold War. One particular form of refugee aid is likely to be permanently phased out, namely large-scale resettlement of refugees from the developing world to the industrialized states. The Viet Nam refugee experience will hardly be repeated. Rather, greater efforts will probably be made to "avert" flows. This can be done either by reducing conflict and flight, as the first root cause debate called for a decade ago, or, negatively, by denying asylum.

What this may mean in practice is indicated by three refugee approaches or regimes established in relation to conflicts in the developing world when the post-Cold War era dawned. Each demonstrates a distinct approach to aid and protection as well as the underlying causes of flight. Slightly formalized and named after the individual cases, they are:

(a) *The Kurdish approach*. An active and innovative regime provided relief and protection, but a comprehensive refugee policy did not follow. The root causes of the problem were old and intractable. There was no ready reference for a political solution, and the UN system was unable to initiate one. The aid function, in other words, lacked a political counterpart to address the root causes.

(b) *The Myanmar approach*. A course of paralysis and neglect was largely set by the states in the region. The refugees received minimal aid, although some correction was provided through the UN system. Despite formal openings for a diplomatic initiative, the regional states made no attempt to address the underlying causes of flight. No leadership emerged in the UN system to chart an alternate course.

(c) *The Haiti approach*. The potential for a comprehensive refugee policy was present but not fully exploited. The regional states utilized the formal openings for a diplomatic initiative to focus collectively on the root causes of flight. Asylum policies, however, were restrictive and determined by one receiving state.

Considered in more detail, it is clear that the Kurdish exodus in 1991 evoked an activist but incomplete aid response which, in political terms, was left suspended. The revolt of the Kurds that year was only the most recent eruption of an old autonomy struggle. The sequence was familiar: a catalytic event brought a long-simmering conflict to the surface, fighting commenced, and a panic-stricken population headed for the border. Yet the timing ensured an innovative response. The revolt came just after an international coalition operating under UN mandate had defeated Iraqi forces. No longer paralysed by the Cold War, the UN Security Council readily authorized an activist refugee policy. When Turkey closed its borders, the Council approved the establishment of a secure zone for refugees on the Iraqi side. The historic resolution of 5 April 1991 declared that international refugees were a matter of international peace and security. A newly defeated Iraq could only acquiesce as allied forces moved in to establish the zone. Subsequently, allied forces withdrew but retained a presence on the Turkish side of the border. The UN retained a presence in the zone through another innovation – UN guards were assigned to protect relief supplies.

It was a highly interventionist refugee policy, departing from the principle of providing asylum outside the state (Refugee Policy Group, 1991). In the longer run, however, the status of the refugee zone was highly uncertain because the root causes of the Kurdish conflict were left as tangled as before. The nature of the problem – an ethnic people dispersed as minorities in four, later six, national states and having armed factions fighting for its own statehood – permitted no ready openings for a UN solution. The international consensus which had carried the UN military action against Iraq was immobilized, its parties recognizing that a continuing Kurdish refugee problem would figure prominently in the post-Cold War order.

From its interventionist, high-profile role in Iraq, the UN approached near paralysis in another minority conflict. Also of long standing, Myanmar's ethnic conflicts erupted in renewed violence in early 1992 (Lintner, 1991; Weiner, 1991; Lawyers' Committee for International Human Rights, 1992). After suspending the results of the 1990 elections, the military junta that ruled Myanmar (SLORC) tightened its grip. On the eastern border fighting between Karen rebels and government forces escalated. On the western border, a long-standing conflict over land and culture led to a violent expulsion of Muslim Arakanese. Earlier, a sizeable number of activists from the pro-democracy movement had fled to Thailand. Their plight was added to the rapidly growing refugee crisis as the Thai Government prepared to return the exiles to Myanmar. Neither Thailand nor Bangladesh did much to facilitate UNHCR access to the refugees.

The junta's decision to suspend the election results provided a formal opening for the international community to impose sanctions, as did repeated and gross violations of human rights. It was also clear that restoration of the democratic process, while hardly sufficient to solve Myanmar's long-standing ethnic conflicts, would at least have established a framework for dealing with these problems in a non-violent manner. However, only mild and uncoordinated international sanctions were applied.

In part, the explanation is found in the structure of international relations in the region. Traditionally a national recluse, Myanmar was of peripheral interest to the superpowers, even during the Cold War. Myanmar's relations with regional powers – India, China and ASEAN – remained more important, but they had no common regional organization that could address the question of Myanmar in the early 1990s. ASEAN could have taken an initiative, but refused to bend the principle of non-intervention. Key states such as Thailand wanted to maintain good relations with Myanmar for economic reasons. All ASEAN members had ethnic problems of their own and feared intrusive external pressures. This stand was shared by China and India. In the UN, the common problems of ethnic minorities inhibited action.

Between the Myanmar approach of paralysis and the Kurdish approach of incomplete activism lies the international response to Haiti's most recent refugee crisis. It also indicates the conditions under which a comprehensive refugee policy can develop.

For years, Haitians had sought to escape misery and violence by migrating.[4] While realizing that Duvalier's rule was at the root of the problem, the United States continued to support him and, after the exodus of 1980, adopted a dual strategy of interdiction and development aid. Interdiction was effective, the attempted root cause strategy less so. Export zones designed to soak up labour generated little development beyond them, and much aid was dissipated by corruption. The export zones probably acted as a magnet for further out-migration. In the main, as Alex Stepick argues, United States policy had the unintended effect of heightening pressure on the Duvalier government, culminating in Baby Doc's downfall in 1986 (Stepick, 1992). Subsequent attempts to develop civil society were cut short. Confrontation between the popularly elected president, Jean-Bertrand Aristide, and the élite-backed military culminated in the September 1991 coup, which again plunged the country into violence. Refugees started to come out in November, reaching a total of 15,000 by February 1992.

Unlike the Asian reactions to the coup in Myanmar, the Organization of American States (OAS) responded with a regional resolve to deny the coup legitimacy and restore democratic rule. In a collective move, the OAS imposed an economic embargo on Haiti and sought to mediate between the contending parties. The illegality of the coup provided a formal opening, and the OAS had both the institutional capacity and legal tradition to act. Despite growing United States hesitancy, this made it possible to formulate a root cause strategy. Restoration of Haiti's elected leadership was seen as the first step towards a political normalization that would permit reduction of both poverty and violence.

The embargo was incomplete, however, and the refugee part of the OAS strategy was poorly developed. The embargo worsened the already desperate conditions in Haiti, and contributed to the exodus. In a situation that required temporary asylum, the failure of the OAS to develop this option left the refugees to the restrictive and much criticized asylum policy of the United States. The most radical course would have been to establish a security zone for refugees inside Haiti, as was done for the Kurds in Iraq. This would have catapulted the OAS more prominently into the Haitian crisis and strengthened the rationale for a comprehensive refugee policy. Owing to the Organization's anti-interventionist concerns, and to United States hesitancy, this was not done.

As the three cases demonstrate, it is easier to obtain international agreement to aid refugees than to address the causes of outflow. The principle of non-interference remains the main obstacle and may in fact have been strengthened in the post-Cold War world as many countries, particularly in the developing world, fear a more assertive UN or regional bodies. Paradoxically, the global developments by the end of the 1980s that enlarged the scope for UN action and made a comprehensive refugee policy possible, simultaneously generated a contrary tendency.

On the other hand, the ideological simplification of a post-Cold War world has created a growing international consensus in favour of liberal democratic norms. This provides a ready opening for the international community to insist on democra-

---

[4] The following section draws heavily on interviews in February 1992 with Profs. Alex Dupuy of Wesleyan University, Alex Stepick of Florida International University, Karen Richmond of the University of Virginia, and Rick Swartz of Swartz & Associates, Washington, DC.

tic principles, especially when their collapse is the immediate cause of conflict and related refugee flows. As the Myanmar and Haiti cases demonstrate, minimal observance of democratic principles and human rights is a prerequisite for dealing with the root cause of many refugee flows. To demand that these principles of governance be observed thus constitutes a central element in a comprehensive refugee policy.

4. New challenges for a comprehensive refugee policy

Two political processes accompanied the dawn of the post-Cold War world – the trend towards greater democratization within some states, and the eruption of old nationality disputes threatening others with violent fragmentation. Both processes are of central concern to the international refugee regime. Failure to stabilize a fragile democratization process could result in a return of social order conflicts and associated refugee flows familiar from the past. Inability to manage nationality questions would encourage a recurrence of refugee flows of another kind.

Democratization

The conditions of democratization are nationally distinct, but in both Africa and Latin America it is evident that the recent democratization process proceeded *despite* generally worsening social and economic conditions. In a socioeconomic sense, the 1980s were "a lost decade" for Latin America, and a decade of decline for most of Africa (Castaneda, 1990; World Bank, 1989; Ravenhill, 1990). The weak material foundation of democratization suggests that economic development must figure prominently in a comprehensive refugee policy. The situation recalls the conclusions of the root cause debate in the early 1980s. For Latin America and much of Africa, perhaps the single most important root cause strategy is to support macroeconomic policies to relieve the debt burden and promote trade.

The trend towards democratization in Latin America has been variously explained (Smith, 1991; O'Donnell and Schmitter, 1986; Lowenthal, 1987). One theory is that the economic difficulties in the early 1980s overwhelmed even authoritarian governments. Debt repayment and restructuring towards market-oriented growth required austerity measures which further undermined the apparent advantages of military regimes in comparison with civil society. Alternatively, the enduring strength of civil society and the accomplishments of political leaders are viewed as the motivating forces towards liberal restoration. More pessimistically, some warn that there is not much to explain as only a civil-democratic veneer has appeared. The military authorities have retained their capacity to seize power but, for the time being, are content to assert their influence indirectly. The result is a fragile democracy with a hard edge, aptly called *democradura*, and possibly a phase in the familiar Latin cycle of authoritarian-democratic rule.

Against this background, the negative socioeconomic trends of the 1980s assume great significance. The debt burden starved most Latin American governments of funds. Regional debt-servicing alone was estimated to be $400 billion for the 1980s. Domestic investment in the region declined by about 30 per cent during the decade; foreign investment fell by 75 per cent. Owing to a lack of investment in infrastructure, future growth was put in danger, perhaps "for years to come", as a former United States ambassador to the region feared (Linowitz, 1988/9, p. 48). The social costs were accentuated by a demographic pattern which released the baby boom generation of the 1960s onto an already weak job market. The proportion of the region's population living in poverty increased from 35 per cent to 40 per cent during the decade, according to ECLA (UN/ECLA, 1991; Stallings and Kaufman, 1989).

Under these conditions, democratization must remain fragile. If it fails, recent history hints at the consequences. Authoritarian regimes in Argentina, Chile and Uruguay in the 1970s produced brutal and widespread repression. Not only the visible members of the opposition were targeted, as often happens when authoritarian rule replaces a *régime des parties*. The very strength of civil society invited widespread repression. Partly because of the common political and linguistic culture, many sought refuge elsewhere in South America. Estimates run to 1 million exiles (Zolberg, Suhrke and Aguayo, 1989, p. 199).

The repression of the 1970s reflected the anti-communist ideology of the times and strong United States support for the military authorities. A return to authoritarian rule in the 1990s would be shaped by a different international and national context. Possibly, economic austerity and socioeconomic discontent would give rise to a populist-fascist ideology as a legitimizing force. One plausible sequence is indicated by the Venezuelan case: urban riots over austerity measures and price increases in 1989 caused more than 300 deaths; in 1992 military factions attempted a coup but failed despite evidence of popular support. Were a coup to succeed, the interim growth of the democratic forces makes it likely that widespread repression and related refugee flows would follow.

Nationality questions

In a post-Cold War world where the permanence of nation states is questioned, nationality problems may progressively worsen. In the former USSR and the Balkans, the situation resembled the post-First World War period when both imperial structures and the political order collapsed, giving way to new principles of organization. In much of Asia and Africa, ethnic divisions have long been politically significant and show signs of becoming more so as aspiring nationalities witness the changing map of Central Asia, the Balkans and the former USSR.

Conditions of economic underdevelopment can easily exacerbate ethnic disputes. Rapid but uneven growth may threaten ethnic compromises. Where development is stagnating, resource scarcity typically sharpens ethnic divisions. In parts of Africa where the combination of weak states and ethnic hierarchies has produced endemic conflict, the result may be a final fragmentation of existing nation states (e.g. Sudan, Chad). In Asia, the generally stronger administrative and coercive capacity of states makes secession difficult, but ethnic conflict will probably remain an enduring source of violence (e.g. in India and Pakistan).

It should be remembered that not all ethnic or nationality conflicts give rise to refugee flows. Continuous tension and temporary violence, followed by a return to the status quo, are common. In fact, considering the frequency of ethnic conflicts in the world, the number of related international refugees is quite low. Only when violence reaches a point where the social contract itself breaks down, and the state is unwilling or unable to provide protection, are people compelled to seek safety outside the country.

When nationality conflicts do generate refugees, the profile is distinct. First of all, there is a "concentration" principle at work. As observers noted after the First World War, the collapse of empires leads to an unmixing of nationalities; ethnic groups move to join their ethnic kin (Annals, 1939). With the collapse of the Austro-Hungarian Empire in the First World War, about 2 million Poles migrated to Poland, 1 million ethnic Germans moved to Germany, and hundreds of thousands of Magyars went to Hungary. The collapse of the Ottoman Empire had a similar impact as Bulgarians from surrounding areas moved into Bulgaria while Greece and Turkey agreed to a formal exchange of populations. Following religious boundaries, Muslims from Bulgaria, Yugoslavia and Romania moved into Turkey.

These are relatively "solvable" refugee flows. The pattern is the same as in liberation struggles when the displaced populations can return to their homeland once the war is over. Population movements of this kind – or even exchanges – can be a solution to stubborn minority questions, and may be the best course of action if the alternative is violent conflict or probable death. In some cases, the central question may be whether to manage the flow (as in the Greek-Turkish exchange of 1922), or whether to let a spontaneous flow with attendant risks of violence unfold (as during the partition of India in 1947). Some contemporary nationality conflicts generate refugee flows that follow the concentration principle, as in the Caucasus. These refugees require protection during passage and assistance for resettlement, and resemble internally displaced persons. They rarely place long-term asylum demands on the international refugee regime.

The massive refugee crisis arising from the former Yugoslavia demonstrates the opposite tendency: the intensity of fighting and lack of local support or absence of an equivalent "homeland", lead to a dispersal of refugees throughout the region and beyond.

In either case, relocation or exchanges can only be "second best" solutions. They may become pretexts for expulsion of minorities. Even when a homeland exists, relocation usually sows seeds of future conflict because the costs of displacement are great, tend to be unevenly divided (even during exchanges), and leave a bitter legacy. The main emphasis, therefore, must be on strategies to contain or regulate conflict.

As the protracted conflict in the former Yugoslavia demonstrates, civil wars of this kind have long and tangled roots that defy easy solutions. A cumulative crisis of uneven economic development, stifled democratization, old ethnic animosities and a sudden collapse of the existing political order culminated in violence in the early 1990s (Golubovic, 1992). Confronting this complex strife was a seemingly paralysed international community. Regional European mechanisms for instituting order were poorly developed, and the UN showed little ability to act independently. More fundamentally, the very principle of international order was in dispute.

The Cold War and its particular balance of power as a source of order had given way to two opposing visions (Myall, 1992; Nye, 1992; Rosecrance, 1992). In the tradition of *realpolitik*, one school of thought sought order in a new balance of power, based on existing nation states regardless of their nature. Against this, the "idealist" view maintained that order must rest on normative principles upholding national self-determination and democracy. The former invoked the dangers of mushrooming violence if existing states were allowed to unravel, revealing an unending series of minority-within-minority relationships and irredentist demands. The latter claimed that an international order which defied nationalist aspirations must eventually fail. As nationalist and democratic forces did not necessarily coincide, confusion mounted and paralysis set in. The international community which had just proclaimed a new era of genuine collective security found it could neither mount an effective peace-making operation in the former Yugoslavia, nor provide adequate relief to civilians.

A comprehensive refugee policy, then, requires minimal agreement on the principle of order. Using an instrumental yardstick of violence and related refugee flows, that means maintaining existing states but demanding internal reforms (Zolberg, Suhrke and Aguayo, 1989). Minorities rarely have sufficient power to achieve statehood; Crawford Young's conclusion in 1976 was that violent secessionist struggles would generally only result in prolonged violence (Young, 1976). The point seems valid today. Existing states can still benefit from a deeply imbedded conservatism in the international system, probably more so after the apparent costs of quick-recognition policies towards successor states in the former Yugoslavia. To assist in the final collapse of imperial territories already in an advanced state of disintegration, on the other hand, might shorten the period of violence, or even prevent it altogether.

While instrumental, this principle of order is normatively anchored. To justify the legality of existing states, and ward off secessionist as well as irredentist demands, mutual restraint and tolerance are required. In a historical period when states are buffeted by the contradictory forces of interdependence and nationalism, institutionalized pluralism or autonomy arguably represents the best framework for regulating nationality conflicts. This imposes a responsibility of restraint on minorities and majorities.

International law does not recognize a minority right to statehood, but the protection of minorities has been codified; in Europe this dates back to the "Capitulations with Turkey" of 1535 (Annals, 1939). More recent attempts were so disastrous in their consequences that the idea itself was discredited. The Minorities Treaties instituted after the First World War were ineffective and unequal, with the result that the "liberation" of German minorities became a pretext for Fascist Germany's territorial expansion. As a reaction, international legal instruments adopted after the Second World War to protect minorities remain weak (Claude, 1955; Thornberry, 1987).

Even under the best of circumstances, a number of nationality or ethnic conflicts will remain unsolvable. Enduring, if fluctuating, violence and related refugee flows will result. A root-cause strategy, therefore, cannot be a substitute for asylum. Failure to provide asylum may in fact encourage repression in the country of origin by conveying a negative evaluation of the target group. The point has often been made with respect to the 1938 Evian Conference – where the United States and

European countries failed to offer liberal resettlement programmes for Jews fleeing Germany and Austria – and has a wider application. As the international refugee regime enters the post-Cold War world, the central challenge is precisely the development of a comprehensive refugee policy which preserves the right of asylum and which encompasses greater efforts to address the causes of flight.

5. Conclusions and policy implications

The international refugee regime currently faces several challenges. The transition to a new era requires, first of all, that the legacy of the past be dealt with. In its last phase, the Cold War intensified local conflicts which produced millions of international refugees. As Cold War tension eased, the regional conflicts were damped down, but some continued to smoulder, and all presented enormous problems of reconstruction and repatriation. Unless reconstruction moves ahead, the poison of old conflicts will remain in the post-Cold War world and produce renewed refugee flows.

The international climate for aid to yesterday's strategic areas is not favourable. Europe is experiencing its own massive refugee crisis, and the former superpowers have either disappeared or show signs of financial exhaustion. To clarify the importance of sustained aid to "old" refugee crises in the developing world, new strategic rationales have to be developed. The premise must be that, if left unattended, defused conflicts can reignite. Unwillingness to deal with what already has the contours of a reconstruction crisis will slow repatriation and probably generate future strife with renewed outflows.

A second challenge for the international refugee regime is presented by repressive governments or anarchic conditions in the developing world. Not all local struggles were "over-determined" by the Cold War: several evolved fairly independently and persisted into the new era. These were recurring struggles of "State v. People" (Hoffman, 1990) formed by their own traditions and social configurations. Whenever these conflicts erupted into violence, refugees followed, as happened in Haiti, Myanmar and the Kurdish areas. A root-cause strategy based on economic sanctions to restore democratic norms and human rights was relevant in at least two of these cases, but only partly implemented in one.

An international refugee regime concerned with the causes of outflows must also consider broader development issues in the post-Cold War world. A third challenge, therefore, is to stabilize the emerging democratization in much of the developing world. From a refugee perspective, democratization with its attendant respect for human rights and tendency to solve conflicts through the political process is obviously positive. The trend towards democratization in Latin America and parts of Asia predates the end of the Cold War; it is more recent in Africa and geographically confined. Future prospects, however, are clouded by adverse conditions such as a crushing foreign debt, socioeconomic inequality associated with market liberalization, demographic pressures and rapid environmental degradation. For many observers, the fact that democratization has proceeded despite these developments is indeed paradoxical. The paradox may yet resolve itself in a return to authoritarianism or civil strife.

A fourth challenge arises from disorders developing in the wake of a vanished era. The rivalry between the nuclear superpowers provided restraints and a certain stability. As the old order disappeared – and before new structures of regional or international order had fully developed – various conflicts erupted to produce both international wars (in the Gulf) and civil wars (in the Balkans). The civil wars in the former Yugoslavia exemplify the ferocity of forces unleashed by the end of the Cold War. By replacing the logic of imperialism with the principle of national self-determination, the disintegration of the USSR threatened existing multi-ethnic states and generated an array of difficult nationality problems within the former USSR itself. New democratic forces were often too weak to restrain a militant nationalism which bred ethnic intolerance and irredentism.

No single strategy can even begin to address the manifold and complex forces of conflict in the post-Cold War era. Economic aid by itself is in most cases of limited relevance; even when expanded to include broader issues of trade and investment, aid strategies would affect only some aspects of strife. It follows that a policy designed to address the sources of refugee flows must be comprehensive in several senses of the word. More specifically, this means a policy which is:

(a) *Multilevel*. Effective root-cause strategies must operate simultaneously on the political, developmental and aid levels. For instance, concern with democratization and human rights is demonstrably relevant to reducing refugee flows in many parts of the world. But the material foundation of democratization must be recognized, including structural economic conditions such as the debt burden. Similarly, aid strategies that emphasize human rights conditionality can, in some cases, reduce outflows by compelling repressive regimes to desist. An imposed human rights conditionality may, however, be less effective than a strategy which reconstructs the aid dialogue to include principles of governance in the broader context of development (*Human Rights in Developing Countries*, 1991; IBRD, 1992).

Internal and international wars are fundamentally questions of military power and diplomacy, but aid strategies are also relevant. Reconstruction aid can be used to promote peace settlements and encourage repatriation, as was tried in Afghanistan and Cambodia. Economic sanctions may be used to compel repressive or illegitimate regimes to observe greater respect for human rights, or to induce warring parties to conclude cease-fires. In fact, economic sanctions have historically been more successful in modifying the conflict behaviour of states than is frequently recognized, the key to impact being the duration and comprehensiveness of the sanctions.

(b) *Cooperative*. Possibilities for dealing cooperatively with international refugee problems have increased in the post-Cold War era. As the UN is freed from the paralysing superpower rivalry of the past, UN agencies have a particularly important role to play in formulating and implementing a comprehensive refugee regime for troubled areas. The leading powers of the new era – notably the United States, the EC and Japan – must recognize that cooperative efforts form the basis of an effective and comprehensive refugee policy.

(c) *Integrative*. Optimally, strategies addressing the causes of conflict should be integrated with aid to the victims. For instance, a blockade designed to coerce a repressive regime and reduce violence in the long term is likely to increase the hardship on ordinary people and increase refugee flows in the short term (as happened in Haiti). Plans to accommodate these refugees should be instituted along with the blockade (as did not happen in the Haitian case). Policy integration is also a prerequisite for reversing refugee flows. Thus, support for economic and political reconstruction will encourage repatriation and prevent renewed refugee flows.

In substantive terms, a comprehensive refugee policy must support principles of order as well as social justice. Two fundamental lessons from the Cold War are particularly relevant in this regard. As the so-called regional conflicts of that period demonstrate, competitive external intervention in local conflicts tends to be counterproductive by intensifying the violence, prolonging the fighting, and inflating the refugee flows. Sales or supplies of arms to conflict areas have similar effects, and undermine both stability and progress when provided to any extent throughout the developing world. The lessons of the past, then, call for restraint on both competitive intervention and global arms supplies.

Beyond that, a comprehensive refugee policy must broadly seek to restrain violence within and among states. This means support for human rights and democratization, minority protection based on mutual respect and tolerance, peaceful change of boundaries, and crisis management wherever possible. These subjects do not fall within the jurisdiction of the international refugee regime, yet the failure of these processes will add to its workload. In order to develop a comprehensive refugee policy, the international refugee community must concern itself with these issues.

Nevertheless, the prolonged crisis in the Balkans exposed certain basic limitations on a root-cause policy designed to modify the causes of contemporary refugee flows. Not only were the principles of international order in dispute and the mechanisms for peacemaking and peacekeeping insufficiently developed. The Yugoslav crisis itself was so complex and intractable that even the best tailored root-cause policy would have seemed inadequate.

In the final analysis, the case for a comprehensive refugee policy must be tempered by two considerations. First, social change – like conflict – is a complex process that often defies predictability and attempts at social engineering. Even forces heralded as pillars of order and stability have historically proved to be deeply subversive institutions, as Benedict Anderson has remarked (Anderson, 1992). Secondly, in so far as social change involves conflict and often violence, attempts to reduce violence could legitimize a commitment to the status quo regardless of its nature. It may be possible to envisage a world where economic equality will reduce international migration; a world without refugees, however, is difficult to imagine and is scarcely to be desired as it implies a world without social change. The international obligation must remain, therefore, to provide asylum to the victims of violence.

Bibliography

Anderson, Benedict. 1992. "The new world disorder", in *New Left Review*, 193, May-June, pp. 3-13.
Annals of the American Academy of Political and Social Sciences. 1939. Special issue on minorities and refugees. Vol. 203.
Arendt, Hannah. 1973. *The origins of totalitarianism* (New York, Harcourt Brace Jovanovich).
Berryman, Phillip. 1984. *The religious roots of rebellion* (Maryknoll, New York, Orbis Books).
Baitenmann, Helga. 1990. "NGOs and the Afghan war: The politicisation of humanitarian aid", in *Third World Quarterly*, XII, 1, pp. 62-85.
Black, Cyril E., et al. 1968. *Neutralization and world politics* (New Jersey, Princeton, University Press).
Castaneda, Jorge. 1990. "Latin America and the end of the Cold War", in *World Policy Journal*, VII, 3, pp. 469-492.
Chan Kwok Bun. 1990. "Getting through suffering. Indochinese refugees in limbo 15 years later", in *Southeast Asian Journal of Social Science*, XVIII, 1, pp. 1-18.
Chanda, Nayan. 1990. "Indochina", in Anthony Lake (ed.): *After the wars* (Washington, DC, Overseas Development Council).
Chandler, David. 1991. *The land and people of Cambodia* (New York, Harper Collins).
Chona, Mark C.; Jeffrey I. Herbst. 1990. "Southern Africa", in Anthony Lake (ed.): *After the wars* (Washington, DC, Overseas Development Council).
Claude, Inis. 1955. *National minorities: An international problem* (Cambridge, Massachusetts, Harvard University Press).
GLASOD (Global Assessment of Soil Degradation). 1991. *World map of the status of human-induced soil degradation* (Wageningen and New York, International Soil Reference and Information Centre and UNEP).
Goldstone, Jack A. 1991. *Revolution and rebellion in the early modern world* (Berkeley, University of California Press).
Goldstone, Jack A.; Ted Robert Gurr; Farrokh Moshiri (eds.). 1991. *Revolutions of the late twentieth century* (Boulder, Colorado, Westview Press).
Golubovic, Zagorka. 1992. "The conditions leading to the breakdown of the Yugoslav State: What has generated the civil war in Yugoslavia", in *Praxis International*, No. 12, July, pp. 129-44.
Harrison, Selig. 1990. "Afghanistan", in Anthony Lake (ed.): *After the wars* (Washington, DC, Overseas Development Council).
Hjort, Anders af Ornäs; M.A. Mohamed Salih (eds.). 1989. *Ecology and politics: Environmental stress and security in Africa* (Uppsala, Scandinavian Institute of African Studies).
Hoffman, Stanley. 1990. "A new world and its troubles", in *Foreign Affairs*, 69:4, Fall, pp. 115-151.
Holborn, Louise W. 1975. *Refugees: A problem of our time: The work of the United Nations High Commissioner for Refugees, 1951-1972* (Metuchen, New Jersey, Scarecrow Press).
Horowitz, Donald L. 1985. *Ethnic groups in conflict* (Berkeley, University of California Press).
Human Rights in Developing Countries. 1991. Yearbook. Bård Anders Andreassen; Theresa Swinehart (eds.) (Oslo, Scandinavian University Press).
IBRD. 1992. *Governance: A report* (Washington, DC).
Kritz, Mary M. (ed.). 1983. *US immigration and refugee policy: Global and domestic issues* (Lexington, Massachusetts, D.C. Heath).
Lake, Anthony. (ed.). 1990. *After the wars* (Washington, DC, Overseas Development Council).
Lawyers' Committee for International Human Rights. 1992. *Burma: The international response to continuing human rights violations* (New York).

LeoGrande, William M. 1990. "After the battle of San Salvador: Breaking the deadlock", in *World Policy Journal*, VIII, 2, pp. 331-356.
Lintner, Bertil. 1991. "The internationalization of Burma's ethnic conflict", in K.M. de Silva and R.J. May (eds.): *Internationalization of ethnic conflict* (London, Pinter).
Linowitz, Sol M. 1988/89. "Latin America: The President's agenda", in *Foreign Affairs*, 67:2, pp. 45-62.
Loescher, Gil; Laila Monahan (eds.). 1988. *Refugees and international relations* (Oxford, Clarendon Press).
Lowenthal, Abraham F. 1987. *Partners in conflict: The United States and Latin America* (Baltimore, Johns Hopkins University Press).
Manz, Beatrice. 1988. *Refugees of a hidden war* (Albany, State University of New York Press).
Marrus, Michael. 1985. *The unwanted: European refugees in the twentieth century* (New York, Oxford University Press).
Martin, David. 1987. "Comparative policies on political asylum: Of facts and law", in Tomasi, L. (ed.): *In defense of the alien* (New York, Center for Migration Studies).
Ministry of Planning and Coordination of Economic and Social Development, the Republic of El Salvador. 1992. *National reconstruction plan of El Salvador*.
Montgomery, Tommie Sue. 1982. *Revolution in El Salvador: Origins and evolution* (Boulder, Colorado, Westview Press).
Moore, Barrington. 1966. *Social origins of dictatorship and democracy: Lord and peasant in the making of the modern world* (Boston, Beacon Press).
Myall, James. 1992. "Nationalism and international security after the Cold War", in *Survival*, Spring, pp. 18-35.
Nye, Joseph. 1992. "What new world order", in *Foreign Affairs*, 71:2, Spring, pp. 83-96.
O'Donnell, Guillermo; Philippe Schmitter. 1986. "Tentative conclusions about uncertain democracies", in O'Donnell, Schmitter and Laurence Whitehead (eds.): *Transition from authoritarian rule: Prospects for democracy* (Baltimore, Johns Hopkins University Press).
Ravenhill, John. 1990. "Reversing Africa's economic decline: No easy answers", in *World Policy Journal*, VII, 4, pp. 703-732.
Roy, Olivier. 1986. *Islam and resistance in Afghanistan* (Cambridge, Cambridge University Press).
Rosecrance, Richard. 1992. "A new concert of power", in *Foreign Affairs*, 71:2, Spring, pp. 64-82.
Refugee Policy Group. 1991. *Human rights protection for internally displaced persons* (Washington, DC).
Rubin, Barnett R. 1989/90. "The fragmentation of Afghanistan", in *Foreign Affairs*, 68:5, pp. 150-168.
Rupert, James. 1989. "Afghanistan's slide towards civil war", in *World Policy Journal*, 6:4, pp. 759-785.
Saikal, A. (ed.). 1989. *The Soviet withdrawal from Afghanistan* (Cambridge, Cambridge University Press).
Schlesinger, James. 1991/92. "New instabilities, new priorities", in *Foreign Policy*, No. 85, Winter, pp. 3-24.
de Silva, K.M.; R.J.May (eds.). 1991. *Internationalization of ethnic conflict* (London, Pinter).
Smith, Peter H. 1991. "Crisis and democracy in Latin America", in *World Politics*, 43:4, pp. 608-634.
Stallings, Barbara; Robert Kaufman (eds.). 1989. *Debt and democracy in Latin America* (Boulder, Colorado, Westview Press).
Stepick, Alex. 1992. "Unintended consequences: Rejecting Haitian boat people and destabilizing Duvalier", in Christopher Mitchell (ed.): *US foreign affairs and immigration policy* (Philadelphia, University of Pennsylvania Press).

Suhrke, Astri. 1990. "Afghanistan: Retribalization of the war", in *Journal of Peace Research*, 27:3, pp. 241-246.
—. 1991. "Refugees in Asia: Problems and practices of asylum for Indochinese and Afghan refugees", paper prepared for ECE\UNFPA meeting, Geneva, 16-19 July.
Sutter, Valerie O'Connor. 1990. *The Indochinese refugee dilemma* (Baton Rouge, Louisiana State University Press).
Thornberry, Patrick. 1987. *Minorities and human rights law*. Report No. 73. (London, The Minority Rights Group).
UN. 1980. "International cooperation to avert new flows of refugees", in *Summary Record*, Special Political Committee of the General Assembly (doc. A/SPC/35/SR.43, 10 Dec. 1980).
—. 1981. *Study on human rights and massive exoduses* (doc. UN/ECOSOC/E/CN.4/1503, 31 Dec. 1981).
—. 1985. *International cooperation to avert new flows of refugees* (doc. A/41/324, 13 May 1985).
UNDP. 1992. *Fourth country programme for Vietnam: 1992-1996* (New York).
UN/ECLA. 1991. Report cited in *Washington Post*, 18 Feb. 1992.
UNOCA. 1988. Office of the UN Coordinator for Humanitarian and Economic Assistance Programs Relating to Afghanistan. *First Consolidated Report* (Geneva).
—. 1989. — *Second Consolidated Report* (Geneva).
United States Committee for Refugees. 1990. *World Refugee Survey* (Washington, DC).
Vernant, Jacques. 1953. *The refugee in the post-war world* (London, Allen and Unwin).
Weiner, Myron. 1991. *Rejected peoples and unwanted migrants: The impact of migration on the politics and security of South Asia*, paper prepared for a conference at the Massachusetts Institute of Technology, Cambridge.
Williams, Michael. 1992. "Beyond the revolution: Indonesia and Vietnam", in Mark Borthwick (ed.): *Pacific century* (Boulder, Colorado, Westview Press).
World Bank. 1989. *Sub-Saharan Africa: From crisis to sustainable growth* (Washington, DC).
Young, Crawford. 1976. *The politics of cultural pluralism* (Madison, University of Wisconsin Press).
Zolberg, Aristide R. 1989. "The next waves: Migration theory for a changing world", in *International Migration Review*, XXIII, 3, pp. 403- 431.
—; Astri Suhrke; Sergio Aguayo. 1989. *Escape from violence: Conflict and the refugee crisis in the developing world* (New York, Oxford University Press).

2

Can foreign aid reduce East-West migration in Europe, with particular reference to Poland?

W.T.M. Molle, J. de Koning and C.Th. Zandvliet

1. Introduction

Basic questions

The question put by this paper is: How large, and in what form, should foreign aid be to reduce significantly over one or two generations the pressure on the labour markets of the Central and Eastern European Countries (CEECs) so as to prevent large-scale migration to Western Europe?

The answer we give relies on an economic assessment of the various determinants of the growth and migration process. We have made the following basic assumptions:

1. Labour migration in Europe is influenced by many factors, comprising *push factors* (e.g. the political situation in the sending country) and *pull factors* (e.g. high wage levels in the receiving country). The economic factors among these, namely, different job access rates and wage levels, are the most important.
2. Wage differences between East and West are very large, so considerable East-West migration is likely to occur.
3. International migration presents more of a problem than a solution to both the sending and the receiving country if the welfare aspects are considered.
4. A reduction of migration is a desirable policy goal. Action should therefore be taken to avoid massive East-West migration.
5. Effective policy-making must not confine itself to setting rules for immigration entry, but must attempt to take away the stimulus to migration.
6. Low-income CEECs need to achieve faster growth than high-income Western countries if differences in wage levels and job access rates are to be reduced.
7. As CEECs' own resources are insufficient to achieve this, international aid is needed.

Specific questions flow from these assumptions:

1. What factors determine migration? Are these different for different categories of migrant? Which of these factors can be influenced by policy measures?
2. How large are these wage differences? Are they much larger for some countries than others? How much migration are they likely to cause? Is this migration permanent or temporary?
3. Are there cases where different positions need to be taken, e.g. for demographic reasons? What type of differentiation by country, age, sex and occupation group should then be made?
4. Who should take action and where will this be done, e.g. the government of the receiving country, or international organizations?
5. Are the rules limiting access of migrants to Western labour markets ineffective? How effective are economic policies in this respect?
6. What factors determine the catching-up process? How does the distribution of income over production factors (labour) come about?
7. Does aid have a positive influence? What is the absorption capacity of the receiving countries? Which types of aid are the most effective? What combinations of aid programmes are practical? What is the role of other determinants in economic growth?

2. Aid and development

Development trends in Europe

History shows a widening of economic inequality over Europe. In 1880 international differences in GDP levels were relatively small but between 1880 and 1913 they increased. GDP per head in the countries of north-western Europe increased on average fourfold, in the countries in the Mediterranean basin it doubled, while in the countries of eastern Europe it increased by only 50 per cent before the First World War (Bairoch, 1976).

Between 1913 and 1950 these trends were partially reversed. Per capita GDP growth in Europe was very low on average, at only 25 per cent. Growth differences between the three main areas were not that great: generally it would seem that western Europe performed slightly better than eastern Europe, which in turn performed slightly better than the south of the continent.

Since the Second World War, the differences between north and south, east and west have tended to decrease (Molle, 1990b). Although difficult to establish, estimates for the years just before the revolutionary events in Central and Eastern Europe (Summers and Heston, 1988) suggest that there was relatively little difference between wealth levels in south-western and Eastern Europe, e.g. Czechoslovakia

Table 2.1. GNP and GNP per capita in Europe, 1989 (based on purchasing power parities)

	GNP per capita (dollars)	GNP (billion dollars)	Population (million)
EC North	**15 476**	**4 327.27**	**279.62**
Luxembourg	24 681	9.30	0.38
France	16 379	919.84	56.16
Germany	15 720	1 232.46	78.40
Germany, Fed. Rep.	17 309	1 074.26	62.06
Germany, Dem. Rep.	9 680	158.20	16.34
Denmark	15 157	77.79	5.13
Belgium	15 119	150.25	9.94
Italy	14 990	862.31	57.53
United Kingdom	14 972	856.95	57.24
Netherlands	14 708	218.36	14.85
EC South	**9 595**	**597.11**	**62.23**
Spain	10 860	422.34	38.89
Ireland	8 334	29.29	3.52
Portugal	7 604	74.46	9.79
Greece	7 078	71.02	10.03
EC 12	14 405	4 924.38	341.85
EFTA	**16 535**	**534.28**	**32.31**
Switzerland	20 918	140.63	6.72
Liechtenstein[1]	20 918	0.59	0.03
Sweden	15 856	134.66	8.49
Finland	15 423	76.56	4.96
Austria	15 236	116.16	7.62
Iceland	14 713	3.72	0.25
Norway	14 658	61.96	4.23
Western Europe	14 589	5 458.67	370.16
East Group 1	**7 890**	**213.10**	**27.01**
Yugoslavia (Slovenia)	12 520	24.50	1.95
Czechoslovakia	7 880	123.30	15.64
Yugoslavia (Croatia)	7 110	33.30	4.69
Yugoslavia (Voivodina)	6 790	13.90	2.05
USSR (Latvia)	6 740	18.10	2.68
East Group 2	**5 097**	**350.50**	**68.77**
USSR (Estonia)	6 240	9.80	1.58
Hungary	6 110	64.70	10.58
USSR (Lithuania)	5 880	21.80	3.71
Bulgaria	5 710	51.30	8.99
Yugoslavia (Serbia[2])	4 950	29.00	5.85
Poland	4 570	173.90	38.06
East Group 3	**3 239**	**129.40**	**39.95**
Yugoslavia (Montenegro)	3 970	2.60	0.65
USSR (Moldova)	3 830	16.70	4.35
Yugoslavia (Bosnia and Herzegovina)	3 590	16.20	4.52
Romania	3 450	79.80	23.14
Yugoslavia (Macedonia)	3 330	7.10	2.13
Yugoslavia (Kosovo)	1 520	3.00	1.99
Albania	1 250	4.00	3.17
Eastern Europe	5 106	693.00	135.73
Total Europe		6 151.11	509.80

[1] GNP is estimated using GNP of Switzerland adjusted in proportion to population.
[2] Excluding Kosovo and Voidovina.

Sources: OECD National Accounts, vol. 1 1960-1990; PLANECON; World Bank Atlas 1990. Adapted from Wijkman, 1992.

Table 2.2. Catch-up rates of growth for East Group countries in relation to the EC, 1990-2020

	1990	%	2020
EC	15 000	2.3	30 000
East Group I	7 000	3.2	18 000
	6 000	3.8	18 000
East Group II	5 000	4.4	18 000
	4 000	5.1	18 000
East Group III	3 000	6.2	18 000
	2 000	7.6	18 000

was on a par with Spain, and Hungary and Poland were in the same group as the lower-income Western European countries of Portugal and Greece.

The economic and political upheavals in Eastern Europe have radically changed the picture. Large sectors of the economy have been cut off from their traditional markets. Production and consumption levels are difficult to establish. On the basis of the partial evidence available (e.g. in Debs, Shapiro and Taylor, 1991) growth in 1989, 1990 and 1991 was negative in most CEECs; in some cases economies shrank by 25 per cent. Given Western Europe's growth, we may conclude that over the past few years the economic disparity between Western and Eastern Europe has significantly increased (by more than 25 per cent).

The 1989 figures on differences in GDP per head in Europe (Table 2.1) are indicative of the present situation: average income levels in the East are only one-third of those of the West. There are significant differences within each of the two groups. The ratio between the richest Western European country (Switzerland) and the poorest Eastern European country (Albania) is 17 (US$ 20,900 to US$ 1,250). However, the ratio between Germany and Poland is 3, equal to the average between Western and Eastern Europe.

Assuming that these figures give a representative picture of the difference between Western and Eastern Europe, we can then calculate the gap that Eastern Europe has to span. To do this, we first assume that the mature economy of Western Europe will grow over the next thirty years (one generation) at its historical long-term growth rate of some 2.3 per cent a year. We next assume (see e.g. Molle and van Mourik, 1989) that an income gap of 1 to 3 can be sustained without giving rise to large-scale migration. With the set-back of recent years, Eastern European countries will have to realize growth rates of 4 per cent to 7 per cent over the next 30 years (see Table 2.2). Such growth rates are realistic by historical standards.

Growth factors

Inputs

Differences in the supply of inputs determine differences in growth rates. According to the neoclassical production function, labour (total employment, hours worked, age and sex distribution, and education), capital (investment in machinery, dwellings and international assets), and productivity growth (residual) are necessary for growth. A disadvantage of this input approach is that the explanatory factors are themselves in need of explanation. Indeed, to state that the postwar growth of the Federal Republic of Germany is due to an increase in immigrant labour is unsatisfactory. An explanation is also needed as to why this country increased output to such an extent that it needed so many additional workers.

Markets

Growth is accelerated by markets. Their influence leads in turn to competition, economies of scale, learning effects, etc.

Growth is also dependent on the relation between import and export prices – the terms of trade. The hypothesis is that countries faced with high prices in their import markets (e.g. because of an oil shock) and with low prices in their export markets, will show lower growth rates than countries in more favourable circumstances.

The "new growth theory" (e.g. Grossman and Helpman, 1990) stresses the interrelation between trade policies based on competition and endogenous human capital improvement and technological progress. Under certain conditions, such trade speeds up growth in both the rich North and the poor South.

Infrastructure

Productive investments are useless if not accompanied by complementary investments in infrastructure. Regional economists stress the need for a good transport infrastructure (ports, airports, roads, railways), and for good telecommunications.

Government and culture

The smooth functioning of the private sector is heavily dependent, among other things, on an efficient legal system, the absence of corruption, and the knowledge that decisions made by the courts will be followed. This can be termed effective political organization and administrative competence (Reynolds, 1983).

Growth is enhanced by institutional flexibility. The rapid postwar growth seen in the Federal Republic of Germany may have been due to the breakup of many special interest groups by the Nazis and the Allied Powers; similarly, the slow growth of the United Kingdom may have been the result of the immobility of its social structure.

Different motivational factors among various religious groups can also lead to differences in growth performance (Hofstede, 1991).

Naturally, many of the growth factors cited here are closely interrelated, so it is difficult to isolate any one of them. Neither is this list exhaustive. In addition, much emphasis has traditionally been given to natural resources, while recently the concern for sustainable development has focused on preserving them.

Aid programmes

Many countries perform very poorly in relation to almost all the above factors, and consequently have very slow growth. In an attempt to accelerate growth, governments have concluded bilateral aid agreements, and international organizations have established multilateral aid programmes. Some programmes help to promote trade (access to developed country markets), while others enhance foreign direct investment (private capital) in less developed countries (LDCs). Although both types of activity are extremely important in the case of Eastern Europe,[1] they will not be discussed here.

International aid is a transfer of resources on concessional terms. Much of it is official development assistance (ODA). This includes concessional loans that are given by official agencies with the objective of promoting the economic development and welfare of the recipient country, and that have a grant element of at least 25 per cent (in terms of the real cost compared to the cost of market loans – see OECD, 1990a). Another important form of aid is technical cooperation. This includes assistance, nearly all in grants, targeted at two types of people: recipient country individuals receiving education and training abroad; and experts working in recipient countries on, e.g. the educational and training system, capital market operations, industrial and infrastructural projects, and policy formation. A third category of aid, emergency food aid, is not discussed here, as it is not a structural entity.

In the past, CEECs did not qualify for developing country international aid; indeed, some of them were aid donors (OECD, 1990a). They received support in the form of loans, and as a consequence some CEECs have a significant external debt.

Countries in the transition period are experiencing difficulties in repaying their debt: for Poland this has led to a debt reduction and rescheduling agreement with creditors. CEECs, in fact, have an urgent need for extra financing for several reasons:

- to improve their capacity to import end products, thereby enhancing competition and improving productivity; this in turn cuts costs and reduces inflation. This policy helps to ensure supplies of consumer goods, and will be a stabilizing factor during the transformation process;
- to increase the stock of modern capital goods; the pace at which machinery is renewed can be accelerated, leading to productivity increases. This often accompanies the transfer of technical know-how and managerial skills;
- to build up a stock of hard currency, needed to underpin the convertibility of the currency.

[1] See in this respect for trade: Collins and Rodrik (1991), Wang and Winters (1991), Hamilton and Winters (1992) and Havrylyshyn and Pritchett (1991). For the importance of FDI in the catching-up process of southern Europe see, for example, Morsink and Molle (1991); for recent changes in the relations between CEECs and the EC see e.g. Gautron (1991) and in a more popular way, Merritt (1991).

It is difficult to assess the extent to which extra capital is needed for the transition process, but requirements are substantial (Debs, Shapiro and Taylor, 1991). It is equally difficult to estimate the amount of foreign capital required to finance the structural development of CEECs to enable them to catch up with the West. Figures range from $20 billion to $200 billion a year (Wersch, 1991). The first is an estimate by the European Community (EC), based on the experience with Structural Funds. The second is by the Centre for Economic Policy Research (CEPR) in London, based on a very high growth assumption. This capital requirement could be met from private or public sources in the form of loans or grants, etc.

The different figures for capital have very different macroeconomic effects. A critical analysis of these effects (Bergeyk, Noe and Oldersma, 1991) leads to the conclusion that aid figures beyond $20 billion exceed the absorption capacity of CEECs. With $20 billion aid, it is estimated that growth of GDP per head in CEECs will be 3 per cent a year for the present decade. EC experience would indicate, however, that support can gradually be stepped up and that, under conditions of integration, growth rates of 4 to 6 per cent are consistent with the "catching up" scenario of the previous era.

Current aid programmes of national governments, the EC, and the international aid agencies take into account many of the determinants of growth, such as providing guarantees for private investments, supporting labour and management training, and technology transfer.

Impact of aid on development

Aid is given to enhance the economic development of the beneficiary. But does it achieve this?

Critics believe it does not (or at least not enough). Some criticisms are that: aid takes away the urgency for reform of the system; it decreases the savings ratio and increases consumption without improving productive capacity; if used for the productive system it is often poorly oriented in technological and market terms; it benefits the donor more than the recipient; and as its objectives are unclear, performance cannot be checked.

However, aid has its supporters (Cassen et al., 1986). By removing bottlenecks to development, in its provision of capital, in terms of infrastructure and in the formation of human capital etc., aid does indeed contribute to economic performance. This is not to say that all aid has been positive, but that, on balance, it has achieved a positive effect. But its effectiveness critically depends on the specific form chosen and on the policies of the recipient countries.

Aid to CEECs has been practically non-existent. Moreover, the economic system in these countries has changed. So an analysis of the effectiveness of past aid schemes to the countries of this region is of little use.

Within the developed world, the aid programmes forming part of the EC "cohesion policy" can be used as a basis for comparison. They are designed to step up the economic growth in member States that are facing either industrial restructuring or underdevelopment in a modern sector. These aid programmes are large and have considerable impact. For example, the total amount of support from structural funds given to countries such as Portugal and Greece amounts to 2 per cent of GDP and 7 per cent of total investment (Commission of the European Communities, 1991). The programmes are thought to be responsible for a significant proportion of recent growth, in Portugal especially. More systematic evaluations of the impact of intra-European aid programmes are rare. One attempt to measure the macroeconomic effects of the structural funds (Marques-Mendes, 1990) reaches a positive conclusion on their influence in reducing disparities, and suggests that more aid would bolster growth even further. Such an increase in resources was agreed upon in Maastricht (the Cohesion Fund).

On the basis of this preliminary evaluation it would seem that:

- aid programmes are, on balance, effective (depending on conditions, etc.);
- aid to Eastern Europe needs to be gradually stepped up to at least $30 billion to $40 billion a year, in order to attain a convergence of GDP levels in 2020 that practically eliminates the need for mass migration from East to West;
- once the transitional stage is over, aid should be oriented towards increasing productive capacity of the recipient countries (see the list of growth factors above);
- aid will be ineffective unless it is set within a framework of liberalization of goods and services between the EC and CEECs.

3. Analysis of migration

Migration trends

The recent new wave of mass migration from Eastern to Western Europe has not reached previous levels, nor is it likely to do so in the next few years. This analysis assumes that East-West migration will continue, and probably grow, in the near future.[2]

The exact number of East-West migrants is hard to establish. There are differences between the statistics of sending and receiving countries, and only a few figures are available on unofficial flows. Figure 2.1 and Table 2.3 give some idea of migration trends. It is not certain that every migrant reported there still lives in a Western European country, but there is no information on the rate of return migration.[3] It must be borne in mind that some people emigrate to other parts of the world, especially to North America. Okólski (1991) estimates that around 80 per cent of the official and 70 per cent of the unofficial emigrants from Poland go to Western European countries.

---

[2] For discussions on the expected size of the migration see van der Kaa (1991a) and proceedings of several conferences on this subject, such as Vienna (24-25 January 1991, Council of Europe, Conference of Ministers and 5-7 March 1992, organized by the Institute for Advanced Studies, the International Institute for Applied Systems Analysis, Laxenburg and the Institute for Future Studies, Luxembourg) and Paris (21-25 October 1991, organized by EAPS/IUSSP/INED).

[3] There is some information on this subject concerning Poland. Okólski (1991) points out that approximately 30 per cent of the people who extended their stay abroad in the period 1981-88 returned to Poland. However, it is after this period that the emigration rate increased.

Figure 2.1. Trends in emigration from Eastern Europe, 1980-89

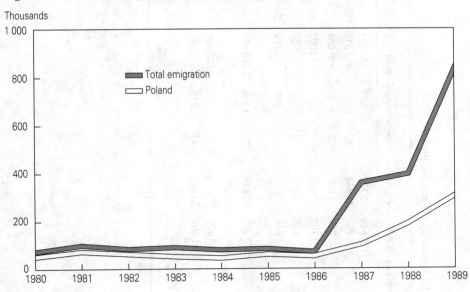

Source: Okólski, 1991.

It is evident that over the last four to five years the number of migrants has risen considerably. These numbers include repatriating Germans (*Aussiedler*), asylum-seekers and tourists who extend their stay in Western Europe in order to find employment or residence. The main sending countries are Poland and the former Yugoslavia and, in recent years, the former USSR. Germany is by far the most important destination country for migrants, both for the *Aussiedler* and others. However, in terms of the size of its population, Austria has experienced the most immigration, in gross, if not net, terms.

Other significant migration flows from Eastern Europe can be found between the former USSR and Israel, and Bulgaria and Turkey. It is very likely that similar flows are occurring within the former USSR, with the building up of new ethnically oriented states, but it is uncertain whether these flows will give rise to East-West migration. This will bring Poland, Czechoslovakia and Hungary to an intermediate position, receiving migrants from the East and sending migrants to the West. People from the former USSR are already working illegally in Poland, especially in construction, small textile enterprises (where women predominate) and housekeeping. According to some estimates there are about 150,000 foreigners working in Poland, mostly in the private sector. This economic migration reflects a willingness by workers to accept low wages, but still earn a relatively good income by converting wages at a high black market dollar exchange rate in the former USSR. Another source of a potential migration flow is the 1.2 million people of Polish origin living in the former USSR (Oschlies, 1989).

Table 2.3. Migration from Eastern to Western Europe: (Estimated) numbers for some major countries, 1980-89

Country of destination		Bulgaria	Hungary	Poland	Romania	Czechoslovakia	USSR	Yugoslavia	Albania	Others	Total	
Germany	Aussiedler[1]		6,620	632 800	151 157	12 727	176 565	3 282		936	984 087	
	Asylum-seekers[1]	1 322	10 226	110 682	13 287	15 380	783	44 948	387		197 015	1981-89
Austria	Asylum-seekers[1]	2 069	15 861	45 924	17 808	19 983	369	2 685	335		105 034	
Sweden	Net-immigration[2]			11 800			1 100	600			13 500	1981-87
France	Asylum-seekers[1]	342	858	7 825	5 119	569	420	1 730	90		16 953	
United Kingdom	Allowance[1]			1 850			270			580	2 700	1984-88
Total		3 733	33 565	810 881	187 371	48 659	179 507	53 245	812	1 516	1 319 289	
Turkey	Allowance[2]	430 000										
Israel	Allowance[2]						158 000				158 000	
Total		433 733	33 565	810 881	187 371	48 659	341 507	53 245	812	1 516	1 477 289	

Source: [1] Chesnais, 1991.
[2] Okólski, 1991.

There is little information on migrant characteristics. The majority are younger or middle-aged, and well-educated (with tertiary or secondary education). The information on Polish migration confirms this picture: in the 1980s emigration absorbed nearly the entire increase in the working age population, while the size of the younger portion of the potential labour force declined. There was also a "brain drain": the number of tertiary educated emigrants was identical to (and for physicians and engineers even higher than) the number of university graduates (Okólski, 1991).

Because of the predominance of the *Aussiedler* in total emigration to Western Europe, the number of emigrating children is comparatively high.

From the scarce information available on emigration from other Eastern European countries, emigration characteristics would appear to be similar to those for Poland.[4] There is no information on the occupational status of the migrants.

Another issue is whether migration is permanent or temporary. There are some indications that under today's circumstances – it is now easier to leave and return to CEECs – the number of temporary migrants to the West is growing; an exact distinction is difficult to make, however, as much "temporary" migration lasts more than several years (Okólski, 1991). Purely temporary residence often coincides with holiday and seasonal work in the West.

Economic, political, demographic and social factors relating to migration sometimes coincide. It is useful to distinguish the following types of Central and Eastern European migrant (Okólski, 1991; van der Kaa, 1991b):

1. legally recruited migrant workers;
2. members of reuniting families;
3. minorities returning to a homeland;
4. those leaving for the home country of a spouse recently married (marriages by partners of different citizenship);
5. political asylum-seekers;
6. migrants settling in the centres of old emigration through extended visits to relatives or friends;
7. illegal migrants not covered by one of the above categories.

Generally speaking, migrants in categories one, and five to seven, are young, well educated and male. The other categories consist mainly of women, children and middle-aged people. This is certainly true for Poland (Okólski, 1991). Until recently, migration to the West consisted primarily of categories one to five, especially legal workers (from Yugoslavia), returning minorities *(Aussiedler* from Poland, Romania and the USSR), and asylum-seekers. Categories six and seven have assumed greater significance in recent years, now that return visits have become less awkward.

Two further elements should be discussed.
(1) The "new" East-West migration adds to the inflow of migrants from Third World countries to Western Europe. Van der Kaa (1991a) estimates that the net

---

[4] See for instance Dovényi (1992) on the characteristics of Hungarian emigration over recent decades.

official inflow of migrants will be between 250,000 and 350,000 people from other continents. These flows are at the moment dominated by the first and second waves of members of reuniting families from the former recruitment countries (e.g. Turkey, Morocco, Tunisia and Algeria). The number of asylum-seekers and, probably, illegal migrants has also increased in recent years. This is of special importance, as it leads to significant problems:
(a) a growing unwillingness among the Western European population to accept immigration;
(b) competition between immigrants from East and South, both on the legal and illegal labour market. This will gave way to the replacement of illegal (and probably legal) employees from the South by illegal workers from Eastern Europe.

(2) It has to be kept in mind that the Western European countries have a long tradition of emigration, but not of immigration. The legal and political system is not well equipped to formulate a consistent immigration policy in the short term. The EC is confronted with different approaches to immigration in its member States – the Treaty of Maastricht does not even include a common policy towards immigration.

A few lessons can be learned by comparing the new migration trends with earlier movements. When labour was first recruited in Mediterranean countries, there was a belief that migrant workers would return to their home country after a period of time, and that their earnings and newly acquired skills would contribute to the growth process there. Neither of these happened to any great extent.

With respect to return migration, a distinction should be drawn between the migrants from developing countries of northern Africa and the countries of southern Europe (Italy, Spain and Portugal). The majority of the guest workers from the first group of countries remained in Western Europe and family members joined them later;[5] a number of those from Spain and Portugal returned in the early 1980s when the economic situation there turned relatively favourable. Is migration from Poland comparable to the first or second group? According to the starting level of per capita income, a comparison with the countries of southern Europe would seem appropriate.

The migrants' contribution to the economic performance of their home country has in all probability been moderate (Keely and Tran, 1989).[6] Only a small part of remittances has been used to enlarge the productive capacity of the home country. So far it seems that the same applies to remittances to Poland, most of which are spent on consumption and house-building; only a small proportion is invested.

Because in the past most guest workers from the South were employed in low-skilled and unskilled work, there was little skills acquisition. It is probable that temporary or seasonal migrants from Poland find themselves in the same position.

---

[5] For example, migration from Turkey and Morocco to the Netherlands was during the 1980s three to five times higher than in the opposite direction. Annually in recent years, only one per cent of the Moroccan and two per cent of the Turkish population in the Netherlands have returned to their home country. This trend will probably continue.

[6] The possible exception to this may be the former Yugoslavia, where remittances have become a source of small-scale capital (Adamkiewicz, cited by Okólski, 1991).

Most of them perform the same kind of job as the early guest workers, and under the same conditions. It is questionable whether such jobs will provide useful skills for restructuring the former communist economies and for improving growth. Apart from any psychological effects,[7] the impression absorbed by these foreign workers of the West's economies and working conditions, etc., will be very biased. Such jobs provide few opportunities for skills enhancement, knowledge of working organizations and experience of market forces.

The recruitment of labour from countries with a totally different culture and language (e.g. Arab countries) during the 1960s and 1970s shows that cultural and language differences, often regarded as significant barriers (the so-called "social distance") to migration, can be overcome by the importance of the economic motive. Low-skilled and unskilled jobs do not require linguistic fluency. Cultural differences between Eastern and Western Europe may also be less important than those between Western Europe and the former recruitment countries.

There is a huge difference between the situation of the labour markets in Western Europe during the 1960s and 1970s, and the present situation. In the 1960s labour shortages slowed economic growth. At the moment unemployment is high nearly everywhere, despite labour shortages in some sectors and occupations.

Push factors

There is little disagreement over the main push factors in the rise in emigration from Eastern Europe. Apart from political refugees, the motives for migration – whether for family reunification, visits to relatives and friends, etc. – seem to be primarily economic: low income, rising unemployment, lack of employment opportunities, the breakdown of old social security systems, bleak employment prospects, and lack of capital. Other factors may be added: disbelief in government institutions, greater inequality in income distribution, lack of good housing, corruption and a poor environmental situation. A belief that the situation will not improve in the coming years is also a pertinent factor (Okólski, 1991; Oschlies, 1989). These factors seem to hold for the whole of Eastern Europe. For Poland two additional factors can be mentioned: the comparatively liberal visa policy adopted in the early 1980s, and the long tradition of emigration.[8] The former Yugoslavia used to have an emigration policy and there are still government agreements with Germany and the Netherlands.

The position of some ethnic minorities, e.g. Jews and Armenians in the former USSR, Turks in Bulgaria, even Russians in the different countries of the former USSR, can be seen as another important push factor. Gypsies in different countries find themselves in a similar position. The assumption is that they will continue their movement to the West (van der Kaa, 1991a).

---

[7] Okólski (1991) mentions the "double-life" aspects of the illegal migrant: hard work in the West as opposed to spurious work in the home country, discrimination as opposed to preference, living and working in humiliating conditions as opposed to displaying "millionaire manners", etc.

[8] There are large so-called "Polonia" in the United States (8.4 million) and Germany (800,000), but also in other Western European countries such as France, Belgium and Sweden, and in the former USSR (Oschlies, 1989).

Because economic motives play an important role in the migration process, developments within the labour market can often give an indication of the scope for earning income in the home country. For reasons of data availability, the discussion will focus on the situation in Poland. Although Poland has a social security system, unemployment and social security benefits are comparatively low and of short-term duration; unemployed people consequently have to search for additional income. Until September 1990, every person registered as unemployed was entitled to receive unemployment benefit. The rules have since changed: someone claiming unemployment benefit must now have worked for at least 180 days during the previous 12 months. Another requirement is that a recipient of unemployment benefit must make a monthly visit to the labour office and be ready to start a job. Since the beginning of 1992, unemployment benefit has been paid at a flat rate of 36 per cent of the average wage; the benefit is paid for 12 months.[9]

The information available on the Polish labour market (Kotowska, 1991; Góra, 1991a) indicates some remarkable developments, many with reference to international migration. The following conclusions can be made:

(1) Over the next few years a substantial rise in the labour force is to be expected, now that more young people are entering the labour market. The working age population will grow by approximately 3.5 million by 2010. This represents 54 per cent of the anticipated increase in Europe's *total* population.[10] The fact that young people are currently remaining in the educational system longer, especially at university, may indicate a worsening of job opportunities for them. Other reasons for this might be to increase their chances of working in Western countries, or to obtain additional income through an educational grant.[11]

(2) As a result of the fast process of restructuring, unemployment increased from around 100,000 at the end of 1989 to 1,845,000 at the end of 1991, i.e. almost 10 per cent of the labour force. It is uncertain when the increase in unemployment will stop. Recent projections indicate a further linear growth up to 3.5 million people, i.e. 18 per cent of the labour force, by the end of 1992.[12] In July and August 1991 nearly 500,000 people lost their jobs, but not all became unemployed. There is no information on the duration of unemployment, but the rise in the unemployment-to-vacancy ratio suggests that most people who lost their jobs are still unemployed. This can be deduced from the fact that during 1990, 1.5 million people became unemployed, but only 300,000 moved from unemployed to employed.[13]

---

[9] Previously, on the basis of the New Law of September 1990, unemployment benefits were 70 per cent of the last wage for the first three months of unemployment, 50 per cent for the next six months and 40 per cent afterwards. A benefit cannot be lower than 95 per cent of the minimum wage level and not higher than the average wage. People who receive a pension or social security benefits, (co-)owners of farms and people who have their own business are excluded from unemployment benefit. Mass redundancies are subject to special legislation; some of those made redundant may receive 100 per cent of the average of their previous six months' wage.

[10] UN, 1991.

[11] According to one of our informants from Poland, the number of first-year students has doubled compared to last year's entrance. She also mentioned that the scholarship grant is significant.

[12] Information received from Prof. Borkowska.

[13] Góra (1991a). Apart from outflows to employment (275,000), in 1990 some 100,000 unemployed people were placed in public works, 10,000 in training schemes, 30,000 received loans to start their own business and 30,000 were employed in new enterprises offered state loans.

(3) The process of restructuring leads to a loss of jobs, especially in the industrial sector. As a consequence, unemployment is comparatively high for people with a vocational education and for young people (those under 25) (see Figures 2.2 and 2.3). For unemployed industrial workers, it is often hard to find jobs in the service sector.

(4) In Poland – as in all CEECs – female participation rates are very high. The transition process has made it very difficult for them to find new jobs. The unemployment-to-vacancy ratio is three times as high for women as for men (Figure 2.4), leading to less family income. However, unemployed women are less likely to emigrate than men. In this sense, higher unemployment need not necessarily mean more emigration.

(5) There are also geographical differences. In general, the unemployment-to-vacancy ratio was by the end of 1990 lower in big cities and in highly industrialized regions (Góra, 1991a). The position of unemployed people in small towns and rural areas is bad; in many cases the enterprise that dismissed them was virtually the only one in the area. A similar problem arises in areas with only one type of industry, e.g. in Lodz (textiles), Walbrzych Katowice (coalmining and metallurgy).

In urban areas unemployment among younger and vocationally educated people is high owing to restructuring, while in rural areas agricultural restructuring will lead to unemployment among older and poorly educated people. More than half

Figure 2.2. Employment and unemployment by education, Poland, 1991, first quarter.

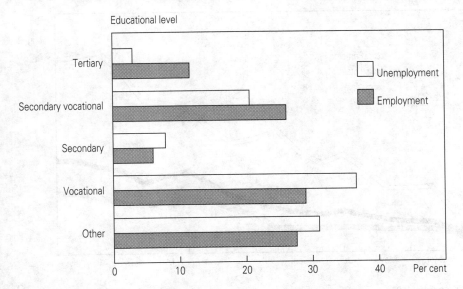

Source: Kotowska, 1991.

Figure 2.3. Percentage unemployment by age group, Poland, 1991, second quarter.

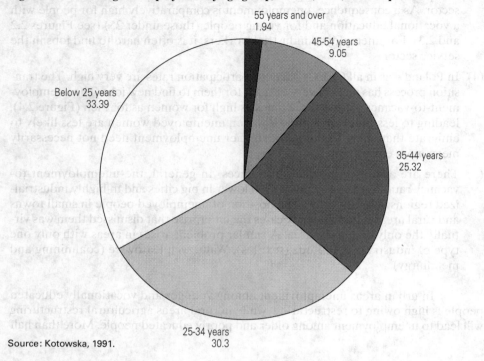

Source: Kotowska, 1991.

Figure 2.4. Unemployment-to-vacancy ratio by gender, Poland, January 1990 – August 1991.

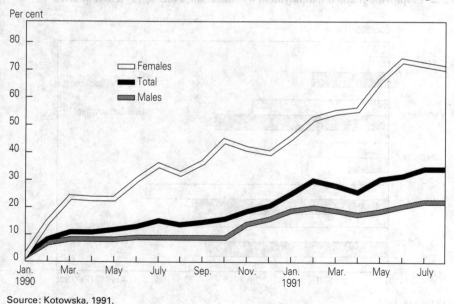

Source: Kotowska, 1991.

the labour force employed in agricultural activities is older than 45, whereas the figure for those in non-agricultural activities is 20 per cent to 25 per cent. The vast majority (80 per cent or more) of these older people are unskilled workers. Among this group there are 2 million "peasant workers" – people who work in industry, but who also own and work small plots of land. They are of particular importance because, according to the law, they are not entitled to receive unemployment benefits. Many peasant workers left their previous job voluntarily, as they had an alternative activity.

Employment in public administration, medical care, education, and cultural activities, i.e. those areas that depend on the state, may fall over the next few years as a result of the growing state deficit. This will occur mainly in larger urban areas.

It cannot be stated with any certainty that unemployment by itself causes a high rate of emigration.[14] The lack of employment opportunities is probably the major influence. However, there is a shift in employment from agriculture and industry to service activities (Góra, 1991b), although the rise in employment in the service sector is too small to make up for the significant losses in agriculture and industry. Neither is it certain where unemployment will peak: through a combination of structural and cyclical components, it is estimated that unemployment could reach 25 per cent to 30 per cent.[15]

The high rate of forecast unemployment suggests that there is a large potential for migration in Poland, especially among younger people. In 1989 Oschlies concluded that younger, more active and better educated Poles had a high incentive to leave; those remaining in Poland understood and often supported this decision. The latest survey (January/February 1992) shows that 60 per cent of young people in Poland (18-24 years) were ready to go abroad.[16]

Pull factors

Apart from the higher standards of living in Western Europe, there are some specific factors that induce higher migration rates. These are:

1. The demographic element. The population in Western Europe will show very little growth over the next few decades, as a result of low fertility rates, often below replacement levels. The populations of the Federal Republic of Germany and France have fallen in recent years. In the Netherlands one of the issues is whether the social security system, especially retirement benefits and the health system, can be financed in the near future. On the labour market employers are confronted with a declining supply of young, relatively cheap, labour.

---

[14] It is even a question of whether migrants are unemployed. Information received indicates that it is possible to obtain a long period of unpaid leave without losing one's job.

[15] Labour hoarding – decisive for the structural component – is estimated to have been around 30 per cent (Góra, 1991b). However, participation rates fell and production declined (GDP sank by 12 per cent in 1990). The outcome of the process is hard to predict, but a maximum rate of unemployment of 30 per cent seems "reasonable".

[16] Information received from Prof. Borkowska; 60 per cent represents almost 3 million people. The question remains how many of them actually take the decision to go.

2. The growing underground economy in Western Europe, with irregular employment opportunities for people from Eastern Europe. They accept wages and labour conditions inferior to the norm.[17]
3. The presence of older emigrants in the countries of destination, especially Germany (the "Polonia").
4. The system of work permits in the EC for non-EC citizens (in the case of Yugoslavia in the form of intergovernmental agreements). This system enlarges the emigration network.

The importance of migration networks, or migration chains for family reunification, should not be overlooked. Preliminary evidence from research into the illegal Netherlands labour market, conducted by the Netherlands Economics Institute (NEI) suggests that a majority of illegal workers from the former recruitment countries of Turkey and Morocco obtain a job through family or friends.

A lack of cultural differences and the ability to speak the language of the destination country also diminish the obstacles to migration. Cultural differences will further decline in importance as sociocultural contacts between East and West increase.

Eastern Europeans can find jobs in the legal labour market through the system of work permits, and in the illegal labour market. The legal opportunities are generally restricted to the lower and unskilled segments of the labour market, as a result of excess supply in other segments of the market in most Western European countries.[18] However, even for some low-skilled jobs, employers have difficulty in finding workers. In recent years in the Netherlands, temporary work permits have been granted to several hundred Polish workers for seasonal work with flower bulbs.

Germany follows a more liberal policy than most Western European countries, especially in the border areas, but legal openings are limited even there. Because employers face difficulties in recruiting personnel, they want a less strict system of work permits for non-EC citizens. There is no doubt that employers cast envious glances at the skilled labour potential in CEECs, especially Poland. The changes in vacancy rates in recent years in the Federal Republic of Germany and the Netherlands (see Tables 2.4 and 2.5) indicate a growing requirement for industrial workers. However, it must be remembered that employers' motives for demanding illegal employees include their needs for flexibility in labour supply, and lower costs (which compensate for lower productivity).[19]

---

[17] Hönekopp (1991) argues that the immigration of recent years has not yet found expression in formal employment of Eastern Europeans in Germany: this has grown from 20,000 in 1980 to 54,000 in 1989. Okólski estimates that in this period 267,800 Poles emigrated unofficially to (the former Federal Republic of) Germany.

[18] European legislation states that non-EC employees can be employed only when labour with the necessary qualifications cannot be hired a) in the home country, or b) in one of the other member countries.

[19] There are no signs that such a productivity gap actually exists. Skilled labour requires practical experience, which most Eastern European skilled workers have.

Table 2.4. Hard-to-fill vacancies by occupational class, the Netherlands, 1990

Occupational class	Total number of vacancies	Vacancy-rate	Number of hard-to-fill vacancies	% hard-to-fill vacancies
Plumbers, welders, etc.	7 100	6.2	5 400	76
Construction workers	6 500	3.7	4 800	74
Electrical mechanics	4 000	3.8	2 400	60
Nurses	4 400	.	2 300	52
Metal workers	3 700	2.4	2 100	57
Hotels and catering	3 300	2.1	1 800	55
Food workers	2 300	3.8	1 700	74
Other domestic professions	2 900	1.4	1 600	55
Architects, engineers, etc.	2 900	.	1 500	52
Agricultural workers	3 500	3.0	1 200	34
Mechanical workers	1 700	3.6	1 200	71
Statisticians, computer specialists, etc.	2 900	2.4	1 200	41
Managers, etc	2 100	0.9	1 000	48
Technicians, etc.	1 500	.	1 000	67
Clothing workers	1 200	4.4	800	67
Painters, etc.	1 100	2.6	800	73
Furniture and wood products workers	1 000	4.5	700	70
Subtotal	52 100	2.2	31 500	60
Total number of vacancies	104 700	1.9	49 300	47

Source: Ministerie van Sociale Zaken en Werkgelegenheid (Ministry of Social Affairs and Employment), Rapportage Arbeidsmarkt (Report on the Labour Market), 1991.

As a consequence of the limited legal demand for Eastern European labour, most Eastern Europeans who are willing to work in the West temporarily depend on the illegal labour market. There are firm indications, especially from the research mentioned above, that the number of such job opportunities is growing. Employers' motives include:
1. The lower cost of this kind of labour, as a result of:
    (a) Strong price competition for products on the local and international markets. This usually occurs in sectors that would not survive in Western Europe under normal conditions.
    (b) The need for higher profits. In this case working conditions are very poor and labour exploitation may be an issue.
2. Problems in finding labour. Three categories can be distinguished:
    (a) Skilled workers (secondary level vocational labour) in which Western Europe is lacking.
    (b) Workers for comparatively bad working conditions, e.g. pay at minimum wage levels, heavy physical labour (in agriculture and some industrial occupations), or bad environments (noise, foul air, etc.).

Table 2.5. Vacancies (1987 and 1990) and vacancy rate (1987) by occupational class, Federal Republic of Germany

Occupational class	Employment ('000) 1987	Number of vacancies 1987	Number of vacancies 1990	Vacancy rate 1987	Average annual growth in number of vacancies (%) 1987-1990
Agricultural, etc.	903.6	7 679	17 158	8.50	26.8
Agricultural	845.7	6 389	15 311	7.55	29.1
Forestry	58	1 290	1 847	22.24	12.0
Mining	93.1	103	120	1.11	5.1
Mining	93.1	103	120	1.11	5.1
Industrial occupations	8 372.5	66 179	135 227	7.90	23.8
Brickworkers	32.3	355	890	10.99	30.6
Building materials	40.6	246	575	6.06	28.3
Chemical workers	239.1	1 468	3 071	6.14	24.6
Paper	46.3	491	1 167	10.60	28.9
Printing industry	148.8	1 288	2 317	8.66	19.6
Wood products	37.7	377	972	10.00	31.6
Metal workers	535.3	3 639	8 512	6.80	28.3
Mechanical workers, etc.	1 941.3	13 844	29 143	7.13	24.8
Electricity	700.1	5 625	12 090	8.03	25.5
Assembly workers	295.2	2 586	6 561	8.76	31.0
Textiles/clothing	316.7	2 378	4 348	7.51	20.1
Leather, etc.	72.9	632	927	8.67	12.8
Food	607	10 469	19 603	17.25	20.9
Construction workers	901.5	12 349	24 635	26.53	52.1
Furniture	301.2	2 884	6 531	9.58	27.2
Painters, etc.	277.8	2 747	5 227	9.89	21.4
Inspectors, dispatch	339.1	1 526	4 018	4.50	32.3
Other production workers	1 197.2	2 111	2 802	1.76	9.4
Train drivers	342.3	1 164	1 838	3.40	15.2
Technical	1 602.1	16 699	18 077	10.42	2.6
Engineers, chemists, etc.	597.4	10 755	9 837	18.00	0.0
Technicians	768	3 636	4 295	4.73	5.6
Specialists	236.8	2 308	3 945	9.75	17.9
Services	15 372.6	81 187	142 885	5.28	18.8
Sales	2 100.4	13 714	23 399	6.53	17.8
Bank employees, etc.	877.1	3 419	4 220	3.90	7.0
Traffic workers	1 037.4	5 012	10 435	4.83	24.4
Transport	464.5	3 028	7 823	6.52	31.6
Administration	5 539.2	17 386	28 514	3.14	16.5
Guards	1 065.6	2 001	3 050	1.88	14.0
Librarians, etc.	98.6	590	514	5.98	0.0
Artists	163.7	769	1 021	4.70	9.4
Doctors, medical	1 264.2	7 785	18 794	6.16	29.4
Socio-cultural work	1 320.5	9 077	13 524	6.87	13.3
Nurses	264	3 171	5 948	12.01	21.0
Hotels and catering	398.8	5 922	9 250	14.85	14.9
Domestic professions	196.3	3 555	6 064	18.11	17.8
Cleaners, etc.	582.4	5 758	10 329	9.89	19.5
Other occupations	563.6	0	0	0.00	.
TOTAL	26 907.6	171 847	313 467	6.39	20.0

Source: Employment: Statistisches Jahrbuch 1990.
Vacancies: Arbeits- und Sozialstatistik Hauptergebnisse 1991, Bundesanstalt für Arbeit.

(c) Workers for irregular and/or unfavourable times, e.g. night work, or for short periods, e.g. seasonal labour in agriculture and tourism, and in peak production in industry; employers need a highly flexible labour supply in these circumstances.

It would seem that the regular labour force in Western Europe shows only a slight interest in the types of job shown under (b) and (c).

Illegal employment does not necessarily lead to financial irregularity; taxes and social security payments are often paid by the employer. The illegal worker is not always directly employed by the employer; it would seem that a large number of the illegally employed work as hired labourers and through labour brokers, a trend apparent in both the Netherlands and Germany.

The NEI research indicates a growth in irregular, low-paid employment under bad conditions in agriculture, industry and services, and in sectors with labour supply problems. The supply of labour from Eastern European (and developing African) countries meets the requirements of Western Europe. It must be stressed, however, that these findings are largely based on qualitative information, and some educated guesses. The number of illegally employed workers is unknown.

Results of the analysis

1. Given the prevailing conditions in both Western and Eastern Europe, there is clearly a large potential for migration. It is, however, difficult to predict the exact number of migrants over the next couple of decades because of the uncertain course of the various underlying factors.

2. The migration phenomenon is based on a combination of push and pull factors of an economic, demographic, social and political nature. The influence of these different factors cannot always be isolated, but the general opinion – and one which we share – is that (if certain migration flows are excluded) economic motives are decisive.[20] It is not the absolute difference in per capita income that rules migration, but, primarily, supply and demand in the labour markets in both the sending and receiving countries; other factors, such as "social distance" and access to jobs, also play a part.[21] An important factor – especially so among young people in Poland – would seem to be a belief in future opportunities in the home country.

3. One of the most important push factors is the situation on the labour market. In Poland, greater unemployment rates are found among young people with a basic or secondary vocational education, and women. There are also geographical differences: unemployment is fairly high in small towns in rural areas and in regions with an industrial monoculture. Another push factor of importance to young people is the lack of good housing.

[20] See for instance Okólski (1991) and van der Kaa (1991a).
[21] See also Heijke (1979).

4. A principal pull factor is the legal and illegal demand for Eastern European labour. This demand is caused by strong price competition on some product markets; and by problems filling vacancies both for skilled workers and for those working in bad conditions or at irregular times.

5. The economic motive appears somewhat attenuated for certain groups emigrating from Eastern Europe. The migration of ethnic minorities is for a large part based on social and political motives (discrimination or ethnic alliance) – for example, ethnic Germans, Jews, Armenians and Gypsies.

6. If we turn to the economic motive as seen in Poland, it seems very likely that, if the economic situation does not change, some 2 million Poles will migrate to the West (70 per cent of them to Western Europe) in the next five to ten years. This guess is based on the results of a recent survey which indicates that nearly 60 per cent of young Poles – some 3 million people – are ready to go abroad. However, not everybody will of course make the move, and this figure also includes people of ethnic German origin (up to 2 million people). This number is also supported by van der Kaa (1991a), who estimates that total yearly net official migration from Eastern to Western Europe (excluding ethnic Germans and illegal migration) could range between 75,000 and 250,000 people, to produce a figure over ten years of between 1 million and 2.5 million people.

4. Policy issues

Introduction

Without intervention, it is likely that some 1.5 million East Europeans will migrate to Western Europe in the next ten years, primarily the young and well-educated. This would be a disaster for CEECs, robbing them of their human capital and future labour force.[22] Neither would it be of great benefit to Western Europe, as it is already confronted with mass migration from other parts of the world.

Is it possible to change this scenario? Economic factors, both in East and West, are the decisive factors behind migration. Part of the change could be effected by removing the pull factors prevalent in Western Europe. One of these factors is the difficulty in finding workers and the consequent acceptance of illegal migrant labour. By inducing a larger number of unemployed people to accept jobs with low wages and bad working conditions, the demand for migrant labour would be decreased. However, it is our opinion that employers will always be tempted to hire people who are willing to accept such jobs. Furthermore, we do not think it realistic to assume that migrants can be kept out of Western Europe; neither would preventing immigration solve the problems in Eastern Europe.

---

[22] Migration at even half this level would be a major problem.

Labour market and educational policy

The creation of jobs and the improvement in living standards must lie with the countries of Central and Eastern Europe themselves. We will now tackle the question of what policies are required, and how foreign aid fits in. Emphasis will be placed on the Polish labour market and educational policy.

The Polish economy is still being transformed from a centrally planned economy to a market economy. The privatization process seems to be constrained to an increasing extent by administrative and organizational factors (Grosfeld and Hare, 1991)[23] so that markets do not function in an efficient way. For instance, there is still a large amount of hidden unemployment in companies, and wages cannot generate equilibrium. The same is true for financial markets.

Under these conditions one should be very careful in applying standard growth theory: this generally assumes efficient markets. In training, for example, it assumes the following: training raises productivity, decreases unit labour costs and product prices, thus resulting in growing product demand and output. However, if employment is virtually fixed, training may have only a potential effect on productivity. Therefore, providing financial capital and education does not automatically generate the results one would expect; it might even increase migration, as unemployed but well-trained people have more opportunities in Western Europe.

Therefore, making markets work more efficiently is an essential precondition for a policy of growth-stimulation. In respect of the labour market this would mean that:

1. Companies should be subjected to market forces. There should be incentives to reduce internal labour reserves to improve flexibility.
2. Wages should be negotiated freely; companies and workers should be able to move away from collective bargaining. It is very important that wages can move freely, so that there is some tendency towards equilibrium on the labour market.
3. There should be an exchange of information on the supply and demand of labour. Labour offices have an important role in collecting information on vacancies and unemployed people, and in matching the two.
4. Social security has to be kept on a minimum level in order to make people accept jobs at wage levels that are realistic in the Polish context. Another reason for this is to avoid the discrepancy between gross and net wages that favours the black economy.

However, making markets work more efficiently does not imply a policy of *laissez faire*. Markets will never function perfectly by themselves. This is especially true for the markets for labour and for education. Long-term policy must therefore include:

---

[23] The best results have been achieved with the so-called "small-scale" privatizations, of shops and commercial activities. Fifty-eight per cent of new private enterprises in 1990 were private shops and retail enterprises (Grosfeld and Hare, 1991).

- a transformation of the economy to a market economy, i.e. strongly curtail the role of the state;
- a new role for the government to deal with market imperfections.

Foreign aid can and should be directed to *both* policies. The first type of aid will make people familiar with the way a market economy functions, ensure that market conditions prevail, and create the necessary institutions and minimum infrastructure.

The second type of aid is to provide capital and know-how to accelerate growth. This presupposes a market economy that is functioning *adequately*, rather than *perfectly*, as perfect markets will never exist. It is, essentially, a matter of timing.

When the preconditions for an efficient labour market are compared with the actual situation in Poland, the following becomes apparent:

1. It is questionable whether legal constraints for laying off workers are at the minimum possible level, because mass redundancies are subject to special laws, and because they are usually unacceptable to the – still strong – workers' councils. As a result, mass redundancies are sometimes very expensive – in some cases workers receive their full wage for a certain period – so enterprises try to avoid them (Góra, 1991b).

2. The high proportion of employment in state-owned companies (Figure 2.5)[24] means that the wage mechanism does not operate, rendering data on moves in real wages inaccurate. There is legislation to prevent real wage increases.[25] Differences in wage levels between state-owned and private enterprises are significant, but there is only fragmentary information on this. There are some indications that real wages in sectors such as education and health is lagging[26] as employment in this sector stabilizes.

3. There are strong indications that social security is being restricted through lower levels and durations of benefits. Other measures in health care (restrictions on free medicines and free care) and transportation (elimination of subsidies) will have consequences for recipients of social benefits. The question is: Will such measures – necessary for the labour market – increase migration pressures in the short term?

---

[24] The share of the private sector in employment rose from 29.6 per cent in 1989 (Góra, 1991a) to 38.2 per cent in 1991 (Kisiel-Lowczyc, personal communication) especially in small-scale trading enterprises.

[25] Nominal wage increases above an indexed increase in consumer prices are heavily taxed. But there is debate as to what should be in the "consumer basket"; neither is the effect of cheap imports certain (Góra, 1991a).

[26] In 1990 average earnings in this sector were comparable to the general average (Boeri and Keese, 1991); in 1991 they were 10 per cent below the general average (Borkowska, 1992).

Figure 2.5. Structure of employment, Poland, 1989.

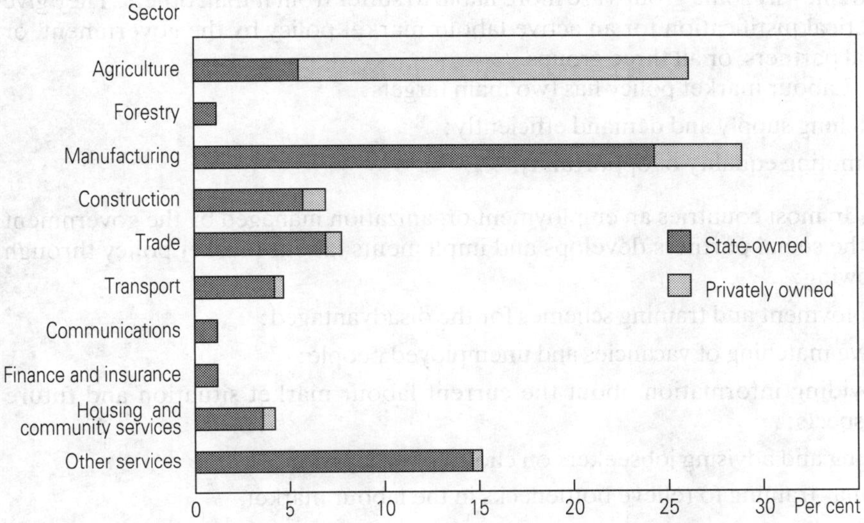

[Bar chart showing employment structure by sector in Poland, 1989, with State-owned and Privately owned categories. Sectors listed: Agriculture, Forestry, Manufacturing, Construction, Trade, Transport, Communications, Finance and insurance, Housing and community services, Other services. X-axis: 0 to 30 Per cent.]

Source: Góra, 1991a.

The labour market

Unemployment and unfilled vacancies are recurrent characteristics of labour markets in market economies. It is important to note that in capitalist systems, government intervention in the labour market was prompted by unemployment rather than the other way round, although in some cases, the cure may have been worse than the disease.

Modern labour market theory has produced a number of explanations for the unemployment phenomenon.[27] First, labour economists have stressed the fact that information on job opportunities and on people seeking employment is not costless, and involves positive unemployment and duration of vacancies.[28] Second, owing to costs of employee turnover, workers have a certain amount of monopoly power, and can set wages above the market clearing level.[29] Third, individual productivity remains largely unrecorded, both for new employees and for current workers. Companies will have to set wages above the market clearing level to keep productivity sufficiently high. So, even in the absence of social security and legal constraints on redundancies, working hours, etc., unemployment would exist.[30]

---

[27] For an interesting overview we refer to Lindbeck (1991).
[28] Phelps (1970).
[29] This is the so-called insider-outsider theory (see Lindbeck, 1991).
[30] Akerlof and Yellen (1986) discuss several variants of these wage-efficiency models.

These new theories explain not only why unemployment exists, but also, to some extent, why some groups are more liable to suffer from it than others. They give a theoretical justification for an active labour market policy by the government, or the social partners, or all three groups.

Labour market policy has two main targets:
- matching supply and demand efficiently;
- promoting equality of opportunity.

In most countries an employment organization managed by the government and/or the social partners develops and implements labour market policy through the following:

(a) employment and training schemes for the disadvantaged;
(b) active matching of vacancies and unemployed people;
(c) providing information about the current labour market situation and future prospects;
(d) testing and advising jobseekers on choice of occupation;
(e) regular training to relieve bottlenecks in the labour market.

Most of these, especially (b), (c) and (e) have a clear economic function. Furthermore, labour market policy has an important training component which overlaps educational policy. Category (a) belongs to the sphere of social policy. However, we argue below that policy for stimulating long-term growth may not be successful unless it is accompanied by short-term social policy.

In theory, Polish labour offices can adopt all these methods. In view of longer-term developments, it is essential that changes in policy are made at the right time. In the short term, these offices are concerned primarily with registering unemployed people. In view of the low vacancy rate they are paying scant attention to matching vacancies and unemployed people. In the short term, greater attention should be devoted to developing and arranging training programmes for the unemployed (connected to private investment schemes) and employment creation schemes.

The labour offices must, however, prepare themselves for the time when unemployment peaks and/or the demand for labour rises. More attention must then be paid to matching (in combination with training schemes). In view of regional differences, policy decisions should be decentralized as much as possible.

Labour offices should always be able to provide up-to-date information on the labour market, both for matching purposes, and to inform employers and employees of job opportunities. Such information can also be used as a basis for educational activities and training schemes.

It is questionable whether the labour offices in Poland are sufficiently equipped for these tasks (Góra, 1991a). The offices are probably understaffed: nearly 400 of them employ some 4,000 people.[31] In addition, equipment, and – especially – experience and expertise are lacking. Foreign aid could be usefully targeted

---

[31] In the Netherlands the same number of officials are working in the labour offices, while employment is about three to four times smaller.

by supporting working visits of several months' duration to labour offices in Western Europe (owing to language problems most probably Germany, France or the United Kingdom). Working visits can also be useful for people in the field of education, especially those developing curricula.

Short-term policies

The transformation process leads to massive unemployment, or rather, makes visible already existing underemployment. It is clear that massive unemployment in Poland is not a temporary phenomenon. This may have a number of drawbacks, including:

- The emergence of long-term unemployment, with its many concomitant negative social and economic effects. From Western Europe's experience we know that long-term unemployment is very hard to combat. Long-term unemployed people lose skills, become less motivated and are subject to prejudice by employers. Wage formation is no longer affected by long-term unemployment (the "hysteresis" phenomenon). Long-term unemployment reduces the quantity and quality of the effective labour supply and consequently has a negative impact on long-term economic growth.
- A further impetus to the black economy. It will be very hard to maintain a social security system as people will try to supplement their social security benefits with unofficial jobs and may be reluctant to accept jobs in the official economy.
- Political instability.
- The "brain drain".

Employment creation programmes designed and carried out by the government (or government-financed organizations) may turn out to be very important, although such measures may not be popular in a country trying to transform itself from a state-controlled to a market economy. These programmes should be designated for infrastructural projects such as roads, environmental improvements, and telecommunications. This ensures that workers keep their skills intact – or improved – and that they have a positive effect on the economy. To optimize the benefit of these projects to unemployed people, the maximum length of participation should be limited, to perhaps no more than 180 days a year.

Migration can help when it is temporary and it relates to economic activity (e.g. learning). Training schemes should be developed within a framework linked to foreign investment. Such investment often introduces into Poland new or modified technology that employees must adapt to. Long-term training should also be considered: for example, part of the training might take place within the Western European head office of a company with an Eastern European subsidiary. Such training schemes might:

- lower vacancy problems in Western Europe, thereby reducing demand for illegal Eastern European labour;

- lower spontaneous labour migration;
- increase Polish human capital, not only by enhancing skills and experience, but also by increasing knowledge of how private organizations function within the market economy.

For the scheme to work successfully certain conditions must be met. First, the trainee's return to Eastern Europe must be assured, i.e. financially, and the company should assume some responsibility for this. Second, such schemes will only be successful when the participants are potential emigrants, otherwise a rise in temporary migration may occur.

If the suggested policies are compared with existing international aid programmes it can be seen that most aid is to projects directed at economic reform and technical assistance. Apart from foreign investment and trade policy, the PHARE programme is responsible for the majority of foreign aid. It consists of long-term projects in agriculture, manufacturing, energy, financial services, privatization, investment, the environment and training. About 80 per cent of the funds are directed to macro-financial support, export credits and support of private investment. Projects and programmes on labour market issues and education are part of the aid on economic reform, and include a project in Poland aimed at strengthening the expertise of local communities in labour offices and social services to promote socioeconomic development at the local level. This will be implemented through demonstration projects.

When we return to the role of ODA for such projects, the political, legal, socioeconomic and cultural environment in CEECs must be considered, because structural change can only be brought about in the countries themselves. The absorption capacity of the system and the individuals acting in it must be borne in mind. There is consequently little point in copying Western educational and labour market structures and institutions and placing them directly in CEECs, but they can be used as a starting point.

It must also be remembered that ODA by itself cannot bring about the desired changes, but it can be of help in improving the framework for the changes. It is beyond the scope of this paper to go into the form and content of foreign aid in greater detail; for this, individual projects and policy proposals have to be considered. However, the following pointers might be of relevance.

1. Adding ODA funds to projects already agreed upon (e.g. for infrastructural improvements). These extra funds might make it possible to devote more attention to the training and education of people working in the project so as to raise their skills level.
2. In projects aimed at improving the educational and labour market structures, attention must be directed at improving the basic skills of people working in these fields. Consequently, it will be more useful if labour market officials know more about the design and implementation of training programmes and the matching process in the labour market (e.g. what employers' criteria are for new employees) and the way to handle them, than that they know how to register the unemployed properly in a well-designed automatic registration system.

3. In the field of education not only must the curricula be adapted to the new needs of the labour market, but all teachers must be instructed: a "train the trainers" programme should accompany any change in the curricula. ODA could be used to realize such additional activities.

Final remarks

We would conclude that, in terms of the Polish experience, the only real solution to the issue of emigration must be brought about in Poland itself. The Polish labour market has to be transformed into a market that functions reasonably well, i.e. one that can create the jobs needed to meet the supply of labour.

However, are the policies suggested above sufficient? Can they induce employment and income growth to such an extent that most people are encouraged to stay in Poland? Can we give some idea of the quantitative impact of these policies? Although these questions cannot be answered with certainty, we feel that it would be unsatisfactory not to give our views on the matter.

In our view there is no reason to be too pessimistic. Let us look at the effects of privatization on employment. To make companies function efficiently, internal labour reserves must be cut drastically, by perhaps as much as 20 per cent initially. However, unit labour costs will drop by the same percentage. If we assume that the long-term wage elasticity of labour demand is in the same order of magnitude as in the Western economies, about -0.5, then the actual drop in employment will be much lower than 20 per cent.[32] Wage flexibility is indeed a powerful tool for job creation. The Netherlands experience, for instance, has shown that refraining from real wage increases over a number of years may – after a few years – lead to substantial employment growth, even in years with moderate growth in output. In 1985 the Netherlands had an unemployment rate of 16 per cent; by 1990 it had fallen to 8 per cent.

Education and training are powerful instruments in stimulating long-term economic growth. It has been often stated that most economic growth can be attributed to the knowledge factor and to improvements in the quality of labour. This is extremely important, because it can induce productivity growth, giving room for real wage increases, which in turn may discourage people from leaving Poland.

If good conditions for private enterprise are established, and well-balanced labour market and educational policies are followed, enough jobs could be created in ten years to absorb a considerable number of the unemployed. At the same time it would be important to ensure growth in productivity and real income, to reduce the income gap between Poland and Western Europe. However, this is a matter for the long run and may take a much longer period. So, the question remains whether the prospect of gradually improving employment opportunities with relatively low wages will be sufficient to make people stay.

---

[32] Assuming, of course, that social security expenses do not lead to high taxes, undoing the reduction in labour costs.

5. Conclusions

First, it is reasonable to assume that in the foreseeable future emigration from CEECs will remain above normal levels, despite international aid of any kind. Any change in the push and pull factors that determine migration will take some time to be felt. The situation on the labour market in both Eastern and Western Europe, rather than political and ethnic motives, are the decisive factors behind these migration trends, aided by the decrease in social distance through ever greater sociocultural contacts. Migration to the West will see CEECs both sending and receiving migrants.

Current and future employment prospects in the home country are probably more important determinants of emigration than wage differences between Eastern and Western Europe. Therefore, to reduce migration to "normal" levels, it is not necessary to close the income gap completely.

Reducing migration has also been shown to be a desirable goal. Because young, well-educated and active people have a high incentive to leave, it is likely that mass migration will significantly reduce the stock of human capital in CEECs. Migration is not very helpful to Western Europe either, as it is already confronted with mass migration from other parts of the world.

Although policy measures in Western Europe can reduce migration to some extent, we believe that the real solution to the problem lies in the creation of jobs and the improvement of living standards in CEECs. Policy should be oriented to stimulating long-term growth, while taking short-term problems into account. In terms of labour market and educational policy, attention should be given to:

1. Transforming the economy to a market economy, that is, strongly diminishing the role of the state. This requires:
   (a) a breakdown of internal labour reserves, largely through privatization;
   (b) freely negotiable wages;
   (c) a system of exchange of information on supply and demand in the labour market;
   (d) social security at a minimum level.
2. Designing a new role for the government to deal with the imperfections of markets. This requires:
   (a) linking the educational and training system to the labour market, through adaption of the curricula and more attention to general education (e.g. inventiveness, self-reliance) in primary education and the first level of secondary education;
   (b) employment creation programmes to avoid loss of skills in the short term and to discourage emigration;
   (c) the development of training schemes for the employed and unemployed. By linking such schemes to foreign investment it is also possible to influence international migration directly.

Projects aimed at increasing the experience and expertise of people working in the educational system and labour offices in CEECS are especially needed.

We strongly believe that much remains to be done before policies implemented at the macroeconomic level and relating to trade matters will give the desired results. But we are sure we can say "Yes" to the question posed in the title of this paper.

To illustrate this we refer to development after the Second World War in Western Europe. As a consequence of high unemployment there, and an active unrestrictive immigration policy in the old settlement countries, people emigrated from Western Europe (and Poland) to the United States, Canada and Australia. However, during the 1950s the economic situation in Western Europe improved dramatically, largely the result of aid from the Marshall Plan. This shows clearly that international aid can play a significant role in eliminating emigration.

Bibliography

Akerlof, G.A.; J.L. Yellen. 1986. *Efficiency wage models of the labour market* (Cambridge, Cambridge University Press).
Bairoch, P. 1976. "Europe's gross national product 1880-1975", in *Journal of European Economic History*, Vol. 5, pp. 273-340.
Barket, T.; M.H. Pesaran. 1990. *Disaggregation in economic modelling* (London, Routledge).
Bergeijk, P.A.G. van. 1990. "Economische hulp aan Oost-Europa", in *Economisch Statistische Berichten*, 18 Apr. 1990, pp. 356-359.
Bergeyk, P. van; W. Noe; H. Oldersma. 1991. *Meer zicht op Oost Europa* (The Hague, Ministerie van Economische Zaken).
Boeri, T.; M. Keese. 1991. *From labour shortage to labour shedding: Some stylised facts of the economic transition in Central and Eastern Europe*, paper prepared for the Third Annual Conference of the European Association of Labour Economists (EALE), Conference Proceedings, Vol. V, *Transition in the labour markets*, Madrid, 26-29 September.
Böhning, W.R.; S. Vieira de Mello. 1991. *International aid as a means to reduce the need for emigration: An ILO-UNHCR initiative*, background paper (Geneva, ILO/UNHCR).
—; P.V. Schaeffer; Th. Straubhaar. 1991. *Migration pressure: What is it? What can one do about it?*, working paper, International Migration for Employment Branch (Geneva, ILO).
Cassen, R., et al. 1986. *Does aid work?* (Oxford, Clarendon Press).
Chenery, H.; S. Robinson; M. Syrquin. 1986. *Industrialisation and growth: A comparative study* (Oxford and New York, Oxford University Press).
Chesnais, J.C. 1991. *Migration from Eastern to Western Europe, past (1946-1989) and future (1990-2000)*, paper for the Conference of Ministers on the movement of persons coming from Central and Eastern European countries, Vienna, 24-25 January 1991 (Strasbourg, Council of Europe).
Collins, Susan M.; Dani Rodrik, 1991. "Eastern Europe and the Soviet Union in the world economy", in *Policy Analysis*, No. 32 (Washington, DC, Institute for International Economics).
Commission of the European Communities. 1991. Directorate-General for Economic and Financial Affairs. "The path of reform in Central and Eastern Europe"; also "Economic situation and economic reform in Eastern Europe", in *European Economy*, Special Edition No. 2; *Supplement A, Recent Economic Trends*, Nos. 8-9, Aug.-Sep. 1991.
Council of Europe. 1990. *Report on the new immigration countries* (doc. 6211, 24 Apr. 1990).
Debs, R.A.; H. Shapiro; C. Taylor. 1991. *Financing Eastern Europe* (Washington, DC, Group of Thirty).

Dekker, L. 1992. "De grote trek uit het oosten: Oosteuropese migranten en hun motieven", in *Oost-Europa Verkenningen*, Jan.-Feb. pp. 3-15.

Denison, E.F. 1967. *Why growth rates differ* (Washington, DC, The Brookings Institution).

Dovényi, Z. 1992. *The role of Hungary in the European migrations of the twentieth century*, paper presented at the conference on mass migration in Europe, Vienna, 5-7 March.

Economic and Social Comittee of the EC. 1992. "Opinion on immigration policy", in *Official Journal of the EC* (Brussels), 17 Feb. 1992, No. C40, pp. 104-112.

Economist Intelligence Unit. 1990. *Poland, Country Report*, No. 4.

—. 1990-91. *Poland, Country Profile*.

Europa van morgen. 1991. "Midden-Europa wil lidmaatschap EG", in *De Europese Gemeenschap en Centraal- en Oost-Europa*, No. 39, 19 Dec. 1991.

Gautron, J-C. 1991. "Les relations Communauté Européenne – Europe de l'Est", in *Economica* (Paris).

Ghosh, B. 1991. "The immigrant tide", in *European Affairs*, 1991, Vol. 4, pp. 78-82.

Góra, M. 1991a. *Labour market in transition: Poland 1990* (Warsaw).

—. 1991b. *Stages of transition: The labour market*, paper prepared for the Third Annual Conference of EALE, Conference Proceedings, Vol. V, *Transition in the labour markets*, Madrid, 26-29 September.

Grosfeld, I.; P. Hare. 1991. "Privatisation in Hungary, Poland and Czechoslovakia", in *European Economy: The path of reform in Central and Eastern Europe*, Special Edition No. 2 (Brussels).

Grossman, G.M.; E. Helpman. 1990. *Trade innovation and growth*, AEA papers and proceedings (Nashville, Tennessee), May, pp. 86-91.

Hamilton, C.B.; L.A. Winters. 1992. "Opening up international trade in Eastern Europe", in *Economic Policy*, forthcoming.

Havrylyshyn, O.; L. Pritchett. 1991. *European trade patterns after the transition*, World Bank working papers No. 748 (Washington, DC).

Heijke, J.A.M. 1979. *Sociaal-economisch aspecten van gastarbeid* (Rotterdam, Netherlands Economics Institute).

Hofstede, G. 1991. *Culture and organisations: Software of the mind* (London, McGraw-Hill).

Hönekopp, E. 1991. *Migratory movements from countries of Central and Eastern Europe: Causes and characteristics, present situation and possible future trends – The cases of Germany and Austria*, paper for the Conference of Ministers on the movement of persons coming from Central and Eastern European countries, Vienna, 24-25 January 1991 (Strasbourg, Council of Europe).

IBRD. 1990. *World Development Report* (Washington, DC).

Kaa, D.J. van der. 1991a. *European migration at the end of history*, PDOD-Paper No. 8, Postdoctorale Onderzoekersopleiding Demografie (Wassenaar).

—. 1991b. *Demografische dilemma's in een democratisch Europa*, speech/statement delivered on the occasion of his acceptance of the Cleveringa professorial Chair in Demography of the State University of Leiden, 26 November 1991 (Leiden, Rijksuniversiteit).

Katz, E.; O. Stark. 1986. *International labour migration under alternative informational regimes: A diagrammatic analysis*, paper, revised version of Harvard Institute of Economic Research, discussion paper No. 1051 and Harvard University Migration and Development Program, discussion paper No. 8 (Harvard University), June.

Keely, C.B.; B.N. Tran. 1989. "Remittances from labor migration: Evaluations, performance and implications", in *International Migration Review*, Vol. XXIII, No. 3, pp. 500-525.

Kennedy, P. 1988. *The rise and fall of the great powers* (London, Fontana).

Kodde, D.A. 1987. "Uncertainty and the demand for education", in *Review of Economics and Statistics*, pp. 460-467.

Koning, J. de. 1991. *Evaluating training at the company level*, paper for the International Conference on the Economics of Training, Cardiff, 23-24 September.

Kotowska, I. 1991. *Demographic determinants of labour market developments in Poland*, paper prepared for the Third Annual Conference of EALE, Madrid, 26-29 September.

Lindbeck, A. 1991. *Microfoundations of unemployment theory*, paper prepared for the Third Annual Conference of EALE, Madrid, 26-29 September.

Marques-Mendes, A.J. 1990. "Economic cohesion in Europe: The impact of the Delors Plan", in *Journal of Common Market Studies*, Vol. 29, pp. 17-36.

Merritt, G. 1991. *Eastern Europe and the USSR: The challenge of freedom* (London, Kogan Page and Commission of the European Communities).

Molle, W. 1990a. *Economics of European integration: Theory, practice, policy* (Aldershot, Dartmouth).

—. 1990b. "Will the completion of the internal market lead to regional divergence?", in H. Siebert (ed.): *The completion of the internal market* (Mohr, Tuebingen), pp. 174-196.

—; A. van Mourik. 1981. "International movements of labour under conditions of economic integration: The case of Western Europe", in *Journal of Common Market Studies*, Vol. 26, 3, pp. 317-339.

—;—. 1989. *Wage differentials in the European Community* (Aldershot, Avebury).

Morsink, R.; W.T.M. Molle. 1991. "Direct investment and monetary integration: The Economics of EMU background studies for one market, one money", in *European Economy*, Special Edition No. 1, pp. 36-56.

Muus, Ph. 1991. "Angst EG voor immigratie Sovjet-Unie onterecht", in *Staatscourant 242*, 12 Dec. 1991, p. 13.

OECD. 1991. *Demographic change and public policy, migration: The demographic aspects* (Paris).

—. 1990a. *Development cooperation: Annual aid statistics* (Paris).

—. 1990b. Directorate for Social Affairs. *Manpower and education: Continuous reporting system on migration* (Paris, SOPEMI, 1989).

Okólski, M. 1991. *Migratory movements from countries of Central and Eastern Europe*, paper for the Conference of Ministers on the movement of persons coming from Central and Eastern European Countries, Vienna, 24-25 January 1991 (Strasbourg, Council of Europe).

Olson, M. 1983. *The rise and decline of nations* (New Haven, Yale University Press).

Oschlies, W. 1989. Polnischer "Drang nach Westen: Dynamik und Motive der jüngsten Emigrationswelle aus Polen", in *Berichte des Bundesinstituts für ostwissenschaftlische und internationale Studien*, No. 30.

Pesaran, M.H.; R.G. Pierse; M.S. Kumar. 1989. "Econometric analysis of aggregation in the context of linear prediction models", in *Econometrica*, 57, pp. 861-888.

Phelps, E.S. (ed.). 1970. *Micro-economic foundations of employment and inflation theory* (London, Penguin).

Reynolds, L.G. 1983. "The spread of economic growth in the Third World", in *Journal of Economic Literature*, Vol. 21.

Ritzen, J.M.M. 1989. *Market failure for general training and remedies*, paper for the Robert M. de la Follette symposium on market failure for training, May 11-12.

Rutkowski, M. 1990. *Labour hoarding and future open unemployment in Eastern Europe: The case of Polish industry*, conference papers for the Second Annual Conference of EALE, Vol. III, Lund, 20-23 September.

Salt, J. 1991. *Current and future international migration trends affecting Europe*, paper for the Fourth Conference of European Ministers responsible for migration affairs, Luxembourg, 17-18 September (Strasbourg, Council of Europe).

Summers, R.; A. Heston. 1988. "A new set of international comparisons of real products and prices, estimates for 130 countries: 1950-1985", in *Review of Income and Wealth*, Vol. 34, pp. 1-25.

UN. 1991. Dept. of International and Social Affairs, *Global Population Estimates and Projections, 1991*, Population Studies No. 122 (New York).

Wang, Z.K.; L.A. Winters. 1991. *The trading potential of Eastern Europe*, discussion paper No. 610 (London, CEPR).

Wersch, M. van. 1991. *De Oost Europese Kapitaalbehoefte*, No. 47c (Amsterdam, De Nederlandse Bank).

Wijkman, P.M. 1992. *Structural change in European production and trade*, paper presented to a conference on Europe into the third millenium (Exeter).

World Bank. 1990. *Poland: Economic management for a new era* (Washington, DC, IBRD).

Zlotnik, H.; B. Hovy. 1990. *Trends in European migration: What the data reveal*, paper prepared for the symposium on the demographic consequences of international migration, held at NIAS, Wassenaar, the Netherlands, 27-29 September.

3

East-West migration in Europe and the role of international aid in reducing emigration

J. Blaschke

Following the crisis in the socialist countries of Eastern Europe[1] it has gradually become clear that the world is facing a new economic and social problem.[2] The outlines may still be rather hazy at the moment, but the specific issues involved will crystallize out over the next few years. At the moment two important aspects should be noted. First, the socialist projects in Eastern Europe represented an attempt to overcome underdevelopment. Contrary to the tenets of Marxist theory, it comprised in essence the industrialization of peasant societies[3] by intellectual avant-gardes. The Central and Eastern European countries (CEECs) demonstrated many features of underdevelopment that we are familiar with in Africa and Latin America today. The socialist projects turned out to be a failure. What we are left with are largely deformed societies whose political systems, economic-industrial complexes and social structures are barely interwoven or related to one another. These societies are becoming increasingly what in development theory has been called "fissured" (Menzel and Senghaas, 1983).

Second, the major outcome of the period of socialist rule was the "depeasantization" of Eastern European societies. Rural proletariats were created which were ultimately no longer in a position to guarantee the food supply in their respective societies. This is in stark contrast to Africa and Asia, where peasants have increasingly been forced to produce more for the international market and thus to neglect food production for domestic purposes. Any development policy in Eastern Europe which takes as its starting-point the food supply of the population must take into account the

---

[1] In his volume *Soviet politics: Struggling with change* (1992) Gordon B. Smith gives a synopsis of all facets of perestroika. We shall refer below only to literature that is of particular importance for the topic being discussed. A list of other publications consulted is appended. The text presented here is an abridged and corrected version of a discussion paper submitted to the joint ILO-UNHCR meeting on international aid as a means to reduce the need for emigration (Geneva, May 1992). Developments after April 1992 are not taken into consideration.

[2] The Western countries were quick to recognize the need for development aid for Eastern Europe. The aid discussed before that date is summarized by J.M.C. Rollo in his essay *Western policy: The room for manoeuvre* (1990, pp. 100ff.). So far involved in development policy programmes are the IMF, the IBRD, GATT, the World Bank, the Paris Club, the UN, the OECD, COCOM, the EC and the G24 and G7 groups.

[3] The industrialization of the Eastern European societies was accompanied by massive urbanization processes. A radical change came about in the 1960s when depeasantization was replaced by the exodus of farm workers. "They hope for better earning and working conditions in the towns, more personal freedom in their way of life and better leisure facilities" (Ruban, 1989, p. 272).

special role of agriculture. A separate perspective for peasants in Eastern Europe can virtually be disregarded (T. Shanin, private communication). Agricultural production cannot build on the social and technical know-how that peasant populations normally possess. It must be regulated by technology from the outset. Two of the main aims of development aid will be to train individual agricultural producers, and to promote other production groups working on their own initiative.

It follows from this that Eastern Europe's prospective migration systems have no historical parallel. In the past such systems were usually bound up with the processes of depeasantization. Migration without peasants is today a feature of many Eastern European migration movements. They can be taken as examples of the migration that will be typical of the regions on the periphery of the world system in future.

The talk of large-scale migration from Eastern Europe has startled politicians and confronted migration researchers with new problems. Research institutes and political agencies in Europe are now greatly concerned with the causes and movements of migration, immigration policy, and issues of integration. The call was raised early on for migration to be regulated by means of development aid and for migrants to be given assistance within the framework of development aid. At the international level there has been a resumption of the debates of the early 1980s[4] which pinpointed this link between migration regulation and development aid with respect to other regions (e.g. Independent Commission on International Humanitarian Issues, [ICIHI] 1986; Lachenmann and Otzen, 1981). The international community has grasped the close links that exist between migration, flight and displacement, on the one hand, and erroneous development policies on the other. It is vital that studies are carried out to look into these links. One of the biggest challenges in the decades ahead is the attainment of development targets in Africa, Asia and Latin America. The significance of this challenge for Eastern Europe is clearly seen in the EC countries: a further raft of development policy is likely, but maintaining peace and integrating the Eastern European states into a pan-European political system will be the larger aim (viz. Senghaas, 1992a).

Using East-West migration since the end of the 1980s as an example, we will now examine the development policy instruments available to regulate migration movements and to provide assistance to migrants. A theoretical approach of this kind can provide no more than a stimulus since both data and theories are rare commodities.[5] Nevertheless, there is a wealth of experience on development aid and migration policy to be drawn on.

[4] Gudrun Lachenmann sticks to the terms of the UNHCR mandate and points out that first, intensified basic-needs-orientated development cooperation could help avert refugee streams and that second, international warning systems could make it easier for development policy institutions to take timely action. Thus development policy remains an independent variable alongside refugee aid. Nothing is said about the integration of the two aid systems (Lachenmann and Otzen, 1981).

[5] The following data were compiled in the course of the establishment of a research group on East-West Migration at the Berlin Institute for Comparative Social Research. A corresponding data bank is now being set up and a publication containing statistics on East-West migration has been published. A revised edition is in preparation. I would like to thank Bernd Rainer, Katrin Becker, Beatrix Bletzer, Bob Bryce, Peter Doherty, Jan-Heeren Grevemeyer, Ewa Helias, Elke Lehnert, Klaus Morner, Renate Rybitzki, Katrin Scherner, Rita Schick, Werner Winter and Inga Wolfram-Trimpert for their help in preparing this report.

Statistical and demographic studies on migration have only just begun to evaluate the figures that are available. There is no justification for postulating a direct connection between population growth and migration. On the contrary, most of the available empirical studies on migration reveal a link between depeasantization and migration, between middle-class orientation and the motives for migration. There is no direct connection between demographic growth and a thwarting of the integration opportunities open to potential migration groups. Rather, political and economic factors are of crucial importance in this respect. This is indicated by the increase in expulsion and migration in the wake of political persecution. It would also be speculative to assume that there will be lower growth rates in labour migration worldwide, but that there will be an exponential increase in the unregulated spatial displacement of people.

1. The evolution of East-West migration

How can East-West migration in the 1990s be regulated? What instruments are suitable for this purpose? The answers to such questions can only be exploratory since little is known about the migration of the 1990s.

The history of East-West migration starts in the nineteenth century. It continued this century with the expulsion of Germans from the former territories of the Reich after the Second World War and the subsequent resettling of war victims as displaced persons. When the Iron Curtain came down, the problem of East-West migration was reduced – in Germany at least – to the immigration of diaspora Germans and the emigration of opponents of the regime from the German Democratic Republic. In other Western European countries this type of East-West migration was negligible.

One exception was the emigration that followed such crises as the Hungarian uprising, the Prague Spring and the Polish troubles. Strict border controls meant that it was virtually impossible to maintain old migration chains. Belgium, France, the United Kingdom, Australia and the United States continued to take in a few Poles and Russians. Another exception was the emigration of Jews who left their countries of origin to go to Israel but who in many cases ended up in Central Europe or in the United States.

It was not until liberalization took place in Hungary and Poland, followed by perestroika, glasnost and the lifting of the Iron Curtain at the end of the 1980s, that there were far-reaching changes in the patterns of migration from East to West. These changes were, indeed, so fundamental that it is certainly justifiable to talk of a completely new system of migration. Characteristic features of this new situation are (a) different types of migrant; (b) different forms of migration; (c) different calls on migration regulation; (d) different problems in the sending and receiving countries; and (e) different expectations of future mobility trends.

The types of migration movement that, to date, can be defined are listed below. Given the diffuse nature of the material available their definition tends to be ad hoc in nature rather than deduced from adequate data. The categorization of migration systems which follows can only serve to determine differing types of migrant groups for the moment. Further research into East-West migration should be able to establish the independent nature of the migration systems and assign the various types of migration movement to them.

Although there are many types of migrant who cannot as yet be clearly isolated, the following may be provisionally distinguished: (1) diaspora migrants; (2) Gypsies;[6] (3) long-standing chain migrants; (4) internal and external refugees and politically displaced people; (5) environmental migrants; (6) migrant workers; (7) illegal, non-documented migrant workers; (8) brain drain migrants; (9) migrant traders; (10) stranded migrants; (11) socially and economically displaced people; (12) West-East migrants. These various types of migrant provide the starting-point for the discussion that follows.

2. Systems of migration

Migration systems display fixed patterns of migration and are largely subordinated to a migration regime. They are institutionalized in a social scientific sense, and regulated. An understanding of the degree of institutionalization and regulation is crucial for an assessment of migration systems.

Only in exceptional cases have systems for international migration movements been established in the Eastern bloc since the Second World War – for instance in Poland under the rule of Gomulka and in the USSR with respect to the Jewish population. The Iron Curtain was designed as a means of preventing migration and, by extension, migration systems. The change came in 1988 with the establishment of a refugee regime in Hungary.[7]

The lack of any sizeable, long-lasting migration movement in Central and Eastern Europe led to a rather odd integration of this region into the international migration regime. There were regulatory bodies at the local level which, in the case of the Jewish organizations, were tied into the supranational networks of Israeli-oriented politics. There were also small groups in the West which, with the help of their sister organizations in the Eastern bloc, attempted to secure emigration for certain groups of people. These migration agencies were organized on a local basis and were so diffuse that it was impossible to maintain an overview of them. National migration agencies were set up in the wake of diaspora migration.

Another important feature of the East-West migration regime in Europe was the political philosophy of the Cold War. The propagation of free international migration was part of the confrontation between East and West. The fact that the East shut itself off from the West was seen as proof of the contempt for the individual that existed under communist regimes. Open borders were a fundamental demand

---

[6] In recent years it has become fashionable to replace the traditional term "Gypsy" with what they are said to call themselves, "Sinti" and "Roma". This is supposed to prevent discrimination against ethnic groups that regard themselves as "Sinti" and "Roma". In our view such a nominalist anti-discrimination policy is misplaced, since it creates new problems and diverts attention from material discrimination. In the case of the Gypsies, the Sinti use the new terminology to marginalize the Roma.

[7] The Hungarian Government is currently publishing a series of information sheets on its refugee policy. The refugee regime in Hungary apparently needs further support in the public health and refugee food aid spheres to supplement the relief payments it has been receiving from UNHCR since 1989.

that was raised with the leadership in Moscow. This value system continues to make it very hard ideologically for Western European governments to close their borders entirely to Eastern Europe.

Migration systems in Eastern Europe are still being established. On the whole, however, we cannot yet speak of the parallel existence of clearly delineated migration systems: the migration processes, types and regimes are changing rapidly. The migration contexts are likewise subject to almost revolutionary social change. Even such established migration systems as those of the Gypsies or of the diaspora minorities seem to be changing radically.

The urbanization processes in Eastern Europe proceeded along different lines from those in other parts of the world. They did not turn peasants into industrial workers, but improved the prospects for peripheral population groups in the centres of nations. Emerging from the regional fragmentation of Eastern Europe are typical migration movements including, among others, highly qualified skilled workers and university graduates, as well as refugees. National borders and ethnic segregation are leading to a migration scenario in which it is becoming increasingly hard to distinguish between internal and external migration movements. Migration systems in Eastern Europe are in a state of flux.[8]

In absolute figures, the largest internal migration system is without doubt in the Commonwealth of Independent States (CIS). In relative terms to the population as a whole, Yugoslavia (or its successor states) comprises the region with the largest internal migration: in the 1970s, 225,000 people a year left the area in which they had settled.

3. Migration policy and development policy

Development policy measures draw on three different sets of instruments: macroeconomic, personnel, and technological (at the microeconomic level). These types of instrument are reflected in development policy institutions and are themselves bound to institutions. Financial, personnel and technical resources have to be channelled via governmental and non-governmental organizations (NGOs). This ensures spatial flexibility for development policy. Development policy measures can be applied *in situ* through the regional and national levels down to the local level.[9]

---

[8] A survey of new internal migration developments in the CIS is given by Ingrid Oswald (1992a; see also the articles by Viktor Voronkov and Igor Ushkalov in the same volume).

[9] The macroeconomic scenarios for Eastern Europe and a possible intervention policy was the subject of a collection of articles entitled *Economic change and the Balkan States* which attempts to systematize the macroeconomic scenarios. The prospects for three countries, according to the authors, seem similar to those of the other Eastern European countries except that the political "sphere" is different. The failure of development strategies could pave the way for a Latin-Americanization of Eastern Europe (Sjöberg and Wyzan, 1991). Concerning Hungary, Roger A. Clarke writes in his omnibus volume that "The major barrier to more fundamental reform of the core economic system in Hungary appears more and more to be the fact that so much of economic decision-making is essentially a political rather than an economic process" (1989, p. 170). Similar conclusions are drawn for Yugoslavia's successor states by James Simmie and Joze Dekleva (1991) and for the former USSR by Nicolas Spulber (1991), who in his comprehensive analysis pleads for rehabilitation of the market but cannot suggest any instruments for such a transition.

Macropolitical measures need state organizations as partners. Donor organizations, such as the World Bank, the International Monetary Fund or the United Nations, can be positioned at the international level. In Eastern Europe, multilateral regional organizations are emerging, based either within the framework of the Conference on Security and Cooperation in Europe (CSCE) or in other European organs. The group of seven leading industrialized nations (G7) and other ad hoc groupings are likewise important in this respect. At the national level, there is a wide range of bilateral and multilateral agreements with Eastern Europe whose primary purpose is to reduce debts and secure investment. At the moment, foreign trade assistance and forms of currency support are being debated, and macroeconomic cooperation is in a transitional phase.

Private economic cooperation also needs to be accommodated in the macroeconomic sphere. In view of the amount of capital required, which cannot be met from state funds, there will be no economic upswing in Eastern Europe without large-scale private investment. The necessary conditions for this investment must be set out within the framework of international accords.

Three areas of technical cooperation are becoming evident. Of undisputed significance is the reversal of damage done to the environment. This ranges from dealing with unsafe nuclear power plants to the redevelopment of the regions of Upper Silesia which have suffered at the hands of the coal and steel industry. It also includes cooperation between municipal sponsors in Western Europe and the former Yugoslav Republic of Macedonia in cleaning up the environmentally unacceptable urban quarters in which Gypsies have been forced to settle.

A second field of technological cooperation is to be found in the establishment of infrastructures. This incorporates improvements in transport and communications, urban development, the supply of water, power and health care, as well as an ecologically acceptable means of sewage and refuse disposal. The opening up of peripheral regions in the CEECs may possibly neutralize internal migration processes through reverse movements. The newly formed states will require functioning infrastructures to ensure efficient government. The best way of stabilizing diaspora minorities, using infrastructure aid, is currently being examined.

Thirdly, technological cooperation is used to set up organizations and train tomorrow's leaders. This would appear to constitute a major field of East-West cooperation in the future. Joint ventures, which not only complement state companies but also create new centres for production and services, require an intensive transfer of knowledge and of practical experience. Given the immense number of colleges, research institutes and academies, as well as the redundancies affecting engineers and scientists in the armaments sector, there is a need to channel potential leaders into new spheres of activity. For these groups in particular, additional qualifications or retraining could be an alternative to migration. Measures of this kind are being carried out by the donor countries in their own interests as they represent an extension of the market for their products. In view of the debate on the return of population groups that have emigrated, training schemes of the kind already under way in developing countries would appear logical.

Personnel measures are implemented almost exclusively by NGOs. Countries such as the United States and the Federal Republic of Germany have set up

NGOs such as the Peace Corps or the Deutscher Entwicklungsdienst (German Development Service). The aim of such personnel development aid was originally political, i.e. to have training and expert knowledge given to people in developing countries by Western staff. This has now been professionalized and constitutes a major pillar of development aid: engineers, technicians, skilled workers, teachers and other specialists are being called upon to help out in these countries.

There is as yet no scientific evidence of the connection between development and migration which might lead to the development of practical models. The sole exception in this respect concerns refugees. Here, though, the discussion on development policy would still appear to be limited because of the "mandate bias" of the international regime. The refugee discussion in the context of development policy is concentrated in three problem areas: first, the settlement of refugees in the first or second country of asylum; second, support for returnees; and, third, the prevention or limitation of refugee movements by combating their causes. An approach based on these three aspects might well be used to deal with migration movements.

Given the various types and systems of migration, there is a requirement for different development schemes for returnees. These schemes will depend on the returnees' motivations and abilities to reintegrate into old social contexts; they will also include resettlement in social milieux with which the migrants were not previously familiar. This obviously applies to a large number of former Soviet military staff who have returned to their country. The repatriation of Gypsies to their accustomed milieux showed that familiarity of the milieux as such, without any consideration of the migration system, is not an adequate category for such measures.

The discussions about the causes of migration seem to be of particular relevance to the overall problem. What is striking here, however, is the separation of the causes from the migration movements themselves. Such a separation is understandable, though, given the definition of refugees as victims of occasional persecution. A socioscientific perspective which distances itself from legalistic casuistry better reveals both the integration of refugee movements into more comprehensive migration systems, and the group orientation of many movements of flight.

Many flight movements are, therefore, simply defined as such because the gates of entry into receiving countries only allow migrant workers to immigrate along the avenue of asylum. Seen from the standpoint of human rights, it may be supposed that these migrant workers have perhaps been subjected to political persecution. Labour emigration often takes place for political reasons. Nevertheless, it is improbable that many of the immigrants would accept a different gate of entry. Refugee movements of this kind consist of a variety of migrants who are forced into a particular migration system because of decisions taken by political regimes.

If the causes of flight and migration are to be combated, the diversity of a migration system must be considered. Any approach must adopt various forms of technical, financial and personnel cooperation, and incorporate protection from human rights violations. In general, it makes sense to regard the migration system itself as an object of political intercession. In the migration system of the Sinti and Roma, for example, protection against discrimination and improvements in the infrastructure in the settlement areas would act, on the one hand, as a brake on migration while, on the other, a relaxation in regulations on temporary migration (via the issue of internationally valid passports or the financing of camp sites) might result in a reduction in the number of migrants. This would require an improved migration system and a greater willingness on the part of receiving countries to accept the social consequences of migration movements.

It is characteristic of development policy measures that either they make themselves felt in macroeconomic terms and, therefore, make the whole economic system of a country their object, or they address themselves in microeconomic terms to a particular clientele in the form of technical or personnel aid. Technical aid for large-scale projects will continue to play a role and have an effect in Eastern Europe in the regulation of migration movements. This applies to ecological measures and the prevention of environmental migration, as well as to the effects of infrastructural measures on migration. As has been the case in the debate on development policy, an example must assert itself in migration theory which defines "strategic groups" as the clientele of such measures. This is the only way in which an evaluation of the effects that development policy has on migration movements can be conducted. The definition of these strategic groups depends on two factors: first, on the threat to them posed by disasters and crises and, second, on their assignment to existing or incipient migration systems.

4. Development policy and migration systems in Eastern Europe

Development policies for diaspora migrants

Diaspora migrants include Germans in Romania, Poland and the CIS, Greeks in the CIS, Yugoslavia, Albania and Bulgaria, Pontus Greeks from the Caucasus, Hungarians in Romania, Yugoslavia and Slovakia, as well as Armenians and Jews.[10] Other minorities deported in the Stalinist era are beginning to define themselves as diaspora migrants. They include, for instance, the Crimean Tartars, 272,000 of whom lived in the USSR in 1989 (Statistical Press Bulletin, 1991). In 1989, there were 847,584 Turks living in Bulgaria, that is, roughly 10 per cent of the total population (Bulgarian Statistical Office, 1992). Their diaspora situation is underlined by the fact that Turkey has a special policy for ethnic Turks living abroad.[11]

---

[10] A standard work on the Jewish diaspora was published in 1992. It traces the emigration from the former USSR in detail and in doing so analyses the structure of the Soviet emigration regime (Salitan, 1992). Salitan sees the ineptitude of the nationality policy that is integrated in the political system as the starting-point for Jewish and German emigration from the former USSR.

[11] The term "diaspora" is used here to refer to the dual political and social loyalties of these population groups. Diasporas are characterized by an orientation towards the country of origin. In the ancient Jewish world this orientation was combined with the expectation of salvation. In view of family, religious, and later on national loyalties, migration chains are certainly of relevance to migration theory. For the most part they are tied up with economic relations. Owing to the shifting of borders and the policy of expulsion that is obviously being pursued in various regions of Eastern Europe, new diasporas are emerging. It is difficult to differentiate between expellees and diaspora migrants within the context of development policy discussions. The individual cases should be discussed separately.

Jews who emigrated from the USSR numbered 1,914 in 1986; 8,155 in 1987; 18,965 in 1988; and 369,385 in 1989 (Salitan, 1992). Pontus Greeks who left the USSR totalled 527 in 1987; 1,365 in 1988; 6,791 in 1989; 13,863 in 1990; and 11,420 in 1991 (Emke-Poulopoulos, 1992). There are currently some 57,000 Greeks living in Albania, although this figure is disputed by Greece. Conservative groups in Greece talk of at least half a million Greeks in southern Albania.

The redefinition of nation state borders and of nationalism has led to other diaspora movements. In Bulgaria, some 400,000 to 500,000 people are expected to arrive from what was formerly Soviet Bessarabia and from Kazakhstan, and there will be others from the former Yugoslav Republic of Macedonia. Efforts to establish a refugee regime in Bulgaria would appear to be linked to these estimates (*Emigrant* [Bulgarian weekly], Nov. 1991).

It is very difficult to assess the diaspora situation of Armenians. In Bulgaria, for instance, discrimination against Armenians has led, on the one hand, to their orientation towards the new Republic of Armenia while, on the other, they have a clear wish to stay in the country. This latter point concerns their function as a "middleman minority" (interview with Stepan Agukyan, an editor with the newspaper *Yerevan*).

The Federal Republic of Germany and Israel had established a migration regime for their diaspora migrants so that when the Iron Curtain fell it was possible for them effectively to regulate and organize the immigration of ethnic Germans and of Jews. In constructing its regime for diaspora Germans, the Government of the Federal Republic of Germany drew on traditions established by the ethnic German minority movement of the Weimar Republic. This migration regime rested on two pillars. One consisted of the established associations of expellees and of a policy of solidarity with ethnic Germans living abroad. The other comprised state agencies which maintained their existence after the end of the Second World War. From 1945, the Federal Republic of Germany had a consistent policy to take in diaspora Germans from the Eastern bloc. The regulatory instruments used included foreign political interventions, immigration assistance and an intricate system of integration.

Greeks living abroad have always played a key role in Greek politics because Greek nationalism embraces the concept of allowing all Greeks to return home. However, re-migration had received scant institutional form in the postwar period, so that chaos reigned in Greek admission policy after 1988. Greece improvised as well as it could in the face of many emigrants' desire to return home. The Office for Overseas Greeks, and a department working with the Foreign Ministry, were simply not prepared for the rush of between 200,000 and 1 million Pontus Greeks wishing to return.

An intricate supranational system of institutions and regulations exists for the emigration of Jews. This runs alongside Israel's immigration policy, and incorporates an aid and intervention system on the part of the United States Government. The USSR and Poland have also been incorporated into this emigration regime.

An informal aid system operates for Armenians; they have also built up an emigration system through their religious and national organizations. Armenians in the Eastern European diaspora were in the unusual situation of being able to migrate within the network of the Armenian diaspora, and of having regained a home country of their own thanks to the resurrection of the Armenian nation state in the Caucasus.

The policies of donor countries for regulating the diaspora migration vary. Israel is pursuing an active strategy to return Jews from the USSR. The position of the Greek Government over the Greek diaspora in Eastern Europe is not yet known. When the new Armenian state is formed, it will try to work together with the diaspora communities in the West to bring Armenians in the CEECs "home". The traditions of Armenians as intermediaries and traders – to some extent this applies to Jews and Greeks as well – will perhaps be used in future to stabilize the diaspora in such countries as Bulgaria, Romania and the Federation of Russia. The dual loyalties of such diaspora populations make them interesting as partners in development aid negotiations. Attention should be given to these groups in discussions over joint ventures.

In the German diaspora – as in others – a small middle class has formed that will be significant for joint venture programmes. This applies equally to returnees from Germany who have gone through the well-developed integration system in the Federal Republic and now hope to have better chances of getting ahead in their regions of origin. In these regions a German-funded network of organizations and lobbies exists; in addition, the desire of political decision-makers in Germany to use funds and other development policy measures to discourage the immigration of Germans from Eastern Europe is apparent.

More than 1.2 million such people have migrated to Germany in the past three years. The number of those remaining, mainly in the CIS, is estimated to be about 3 million. If the non-German members of their families come with them a total of 7 million migrants can be expected. The Stalinist displacement policy deprived the German diaspora of its hereditary settlement areas. The diaspora policy now being developed by the Ministry of the Interior in Germany is intended to re-establish those settlement areas on a smaller scale.

There are two motivations. The first concerns making reparations to the displaced people and propagating the "homeland" concept enshrined in the German nationalist theory of the nation. Second, it is assumed that discrimination against Germans where they are now living will lead to more extensive migration to Germany.

The reconstruction of the old settlement areas is currently being supported through generous financial backing. However, negotiations between Ukraine, the Russian Federation and Germany have run into a number of serious problems, similar to those encountered by repatriation programmes for developing country refugees: the desired areas are occupied by other people, while the areas offered are economically unattractive. Repatriation thus becomes resettlement and involves a risk that is hard to calculate both for the migrants and for the surrounding population. The German Government is not in a position to predict the cost either; it has to rely on the intermediary agencies that are still being formed. These include the organizations of diaspora Germans and local institutions in Ukraine and the Russian Federation that expect the German settlers to stimulate the economy. Given these difficulties and the overall context of the migration system of the diaspora Germans, it is difficult to forecast success at the moment.

There are two models that might be exceptions. The St. Petersburg municipal government has announced that German colonies can be established on the outskirts to help supply the city. It should be possible to offer prospects for diaspora Germans there if concrete support is given to individual enterprises, if infrastructural projects and housing construction are funded, and if measures are taken to promote solidarity among the local population.

Such a colonial solution resulting from the settlement of migrants would be in the tradition of the old Russian Empire and could be functionally situated within a calculable context of regional development strategies. It would thus be possible to ensure political support for the project among the population, to provide the migrants with a motive for resettling there, and to give the designated regions a broad development policy impetus. The project calls for close cooperation with the old organizations of the diaspora minorities and cooperation at local, regional and national level on the part of the countries concerned. The latter would have to establish a control system and it would have to be situated outside the international agencies, as it would draw its legitimacy from the diaspora situation.

Various problems seem to be involved in the discussion about a free trade area in Kaliningrad (formerly Königsberg). The social development of a small peripheral region cut off from the future economic and social system is the first issue involved. The second is the establishment of a free trade zone and its concomitant stimuli for industrialization in the Baltic Sea region, currently being debated by international firms. Third, in Germany at the moment there is debate among groups displaced from the region about the special responsibility of the German Government. Two concrete proposals have so far emerged. First, German financial institutions and industrial firms want to become involved in the region if the necessary political safeguards are provided. Second, some Russian politicians want to settle diaspora Germans there. Under such circumstances concerted development activities, which would of course have to be controlled bilaterally, might be reasonable from the point of view of migration policy. This strategy is, however, open to criticism with respect to national security, because of the long-term effects of such a policy on German-Polish relations and on the possibility of a German bridgehead being established in what used to be East Prussia.

Development policies for Gypsies

Gypsies, most of whom are Sinti and Roma, have been roaming Central Europe since the Middle Ages. In the countries behind the Iron Curtain they were usually forced to settle in one place and lived in poor social conditions. Nevertheless, the borders were always sufficiently open to permit at least small-scale population movements. This situation has changed radically since 1989. The Roma in Eastern Europe are on the move, trying to improve their social situation by moving to Western Europe. The Gypsies' social system is experiencing a fundamental transformation.

A total of 404,461 Gypsies were registered in Hungary in 1986, 74,912 of whom lived in Budapest and the surrounding area (Fact sheets on Hungary, 1991). According to the Federal Statistical Office of Germany (1990 Report on Albania), there are some 6,000 Gypsies living in Albania. The number of Gypsies living in Bulgaria is estimated to be around 800,000 (interview with Elena Marushiakova).

The official figure in 1989 was 576,927 (Bulgarian Statistical Office, 1992). In 1987 there were 47,223 Roma living in Macedonia (Poulton, 1991). The same source puts the number of Gypsies living in the former Yugoslavia at 850,000, including 150,000 in Croatia. The overall estimate for the number of Gypsies living in Eastern Europe is 2 million to 3 million. Chesnais (1990) mentions in addition 200,000 to 500,000 Gypsies in the CIS, 300,000 to 400,000 in Czechoslovakia, and 10,000 to 15,000 in Poland. There are probably between 500,000 and 900,000 Roma living in Romania.

It is mainly Roma – occasionally Sinti – who emigrate from Eastern Europe. The Gypsies' own definition of themselves is based on their migration systems. Gypsies have never taken any notice of national borders. This violation of a basic nationalist consensus has not only demonstrated a lack of obedience to the nation state regimes, but also reflected traditional modes of conduct. Violations of the border regime, however, have been primarily a result of the discrimination against Gypsies within the nation states themselves: Roma and Sinti have regularly had to flee as refugees from their countries of origin and have become stateless as a result.

In addition to this, religious and cultural traditions would appear to be of importance. Some of the bigger social associations of the Gypsies hold large festivals in the Balkans. Regular border crossings are part of the annual pattern of events. Over the past few decades there have apparently been no East-West migration movements. In Roma literature, however, there is mention of regular and frequent border crossings by Western Gypsy groups. It can be assumed, therefore, that there must have been East-West movements from the Balkans, too.[12] It is unlikely that Roma from the Balkans would have failed to avail themselves of the opportunities to cross borders over the past few decades. A certain degree of East-West migration is plausible in that there are festival sites in both France and Spain. Here, cultural pull factors are at work. Reasons for the international migration of Gypsies are to be found not just in the cultural and political sphere but also in family ties. These have been established in the wake of migration movements and could in theory be interpreted in the context of chain patterns.

It is possible to regard the migration of Gypsies after 1988 as an escape along traditional lines of flight by a pariah population that had been left to its own cultural devices and forced to live in abnormal conditions. Clandestine migration traditions were transformed ad hoc into a comprehensive migration system.

These remarks can only be interpreted in the context of other suppositions. The social system of the Gypsies in Europe has been distinguished in particular by an unsuccessful adaptation to modern ways of life. Peasant professions were only partially adjusted to the demands of industrial societies. Tinkers and scissor grinders became factory workers but they avoided any long-term working contracts. Family structures and ways of life were not fundamentally changed. Horse-dealers began trading in automobiles in the hope of being able to preserve their traditional way of life. Acculturation to and integration into nation states does not appear to have suc-

---

[12] A general picture of migration problems in the Balkans is given by Christopher Cviic (1991). He shows that first, the migration movements have not yet been precisely defined and that second, a policy for this region would have to form "networks for the new millennium" (p. 104).

ceeded so far. The end of industrialism and the establishment of economic postmodernity would appear to have brought with it the launching of a fundamental change in the Gypsies' social structures.

Their flight to the West should be seen in this context. There is, however, scant information on more far-reaching developments – especially the links between social change and the establishment of a migration system for European Gypsies.

We know little about the history of the migration system of the south-east European Roma. In this regard, it would be of interest to launch a range of scientific projects in which the intellectual élites of these population groups could play a key role. Not until this history is known will it be possible to answer the questions on the significance of the migration process itself: Do the Gypsies themselves regard their migration as provisional? Are their movements important for reconstructing their social systems?

Until then, in terms of development policy, we will only be able to point to the various causes of emigration. Human rights violations of these minorities have increased in the past year and continue to represent a latent threat. In every development policy measure, care must therefore be taken to prevent human rights violations. For that reason it will be essential, particularly in the case of groups like the Gypsies that are exposed to such extensive discrimination, to involve the surrounding population in the concrete development of policy measures. If rejection of a pariah population were compounded by envy of their development policy privileges, then an explosive situation could arise.

Until now the decisive reason for Roma migration has probably been the hopeless situation in the suburban ghetto settlements. Poor hygiene, the lack of infrastructures (e.g. water, electricity, transport) and the almost total lack of job opportunities make it almost impossible to survive in such areas. Consequently, fear of persecution, poverty migration, and the revival of traditional migration systems supplement one another. It cannot be assumed that these populations are "born to travel". All sociological investigations into the situation of Gypsies have shown that a solid focal point of life is part of the "life dream" of these populations. Migration-oriented development policy would have to improve that focal point within the context of local patterns of life. Massive infrastructural and construction programmes, linked with a local labour market policy, could well be seen as instruments for regulating migration. Almost all settlement areas are close to urban agglomerations, and consequently the incorporation of such an employment programme into regional development concepts becomes reasonable.

Pilot projects of this type are yet to be undertaken. Action so far has been limited to structural improvements in housing and financial assistance. The Federal State of North Rhine-Westphalia has begun a project for migration-oriented development policy in the former Yugoslav Republic of Macedonia for Gypsies expelled from Germany. The project will probably be supplemented by more far-reaching measures. No long-term success is foreseeable at the moment, as the project is limited to improvements in infrastructural activities. Without labour market policy instruments the situation will not improve. There even seems to be a tendency for the returnees settled there to re-immigrate. Future projects should build on this experience.

Development policies for long-standing chain migrants

The way the old migration chains have been maintained within the framework of East-West migration is striking. Many of these chains were or seemed to have been broken, such as the Polish[13] and Russian links with Western Europe. During the 1950s, the migration movements from Poland were quite obviously steered by Polish organizations to North America.

In the late 1980s, the old links seemed to be reappearing in Germany. This was encouraged among the Poles by the intellectuals who had emigrated in the wake of the Polish political crises. The increase in Polish chain migration remained slow until 1988, when it speeded up. Russian immigrant colonies also seem to have been renewed in recent years. The apparent reticence of Russian immigrants contributed to the view that they were inclined to assimilate. In recent years, Russians who have lived for a long time in the industrialized countries have acted as intermediaries for newcomers, and as interpreters.

The established immigrant minorities in the West have become centres of immigration. Repairs are now being made to migration chains that were severed for over 40 years. Particularly affected in this respect are Poles, Ukrainians, Baltic peoples and Russians, in both the classical immigration countries and the industrial areas of Western Europe. People from areas of former Yugoslavia who were recruited as migrant workers and went to Western Europe also belong to the category of chain migrants. The latest migration movements are following the chains of migration established earlier.

In 1989, for example, there were more than 1 million Yugoslavs living in the Federal Republic of Germany, Sweden, France and Switzerland (Chesnais and Council of Europe, 1990). Some 1.5 million Yugoslavs live overseas (*Facts on Yugoslavia*, 1985). According to newspaper reports in 1992, Croat aid organizations assume that the Croatian diaspora in the United States comprises 2 million people (*Vecernji List*, 21 Feb. 1992).

Not all chain migration systems can be dealt with here. Moreover, as mentioned above, we know little about these networks. The structure of such migration systems, however, suggests the building of return migration gates via development policy measures. These would include participation of such migrants in joint venture firms and the use of development policy resources as safeguards for that participation. It would also be useful to examine individual chain migration movements, to find out in what sequence the migrations take place and the gates of entry change, and how the push factors have changed during specific periods. The way those remaining behind profit from the chain migrants should also be investigated. Only when such case studies have been completed will it be possible to include chain migrants in development policy strategies.

---

[13] An introduction to the problem of Polish chain migration is given by Beatrix Bletzer in her essay on the Polish community in Berlin (Bletzer, 1991), and by Ewa Helias in her working paper for the Berliner Institut für Vergleichende Sozialforschung on the continuity of Polish labour immigration in the new states of Germany.

Development policies for internal and external refugees and politically displaced people

Eastern Europe is a region in which nation states were formed comparatively late. They were plagued by political crises, violence and discrimination.[14]

There is hardly a population group that will allow itself to be made into a minority without exercising vigorous protest, but democratic popular sovereignty requires power to be exercised by the majority. In the history of nationalism, the establishment of national homogeneity has always been accompanied by expulsion and migration of minorities. Typical are the refugee movements of minorities from Croatia, Serbia, and Bosnia and Herzegovina. The same applies to Russian minorities in the new states of the CIS and to refugees from Moldova, Azerbaijan, Georgia and Romania.

The changes in Eastern Europe are revolutionary. In addition to minorities who are suffering persecution because of their ethnic background or their religious creed, some people are fleeing civil wars merely to ensure their survival. Civil wars do not distinguish between civilians and soldiers. For the most part the victims are those who have been bombed out of their homes or expelled. The numbers of migrants have increased during the upheavals and changes in regimes.

The civil war in former Yugoslavia, resulting from the formation of the nation states of Croatia and later Bosnia and Herzegovina, resulted in expulsions. The emigration that was involved was clearly a step-by-step process. The refugees remained in the country for a considerable time, then migrated to Hungary, then to Austria, and later – most of them – to Germany. These migration movements are contributing to the expansion and restructuring of the system of Yugoslav migration in Europe. Chain migration following Yugoslav labour migration, refuge-seeking as a result of minority conflicts and nation state formation, and old and new refugee regimes, are all decisive factors in the changes in the Yugoslav migration system.

There is little to be said so far about the refugee regimes in the CIS. The large number of internal refugees in that region makes such a regime necessary. In addition to looking after the victims of civil war, it will be responsible for the small number of stranded refugees and transit migrants. There is no way of knowing what form the establishment of the refugee regime will take in the former USSR. Traces of old systems that are being revived can be detected, but in most cases the attempts at refugee control are both new and local. It appears that a policy of resettlement in the rural environment offers the best prospects for success.

The process of state formation in Croatia and the problems of disengagement from the institutions of the formal centralized state connected with it, the minority policy in the regions occupied by Serbs and other minorities, and the intervention of Serbian militia, have all resulted in population shifts in the civil war that could have been prevented through timely international intervention. Such a policy of intervention would have had to be accompanied by safeguards for minorities and programmes to break up the armed forces. This opportunity went unexploited, so

---

[14] Nation states identify themselves as such by claiming to link the sovereignty of the people with cultural homogeneity in the confines of a clearly delineated territory.

that it has become necessary to repatriate refugees in the combat regions. The same can be argued for the migration disasters after Bosnia and Herzegovina's independence and Serbia's expulsion policies.

Experience in repatriation in other parts of the world can certainly be utilized in this context. Success is made harder to achieve both by continuing local fighting and by the refugee reception structures in receiving countries. The lack of provision for short-term asylum in non-combatant areas and in neighbouring countries forces the migrants from that crisis region into proceedings that take several years in some Western European countries and that consolidate the immigration predicament. In this situation, it is probable that immediate resettlement programmes need to be supplemented by training (and further training) measures.

A second refugee system has developed in the CIS countries. Long-term conflicts in Azerbaijan, Armenia and Georgia, as well as in other crisis regions, have made hundreds of thousands of people homeless inside the CIS. Reliable estimates suggest that 2 million to 3 million people have been caught up in these refugee movements. A policy of repatriation is not feasible, as internal flight movements inside the CIS have predominantly been transformed into external displacement phenomena. Structured refugee regimes have not yet emerged. In the main it will be the Ministry for Agricultural Development that will be responsible for these refugees in the Russian Federation. Preparations are being made for resettlement programmes in cooperation with Western European countries. Ideas for corresponding agrarian projects are still in short supply. Nor is it clear how these projects are to be incorporated in the overall Russian development process. It would seem to be in the interests of peace in the region that these projects be given international support. New development policy concepts are required to provide for the direct transformation of industrial workers or industrialized farm workers into farmers. The lack of prospects for these people makes it necessary to test long-term strategies, however sceptical the scientific community may be. It is incumbent upon the UN system to provide support for the establishment of national migration and refugee regimes.[15]

The processes of state formation within the former USSR are likely to result in further expulsion and refugee movements. This is especially true for the Russian population groups in the new states outside the Russian Federation. Nationalism will cause new emigration movements which, under certain circumstances, could take a violent course. In Moldova we can already see how implacable such a conflict can be. The Russian part of the population is trying forcibly to safeguard its privileges there by separating the territories it occupies from the rest of the new state. One reason for the severity of these conflicts may be that the territories are relatively homogeneous ethnically, and geographically it would be possible to annex parts of them to the Russian Federation. All observers predict expulsion and flight movements.

The international organizations should draw attention to the humanitarian and social consequences of such processes. It is quite possible for the issue of the Russian minorities to be discussed through consultative means when the legal and adminis-

---

[15] In 1990 Louise Drüke presented an initial summary of possible strategies for timely intervention in refugee-producing situations. Her work refers to a large number of instruments in this field but limits itself to a presentation of the activities of individual organizations.

trative institutions are developed in the new states. It would likewise be sensible to use development projects to encourage the new states to adopt a minority-friendly policy. The arrival of Russians from the peripheral states will have to be a central topic in the establishment of a Russian migration regime.[16] In Armenia about 3 per cent of the inhabitants are Russian, in Georgia and Lithuania 9 per cent, 10 per cent in Azerbaijan and Belarus, 12 per cent in Moldova and Tajikistan, 13 per cent in Uzbekistan, 15 per cent in Turkmenistan, 19 per cent in Ukraine, 25 per cent in Estonia, 29 per cent in Kyrgyzstan, 30 per cent in Latvia and 42 per cent in Kazakhstan. In the Russian Federation itself, 83 per cent of the inhabitants are Russians (1979 census figures).

The aggressive behaviour that is typical of irredentist movements is reason enough to consider the role of international peacekeeping in the formation of new states. Development policy should also see itself as a peacekeeping instrument.

The emergence of migration and refugee systems will be an important political talking-point in the CEECs. International discussion on the link between external and internal flight will therefore have an effect on migration regulation in Eastern Europe. It is evident that internal and external migration movements often belong to the same migration systems. Poland, Hungary and Czechoslovakia – all of which will be helped by a number of development policy measures in the coming years – should set aside part of this aid for refugees and other emigrant groups.

Development policies for environmental refugees

The issue of environmental displacement first arose only a few years ago. Mass migrations of this kind can be expected in the CEECs. Chernobyl, the southern Urals and Murmansk with their nuclear catastrophes seem to represent one side of the coin, while the other is reflected in the desertification of Central Asia and the depopulation of polluted industrial cities. Environmental catastrophes and their consequences will lead to the displacement of hundreds of thousands of people. The condition of industrial plants indicates that further environmental displacements can be expected. Disaster aid agencies are currently interceding in such migrations. We know of no planning in anticipation of such migration movements. The relevant regimes and systems are still in the process of formation.

Technical cooperation between the industrialized states and the CEECs is obviously necessary. The redevelopment of polluted industrial regions will be a foundation for reindustrialization processes. Action has already begun to make nuclear plants and other disaster-producing technological behemoths safe. The land recovery projects in Central Asia will obviously require extensive development policy efforts to become functioning agricultural systems. These are problems that can hardly all be resolved in one go, but each individual case should have access to technical cooperation provided by large development policy institutions. Within the context of a suitable development policy the consequences of past environmental migrations should be examined and priority given to disaster relief and public health care. In these spheres too, appropriate regimes will have to be installed with the aid of regional initiatives.

---

[16] This was pointed out at an early date (1984) by Jones and Grupp.

Development policies for migrant workers

Recruited Yugoslav migrant workers of the first generation still constitute significant immigrant populations in Western European cities. The need for labour in Western Europe has led to new recruitment contracts, for nurses from Yugoslavia for example. Seasonal workers from Poland and Czechoslovakia are contracted for the building trades and agriculture. Company contract workers from Albania, Bulgaria, Czechoslovakia, Poland and Hungary are filling gaps in Western Europe's labour markets. In Germany, immigrants with limited residence permits are given a general work permit as short-term workers (for three months). However, the labour administrations are required to give their approval for special employment.

A differentiation in the gates of entry for migrant workers is of special importance. In 1990 and 1991, employment was arranged for no more than 600 Polish "guest workers", although in October 1991 alone 70,289 Polish workers were requested by German employers for seasonal jobs, cross-border commuter employment and student holiday work; 98 per cent of them were requested by name. In the same month, 114,100 short-term employees requiring an entry visa were registered with the Federal Institute of Labour. More than half of these came from Poland. In December 1991, there were 41,945 Polish company contract employees working in Germany, mostly in the building trades. The number of workers required in this sector is increasing. In the States of Brandenburg and Berlin, the number of these contracts rose from 28 to 1,000 between 1990 and 1991, of which some 600 were with Polish firms in Germany. These figures are high and rising because the borders between Poland and Germany are fairly open for citizens of both countries, and because high quotas have been bilaterally agreed (Working Group on East-West Migration at the Berlin Institute for Comparative Social Research, 1992).

It is striking how little influence the international migration regime, that is, the ILO and other human rights organizations, have on conditions of labour immigration in the East-West context. Western Europe's gates of entry for labour migration are currently being defined ad hoc and depend on the labour market requirements of any given moment. Labour migration is regulated on the basis of need by the countries affected and conducted within the context of established labour migration policies. Recruitment campaigns targeting specific professions are the exception.

Case studies on the more recent forms of labour migration from CEECs will have to be carried out before relevant conclusions can be drawn. The little information we have on labour migrants, especially from Poland, suggests that labour migration has implications for development policy even in the framework of concrete migration systems. Of course this does not apply to the national economic system as a whole: we might mention the teacher who as a commuter supplements her income by providing services and in that way makes an indirect contribution to the stability of the school system in Poland. This applies equally to the many illegally employed Poles in agriculture, forestry and other branches of the informal sector. In terms of development policy, it might be considered useful not to erect further obstacles to such forms of work. The provision of social safeguards for these labour migrants through bilateral agreements and the implementation of at least the basic requirements of the ILO Conventions would seem to be important in this regard.

Development policies for illegal, non-documented migrants

This type of migrant comprises illegal workers from various CEECs, but in particular from Poland, who can be assigned to the general category of migrant workers. The number of illegal workers employed in Berlin and Brandenburg alone is estimated at 100,000.

The regime for illegal immigrants is just coming into existence. There has been a conference on the subject at the European level which proposed little for combating its causes or for controlling migration, but much to say about policing action in non-specific terms. Progress has been made in labour market monitoring over the employment of illegal labour, but such monitoring is unlikely to be very successful in the informal sectors of Europe's economies.

These migrants can either be assigned to older migration systems or else they begin to construct new migration systems. Owing to the lack of statistics and the tacit acceptance of the groups involved, too little is currently known about them. It is difficult to point to these migrants as a strategic group qualifying for development aid. However, great numbers of them will be subject to repatriation. It would be worthwhile to combine repatriation policies with development strategies. The forecast number of illegal migrants and their low social position justify their definition as strategic groups *sui generis*.

Development policies against the "brain drain"

According to the criteria of international law, emigrating technicians, academics and other highly qualified experts belong to the migrant worker category.[17] However, for the purposes of socioscientific studies on the regulation of migration, this group of migrants needs to be analysed separately. Of the Jewish diaspora, 44.8 per cent are scientists, 30 per cent engineers and architects, 5.2 per cent doctors and dentists, and 4.1 per cent teachers. This shows the overwhelming tendency towards brain drain migration among diaspora migrants.

As early as the 1970s, selected students and researchers were given the chance to cross the Iron Curtain to the West. There were close ties between Western and Eastern European universities. The quality and quantity of the exchange and the restrictions imposed on it varied from one CEEC to the next, but the old paths of sci-

---

[17] Reinhard Lohrmann (1991) summarizes the brain drain phenomenon in Eastern Europe, noting that the problem has been exaggerated but will no doubt become more important in the future. Lohrmann claims that intensive research is needed here. Dieter Vogeley (1991) refers to the connection between the brain drain and older chain migration and suggests that while there could be a repetition of developments of the 1920s we have too little information to be able to predict it.

entific exchange were still the decisive starting-points for the brain drain migration movements that are currently in progress.[18]

The scientists' networks that were conceived as exchange networks now run the risk of becoming emigration agencies, in view of the excessive income differences between East and West. Public and private research institutions in the West and in developing countries have begun recruiting personnel in Eastern Europe. The natural sciences and technology are the most attractive areas. There are already highly specialized computer scientists from Eastern Europe working in many Western European research institutes.

The brain drain movement also extends to other professions, with technicians and engineers from Eastern European industry much in demand. The emigration of such specialists is still in its early stages as there are no established migration systems. Only a few migration movements, e.g. those from Poland and Hungary, have developed from established chains.

It is reasonable to suppose that a high standard of education facilitates not only vertical, but also horizontal, mobility. Many university graduates among the commuters and seasonal workers from Eastern Europe are performing tasks that require only a low level of education. Polish university staff and teachers are working in the services sector in Western Europe. The economists' notion of the establishment of migration systems through income differentials is certainly confirmed with respect to the brain drain.

The tradition of the intelligentsia in CEECs is determined either by technological formalism or by educational patterns based on the history of ideas. A flexible educational content was largely unknown. This educational élite, however, together with the rising generation, is the source of tomorrow's leaders. Education, training and retraining institutions are required to begin this process of social change as quickly as possible.

Such educational establishments should be a central objective of joint ventures. The British-Russian University and existing private initiatives are examples of such ventures. It is particularly important that Eastern Europeans should be involved in administration and teaching at such institutions. The activities of individual national associations and chambers of industry that have – in their own interests – pledged to provide advanced management training are also important. There seems to be a link between a commitment to development policy and an interest in having intermediaries for future investments. Trade unions could, for example, take on the training of some of tomorrow's top civil servants for democratic political systems, as could other associations and special interest groups. Development policy institutions have already started to help finance such activities.

Arms conversion has a decisive role to play within the context of the vast military-industrial complex with its military and civilian production, its service sec-

---

[18] See Rhode (1991) for the historical background to this type of migration, available figures and possible research prospects. Although Bulgaria has closed its borders to emigrants, the brain drain from that country seems to be significant (see Zlatanova, 1992 and for an alternative view, Bobeva, 1991). About 40 per cent of all brain drain migration to Austria is from Eastern Europe (Fasmann, undated). The EC is contemplating research work and development policy measures in this connection as part of its COST programme (see Rhode, 1991).

tors and its research institutions (see Cooper, 1991). One could even speak of the "conversion of human capital". The Western European and American anxieties that led to the early introduction of well-funded anti-migration programmes are having certain effects here. One of these is the establishment of an Academy of Atomic Science to prevent experts in that field from going to third countries. It might be pertinent to discuss whether such academies could not be transformed, with the help of international agencies, from pure job creation measures into useful development policy projects.

The large number of technicians and engineers should also be incorporated into the strategies for forming a new élite. These segments of the population, together with retrained economists and arts scholars, could build up small, middle-class-oriented businesses with Western support. Western development agencies have a crucial counselling and funding role in this respect. Cooperative and enterprise-based elements will have to be introduced, as in Western countries. Among these are state-subsidized credit institutions and distribution agencies. Although required in classical development policy, Eastern Europe offers no precursors for small business structures except in Hungary, Poland and Yugoslavia's successor states; it would, however, be appropriate to investigate whether the informal sector could not be the basis for establishing such firms in all CEECs.[19]

Since by definition the brain drain is part of a regulated migration system, it seems reasonable to develop elements from it into a migration policy. It would certainly be useful, for instance, to couple long-term research projects that tie the intelligentsia to a particular place with short-term visits to the West and in this way to make social imitation possible. The purely abstract, people-less transfer of Western experience would not be enough on its own to launch new research establishments successfully.

Development policies for migrant traders

Migrant traders from Eastern Europe move westward for short periods to conduct small-scale business at "poverty markets". These markets, held in Germany, France, Austria and Italy, have also been set up at various locations in Poland near the border with the CIS, as well as in Hungary and former Czechoslovakia. This category also covers other traders whose activities are more certainly illegal, including prostitutes or small-time criminals who use ethnic networks for their short-term work in the West. Migrants who move because they wish to carry on an independent trade also belong to this category.

---

[19] The PHARE Programme adopted by the EC in July 1989 is an initial comprehensive programme in this sphere. Scholarships and grants are to be used in Eastern Europe to promote first, privatization and the establishment of firms; second, the expansion of banking and finance institutions; third, the development of small and medium-sized business; and fourth, labour market policy. The Eastern European intellectual élite is given a crucial intermediary function in the PHARE programme. The programme is expressly designed to promote the establishment of a "civil society". Community facilities, NGOs and lobbies are to be involved in this effort (see Pinder, 1991 on the general problem of European aid for Eastern Europe).

A good synopsis of the experience with development policy measures in this area and the role of international organizations is given by Fuhr and Späth (1990); see also Giaoutzi et al., 1988).

When the Iron Curtain fell, the so-called "Polish markets" (in e.g. Berlin, Istanbul, Vienna and Budapest) were soon a striking feature of the landscape. Migrants tried to sell consumer goods from their suitcases for convertible currency to finance a medium-term stay or to send money home. This system of "suitcase traders" is now a characteristic feature of both sides of the CEEC borders. A small-business migration and trading system, such as existed in the 1920s and 1930s, will probably take root in the next few years. Whole districts of large Western cities are dominated by second-hand stores, import firms and restaurants run by migrant traders from Eastern Europe.

The excessive income differentials between East and West and the new markets arising out of industrial reconstruction in Western Europe attract other types of commercial migrant, such as entertainers and artists who, like scientists, are very mobile. The borderline between these and other trades is not always clearly defined.

There is also trades migration in areas regarded as criminal in Western Europe. Owing to supply planning deficits, some minorities in the former USSR in particular have specialized in smuggling and black market dealing. The structures reflect the economic networks thrown up during economic crises and after the World Wars. These minorities are in the process of internationalizing their networks towards Western Europe, assisted by the demand for illegal merchandise and services there. Drugs, illegal employment and the distribution of smuggled goods are major areas. Another rapidly growing area is traffic in girls. Western European brothels that used to recruit in south-east Asia and Latin America are now drawing their staff increasingly from Eastern Europe. This also applies to the international marriage market. There are indications that affluent and childless families in Western Europe are now being supplied with more adoptive children from Eastern Europe than from developing countries. The criminality of these operations has consolidated the networks: mafia-type migration systems have formed in the space of a few months.

In the 1980s, an important political topic in Western Europe was the desire to push back the migrant traders. The system of "suitcase migrants" could be limited, but not prevented, through police action. Development policy would have to aim at removing both the criminal aspect, and restrictions for the customer. The introduction of stable markets with food controls, hygiene and conserving facilities appears to be essential. Development policy investments could meet this need. A thought to consider is whether migrant traders ought to be given support as small businessmen in their countries of origin: conceivably, they might come to be regarded as the precursors of East-West free trade.

Development policies for stranded people

Subsumed in the category of "stranded" are those termed "refugees in orbit", and transit migrants who have been prevented from entering their chosen country of destination and who do not wish to return to their country of origin. This applies to people from developing countries who came to Eastern Europe as migrant workers, and transit migrants whose movements were interrupted in Eastern Europe. In Bulgaria, there are between 14,000 and 15,000 transit migrants from Sri

Lanka, India, Bangladesh, Nigeria and Ghana who are currently housed in temporary accommodation in Sofia. In Poland on 15 January 1991, 511 refugees were counted. Some 700 applicants have so far received recognition as refugees. There are no figures available for the much larger numbers of transit migrants. While some come from developing countries, the majority are from CEECs. In 1990, 4,251,282 people travelled to Poland from the USSR, 143,280 from Bulgaria and 323,926 from Romania. Some of these visitors to Poland will have travelled further west or will be waiting for a favourable opportunity to cross the border illegally.

In the 1980s, airline companies belonging to the International Air Transport Association (IATA) were integrated into a strict system of migration control. International flights without the necessary visas became almost impossible. Only Eastern bloc airlines, and a few in developing countries using Eastern bloc air space to reach Western Europe, allowed illegal migrants and refugees to reach stopping-off points in CEECs first and subsequently their Western European destinations. Under international law, such migrants are turned back at the borders of Western European countries or are prevented from continuing their journey. For that reason there are many "migrants in orbit" in all the CEECs. They receive very little assistance as the relevant international regimes are effective to only a limited extent in the CEECs (with the exception of Hungary).

Until the end of the 1980s many CEECs employed labour migrants from the "fraternal countries". The majority of these labour migrants – in the former German Democratic Republic at least – have lost their jobs and often their accommodation as well. They comprise a population that is, potentially, increasingly obliged to engage in illegal activities. There is no migration regime, and certainly no migration system for such migrants.

The movement of Eastern European migrants to the West has, in recent years, spawned immigrant minorities in Hungary, former Czechoslovakia and Poland whose intention is to cross into Western Europe illegally. To date, these refugees in orbit have been registered neither by aid agencies nor by the regulatory authorities. To help them, the refugee regimes in Eastern Europe must first be improved. Their repatriation or their resettlement in a third country is part of the international agencies' mandate that must be fulfilled through new refugee conventions and adequate resources.

Development policies for economic and socially displaced migrants

Large numbers of people have become displaced following the collapse of the Eastern European regimes in a manner similar to that which occurred at the end of the Second World War. They are demobilized soldiers, regime opponents from the *gulags* and psychiatric clinics, victims of housing speculation, and immigrants in cities who have lost their legal status as temporary residents. The CIS in particular seems to have millions of displaced persons.

Among the few statistics that provide an indication of the number of displaced persons are police figures for people of no fixed address (although they are only a very small minority group in this type of migration). From 1987 to 1990, between 110,000 and 120,000 people of no fixed address were arrested annually in the USSR; 76,566 were picked up by the police in the Russian Federation in 1990 (*USSR in Figures*, 1991).

The characteristic feature of displaced persons is that they cannot be assigned to a migration regime. From the point of view of migration theory, there is an implicit contradiction here: displaced persons have been the target group of the largest institutionalization processes of the migration regime. This experience can perhaps be of use in establishing functioning migration control institutions.

Development policies for returnees

The category of returnees is extremely broad and as such is indeterminate. They include members of the Soviet Army returning home, whose reintegration after the collapse of the USSR has similarities with the return of mercenary armies. There are people returning from diasporas who wish to contribute to the process of reconstruction in their countries of origin by using the capital and skills they have acquired in exile. There is likely to be an increase in the numbers of returning religious and political refugees who see their home country as some sort of utopia.

The return of Soviet soldiers to the CIS is in almost all cases regulated by contract and subject to a military regime. The social and economic aspects of this return are also subject to such planning. The resources of the CIS will in all likelihood permit no more than a very limited level of integration of the returnees. The international assistance so far given is inadequate.

In the case of Germany, development policy measures are envisaged for the members of the former Soviet Army. International syndicates are involved, mostly in the construction of housing. In Poland, former Czechoslovakia and Hungary the withdrawal of the former USSR's troops has led to the discovery of environmental damage with unforeseeable consequences. International and national development policy institutions should assist the regions affected in undoing the damage.

Until the end of the 1980s there was a stringent immigration policy in the CEECs for returning businessmen and refugees. The relevant institutions have since collapsed, and nothing so far has replaced them. Instead, political "grey zones" have come into being. In East-West migration there are currently indications of return migration or temporary return within individual migration systems. In terms of development policy, these returnees have a special entrepreneurial or intermediary function. They establish networks between Western Europe and the regions they return to.

5. Summary

Macroeconomic measures are necessary for the economic development of Eastern Europe, to the extent that they can be funded, planned and implemented politically. These measures would have to include debt reduction, the establishment of a convertible currency system, and almost superhuman efforts in the field of infrastructural assistance. Macroeconomic improvements will affect migration behaviour.

New job opportunities, improved conditions of employment and higher incomes will reduce the number of economically motivated migration decisions in the long run. However, such an economic upswing is not yet in sight.

Even if macroeconomic measures are successful, a migrant-oriented development policy will be needed if progress is to be made towards the goals of migration control, improvement of migrants' living conditions, and protection from persecution. Economic developments can themselves encourage migration, and migration systems sometimes operate to such a limited extent that their only effect is to motivate migration through modernization of the social context. A strategic approach to development policy measures is therefore necessary. The target groups have to be supported in the context of their migration systems and themselves involved in the implementation of development policy. We know too little about the new migration paths and systems in Eastern Europe to be capable of large-scale conceptual planning from the outside.

The confused state of the overall situation in Eastern Europe makes it necessary to proceed with caution and understanding. A euphoric approach that ignores all developing country experience should be avoided.[20] Since resources are limited and the tasks huge, such development projects will inevitably have to be limited to regions where they are most likely to succeed.

The anxieties and economic power of Western Europe are advantageous for development policy, migration control and support for migrants (Blaschke, 1991). It seems to be possible for a variety of pilot projects to be undertaken within this context. It needs to be pointed out, however, that this discussion has to date been conducted largely at the symbolic policy level. The few activities that have been undertaken do not seem to have been planned and implemented consistently. The problem could be somewhat resolved, however, through pan-European coordination and evaluation of the measures taken.

Unlike the countries of Africa, Latin America and Asia, the CEECs are recipients of assistance channelled mainly through institutions that are based on the "European idea". The admission talks between the European Community and Poland, former Czechoslovakia and Hungary point to a fundamentally different basis for economic cooperation and aid for development. The deeply rooted fear of hordes of migrants from the East reinforces this.

In view of the formation of nation states, democratization, and the continuing pauperization of Eastern Europe, an increase in human rights violations, persecution of minorities, and civil wars can be expected. It is important therefore to refer to the need for changes in the UN system of conflict reduction, human rights protection and early detection of violent tendencies and expulsions. New political regimes need to be established at the international level.

At the national level, it would seem that the establishment of refugee and migration regimes should be given priority so as to protect and support migrant groups. The large number of internal migrants and displaced populations should be given special consideration. We know little about these population movements and less about their sociostructural environments.

---

[20] For a good introduction to the underdevelopment and migration literature, see Appleyard, 1992.

Bibliography

Amin, Samir. 1975a. "The early roots of unequal exchange", in *Monthly Review* 27:7, pp. 43-45.
—. 1975b. *Unequal development* (Brighton, Sussex, Harvester Press).
—. 1981. "Die ungleiche Entwicklung in den kapitalistischen Zentren: Die nationale Frage und die regionalen Fragen im Zentrum", in Fröbel, Folker; Heinrichs, Jürgen; Kreye, Otto (ed.): *Krisen in der kapitalistischen Weltökonomie* (Reinbek, Rowohlt), pp. 76-99.
Appleyard, R.T. 1992. "Migration and development: A critical relationship", in *Asian and Pacific Migration Journal*, 1:1.
Blaschke, Jochen. 1981. "Zwischen staatlicher Planung und autonomer Organisation – Bruchstellen der Entwicklungspolitik", in Berliner Institut für Vergleichende Sozialforschung (ed.): *Bruchstellen, Industrialisierung und Planung in der Dritten Welt* (Berlin), pp. 7-28.
—. 1991. "International migration and East-West migration: Political and economic paradoxes", in *Migration*, 11-12.
Bletzer, Beatrix. 1991. *Interessenlage und Eigenorganisation der Polen in Berlin – Analyse der Entwicklung seit den 80er Jahren*, Ph.D. thesis (Fachbereich Politische Wissenschaft an der FU Berlin).
Bobeva, Daniela. 1991. *Brain drain problem in Bulgaria* (mimeo).
Cviic, Christopher. 1991. *Remaking the Balkans* (London, Chatham House Papers; New York, Council on Foreign Relations).
Chesnais, J.C.; Council of Europe. 1990. *Migration from Eastern to Western Europe, past (1946-1986) and future (1990-2000)*, paper for the second meeting of senior officials entrusted with preparing the Conference of Ministers on the movement of persons from Central and Eastern European countries, Strasbourg, 8-9 November 1990.
Clarke, R.A. (ed.). 1989. *Hungary: The second decade of economic reform: Perspectives on Eastern Europe* (London).
Cooper, Julian. 1991. *The Soviet defence industry: Conversion and reform* (London, Chatham House Papers).
Council of Europe. 1991. Conference of Ministers on the movement of persons from Central and Eastern European countries, Vienna, 24-25 January 1991, in *AWR-Bulletin*, 29(38):1, pp. 4-7.
Drüke, L. 1990. *Preventive action for refugee producing situations* (Frankfurt-am-Main, Peter Lang).
Emke-Poulopoulos, Ira. 1992. *The gates of entry of immigrants and refugees in Greece*. Vortrag auf der Europäischen Konferenz: Zwei Welten: Migranten – Entwicklungen – Metropolen, 26-29 March 1992, Berlin.
Fuhr, Harald; Brigitte Späth. 1990. "Internationale Organisationen und Kleingewerbeförderung: Herausbildung, Implementation und Wandel einer entwicklungspolitischen Konzeption", in Glasgow, Manfred (eds.): *Deutsche und internationale Entwicklungspolitik. Zur Rolle staatlicher, supranationaler und nicht-regierungsabhängiger Organisationen im Entwicklungsprozeß der Dritten Welt* (Opladen), pp. 121-141.
Gellner, Ernest. 1991. "Ethnicity and faith in Eastern Europe", in Graubard, R.; S. Richards. (eds.): *Eastern Europe, Central Europe, Europe* (Boulder, Colorado, Westview Press), pp. 267-282.
Giaoutzi, Maria; Peter Nijkamp; David J. Storey (eds.). 1988. *Small and medium-size enterprises and regional development* (London, Routledge).
Graubard, Stephen R. (ed.). 1991. *Eastern Europe... Central Europe... Europe* (Boulder, Colorado, Westview Press).

Independent Commission on International Humanitarian Issues (ICIHI) (ed.). Working Group on Refugees and Displaced People. 1986. *Refugees: Dynamics of displacement*. A report for the ICIHI (London and New Jersey, ICIHI).
Jones, E.; F.W. Grupp. 1984. "Modernization and ethnic equalisation in the USSR", in *Soviet Studies*, No. 36, pp. 159-184.
Lachenmann, Gudrun; Uwe Otzen. 1981. *Die Weltflüchtlingsproblematik – eine Herausforderung für die Entwicklungspolitik* (Berlin, Deutsches Institut für Entwicklungspolitik).
Lohrmann, Reinhard. 1991. *Brain-drain migration from Eastern Europe: Notes on a questionnaire* (mimeo).
Menzel, Ulrich; Dieter Senghaas. 1983. "Autozentrierte Entwicklung im Weltsystem – Versuch einer Typologie", in Blaschke, Jochen (ed.): *Perspektiven des Weltsystems. Materialien zu Immanuel Wallerstein "Das moderne Weltsystem"* (Frankfurt, Campus), pp. 142-188.
Oswald, Ingrid. 1991. "Die Öffnung der osteuropäischen Grenzen – Folgen für Osteuropa", in *Die Neue Gesellschaft/Frankfurter Hefte*, 38:5, pp. 423-428.
—. 1992a. "New migration patterns in the former Soviet Union", in *Migration*, 11-12.
—; Osteuropa-Institut Berlin. 1992b. *How far is Eastern Europe from Germany?*, paper for the symposium on Multiculturality – Threat or resource? 5-6 March 1992 (Gothenburg).
Pinder, John. 1991. *The European Community and Eastern Europe* (London, Chatham House Papers).
Poulton, Hugh. 1991. *The Balkans: Minorities and states in conflict* (London, Minority Rights Group).
Rhode, Barbara. 1991. *East-West migration/brain drain: Mapping the available knowledge and recommendations for a European research programme* (Brussels, European Cooperation in the Field of Scientific and Technical Research).
Rollo, J.M.C. 1990. "Western policy: The room for manoeuvre", in Royal Institute of International Affairs (ed.): *The new Eastern Europe: Western responses* (London, Chatham House Papers), pp. 100-115.
Ruban, Elisabeth. 1989. "Demographic development", in German Institute for Economic Research (DIW) (ed.): *GDR and Eastern Europe: A handbook* (Aldershot, Gower), pp. 267ff.
Salitan, L.P. 1992. *Politics and nationality in contemporary Soviet-Jewish emigration, 1968-89* (New York, St. Martin's Press).
Senghaas, Dieter; Stiftung Entwicklung und Frieden (SEF) (eds.). 1992a. *Die Zukunft der internationalen Politik: Überlegungen zur Friedensproblematik nach dem Ende des Ost-West-Konfliktes* (Bonn, SEF).
—. 1992b. *Friedensprojekt Europa* (Frankfurt-am-Main, Suhrkamp).
—. 1992c. "Entwicklungshilfe für Osteuropa und die Mitglieder der GUS?", in *Der Überblick*, 2, pp. 24-25.
Simmie, James; Joze Dekleva. 1991. *Yugoslavia in turmoil: After self-management* (London, Pinter and New York, St. Martin's Press).
Sjöberg, Örjan; M.L. Wyzan. 1991. *Economic crisis and reform in the Balkan states: Albania, Bulgaria, Romania and Yugoslavia facing the 1990s* (New York, St. Martin's Press).
Smith, G.B. 1992. *Soviet politics: Struggling with change*, second edition (Basingstoke and London, Macmillan).
Spulber, Nicolas. 1991. *Restructuring the Soviet economy: In search of the market* (Ann Arbor, University of Michigan Press).
Todaro, M.P. 1985. *Economic development in the Third World* (New York, Longman).

Ushkalov, Igor G. 1991. "Inter-state migrations in the former USSR and Eastern Europe: The past, the present and the future", in *Migration*, 11-12.

Vogeley, Dieter. 1991. "Nach Öffnung der osteuropäischen Grenzen: Westeuropa vor neuen Migrationsfluten oder -rinnsalen?", in Deutschen Gesellschaft für die Vereinten Nationen (ed.): *Massenansturm aus dem Osten? Ursachen und Herausforderungen der Ost-West-Migration*, 14 May (Bonn), 15 pp.

Voronkov, Viktor M. 1991. "Leningrad/St. Petersburg – Metropole und Zentrum für Migranten", in *Migration*, 11-12.

Zlatanova, Valentina. 1992. "The Bulgarian brain drain", in *Migration*, 11-12, pp. 7-17.

4

Displacement-generating conflicts and international assistance in the Horn of Africa

A. Zolberg and A. Callamard

1. Introduction

For several decades now, wars and famines have ravaged the Horn of Africa,[1] resulting in loss of life and massive displacements of dispossessed people both within their own countries and across international borders. According to the UN Special Emergency Programme for the Horn of Africa, a total of 22 million persons are today in immediate need of emergency assistance, including more than 7 million internally displaced, 1.5 million refugees, 700,000 returnees and 13 million severely affected by drought.[2]

For several decades also, multilateral and bilateral donors have showered enormous resources to alleviate human suffering and develop the region. Given the gravity of the current economic and political crisis in all four countries, it can be argued that international assistance has largely failed to achieve its objectives. Two major questions therefore arise: First, to what extent is this failure attributable to internal deficiencies, and how much to external forces? And in that light, what should be the future role of international assistance in this region, and what reforms should be undertaken to overcome the mistakes and failures of the past?

The objective of this paper is to provide some preliminary answers to these questions. Beginning with an analysis of the root causes of the forced movements of populations, we show that the conflicts that have plagued the Horn for several decades arise mostly from the difficulties of state-building under conditions of extreme underdevelopment, exacerbated by the direct and indirect involvement of the superpowers. We suggest in particular that military assistance is a root cause of forced internal and external population displacements and a major impediment to the successful accomplishment of international assistance. With regard to the latter, we identify obstacles arising at four distinct levels, namely local, national, international and the UN itself. Accordingly, strategies for preventing forced movements

---

[1] As used in this paper, the Horn of Africa refers to Sudan, Ethiopia, Djibouti and Somalia. However, we do not deal with Djibouti both because of limited space and difficulties in obtaining adequate information.

[2] UNDP, 1991a, p. 12.

and for improving the effectiveness of international assistance should not be limited to one or two of these levels but must embrace all of them. But the foremost condition for any such undertaking is the achievement of generalized peace.

The crisis that has engulfed the Horn of Africa (and Sudan) in the past three decades is rooted in the region's distinctive political history, its contemporary geopolitical status, as well as economic conditions determined by a combination of poor natural endowment, social factors including demography, and detrimental effects generated by the world economy. The tensions experienced by the countries arise in large part from the difficulties of constructing modern states in ethnically diverse societies under problematic economic conditions and within a politically divided world. Not only has each of them experienced protracted internal conflicts of its own, but these have been exacerbated by interactions among them, as well as by the direct and indirect involvement of a variety of external powers. The latter phenomenon is attributable to the fact that, from a geopolitical perspective, the region constitutes the western flank of the explosive Middle East.

2. International assistance: Trends and implications

The starting point for any realistic assessment of the role of international assistance is that the Horn of Africa is one of the very poorest and least developed regions of the world.[3] Although in the past three decades it has received considerable official development assistance (ODA) from bilateral and multilateral donors, this has been outweighed during the same period by military assistance, which has in effect triggered a regional arms race.[4] Although conventionally, development assistance and military assistance are considered separately, in this case it is essential to view them as interactive factors. As demonstrated in section 2, military assistance is a major contributing factor to the Horn's conflicts, and consequently ranks high as a cause of its forced internal and external population displacements. Thus, ODA is faced with the task of helping to reconstruct extremely underdeveloped societies whose predicament has been rendered even more desperate by an arms build-up. Under such conditions, it can do little more than pick up the pieces.

---

[3] According to the Human Development Index scale of the *Human Development Report*, (UNDP, 1991b), whose lowest number is 160, the countries under consideration rank as follows: Ethiopia 141, Sudan 143, Somalia 149, and Djibouti 153. These conditions are corroborated by the World Bank's differently constituted *World Development Report* (World Bank, 1991).

[4] Although official figures suggest roughly the same order of size for the two types of assistance, the military side undoubtedly outweighs the other because much of it went to various anti-governmental organizations (e.g., EPLF in Eritrea, SPLA in Sudan), and hence does not appear in conventional sources.

Types and sources of assistance: A summary overview [5]

Development assistance. Overall, bilateral development assistance from the 1960s onwards closely reflected changing international political alignments in the region. The main trends can be briefly summarized as follows.

- During the period 1970-79, the net flow of resources granted to the three countries fluctuated from one year to another. The country which experienced the highest and most regular increase was Sudan, for which ODA jumped from US$ 16 million in 1970 to US$ 410 million in 1978 (Table 4.1).

- During the period 1980-89, Ethiopia experienced the highest increase of total net ODA, from $ 216 million to $ 702 million. As far as Somalia and Sudan are concerned, the figures fluctuated on a yearly basis but remained quite constant around $ 440 million for Somalia and $ 700 million for Sudan (Tables 4.2 and 4.3).

- For the period 1969-72, Ethiopia was the highest recipient of ODA originating from DAC (OECD Development Assistance Committee) countries, with the United States in the lead. In contrast, Sudan did not receive any development assistance from the United States during this period. The amount of ODA granted by the UN slightly counterbalanced the difference: $ 5 million was annually granted to Ethiopia, and $ 3.6 million to Somalia as against $ 11 million to Sudan (Table 4.4). Nevertheless, the total gross receipt of ODA for Ethiopia, $ 43.6 million, was much higher than for either Somalia ($ 29.5 million) or Sudan ($ 19.8 million).[6]

- Ten years later, the situation was reversed: Sudan received 1.3 per cent of total ODA allocated by DAC countries (no figures are available for Ethiopia and Somalia), 1.4 per cent of ODA allocated by the United States, and 4.4 per cent of ODA granted by OPEC countries (Table 4.5). Ethiopia and Sudan ranked among the top four recipients of UNDP development assistance (the first two being India and Bangladesh, with respectively 4.5 per cent and 3.8 per cent of the total).

- Another important feature of the 1970s and 1980s was the rise of the OPEC countries as a main source of bilateral aid for Sudan and Somalia. Although the Syrian Arab Republic and Jordan received the bulk of OPEC's bilateral assistance in 1981-82 (respectively 25 per cent and 17 per cent), both Sudan and Somalia were granted large amounts: 4.4 per cent for Sudan and 2.7 for Somalia. Furthermore, according to data compiled by Laitin and Samatar, after 1976 Somalia was increasingly tied to the Arab world, and bilateral aid from OPEC states outpaced funds from the OECD countries (Table 4.6).

---

[5] Because of the variations in the manner in which OECD aggregated its statistics on ODA from one annual report to another, there is some overlap of years and figures over the 20 years, and this period should not be totalled. Furthermore, because the total flow of ODA has been aggregated either as a gross receipt, a net receipt, or a net flow of resources, figures should not be compared from one table to another.

[6] OECD, 1974.

Table 4.1. Total recorded net flow of resources from OECD Development Assistance Committee (DAC) countries and from international agencies, 1970-77 (US$ million)

	1970	1971	1972	1973	1974	1975	1976	1977
Ethiopia	47.67	59.06	47.79	65.30	96.93	130.4	137.1	105.6
Somalia	30.04	34.28	31.33	31.09	19.78	92.1	77.8	178.5
Sudan	16.41	16.90	45.01	94.51	110.30	411.7	335.1	278.3
Total Africa	3 078	3 760	3 548	4 073	4 752	9 327	9 969	13 700

Source: OECD Development Assistance Committee, Development Cooperation Reports (various years).

Table 4.2. Total net ODA from DAC countries, multilateral agencies and OPEC, 1980-83 (US$ million)

	1980	1981	1982	1983
Ethiopia	216	241	200	251
Somalia	446	374	462	276
Sudan	620	681	740	929
Total Africa	10 768	10 572	10 597	10 048

Source: As Table 4.1.

Table 4.3. Total net ODA from DAC countries, multilateral agencies and OPEC, 1985-89 (US$ million)

	1985	1986	1987	1988	1989
Ethiopia	715	636	635	970	702
Somalia	353	511	580	433	440
Sudan	1 129	945	898	937	760
Total Africa	12 846	14 434	16 255	17 694	18 123

Source: As Table 4.1.

Table 4.4. Gross receipts of ODA by donor, annual average, 1969-72 (US$ million)

	United States	Total DAC	UN	Total multilateral agencies
Ethiopia	16.3	34.7	5.1	8.9
Somalia	6	18.8	3.6	10.7
Sudan	0	6.6	11.1	13.2

Source: As Table 4.1.

Table 4.5. ODA by donor, annual average, 1981-82 (percentage of total allocated ODA)

	United States	DAC	OPEC	UNDP	WFP	Total multilateral agencies
Ethiopia	-	-	-	3.0	5.0	2.1
Somalia	0.7	-	2.7	1.2	5.8	2.3
Sudan	1.4	1.3	4.4	3.0	1.8	2.9

Source: As Table 4.1.

- The figures provided by the OECD do not include economic assistance provided by the USSR. According to Paul Henze,[7] this was quite limited for all three countries from the beginning of the 1960s, especially if compared with the ODA provided by DAC and OPEC countries and multilateral agencies (Table 4.7). Henze's general assessment seems to be corroborated by other sources.[8] In 1975, the USSR granted $52 million for development projects in Somalia.[9] However, after 1978, Ethiopia was the only country in the Horn to receive Soviet economic aid. In response to the great famine of 1985-86, 10,000 tons of rice and medical supplies were donated, and 250,000 tons of wheat valued at $50 million in 1988.[10]

- From 1975 to 1989, Ethiopia, Sudan and Somalia were among the African countries which received the largest share of total ODA granted to the continent, surpassed only by the Sahel countries, Mozambique, the United Republic of Tanzania and Kenya (Table 4.8).

- Almost half of Somalia's GNP consists of ODA, a proportion which is surpassed only by Mozambique (76 per cent), and which has been similar since 1980 (45 per cent of GNP, as against 7 per cent at that time for Mozambique). The share of ODA in Ethiopia's GNP more than doubled between 1980/81 and 1988/89 from 7 per cent to 16 per cent, while for Sudan it remained almost constant at around 10 per cent (Table 4.9).

Emergency assistance. On many occasions the UN provided the region with emergency and refugee assistance to contain the worst consequences of drought, famines and forced displacements. Given the large number of donors (from bilateral donors to all the multilateral agencies) it is difficult to assess the exact amount disbursed.

In 1991, the region was in yet another catastrophic situation, resulting from 20 years of civil wars, recurring drought, and severe social and economic deterioration. In September 1991, a UN-consolidated interagency appeal was made, requesting $400 million for all UN agencies to organize and accelerate emergency relief. However, one month after the appeal, only $110 million had been provided, well below what the emergency situation for Ethiopia alone required six years earlier; and five months later (February 1992), a little over half the amount requested had been supplied ($260 million), while conditions in the Horn continued to worsen and its financial needs increase.[11]

Refugee assistance. For the past 30 years, although fluctuating from year to year, total UNHCR aid has always been important; and in recent years the Horn has received the bulk of refugee assistance committed to Africa. For the 1963-81 period, Somalia outranked any other African recipient: an average of $4.8 million (in constant 1970 dollars), followed by Cameroon ($1.6 million), Mozambique ($1.2 mil-

---

[7] Henze, 1991.
[8] Patman, 1990; Ottaway, 1982; Korn, 1986.
[9] Patman, 1990, p. 180.
[10] Henze, 1991, p. 128.
[11] UNDP, 1991c, 1992.

Table 4.6. Bilateral foreign aid to Somalia by source (US$ million)

	1973	1976	1979
OECD	19.32	20.07	49.8
OPEC	n.a.	33.40	94.8

Source: Laitin and Samatar, "Somalia and the World Economy" in *Review of African Political Economy*, No. 30, Sept. 1984, p.71.

Table 4.7. Soviet economic aid, 1959 to 1983
(converted to millions of constant 1987 US dollars)

	Initial agreement	Offered	Disbursed
Ethiopia	1959	468	247
Kenya	1964	44.3	12.3
Somalia	1962	150	93
Sudan	1961	40	38
Total		702.3	390.3
Total in 1987 dollars		2 106.3	1 170.9

Source: Henze, 1991, p.129.

Table 4.8. Percentage of total ODA per country

	1975-76	1980-81	1988-89
Sub-Saharan Africa	19.7	26	35.9
Ethiopia	0.8	1.0	2.1
Somalia	0.8	1.3	1.1
Sudan	1.4	2.1	2.1
Sahel[1]	4.0	4.6	6.0
Mozambique	0.3	0.5	2.2
Tanzania	1.6	2.2	2.4
Kenya	0.8	1.4	2.2
Zaire	1.1	1.3	1.5

[1] Burkina Faso, Cape Verde, Chad, Gambia, Mali, Mauritania, Niger, Senegal.
Source: As Table 4.1.

Table 4.9. ODA as a percentage of GNP

	1980-81	1988-89
Ethiopia	7.2	15.8
Somalia	44.7	46
Sudan	8.9	10
Mozambique	7.2	76.1
Sahel[1]	14.8	17.8
Rwanda	12.4	11.4
Kenya	6.3	11.1
Zaire	4.3	11
Ghana	3.9	10.2

[1] Burkina Faso, Cape Verde, Chad, Gambia, Mali, Mauritania, Niger, Senegal.
Source: As Table 4.1.

lion), Sudan ($1.0 million) and Djibouti ($0.8 million). However, during this period Ethiopia received relatively little refugee assistance ($0.4 million).[12] At the beginning of the 1990s, however, Ethiopia rose to the top of this table: in 1991, general and special programmes totalled $98 million (Malawi, the second largest recipient, received about a third of this amount, $32 million). Some $23 million was originally approved for Somalia; less than a fifth of this was actually allocated because the deteriorating security situation made delivery impossible.[13] Sudan came third in the amount of resources allocated ($21 million); Djibouti received a small amount ($2 million).

Military assistance.[14] At the same time as international assistance was pouring in, a build-up of military forces was taking place. From the 1960s onwards, all three countries obtained large amounts of military aid, mainly from the USSR and the United States. During the 1960s, 94 per cent of United States military aid for north-eastern Africa – which includes Kenya – went to Ethiopia ($104 million); the USSR provided $110 million to Sudan and Somalia. Somalia emerged as the most militarized of the three countries in the per capita value of foreign military aid. In 1970, military expenditure (exclusive of foreign military assistance) represented 5 per cent of its GNP, as against 6.1 per cent for Sudan and 2.4 per cent for Ethiopia.

The militarization process intensified during the 1970s, resulting from enormous increases in foreign military assistance both to governments and insurgency organizations. For instance, Henze estimates that the Eritrean insurgency absorbed at least $50 million worth of arms up to 1980. When the Ogaden war began in June 1977, the USSR shifted its support to Ethiopia while the Carter administration refused to provide military assistance to Somalia as long as it remained in the Ogaden. In August 1980 the United States and Somalia signed an agreement for the use of military facilities at the port of Berbera by the United States newly created Rapid Deployment Force. In return, Somalia was to receive $20 million in military credits, $5 million in budget support and $20 million in general credit. However, in 1987 United States military aid was cut to $8.7 million.[15]

Theoretical and political implications

This brief summary highlights two fundamental aspects of international assistance in the Horn of Africa. It took on an international character (a) in terms of its relative importance in ODA, and emergency and refugee assistance granted to the rest of the developing world, and (b) as one of the variables within superpower rivalry. It also acquired a domestic and regional significance, given its fundamental input into the economies of all three countries and its repeated role in alleviating human suffering.

In the course of the past 20 years or so, the economies of Ethiopia, Sudan and Somalia have been highly dependent upon the resources provided by bilateral

---

[12] Annual Report of the UNHCR to the UNGA and Annual Report on UNHCR Activities to the Executive Committee.
[13] UNHCR, 1991, pp. 90-96.
[14] The principal sources for this section are Henze, 1991; Patman, 1990; Ottaway, 1982; Korn, 1986.
[15] Patman, 1990, pp. 262, 293, 294.

and multilateral donors. Yet such assistance was not sufficient to prevent recurrent famines and the multiple displacements of impoverished populations within or outside their countries of origin. This situation is of course not unique to this region. Although for some four decades a variety of bilateral and multilateral organizations, as well as non-governmental organizations (NGOs), have showered enormous financial, technical and human resources on the developing world – with the ostensible goal of eradicating poverty, malnutrition, and illiteracy – in 1991, there were about 1.2 billion "poor" people in the developing world; 77 per cent of the world's population shared a mere 15 per cent of its income. Sub-Saharan Africa is currently the most impoverished region: its share of the world's poor will rise from 30 per cent to 40 per cent by the year 2000.[16]

Although the situation would be much worse without international assistance, its overall effectiveness has been extremely limited. For several years now, practitioners and academics have gone to great lengths attempting to provide some explanations for this situation. All aspects of international assistance have been scrutinized and criticized, and a variety of recommendations has been made, ranging from increased local participation in the design and implementation of projects to the creation of a new international economic order and a restructuring of the United Nations.[17] The explanations of failure and recommendations for reform can be categorized at four levels: local, national, international and organizational.

Local explanations. In the past decade, a number of analyses have purported to demonstrate that international assistance has failed because it did not take into account the local needs of the population, did not integrate the local populations within the design and implementation of development programmes, and relied exclusively on the state and the public sector. Hence community development, as opposed to national development, and community participation, as opposed to a top-down approach, are put forward as the only viable path towards the alleviation of world poverty. This approach was popularized by the Dag Hammarskjöld Foundation and the Basic Need Approach of the ILO, which called for the incorporation of a sort of "development guarantee" for the weakest social groups and the promotion of local populations' self-sufficiency.[18]

With regard to the Horn specifically, a paper recently published by Bread for the World argues that the causes of war, famine and underdevelopment in the region are all rooted in inequitable control over resources and decision-making.[19] The author suggests that the Horn needs alternatives to centralized economies and government-controlled development processes and that strengthening the capacity of existing and emerging NGOs is a prerequisite for development and peace.

National explanations revolve around the application of the principle of national sovereignty, which is said to be a significant obstacle to the implementation

---

[16] UNDP, 1991b, p. 23.

[17] See especially the special issue of *Development*, entitled "We the Peoples of the United Nations...", 1986, pp. 1-2.

[18] For a theoretical account of community and national development, see Hettne, 1990; Kitching, 1989.

[19] Pauling, 1991.

and success of international assistance because it limits the reach and content of development programmes and humanitarian relief. In the case of Ethiopia, the forced resettlement of populations during the 1985 drought exemplifies such a situation, as does the use of international assistance for purposes other than the ones for which it was intended. Similarly, during the numerous famines that have plagued the region in the past two decades, the destination of emergency assistance was controlled by the various governments, who manipulated food relief as a weapon to repress dissidence. As highlighted by Operation Lifeline, it is possible to limit the invocation of sovereignty as a block to humanitarian activities. Yet, considerations of sovereignty exercised a major constraint on the effectiveness of the UN system in responding to the humanitarian crisis in Sudan.[20]

The current situation in Somalia tragically highlights another limitation of international assistance, one which arises from continuous warfare, the division of national territory into many areas controlled by opposing factions well supplied with weapons, and the disappearance of central government: in short, anarchy.[21] In September 1991, the UN withdrew from Mogadishu because of concerns over the security of UN personnel. However, ICRC and several private humanitarian organizations continued to operate there, while UNICEF and UNHCR maintained their field presence wherever feasible.[22] The UN decision to withdraw was attacked by NGOs and human rights organizations, especially Africa Watch. We will return to this subject in the conclusion. Suffice it to note at this point that in addition to the principle of national sovereignty, the *principle of self-determination* and the civil conflicts its application necessarily gives rise to, can limit the operations and objectives of international assistance militarily and politically, if not legally.

The *international* economic and political system is also a significant impediment to the successful implementation of international assistance. First, international assistance cannot counteract the overall effects of the international economic order, especially negative terms of trade for developing countries and the exploitation of their resources by multinational enterprises. Even if international assistance does provide some benefits, its positive outcomes are swept away by broader trends.

Second, the failure of international assistance may be analysed within the context of the Cold War and superpower rivalries. As revealed by our examination of military assistance, in the past three decades both the United States and the USSR supplied weapons to Ethiopia, Sudan and Somalia, thereby feeding endless wars and civil conflicts, and directly contributing to the displacement of populations in search of security. A product of the Cold War, this extensive military assistance contradicted the objectives of development and humanitarian assistance, and hampered the effectiveness of whatever assistance was distributed. Although the Cold War has now ended, its legacy still survives in extensive stocks of weapons, which

---

[20] For instance, in October 1989, the Sudanese Government closed Sudan airspace to all relief flights (with the exception of the ones for government-controlled Juba) therefore crippling many relief operations. See Minear, 1991.

[21] Zolberg, 1992, pp. 303-11.

[22] See "Somalia: A fight to the death? Leaving civilians at the mercy of terror and starvation", in *Africa Watch*, 13 Feb. 1992, Vol. 4, No. 2.

simultaneously increase the governments' capacity for repression, foster the emergence of armed bands that terrorize populations, and prevent the implementation of emergency relief.

Finally, the current problems of international assistance in the Horn of Africa can be considered within the context of the "new world order". As Aryeh Neier has put it, "Now that superpower rivalry for geopolitical advantage is no longer a factor, the funds that previously flowed so plentifully to finance these wars are in short supply for the rebuilding of those devastated countries. They will have to struggle largely on their own to clear their fields of land mines, to cope with the enormous quantities of high-powered weapons in the hands of demobilized and unemployed young men, and to rebuild their economies."[23]

The current difficulties in financing emergency assistance to the Horn of Africa highlights the general lack of interest among Western donor countries to help create peace and security, and to bring an end to the massacres in Somalia.

Moreover, some political analysts argue that the end of the Cold War, far from reducing the incidence of internal and regional conflicts, removes some of the constraints that previously acted to restrain regional aggressions.[24]

Finally, the *United Nations* must also bear some responsibility for the failure of multilateral assistance. Two main internal reproaches are generally addressed to the United Nations: the absence of coordination mechanisms among UN agencies, and its dependence on Western countries.

The lack of coordination and cooperation among UN agencies refers to the duplication of efforts, the conflicts over resources and programmes, and the absence of coordination in the course of emergency relief. As the authors of *Humanitarianism under siege* point out, "Inter-agency differences, while harmonized a bit, were never really resolved. Basic decisions about program objectives, funding, media, and reporting were seldom reached through collegial inter-agency discussions. As a result, information remains far less readily available about Lifeline as a whole than about the activities of a given UN agency."[25]

It is difficult to assess how much the lack of coordination among UN agencies is directly responsible for the poor success rate of development programmes, refugee assistance or emergency relief. However, given the increasingly publicized debate within and outside the United Nations over this issue and the recent General Assembly Resolution 46/182 aimed at strengthening the coordination of humanitarian emergency assistance of the United Nations, it is evident that coordination stands first among the internal UN mechanisms hampering the effective implementation of all types of international assistance.

---

[23] Aryeh Neier, "Watching rights", in *The Nation*, 3 Feb. 1992, p. 115.

[24] See especially Mearsheimer, 1991.

[25] Minear, 1991, p. 51.

3. Conclusion: The future role of international assistance in the Horn of Africa

As demonstrated in the previous section, the effectiveness of international assistance in preventing forced displacements of population is hampered by obstacles arising at four distinct levels; consequently, any attempt to address the root causes of these movements must embrace all of them in a coordinated and coherent manner. Not only are actions that focus exclusively on any one of these levels likely to fail to provide long-term solutions to the problems that have plagued the Horn for too many years, but a limited approach may have negative consequences in discouraging donors from continuing their actions and in creating imbalances that may themselves provoke further conflicts and resulting displacements.

International obstacles

It is now widely acknowledged that violence plays a major role in the onset of African famines. A key to the success of any future undertaking is to achieve balanced reconstruction of civil society in each of the countries concerned; but that is itself possible only under conditions of generalized peace. In our review of root causes, we argued that in every one of the countries of the Horn, the conflicts of the past three decades are related to state-building problems, which have taken the form of confrontations between a "centre" and one or more ethnically and culturally distinct "peripheries". No proposed solution can ignore these issues, even though a consideration of them raises delicate matters of sovereignty. It was shown also that direct and indirect involvement by the superpowers, as well as other external powers that view the region from the perspective of Middle East politics, have exacerbated these conflicts. With the Cold War over, the first of these factors has in effect disappeared – except for its destructive legacy, in the form of stocks of arms – but the other is likely to remain important in the foreseeable future. It is evident that the Horn would benefit considerably from a reduction of tensions in the Middle East; but while such a development can be hoped for, it cannot be expected to materialize in the near future. Hence, the focus must be on the Horn itself.

The central issue is the question of autonomy for the regions in question. This can range from devolution of power from the centre to the regions within the framework of a federal state (with varying possible degrees of autonomy), to outright separation and the creation of new states.

How are these matters to be decided? Preferably by the populations concerned, acting through their representatives within the framework of a democratic state. However, these conditions are not currently realized in any of the countries concerned; and although in theory they could be brought about by internal processes alone, in practice this seems rather unlikely. Hence the question arises of which international agencies and actors should intervene, and what role they should play.

The initial actions required are essentially *political*, and the most appropriate bodies for this are regional organizations, mainly the Organization of African

Unity (OAU); because of the region's ties with the Middle East, the Arab League will probably be involved as well.

But to deal effectively with this problem, and to avoid being overtaken by events that might lead to a renewed scramble for Africa, the OAU ought to reconsider its principle of the inviolability of colonial borders. It should be noted that two of the situations in the Horn are ambiguous in this regard: (a) Eritrea was at one time a separate colony, and entrusted to Ethiopia by the United Nations under certain specific conditions; (b) Somalia was constituted by the voluntary merger of two distinct territories, the Somali Republic and British Somaliland. These two can be termed exceptional cases, where separation would not amount to an unacceptable precedent.

Since by 1992 the Eritrean case appeared to be on the way towards resolution along these lines, the peacemaking role of the international community should be focused on the other problem, Somalia. In the absence of internal interlocutors able and willing to negotiate, there is an urgent need for international humanitarian intervention. Once again, the preferable approach is a regional one, as in the case of ECOWAS with regard to Liberia. But because of overall conditions in the Horn, there are no countries with the capacity to undertake such a major task. The second best solution is action by the OAU. Should it be unwilling or unable to perform this function, the matter must be dealt with at the level of the United Nations. Matters have in fact moved in this direction.

Having adopted a role in Somalia, the UN should consider taking action similar in scope to that currently pursued in Cambodia, ranging from the repatriation of refugees to de-mining, and organizing elections, etc. Although a UN mediator is currently searching for political settlement to the conflicts, the sending of UN peacekeeping forces has been held up by financial constraints and lack of commitment on part of member States. As pointed out by *The New York Times*, "Having contributed to this calamity, Somalia's former armourers cannot with decency sit on their hands" (9 Feb. 1992, p. E16). As under present conditions, the countries of the former USSR cannot be expected to act, the responsibility rests by default with the United States. Indeed, all Western powers with special concerns in the region (especially France and Italy) share an interest in restoring peace.

In the other cases, namely Ethiopia and Sudan – as well as within distinct Somali states, should these come into being – ongoing centre-periphery conflicts might be settled short of separation by way of federal solutions. Because the provisional Ethiopian Government appears inclined to move in the direction of federalism, the role of the international community should for the time being be limited to facilitating its efforts to draw up an adequate constitution. The most intractable case is Sudan, where a limited federalism was attempted in 1967, but did not last. The subsequent resumption of civil war effectively demonstrates the positive value of federalism. If the objective of the international community is to reduce the flow of refugees, it has little choice but to put pressure on the various parties to come to the negotiating table, as they have occasionally done in the past. The situation is complicated by the involvement in the conflict of most of the Middle Eastern powers, including Israel and the Islamic Republic of Iran, as well as China (as an arms supplier). The case of Sudan might be approached within the context of a Middle East settlement.

The ongoing conflicts continue to be fuelled by the widespread availability of weapons. This is in part a legacy of the arms race that engulfed the region during the Cold War, and of continued supplies from external sources. The goal should be an effectively enforced arms embargo, coupled with disarmament of fighters when alternative constitutional channels for dealing with their grievances become available. If that happens, several possibilities arise: incorporating fighters into national armies, buying up their arms, instituting a "food for arms" programme, and so on. To be efficient, however, the disarmament process must accompany the creation of alternative means of survival and of economic self-sufficiency. This highlights the fact that economic reconstruction and development are necessary components of any programme of political reconstruction.

National obstacles

As seen above, the central issue in the Horn of Africa is the question of autonomy. The future political configuration – federalism or outright separation – of all the countries under consideration will in effect determine the prospects for long-term peace.

Federalism entails more than administrative decentralization, but a genuine deconcentration of power, according to rules set in a constitution. The formation of relatively autonomous power centres is tantamount to the reinforcement of civil society. Thus, genuine federalism goes hand in hand with democratization, as well as the promotion of human rights, and each process feeds into the other.

It is sometimes argued that federalism is costly, in that ministries and government services must be duplicated, and hence that it constitutes a luxury that developing countries can ill afford. This, though, is a short-sighted vision, as it neglects the role of federalism in the democratic management of ethnic and cultural differences, and as the alternative to such an approach is often very costly in terms of human suffering and of government apparatus for repression. However, it is true that federalism requires properly trained regional and local *political* as well as administrative personnel. The same holds true for the creation of a new State, such as Eritrea. Training such personnel should be one of the priorities of international assistance.

In both cases – federalism and separation – the drafting of a constitution is the primary step towards the emergence of a legitimate State. A number of developing countries, including Namibia, Nigeria (after the civil war) and India have achieved relative success in settling at an institutional and constitutional level problems between ethnic groups. Their experiences should be called upon. While the constitutions of the countries of the Horn cannot be borrowed from other contexts, it is evident that the current leaders in charge of the first crucial steps towards statehood could learn a great deal from past experiences and mistakes.

In addition to facilitating the process towards political reconstruction, international assistance is required for the economic reconstruction and development of the areas under consideration. It has already contributed to the completion of a series of national strategies on critical sectors of the Ethiopian economy, including National Disaster Preparedness and Prevention, Conservation, Food Security and Nutrition. The design of each strategy was preceded by comprehensive studies of the issues involved and by conferences in which both national and international experts participated.[26]

Economic aid should take into account two interlinked factors it has generally ignored in the past:

- As indicated on the first part of this paper, economic factors fuelled the political struggles of the past 30 years. Uneven development, resulting from government policies favouring some regions over others, and the unequal redistribution of resources (education, health facilities, public infrastructure, etc.) have activated separatist demands and weakened populations to the extent that they are unable to face droughts and escape famines.

- Development planners ought to take into consideration the realities of ethnic configurations.[27] Where ethnic identities are territorially based, projects that exclusively benefit certain regions and populations or that threaten the ecological conditions of some areas, are likely to result in ethnically based conflicts.[28] International agencies and bilateral donors in charge of economic assistance and development programmes should strive towards a territorially based distribution. While federalism might facilitate the integration of these questions, the process towards even development will be conditioned by other factors, including the distribution of resources among and *within* federations. Finally, it should be emphasized that such an approach does not rule out the necessity of positive discrimination. In fact, it is evident that international assistance should at first discriminate in favour of populations most in need and at risk.

Local obstacles

After decades of heated debate over the respective merits of national development and community-oriented development, it is evident that neither can be effective without the other. Nationally based programmes cannot be sustained without the active political and economic participation of local communities. Conversely, local development and self-reliance necessitate a degree of state power. As Björn Hettne has pointed out, some economic planning will always be necessary even in an extremely decentralized economy: the state must provide adequate infrastructure for any cooperation between local units to be possible, and may have to intervene to correct imbalances in resource endowments.[29]

With regard to preventing future migration flows, it is necessary to identify the most vulnerable regions and communities, and design strategies appropriate for

---

[26] Raven-Roberts, 1992, p. 11.

[27] Björn Hettne makes a distinction between functional and territorial principles of development. The former is a result of specialization and advanced division of labour, while according to the latter, it is the regions themselves which are to be developed, not the larger functional system. The territorial approach is inherently cultural (Hettne, 1990, p. 193).

[28] See Stavenhagen, 1986; Thompson and Ronen, 1986.

[29] Hettne, 1990, p. 177.

diverse local situations. As Angela Raven-Robert points out with regard to Ethiopia, "The Ethiopian rural economy is made up of different production types, each affected differently by drought conditions and each has specific nuances that have to be catered for in the design of relevant strategies."[30]

One issue that must be faced is whether the populations in question can be helped in their present locale (or locale of origin, if they are returnees). If the area in question is beyond help, i.e. does not offer any realistic prospect of providing an environment for long-term self-reliance, ways must be found to resettle the population permanently. However, care must be given to avoid authoritarian solutions that usually inflict great suffering on the target populations and are economically counter-productive. Once again, there is no substitute for a relatively democratic process which, in this instance, would take the form of consultation with representative groups of displaced persons (or candidates for relocation). The experience of negotiations involved in the relocation of populations threatened by dams might provide useful knowledge as to what does, and does not, work. Since the formation of a balanced state and civil society requires self-reliant, democratic and participatory communities, international assistance can contribute to the process by channelling a significant part of its funds to these communities. It should facilitate the emergence and strengthening of local counterparts, to be accountable for local development programmes. National and international NGOs could play a major role in this process by identifying promising local associations or by contributing to the creation of organizational frameworks that will represent the interests of rural populations.

United Nations obstacles

With regard to the Horn of Africa, the immediate requirements are of an emergency nature – food relief, shelter, health facilities – coupled with the repatriation of many thousands of refugees and displaced persons. In this regard, it is imperative for UN agencies to overcome organizational structures and practices that hamper interagency cooperation and coordination. This does not require starting from scratch. Effective experiences must be recalled and replicated.

For instance, the Office for Emergency Operations in Africa (OEOA) is widely regarded as one of the most effective UN endeavours in the region and as a model of coordination to be emulated. According to Maurice Strong, its former Executive Director, there are three main reasons behind OEOA's success: personal involvement of senior UN agency officials, fast decision-making, and successful coordination. A computerized database provides up-to-date information for governments, UN agencies, and NGOs on country needs, supply lines and port congestion; and a concerted fund-raising drive raised $4 billion over a two-year period for the 20 countries or so needing emergency assistance.[31]

[30] Raven-Roberts, 1992, p. 11.
[31] See the article "UN Role in African crises debated", in *Africa Recovery*, June 1991, pp. 30-31. The article summarizes the discussions and findings of a North-South round table meeting in New York in February 1991.

Another concrete success, according to participants in a February 1991 North-South round table, was the UN's Inter-Agency Task Force on Africa which "articulated Africa's concern brilliantly and supported several historic initiatives, including the African Alternative Framework to Structural Adjustment Programmes and the Arusha Charter for popular participation".[32] The more recent Special Emergency Programmes for the Horn of Africa (SEPHA) constitute another positive UN attempt to address emergency issues. Of special importance were the reports published on a regular basis from September 1991 to February 1992, which served two crucial purposes: (a) providing a centralized database on emergency needs and financial resources required, pledged and available; (b) conceptualizing innovative operational modalities, including interagency coordination, needs prioritization, and strategies tailored for specific groups.[33]

UN emergency efforts should be coordinated through the creation of a single unit with four main functions:

Financial: interagency appeals, fund-raising;
Political: lobbying with donors, General Assembly, General Secretariat;
Conceptual: needs assessment and prioritization, design of innovative methods and strategies;
Operational: coordination of modalities among UN agencies, and between UN and NGOs.

All four functions matter. *A political and financial entity which has no operational or conceptual role will have very little success in resolving the situation in the field*. The effective pursuit of these four functions requires resources, commitment, and experienced staff. The first two are strongly interlinked. The availability of sufficient resources is determined by the donor countries (hence the importance of the "political" function) and by the funds provided by the UN itself. Commitment refers to political support on the part of the UN Secretariat and donor countries. This in turn necessitates attributing to the Horn of Africa a high priority on the international agenda. Finally, all these efforts will be of little use unless they are placed under the leadership of a team of professionals with thorough experience of both the areas under consideration and of emergency relief.

It should be emphasized once again that successful strategies and ideas for preventing emergency situations (through disaster preparedness and prevention measures, for example) and for organizing emergency relief, exist. What is required, therefore, is not so much innovation, as learning from past experiences, integrating them within the design and implementation of new policies, and the emulation of successful models, such as OEOA and SEPHA.

---

[32] Ibid.
[33] See SEPHA, Consolidated Interagency Appeal of September 1991 and February 1992; Situation Reports from October 1991 to January 1992 (see notes 2 and 11, above).

As Cleveland reminds us, "Knowledge has always been power."[34] Within the global system, knowledge provides human beings and institutions with ways of interrogating, comprehending, influencing, and transforming world affairs. In the course of its nearly half century of existence, the UN has accumulated a broad range of experience ranging from peacemaking efforts to humanitarian relief and development assistance. *It is crucial that these experiences be translated into knowledge through systematic and continuous learning mechanisms if the UN is to face the numerous challenges resulting from the end of the Cold War and seize the opportunity this presents for ensuring peace and security.*

Bibliography

Cleveland, H. 1991. "Rethinking international governance: Coalition politics in an unruly world", in *The Futurist*, May-June 1991, Vol. 25, No.3.
Henze, Paul. 1991. *The Horn of Africa: From war to peace* (New York, St Martin's Press).
Hettne, Björn. 1990. *Development theory and the three worlds* (New York, Longman Scientific and Technical).
Kitching, Gavin. 1989. *Development and underdevelopment in historical perspective* (London, Routledge).
Korn, David A. 1986. *Ethiopia, the United States and the Soviet Union* (Carbondale and Edwardsville, Southern Illinois University Press).
Mearsheimer, John. 1991. *International strategy* (Ithaca, New York, Cornell University Press).
Minear, Larry. 1991. *Humanitarianism under siege: A critical review of Operation Lifeline Sudan* (Trenton, The Red Sea Press).
OECD. Various years. *Development Cooperation Review*.
Ottaway, Marina. 1982. *Soviet and American influence in the Horn of Africa* (New York, Praeger).
Patman, Robert. 1990. *The Soviet Union in the Horn of Africa* (Cambridge, Cambridge University Press).
Pauling, Sharon. 1991. *Ending war and famine in the Horn of Africa through grassroots initiatives* (Bread for the World background paper, No. 119, Mar.).
Raven-Roberts, Angela. 1992. *Community development and the new State. Prospects for community initiatives in a new structure of Ethiopia: More questions than answers.* Paper presented at the conference on the Horn of Africa, organized by Michigan State University, April 1992, p. 11.
Stavenhagen, Rodolfo. 1986. "Ethnodevelopment: A neglected dimension in development thinking", in R. Apthorpe and A. Krahl (eds.): *Development studies: Critique and renewal* (Leiden, E.J. Brill).
Thompson, B.R.; Ronen, D. 1986. *Ethnicity, politics and development* (Boulder, Colorado, Lynn Rienner).
UNDP. 1991a. Special Emergency Programme for the Horn of Africa (SEPHA) *Situation Report No.1, Oct. 1991* (New York).
—. 1991b. *Human Development Report* (New York, Oxford University Press).

---

[34] Cleveland, 1991. Cleveland suggests building new global institutions, including a collective executive able to perform policy analysis and to negotiate consensus on standards, etc.; international taxes; an international panel of conflict conciliators designated ahead of time by the UN, etc. He also advocates an increasing role for NGOs and UN peacekeeping forces.

—. 1991c. SEPHA, Consolidated Interagency Appeals of 1 September 1991, and 1 February 1992 (New York).
UNHCR. 1991. *Annual Report.*
World Bank. 1991. *World Development Report* (New York, Oxford University Press).
Zolberg, Aristide. 1992. "The specter of anarchy: African States verging on dissolution", in *Dissent*, Summer, pp. 303-11.

5

The use of foreign aid for reducing incentives to emigrate from Central America

S. Weintraub and S. Díaz-Briquets

1. Introduction

The premise on which this study is based is that the supply of prospective immigrants from Central America is substantially greater than the willingness of receiving countries to allow them entry. Central America is defined here as comprising Costa Rica, El Salvador, Guatemala, Honduras, and Nicaragua, the five countries of the Central American Common Market.[1] The United States is the main migrant-receiving country outside Central America. Those coming overland to the United States must traverse Mexico and some migrants remain there, many at the border with Guatemala. The combined population of the five Central American countries is now 27 million,[2] and the number of Central Americans (other than tourists) estimated to be in the United States is about one million (plus perhaps another 500,000 in Mexico).[3]

Migration takes many forms. These include legal immigration into the country of destination, illegal or undocumented immigration, refugee flows, movement with the original purpose of temporary labour, and tourist or business travel with the intent to remain only temporarily in the receiving country. The concern of this study is with emigration for the purpose of indefinite residence in the country of destination, as would be the case for many persons seeking refugee status, and many undocumented immigrants. Legal immigration for permanent residence in the United States, while not the theme of this study, would presumably also be affected if emigration pressures in Central America were reduced. The desire to reduce emigration pressures does not pertain to temporary movement of persons for tourism or business. Indeed, one would expect that as incentives for permanent emigration declined

---

[1] Central America could be defined more expansively to include Panama and Belize. They were omitted to permit discussion later in this paper of the Central American Common Market. There is also more similarity in the nature of the economies among the five countries covered than there is between any one of them and either Panama or Belize. There are also historical reasons for treating the five countries separately from Panama and Belize. In other respects, the analysis in the paper would not be altered if the definition of Central America were expanded.

[2] If Panama and Belize were added the population would be about 30 million.

[3] In addition to persons who have emigrated out of the region, there are now hundreds of thousands of Central Americans who live in the region outside their own country. There has long been much emigration from El Salvador to neighbouring countries, particularly Honduras, but the unsettled situation in the region since 1979 has led to a vast increase in intraregional migration.

because of greater economic opportunity at home, temporary visits would increase because of the higher income in the former sending countries.

Other than permitting large-scale immigration, an industrialized receiving country has two broad ranges of instruments for influencing economic and social outcomes in developing sending countries. These are policies dealing with the current account of the balance of payments, namely, with the movement of goods and services, and those affecting the capital account (see *Unauthorized migration: An economic development response*, 1990). The two sets of policy instruments can be separated analytically, but not in practice. The provision of official development assistance (ODA), debt relief, and the encouragement of private foreign direct investment (FDI) to a sending country, all of which involve some actual or implicit flow of capital resources, are intended to augment economic activity, including the expansion of exports. This would be particularly true for Central America, where the economies are largely open and earnings from merchandise exports in years of satisfactory economic growth range between 20 per cent and 35 per cent of GDP (Weeks, 1985, p. 52). What this means is that the use of foreign aid – the transfer of capital and technical resources to achieve the kind of self-sustaining growth that would reduce or eliminate the incentive to emigrate – requires as a corollary keeping import markets open in the United States and other industrial countries. "Aid, not trade", cannot be a complete policy formulation, certainly not with respect to Central America.

The United States, when formulating foreign economic policy, or foreign policy generally for that matter, has rarely considered the migration implications of its actions (see Díaz-Briquets and Weintraub, 1991e, p. 3). United States involvement in Viet Nam in the 1970s and in Central America during the 1980s had substantial migration consequences. Indeed, the destination of migrants from sending countries is often largely determined by past relationships, as exemplified by Filipinos emigrating to the United States, north Africans to France, and south Asians to the United Kingdom. This paper assumes that reducing migration pressure should be made an explicit goal of the foreign economic policy of the United States. If such a policy objective were adopted, foreign assistance would have a decided advantage over other instruments in that it can be pinpointed to migrant-sending countries and, to some extent, even to major sending regions in the sending countries (Weintraub, 1983, p. 227). Trade policy can also be targeted to some extent, but this may require preferential treatment and lead to the alienation of those countries that are discriminated against. It remains to be seen whether the United States will provide trade preferences to Mexico, the main migrant-sending country, by means of a free-trade agreement. The United States provides trade preferences to Central American countries under the Caribbean Basin Initiative (CBI) and the European Community (EC) does the same for African, Caribbean and Pacific countries under Lomé. In both instances, under CBI and Lomé, foreign aid is also a major part of the development package.

Foreign direct investment is even more limited than trade as an official means to staunch migration because it is essentially under the control of private persons rather than governments.

There is a major difference between the United States and the countries of the EC in the choice of the primary instrument for reducing emigration pressures in sending countries. In Europe, growing out of concern over potential migrant flows from Eastern Europe, southern Europe (largely Turkey; see Martin, 1991), north Africa, and south Asia, there is much discussion about using aid as the key corrective action (Tapinos, 1991a and 1991b). The United States, by contrast, has opted instead for trade measures to stimulate economic development in those countries which send most migrants to the United States. This is evident from the fashioning of President George Bush's Enterprise for the Americas, which holds out the promise of free trade in the Western Hemisphere, but not of significant new bilateral aid. One reason for the United States preference for trade measures is clearly the parlous state of the United States budget and the unwillingness to incur increased deficits. This sentiment against augmented budgetary appropriations for foreign assistance will have to be overcome if foreign aid is, indeed, to become the measure of choice for United States development policy in Central America. Foreign aid to Central America was the instrument of choice earlier, during the Reagan administration (*Report of the President's National Bipartisan Commission on Central America*, or the Kissinger Commission, 1984), but that was before the steady progression of fiscal deficits whose end is nowhere in sight.

The development task in Central America is formidable. As one commentator put it: "The 1980s have been struggling, immiserizing years in Central America" (Saborio, 1990, p. 295). The regional agenda includes the need to reconstruct political systems, re-establish institutions devastated by civil wars, restore social harmony after tens of thousands of deaths, and then rebuild economies in such a way as to instil some semblance of social justice (Crosby, 1990, p. 105). Hundreds of thousands of persons were displaced by conflicts in Nicaragua and El Salvador, many of them internally in the region and others to countries outside Central America (Lake, 1990, p. 6). Many of these people may never return, particularly those displaced outside the region, but others are already coming home, as in Nicaragua. Furthermore, if migrants return to war-devastated economies, they can aggravate the development problem in the near to medium term. Fortunately, the civil war has ended in Nicaragua and an agreement to terminate hostilities that have been going on since 1979 has been reached between the Government and the rebellious Farabundo Marti National Liberation Front (FMLN) in El Salvador. Thus, while the development problems are colossal, the circumstances for renewal of economic growth are more favourable today than they have been for more than a decade.

What follows is an analysis of the feasibility of using international aid as a means of reducing the need for emigration from Central America. The time period adopted is a long one – 20 to perhaps 40 years of consistent flows of aid to the five countries. The study will cover, in sequence: demographic and employment projections in Central America over this long period to define the dimensions of the problem that must be confronted; a brief review of Central American emigration to the United States; developments in the region since the Second World War to provide the antecedents of the current situation; a description of past foreign aid to Central America; and an evaluation of successes and failures of past foreign assistance and an examination of the features necessary to optimize future aid flows. The final section will discuss the central theme of the study: "What forms, contents, and dimensions would foreign aid have to take in the case of Central American countries to reduce drastically, in one or two generations, the desire of their citizens to seek work in the United States?"

2. Demographic overview of Central America, 1990 and 2025

Central America has had one of the fastest demographic growth rates in the world in the postwar period; until recently, population growth was as high as 3 per cent per year. Between 1950 and 1990, the population of the five Central American countries increased by more than 200 percent, from 8.3 million to 26.5 million. The reasons for this dramatic increase are familiar. A sustained mortality decline and persistently high fertility led to a steep rise in natural increase rates. As is typical with such a demographic growth rate, there is a young age structure and a high dependency ratio in Central America: more than 40 per cent of the population are now below 15 years of age. Although birth rates have begun to diminish in the region, only Costa Rica has experienced substantial fertility decline.

Current United Nations (1991) and International Labour Office (1986) population and labour force projections extend to the year 2025, or approximately the two generations with which this paper is concerned. The United Nations projections in Table 5.1 are the medium variant; they describe some basic features of the Central American population in 1990 and two generations from now. The most striking aspect is the large increase in population, from 26.5 million in 1990 to 59 million in 2025, or 127 per cent. This increase is anticipated even though the United Nations assumes that annual population growth rates in all five countries will have fallen below two per cent by the end of the projection period because of fertility declines. Because of this, the median age in the Central American countries is projected to rise appreciably. Only in Costa Rica, however, will it exceed 30 years in 2025.[4] For decades to come, Central America will remain a high demographic growth region with a youthful population and a rapidly expanding labour force.

Central America's economically active population (EAP) follows a growth pattern roughly similar to that of population growth. The EAP is expected to increase by more than 16 million workers between 1990 and 2025, or by 189 per cent. The relatively higher increase in EAP than in population growth is the result of declining population growth and increasing female labour force participation. Female labour force participation rates are forecast to double over the projection period. Owing to population growth momentum (the triangular shape of the regional age distribution), net average annual EAP increments (the balance of new entrants and those exiting from the labour force owing to retirement, death or other causes) increase progressively up to the end of the projection period (see Table 5.2). Whereas during the 1990-2000 period, an average of 341,000 workers will be added annually to the EAP on a net basis, the annual average net additions to the EAP will increase to 581,000 workers in the period 2020-2025. In future years, the Central American countries will be in the unenviable position of having to increase the number of job opportunities at a much faster pace than today.

Open unemployment rates are not high in Central America. During the 1960s and 1970s, official urban open unemployment rates were generally below 10 per cent, occasionally rising above that level, as in Managua in 1979 (PREALC,

---

[4] By way of comparison, the median age in the United States is now 33 years.

Table 5.1. Central America: Basic demographic data, 1990 and 2025

	1990	2025
Costa Rica		
Population (thousands)	3 015	5 250
Median age (in years)	22.3	31.6
Economically active population (thousands)	1 023	1 958
Per cent urban	47.1	68.5
Population density (km^2)	59	103
El Salvador		
Population (thousands)	5 252	11 299
Median age (in years)	17.3	24.4
Economically active population (thousands)	2 155	5 699
Per cent urban	44.4	66.0
Population density (km^2)	250	537
Guatemala		
Population (thousands)	9 197	21 668
Median age (in years)	17.1	23.9
Economically active population (thousands)	2 628	8 230
Per cent urban	39.4	61.8
Population density (km^2)	84	199
Honduras		
Population (thousands)	5 138	11 510
Median age (in years)	17.4	26.0
Economically active population (thousands)	1 576	5 268
Per cent urban	43.7	68.3
Population density (km2)	46	103
Nicaragua		
Population (thousands)	3 871	9 219
Median age (in years)	16.9	24.9
Economically active population (in thousands)	1 204	3 673
Per cent urban	59.8	77.9
Population density (km^2)	30	71

Source: UN, 1991; ILO, 1986.

1982). Underemployment, on the other hand, is widespread, leading to high equivalent joblessness rates, often in excess of 30 per cent of the EAP. In 1989, in Guatemala, for example, the open unemployment rate was 6.3 per cent, whereas the equivalent underemployment rate was estimated at 35.4 per cent (CEPAL, 1990, p. 6). There is general consensus that Central America's labour supply is likely to continue to outstrip labour demand, and that unemployment and underemployment will become more acute (Gendell, 1986; Espenshade, 1989; Tucker, 1991).

Table 5.2. Growth of the economically active population, 1990-2025 (thousands)

Country or region	1990	2000	2010	2020	2025
Costa Rica	1 023	1 297	1 608	1 857	1 958
El Salvador	2 155	2 964	3 961	5 104	5 699
Guatemala	2 628	3 665	5 152	7 112	8 230
Honduras	1 576	2 299	3 261	4 601	5 268
Nicaragua	1 204	1 774	2 447	3 250	3 673
Central America	8 586	11 999	16 429	21 924	24 828
Avg. annual increment	—	341	443	550	581

Source: ILO, 1986.

The increases in urbanization, population density and the economically active population suggested by the projections in Tables 5.1 and 5.2 are particularly significant in understanding employment and emigration pressures. By 2025, Central America will be highly urbanized. Nearly three out of every four inhabitants will reside in cities. In 1990, by contrast, only in Nicaragua did the urban population exceed 50 per cent of the total. Population densities are expected to increase by over 100 per cent in all the countries except Costa Rica. El Salvador will become an exceptionally crowded country, with a population density in 2025 nearly as high as Bangladesh today. Even where population density figures are relatively low, Central America's ability to absorb future population increments is constrained in rural areas. The rough topography of the region precludes agricultural use of the major part of the region's land surface (Leonard, 1987). As will be highlighted later, the limits of the agricultural frontier and the rising urbanization trend imply that an effort must be made to absorb future Central American labour force increments in non-farm rural, urban, and regional activities.

3. Emigration from Central America

Before the 1970s, emigration from Central America was relatively modest, and only small numbers of Central Americans emigrated outside the region. Within the region, the migratory story was different. Many Salvadorians emigrated to Honduras, and other migratory flows among neighbouring countries were common. By the mid-1970s, however, Central Americans, Salvadorians and Guatemalans in particular, began to emigrate in increasing numbers to Mexico and the United States. The 1980 United States census enumerated 94,447 Salvadorians and 63,073 Guatemalans in the country. Close to half of these immigrants had arrived in the 1975-80 period, many of them illegally. In 1977, the first year for which separate figures are available for Central Americans, more than 7,000 Salvadorian and over 5,000 Guatemalan undocumented immigrants were apprehended along the United States-Mexico border. Many more presumably escaped apprehension.

With the civil wars of the early 1980s, what had been a modest but growing emigration trickle became a flood. While most international attention was devoted to the refugees seeking sanctuary beyond Central America, the vast majority of those uprooted escaped rural violence by moving to cities within the region.

There is much debate on the relative weights to assign to different causes for the rise in Central American emigration, particularly to the United States. Some observers focus on the relationship between violence and the associated economic crisis, and emigration. Other observers point to the rising emigration trend before the 1980s, and conclude that most Central Americans emigrate primarily for economic reasons. The majority of emigrants, in this view, would have left Central America in search of economic opportunities regardless of the political situation. There are surely elements of truth in both assertions (Stanley, 1987). But regardless of the weights assigned to the initial determinants, social networks between Central America and the United States have now been established. With the regional violence abating, economic factors should reclaim their undisputed pre-1980 significance.

An indicator of the increase in Central American emigration to the United States is the number of applications submitted under the legalization provisions of the Immigration Reform and Control Act (IRCA) of 1986. Of the 277,642 Central American applications, 168,014, or 60 per cent, were filed by Salvadorians, and 70,967, or 25.4 per cent, by Guatemalans. The remainder were from Costa Rica (3,781; 1.4 per cent), Honduras (18,121; 6.5 per cent), and Nicaragua (16,759; 6.0 per cent). Over 90 per cent of these applications are expected to be approved, leading to the eventual granting of permanent resident status to some 250,000 Central Americans. A further 184,798 Salvadorians were awarded temporary protected status in 1991 under a special provision of the Immigration Act (IA) of 1990 (and an additional 2,216 cases are pending). This temporary status lasts 18 months and is due to expire on June 30, 1992.[5] As a result of IRCA and IA, the status of over 450,000 Central Americans was regularized, either on a temporary or a permanent basis. This figure is the equivalent of approximately 3 per cent of Central America's EAP in 1990.

In addition, the number of Central Americans admitted as landed immigrants in the United States is increasing. Over 25,000 Central American immigrants were admitted in 1988, as compared to 15,000 in 1977. Future years should see further increases as the immigrants legalized under IRCA become naturalized United States citizens and claim their relatives abroad through the family reunification provisions of United States immigration law.

Although the number of attempted illegal entries by Central Americans – mostly through the United States-Mexico border – experienced a sharp decline in the years following the passage of IRCA, at least as evidenced by apprehension data, unauthorized Central American immigration is still taking place, as indicated by the continued apprehensions of undocumented immigrants (Table 5.3). In 1991, more than 23,000 Central Americans were apprehended, including 10,924 Salvadorians

[5] In early 1992, the US Immigration and Naturalization Service (INS) began notifying the Salvadorians awarded temporary protected status that they could be deported after 30 June 1992. No deportations, however, were anticipated before 1993. Advocates for the migrants are requesting an 18-month extension at a minimum, before the migrants are forced to return home to allow the Salvadorian economy to recover now that a peace accord has been signed (*Washington Post*, 11 Jan. 1992, p. A12, "US warns Salvadorans of deportation"). In May 1992, the Bush administration announced that the Salvadorians would be granted at least a one-year extension (*Washington Post*, 15 May 1992, p. A18, "US allows Salvadorans to stay").

Table 5.3. Central Americans apprehended, fiscal years 1986-91

Year	Costa Rica	El Salvador	Guatemala	Honduras	Nicaragua
1986	...	20 604	9 927	...	...
1987	207	9 780	6 722	2 602	4 819
1988	236	14 322	9 246	3 943	3 280
1989	423	20 242	13 431	7 133	9 348
1990	309	16 953	9 707	5 695	4 457
1991	298	10 924	6 574	4 425	1 094

... = figures not available.

Source: US Immigration and Naturalization Service.

and 6,574 Guatemalans. In 1986, the year before IRCA went into effect, the border patrol apprehended more than 20,000 Salvadorians and close to 10,000 Guatemalans. Annual apprehensions by country of origin have fluctuated since then, although the number of apprehensions seems to be on the decline. The trend is consistent with what one would expect from the gradual pacification of Central America. Since the 1990 electoral defeat of the Sandinista Government in Nicaragua, the number of Nicaraguans apprehended has dropped substantially – only 1,094 Nicaraguans were apprehended in 1991.

There is no conclusive evidence regarding the socioeconomic characteristics of Central American migrants to the United States. However, on the basis of the few studies that exist and the results of investigations of other emigrating nationalities, it can be posited that most migrants – even those fleeing for political motives – originate from urban localities and have socioeconomic characteristics above the norm in countries of origin. Wallace (1986) found, for example, that the educational and labour force characteristics of a sample of Central American immigrants he studied in California were above average and that most had an urban background. Comparable findings were reported by Montes Mozo and Garcia Vasquez (1988) in their study of Salvadorian emigration to the United States. These investigators found a strong migration selectivity in terms of educational and occupational background. About half of the Salvadorian refugee respondents interviewed in the United States had urban origins. The background of the emigrants has implications for the types of employment that must be created at home if emigration incentives are to be gradually reduced.

4. Post-Second World War developments in Central America

The Central American countries have small, open economies and are thus extremely vulnerable to developments abroad. Until the 1940s, the region was highly dependent on the export of two traditional commodities – coffee and bananas – and imported almost all of the manufactured goods it consumed. The region's agricultural export structure broadened significantly in the postwar period as cotton, sugar and beef supplemented coffee and bananas as important regional exports. Industrial

Table 5.4.   Gross domestic product: Average annual growth rates, 1961-70 to 1981-90 (per cent)

Year	1961-70	1971-80	1981-90
Costa Rica	6.0	5.4	2.3
El Salvador	5.8	2.6	-0.4
Guatemala	5.5	5.7	0.9
Honduras	5.3	5.7	2.0
Nicaragua	7.1	-0.1	-2.4

Source: IDB, 1991b, Table B.1, p. 273.

development was modest until the 1960s, when the countries of Central America, like other Latin American countries, embraced import-substitution policies. Central America did so within the expanded internal regional market provided by the Central American Common Market (CACM).

Commodity exports and the economic dynamism arising from import-substitution industrialization led to a period of rapid growth (Table 5.4). The United States-sponsored Alliance for Progress of the 1960s gave an added boost to the region by providing, among other things, an impetus to several regional organizations. These included the institutional infrastructure for Central American integration and the Inter-American Bank; these institutions contributed greatly to the region's economic development during the 1960s and early 1970s. Between 1961 and 1970, gross domestic product in every Central American country grew by more than 5 per cent annually, or about 2 per cent a year on a per capita basis. High growth rates were sustained during the 1970s by Costa Rica, Guatemala and Honduras, but not by El Salvador and Nicaragua.

Not everyone benefited from the years of prosperity. Income distribution worsened and competition for land between modern producers of commodity exports and the rural poor, further aggravated by rapid population growth, intensified (Durham, 1979; Williams, 1986). Attempts to redress the demand for farm land became manifest with the agrarian reform programmes implemented in the 1980s in El Salvador and Nicaragua (as well as in Costa Rica and Honduras to a lesser extent).

By the mid-1970s, Central America felt the effect of rising international oil prices. Nicaragua had suffered much economic damage in 1972, when a violent earthquake devastated Managua. El Salvador was one of the principal beneficiaries of the CACM, and its poor economic performance by the middle of the decade was associated with the gradual collapse of the common market. The 1969 war with Honduras, which led to the forced repatriation of numerous Salvadorian emigrants and increasing political instability, contributed to the economic decline. Despite the relatively poor performance of El Salvador and Nicaragua during the 1970s, regional real per capita income doubled between 1950 and 1978 (Feinberg and Pastor, 1984).[6]

The recent violent history of the region is well known. There was a short but bloody conflict in Nicaragua in 1979 that led to the Sandinista overthrow of the

---

[6] This calculation includes Panama, as well as the five Central American countries.

Somoza dictatorship. By then, El Salvador was simmering in the political cauldron that in a couple of years would engulf the country in a brutal civil war. The Contra wars erupted later in Nicaragua.

These developments were the final straw that broke the back of the nearly defunct CACM. It had become increasingly clear that the CACM was not functioning as its architects had hoped. Not only were the benefits of regional trade unequally distributed among the various member countries, but because of the protective walls erected by high tariffs, Central American industries were producing low-quality goods at high cost. Import dependency continued, but it was now for intermediate and capital goods rather than for consumer goods. The drive to increase the volume of non-traditional exports gave rise to troublesome unanticipated consequences. The natural resource base of the region was abused, with grave consequences for the long-term sustainability of many agricultural activities (Leonard, 1987). Extensive tracts of tropical forests were converted to low-productivity pastures, and the overuse of herbicides, pesticides and other chemical inputs contributed to environmental damage in many cotton-growing areas of the Pacific coasts of Guatemala and Nicaragua.

The economic crisis of the region was deepened by the collapse in prices of the region's export commodities and the steep rise in oil prices and interest rates. Between 1981 and 1990, annual economic growth rates in Central America were either negative or minimally positive; on a per capita basis, every country experienced declines. By the mid-1980s, major declines in exports of goods and services had been recorded in El Salvador, Guatemala and Nicaragua. Costa Rica and Honduras – the two countries not engulfed in major civil conflicts – were able to withstand this trend.

For El Salvador and Nicaragua, the economic consequences of the civil wars were disastrous. Between 1977 and 1983, per capita income in El Salvador declined by 40 per cent (Weeks, 1985, p. 191), while the economy of Nicaragua has been in a virtual free fall since the 1970s: GDP per capita declined by 3.1 per cent annually during the 1970s and by 5.6 per cent annually during the 1980s. Despite unprecedented amounts of foreign assistance, per capita GDP in El Salvador remained essentially unchanged at about US$ 1,090 in 1990 dollars between 1983 and 1990 (IDB, 1991, p. 273).[7] In Nicaragua, GDP per capita in 1990 was about half of what it had been in 1981 – $ 505 compared with $ 922. The Central American countries, with the exception of Sandinista Nicaragua, began to look outward during the 1980s to seek foreign investment to develop non-traditional agricultural and manufactured exports as a way out of their economic difficulties. President Reagan's CBI was a catalyst for the new economic development strategy. Protective barriers erected during the heyday of the CACM were reduced, but still hesitantly. Thus far, the only country that appears to have benefited from the export promotion strategy is Costa Rica: in constant 1988 dollars, Costa Rican exports of goods and services increased by 67 per cent between 1981 and 1990, from $ 1,191 million to $ 1,987 million. In the other Central American countries, export volume has stagnated or actually declined.

It remains to be seen if the other Central American countries can succeed in attracting foreign investment and in exporting non-traditional exports. Peace may be a necessary – but on its own insufficient – condition to achieve these goals. The envi-

---

[7] All dollars in this paper are U.S. dollars.

Table 5.5. Total net resource flows: Central American countries, 1980-89 (millions of US dollars)

Year	Costa Rica	El Salvador	Guatemala	Honduras	Nicaragua
1980	164.3	134.9	136.6	198.3	40.1
1981	99.7	188.4	222.0	216.9	307.8
1982	134.7	259.4	203.6	179.2	170.6
1983	288.4	337.4	215.7	259.5	171.0
1984	305.5	303.1	174.2	391.5	153.4
1985	413.5	379.0	337.7	386.1	116.5
1986	331.8	330.8	126.1	297.9	171.8
1987	242.7	422.2	160.6	243.6	176.4
1988	161.3	413.0	259.2	376.4	242.4
1989	229.1	427.8	206.8	242.9	182.9

Source: OECD, 1984, 1987, and 1991.

ronment for private investment in Nicaragua remains inhospitable despite the transition to democratic government in the 1990 elections. Instability there continues because of disputes over property rights and the deep political polarization of the country. The political cleavage in El Salvador is equally deep and the truce in the civil war is too new to determine its durability. The social tensions of Guatemala are not likely to disappear. There is some danger that foreign aid flows to Honduras, the most backward Central American country, will decline because the region no longer commands the international attention it received during the 1980s.

5. Past foreign aid

Net resource flows from all sources to Central America, 1980 to 1989

During the 1980s, the five Central American countries received $12.3 billion dollars in net resource flows from bilateral and multilateral sources, including direct private investment and export credits (see Table 5.5). Most of these flows came from OECD countries, primarily the United States. Nicaragua received an estimated $3.5 billion in economic aid from the former USSR and its Eastern European allies, plus billions more in military aid (FBIS, 1992a). The Inter-American Development Bank (IDB) was the main source of net multilateral assistance to the region ($1.82 billion),[8] followed by the United Nations through some of its specialized agencies ($618 million), and then by the World Bank ($528 million). During this period, Mexico and Venezuela also provided oil credits valued at several hundred million dollars to Cen-

---
[8] The Inter-American Development Bank provided Central America with a total of $5.2 billion between 1961 and 1990 (IDB, 1991a, p. 12).

tral America. Private flows were $686 million, but were becoming increasingly negative by the end of the decade as interest and payments of principal fell due.

In current dollars, El Salvador, with 25.9 per cent of the total, or $3.2 billion, was the main recipient of financial resources, followed by Honduras (22.6 per cent), Costa Rica (19.2 per cent), Guatemala (16.6 per cent), and Nicaragua (15.7 per cent). In per capita terms (i.e. net resource flows received between 1980 and 1989 over the 1990 population), the ranking is different: Costa Rica received the most substantial flows ($786 per capita), followed by El Salvador ($608), Nicaragua ($499), Honduras ($304), and Guatemala ($222).

United States bilateral assistance

Between 1980 and 1989, United States bilateral assistance (including the economic support fund) amounted to $6 billion, or about 50 per cent of total net resource flows (exclusive of direct private investment).[9] The main recipient of United States bilateral assistance was El Salvador with $2.7 billion, or 44.3 per cent of the total, followed by Costa Rica and Honduras, with about 20 per cent each. Guatemala obtained $772 million or 13 per cent, while Nicaragua received only $112 million, or 2 per cent. During this same period, the United States also provided Central America with $1.47 billion in military assistance. El Salvador was the main recipient of this with $949 million, or 65 per cent of the total, followed by Honduras with $454 million or 31 per cent. Costa Rica and Guatemala each received about 2 per cent of the total. Of the total United States assistance of $7.5 billion, 80.4 per cent was allocated for economic assistance and 19.6 per cent for military assistance.

Trends in United States assistance in constant 1990 dollars

The level of United States assistance to Central America during the 1980s (in 1990 dollars) was considerably above the historical trend (Figure 5.1). United States assistance to Central America rose during the 1960s under the Alliance for Progress. It declined during most of the 1970s, only to rise again during the 1980s in response to national security concerns. United States assistance reached its peak in the mid-1980s following the recommendations of the Kissinger Commission, appointed by President Reagan. The Commission recommended $6 billion in immediate economic assistance to Central America, excluding Nicaragua, between United States fiscal years 1985 and 1989, plus military assistance. While the target figure for economic assistance was not reached, Central America did receive $4.1 billion, or 68.5 per cent of the suggested figure. This was a considerable share of global United States economic assistance in light of Central America's population.

Most of the economic assistance went to El Salvador, Honduras and Costa Rica, with only limited amounts allocated to Guatemala and Nicaragua. Several hun-

[9] Between 1990 and 1992, the United States will have provided an additional $2.6 billion in economic aid to Central America distributed as follows: Costa Rica $173.8 million; El Salvador $912.2 million; Guatemala $266.3 million; Honduras $495 million; and Nicaragua $730.4 million.

Figure 5.1. United States aid to Central America, 1962 to 1990 (1990 dollars)

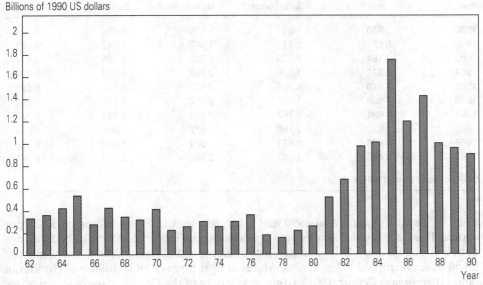

Source: Sanford, 1989, p. 10.

dred million dollars were also assigned to Central American regional programmes, including funds for Belize and Panama. The bulk of the assistance was granted under the Economic Support Fund (ESF). While ESF aid is provided to assist countries facing national security problems – and hence is equated with military assistance by critics of the United States foreign assistance programme – it is usually granted as balance-of-payments support to help with a country's economic development objectives. Most ESF resources earmarked for Central America during the 1980s were used to assist the private sector acquire needed imports (Sanford, 1989, pp. 44-45).

United States aid provided to Central America during the decade shifted from concessional loans to grants. Military assistance to Central America was mostly in grants as well. The major portion of United States development assistance to Central America during the 1980s was for agricultural programmes, followed by a miscellaneous category called selected development activities (SDA), and health and education activities. SDA included aid designed to support the development of the private sector, and to help Central America take advantage of the export opportunities provided by the Caribbean Basin Initiative. The export focus explains why agricultural assistance shifted from support to meeting basic human needs and promoting rural development, to the promotion of commercial agriculture and non-traditional exports (Sanford, 1989, p. 51). A marked increase in education programmes followed the Kissinger Commission's recommendation to increase the number of scholarships for Central American students to attend United States educational institutions.

Table 5.6. Total debt stocks, Central America, 1980 and 1982-90 (millions of US dollars)

Year	Costa Rica	El Salvador	Guatemala	Honduras	Nicaragua
1980	2 735	911	1 166	1 470	2 171
1982	3 627	1 419	1 537	1 842	3 331
1983	4 164	1 673	1 799	2 126	4 174
1984	3 973	1 730	2 353	2 284	5 106
1985	4 370	1 757	2 623	2 731	5 691
1986	4 529	1 713	2 752	2 974	6 181
1987	4 691	1 752	2 770	3 302	7 322
1988	4 532	1 760	2 577	3 304	8 052
1989	4 468	1 851	2 601	3 350	9 205
1990	3 490	1 863	2 702	3 449	10 281

Source: World Bank, 1990a; IDB, 1991b.

Central America in 1990 had a foreign debt of $21.8 billion or $822 per capita. The debt breakdown by country is shown in Table 5.6. Much of Nicaragua's debt is to the former USSR and its Eastern European allies and, most likely, most of it will never be repaid.[10] The United States in 1991 forgave $457 million of Honduran debt (*Washington Report*, 1991). Commercial debt of the Central American countries is traded in secondary markets at a fraction of nominal value. By taking advantage of the Brady Plan, Costa Rica, the Central American country most indebted to private banks, was able to reduce its foreign debt by 22 per cent in 1990, or by about $1 billion (IDB, 1991b, p. 69). But even with such a reduction, Costa Rica faced interest payments in 1990 equivalent to 17 per cent of exports. The 1990 debt service ratios (debt service due, although not necessarily met, in relation to exports of goods and services) was 63 per cent for Nicaragua and 30 per cent for Honduras, which are extremely high. The ratios are more modest for Guatemala (9 per cent) and El Salvador (12 per cent).

6. Evaluation of past foreign aid and optimizing future assistance

As is evident from the preceding, aid flows to Central America jumped sharply during the 1980s and this coincided with a drastic decline in per capita GDP in every country. The reasons for the per capita GDP decline have already been discussed. They included open warfare, deterioration in the terms of trade, and the collapse of the CACM.[11]

[10] In a letter from the Government of the Federation of Russia printed in the Managua daily newspaper *La Prensa*, the level of Nicaragua's debt to the Federation of Russia was given as $2.671 billion, and overdue repayments were put at $458.9 million. Some of these loans were described as being in United States dollars and German marks, which the USSR had to borrow on world money markets and on which the Federation of Russia is still meeting service payments (FBIS, 1992b, p. 25).

[11] The deterioration in the terms of trade was most sharp in El Salvador, where the index was 62 in 1988 on a scale 1988=100 (Saborio, 1990, p. 283).

For all these reasons, the relationship between foreign aid received and economic growth during the 1980s was distorted. However, this very distortion makes evident that foreign aid cannot be assessed in a vacuum. There is no assurance that there will not be comparable distortions in the future. It is thus necessary to ask what conditions are necessary internally within Central America to make the sustained provision of foreign aid effective as a migrant-reducing tool. Because the external factors that Central America must confront are beyond its control, the required internal changes must also serve to mitigate the regional effects of an adverse external situation, for example, by diversifying the composition of the region's exports and reinvigorating the CACM.

Various commentators use different words and have their own priorities among the several themes, but stresses are similar on what must be done to create the conditions for recovery, and hence for effective use of foreign assistance to reduce emigration incentives. These are the restoration of internal peace and security, the strengthening of democratic institutions, economic reforms, and social justice (see Washington Institute Task Force Report, 1984; *Report of the International Commission for Central American Recovery and Development*, the Sanford Commission, 1989; and Smith, 1991.) The Esquipulas II accords of 1987 of the five Central American presidents, spearheaded by the then president of Costa Rica Oscar Arias, gave pride of place to establishing firm and lasting peace in the region and democratization (see *Report of the International Commission*, 1989, pp. 121-126 for the text of Esquipulas II).[12] We will deal with these issues first as well.[13]

Latin America as a whole, and even most countries in Central America, spend relatively modest sums on arms. In the period 1972-78, the Latin American and Caribbean countries spent on average 2.3 per cent of GDP on the military, compared with 5.9 per cent for developing countries generally and 3.8 per cent for industrial countries (Hewitt, 1991, p. 23). Nicaragua was the big spender in Central America during this period, devoting 10 per cent to 20 per cent of GDP to the military; at the other end of the scale, Costa Rica spent less than 1.6 per cent of GDP for military purposes (Hewitt, 1991, p. 25). The industrial countries contributed to the military build-up in Central America, particularly the United States and the USSR. Indeed, developments in Central America in the 1980s were dominated by Cold War rivalries. These have obviously now dissipated, although each Central American country continued to receive some arms transfers in 1990 (Grimmett, 1991, p. 82).

However, the budgetary aspect is far from the full story of the cost of military action in the region. By the time the Government of El Salvador and the guerrilla opposition reached agreement in January 1992, some 75,000 people had been killed during the 12 years of conflict (*Washington Post*, 1 Jan. 1992, p. 1). Economic and social development could not proceed under these circumstances, any more than they could in Nicaragua during the long civil war abetted by foreign intervention.

---

[12] President Arias received the Nobel Peace Prize largely in recognition of his achievement in bringing about this agreement.

[13] Germany is apparently also placing heavy emphasis on this aspect of development by proposing to reduce its foreign assistance to countries that spend heavily on weapons (*New York Times*, 3 Aug. 1991, p. 3).

However, peace may be coming back to the region and this should end most of the bloodshed and permit the reduction of military expenditures.

The interplay between the military and civilian government leaders remains a formidable issue in all the countries of Central America, save for Costa Rica. Military-civilian relations have changed considerably since the early 1980s, but the division of power between the two remains uncertain throughout the region (Millett, 1991). This uncertainty cuts across two themes, the restoration of order and the consequent reduction of resource use for military purposes, and the vigour of democratic regimes in the region. The thesis of the Sanford Commission is that "without democracy, there will be no lasting peace" (*Report of the International Commission*, 1989, p. 10). The argument of the Kissinger Commission was that economic and social development requires the "legitimation of governments by free consent," which entails political pluralism, freedom of expression, respect for human rights, an independent and effective system of justice, and free elections without repression (*Report of the President's National Bipartisan Commission*, 1984, p. 16). The connection between democracy and legitimacy is quite complex in Central America. It obviously entails other variables as well, such as the rate of economic growth, how the benefits of this growth are distributed, and the acceptance of these outcomes by powerful groups in society. One author has put this last point in different terms, namely, that powerful non-governmental actors must cooperate with the government in carrying out the economic development strategy, or at least not seek to thwart it (Crosby, 1990, p. 126).

We will make only a few comments here on the link between democracy and development in Central America. The most successful government in the region in terms of economic growth during the past decade, Costa Rica, is also the most democratic, the one whose legitimacy is not really in question. Yet it is hard to attribute Costa Rica's growth solely to the existence of a democratic regime. Costa Rica was also the one country that either did not have an insurgency movement or was not pulled deeply into the conflict in Nicaragua. It was therefore able to devote most of its efforts to internal economic and social problems. The fact that Costa Rica did not share the political-military turmoil of the other countries may have been due to the fact that its government was seen as legitimate.

The decade of the 1980s in Latin America was notable for the growth of democratic regimes. This was true in Central America as well. Many Latin American democracies are quite fragile and it is far from clear that they are durable. Yet they emerged at a time of economic decline unprecedented since the great depression and, in Central America, during a period of conflict. The political ethos of Latin America may be more democratic today than at any previous time in the hemisphere's history. In our view, this is a propitious climate for making the kinds of economic adjustments that are necessary to reduce emigration pressures.

We do not wish to oversimplify. There is much social injustice in the region and this dilutes the meaning of free political choice. The military remains a powerful group in all the countries other than Costa Rica, and this will strain the growth of democratic structures. Powerful economic groups may resist the structural changes that are required to secure sustained economic growth whose benefits are equitably distributed and this can frustrate the task of governments. Finally, because of the lack of experience with democratic norms, one should not expect democracy to flourish in Central America along the lines of the European or United States model.

While many commentators have argued for simultaneous structural economic change and the establishment of democracies, recent experience in the region itself (e.g. Chile and now Mexico) and elsewhere (in east Asia, Eastern Europe, and the former USSR) makes it clear that there is a sequencing of progression, that glasnost and perestroika do not move at the same pace or occur in the same sequence in all countries. Our judgement is that the necessary economic and social restructuring should not be deferred until the political opening is complete.

Ultimately, the case for providing sustained foreign aid over several generations as a way to drastically reduce emigration pressure from Central America must rest on the conviction that the assistance will itself lead to significant, sustained economic growth with greater social justice. The end to military conflict is a necessary condition for attaining this outcome, but obviously not sufficient unto itself. Flourishing of democracy is necessary to legitimate governments that will be forced to take what at times will be painful and controversial actions; and the very process of economic and social development should strengthen democratic institutions.

In addition to the apparent decline in military conflict in Central America and the emergence of fragile democracies, the region is undergoing a significant change in development philosophy, shifting from regimes of high import protection to efforts to promote non-traditional exports. As was noted earlier, Central America's eco-system limits the extent to which agricultural exports can be expanded and past environmental degradation may even lead to reductions in the existing level of these exports. To date, Central America has moved somewhat hesitantly to reduce its import barriers, tariff and non-tariff, but the direction is clearly toward liberalization (ECLAC, 1991a, pp. 4-5). In our view, looking outward in the production and export of non-traditional products is a necessary step in the reinvigoration of the Central American Common Market.

The promise that now exists is that the CACM may truly become a trade liberalizing integration arrangement. If the common external tariff and the import barriers against non-members are low, this will facilitate non-traditional exports not only within the region, but outside as well, and will reduce the import penalty on the less competitive member countries. This implies that future foreign assistance should put much emphasis on restructuring the CACM in such a way as to encourage non-traditional exports, and thereby augment employment. However, the employment-creation aspects of manufactured exports should not be overstated. Job creation in manufacturing export activities are unlikely, even in the best of circumstances, to exceed 10 per cent of additions to the labour force in the region (Tucker, 1991, p. 103). This is not negligible, but neither is it a panacea.

We wish to amplify the earlier discussion on the limits to using the land to provide a basis for absorbing the region's growing labour force. Central America is dominated by hilly and highland zones which together make up between 73 and 95 per cent of the total land area in the individual countries (Leonard, 1987, p. 4). Depletion rates of forests, soils, fisheries, and other resources exceed renewal rates, and water pollution has reached critical levels in many parts of Central America (ibid., p. xvi). One estimate is that less than 40 per cent of the region's original forests remain and that two-thirds of the loss has occurred since 1950 (ibid. p. xi). These realities imply that increases in earnings from agricultural exports cannot be based on expansion of the area devoted to export agriculture, but rather require increased yields. This outcome, in turn, is constricted by the soil depletion and water pollution that can ensue. Leonard further argues that without drastic changes in land-use patterns, agricultural production in Central America will continue to lag behind population growth (p. 109). These circumstances, coupled with the problem of creating sufficient employment in urban areas, led Leonard to conclude that what is needed are sharp increases in off-farm rural employment, stimulated by investment in infrastructure and the encouragement of small and medium-sized enterprises (p. 177). The value of taking this direction in future aid programmes will be discussed in the next section.

Bulmer-Thomas (1987) has criticized past foreign aid to Central America for embedding the resources received into national budgets and failing to obtain financial commitments from national governments. This shortcoming, he argues, was compounded by the fact that many of the institutions created operated as foreign enclaves and could not function once the foreign financing was terminated (pp. 178-9). Leonard argues that much of the assistance provided to the beef cattle industry contributed little to export receipts in relation to the huge amounts of land devoted to pasture, much of which could have been more productive as farmland in land-scarce Central America (ibid., pp. 102-3). Many of the important institutions that could have been strengthened with foreign assistance, such as those related to the CACM, fell instead into desuetude.

Perhaps the most significant shortcoming of development patterns in most Central American countries has been insufficient attention to social issues. In the mid-1980s, the poorest 20 per cent of the population in the five countries received between 2 per cent and 5 per cent of national income, and the richest 20 per cent between 50 per cent and 65 per cent (Leonard, 1987, p. 205). The middle-income groups, the 60 per cent between these two extremes, were thereby constrained in their participation in national economies. This undoubtedly contributed to the political polarization that was evident in all the countries other than Costa Rica. The skewed income distribution contributed as well to emigration from the region once military conflict began and incomes generally declined. In the countryside, from which people emigrated either to urban areas or outside the region, emigration itself, plus the distorted land-use patterns, presumably increased relative deprivation (Stark and Taylor, 1991) and stimulated further emigration out of Central America.

It will certainly not be easy to devise aid programmes for Central America which will be optimal in terms of income and employment generation, and hence for staunching the pressure to emigrate, but it is important to learn some lessons about what not to do. The future task is inherently formidable because of the devastation of the last decade and the immensity of the development problem. This task will be complicated by three other problems that must be taken into account.

First, it is clear that the main aid donor to Central America, the United States, is losing its appetite for foreign aid. This is particularly true now that the Cold War, which was the stimulus for the large aid to Central America during the 1980s, has ended. United States attention on Central America has always been episodic and is now in one of its trough periods (see Nuccio, 1991). It remains to be seen whether the immigration focus – the focus on the reduction of emigration from the region – can attract the attention of the United States Government and legislature in the same way that the Cold War did.

Second, there is much evidence that funds to multilateral development agencies will not only not increase, but in fact decline. This has led to the position that what are needed are better development strategies to compensate for the shortfall in resources (Summers, 1991).[14]

Third, if resource flows are in fact constrained, this will limit the influence of the aid donors in reaching agreement with aid recipients on the conditions that will be most effective in achieving development, or put differently, in raising income and employment sufficiently to eliminate the pressure to emigrate from Central America (Weintraub, 1991).

7. Needed future foreign aid to staunch emigration pressures

The discussion that follows assumes that there will be no military conflict in Central America over the next two generations. This will permit the dedication of resources to economic and social development; and the emigration from Nicaragua, El Salvador, and to some extent from Guatemala, that was induced by internal conflicts during the 1980s, will not recur. It assumes as well that the process of democratization that has begun in the region will intensify.

No assumption is made that the amount of aid needed will in fact be forthcoming. Rather, the analysis seeks to determine the level and the nature of aid that is necessary to accomplish the purpose set out in the terms of reference: "What forms, contents and dimensions would foreign aid have to take in the case of Central American countries to reduce drastically, in one or two generations, the desire of their citizens to seek work in the United States?"

In summarizing the lessons learned from past experience with development programmes, the economist who directed the work for the World Bank's *World Development Report 1991* said that growth in total factor productivity was more important than capital growth. An important feature of the policy atmosphere to accomplish this, he argued, was for governments to do less where markets can work and do more where the markets cannot, such as in fostering education, environmental protection, and the development of social and physical infrastructure. At the macroeconomic level, the emphasis in this analysis was on stability, and at the microeconomic level, on developing a competitive economy, including competition from imports (Thomas, 1991). This analysis is accepted in what follows.[15]

---

[14] To quote from page 3 of Summers' article: "This suggests that, in the end, what will make the greatest difference for development are well-implemented, good strategies, and not simply in the transfer of resources." Lawrence Summers is the chief economist of the World Bank.

[15] This prescription is World Bank orthodoxy, but that does not make it wrong.

Foreign assistance to Central America will come from a variety of official sources – bilaterally from governments, especially from the United States, and from international financial institutions. While the assumption on which this study is based is that a reduction in emigration pressure in Central America will be the major objective of United States aid there, this is unlikely to be the regional objective for other countries or for the multilateral development banks. If eliminating the pressure for emigration from other regions, say Africa, is the major objective of European countries, there is thus a basis for what in the United States is referred to as "log rolling", that is, the United States contributing to African aid with objectives other than staunching emigration and the Europeans to Central America on the same basis. Because donor countries have different objectives and styles in providing aid, and the multilateral organizations still other ways of operating, there will have to be a division of labour, but some assurance will be needed that the whole induces some consistency of policy by recipient countries. This is probably best managed by a coordinating or consultative group, presumably chaired by one of the international organizations – logically either the World Bank or the IDB.

How much aid is needed?

Calculating the amount of foreign assistance needed to accomplish a complex task of economic, social, and political development is an inexact art. And, as noted, practitioners engaged in this process are not even sure that the aid volume is the critical variable.

The Kissinger Commission, apart from its immediate programme, calculated that $20.8 billion in external finance (that is, not merely ODA from the United States) was needed over the period 1984-90 (*Report of the President's National Bipartisan Commission*, 1984, p. 78). The economic objective was to restore per capita GDP in 1990 to levels achieved in 1980. The technique used to calculate external financing needs was a two-gap model, that is to provide external resources to close the savings and balance-of-payments gaps of the Central American countries, although the figures were adjusted for political and other considerations deemed important by the Commission. The two-gap model was a favoured technique in the 1960s for estimating foreign aid needs. It is by no means a foolproof method in that it requires assumptions on shifting variables, such as the incremental capital-output ratio; and the estimate leaves static the changes in capital requirements brought about by changing factor productivity. In any event, while United States foreign aid increased sharply following the release of the Kissinger Commission report, it did not reach the levels recommended. In addition, a proposal considered even more important than the aid level, that of establishing a multilateral Central American Development Organization to evaluate country policies and to coordinate aid disbursements, never came into existence.[16]

---

[16] An ambitious CADO, with significant independent powers, was killed by the U.S. Agency for International Development, which feared its loss of authority.

The Sanford Commission, apart from its immediate action plan, recommended that external financial flows of $2 billion a year for five years were needed, starting in 1990, with the objective of attaining GDP growth of 5.5 per cent a year (*Report of the International Commission*, 1989, pp. 81-82). The technique used in this calculation was based primarily on filling a balance-of-payments gap.[17] This analysis is obviously no more precise than that of the Kissinger Commission. The total amounts of external assistance set forth by the two commissions are quite close to each other, but their distribution among countries differs, as do their assumptions about debt relief.

We have approached the resource requirements from the perspective of demography and job creation. The quantitative dimensions of the job-creation problem are set forth in the second section of this report showing the future growth of the economically active population. Based on past performance, the rough relationship between job creation and GDP growth is the following:

$$\frac{\Delta GDP}{2} = \Delta \text{job creation}$$

This can be expressed in percentage terms: a 6 per cent increase in GDP leads to a 3 per cent increase in job creation. The relationship was taken from experience in the region before the turmoil in the 1980s.

Our demographic and labour force projections to the year 2025 indicate that the five Central American countries will have to create at least 340,000 jobs a year during the 1990s just to handle net additions into the economically active population. This number will rise to 560,000 annually by 2020-2025, the end of the projection period (see Table 5.2 above). Official data on open urban unemployment for Costa Rica, El Salvador, Guatemala and Honduras are relatively low, between 5 per cent and 10 per cent, although the figures are much higher in Nicaragua (ECLAC, 1991b, p. 39). However, as noted earlier, underemployment is substantial, both in the countryside and the cities. Unemployment data in Central America are highly unreliable and we therefore do not place much significance on them (Bulmer-Thomas, 1987, p. 252). What we do assume, however, is that the 340,000 annual figure for net additions to the EAP during the next decade probably understates the requirement for job creation by as much as 50,000 to 100,000 a year until the unemployment/underemployment backlog is eliminated.

The EAP in Central America now numbers about 9 million persons. It would take an annual GDP increase of 8 per cent to increase the demand for labour by 360,000 each year (9 million x .04). Put differently, every 1 per cent increase in annual GDP leads to the creation of about 45,000 jobs, and it would thus take about an 8 per cent increase in GDP to provide about 360,000 new jobs.

These are admittedly rough estimates of the need for job creation. The relationship between the change in GDP and the change in demand for labour is not the same in all sectors, nor is it constant over time. But the estimates are no more rough

---

[17] The methodology is given briefly in Appendix 2 of the Commission's report. More detailed calculations are contained in Bradford, 1989, which gives a range of aid requirements depending on the level of debt relief granted to the countries of Central America.

than using other techniques with equally questionable assumptions.[18] If we assume that the investment required for each new job is $30,000, this implies a need for $10.8 billion of investment per year, or more than 40 per cent of GDP. If each new job requires only $20,000 of investment, the required investment/GDP ratio falls to 29 per cent. This calculation permits us to derive a savings gap. Gross fixed capital formation as a proportion of GDP is substantially lower than either figure calculated above in each of the five countries: about 22 per cent in Costa Rica; 12 per cent in El Salvador; 15 per cent in Guatemala; 13 per cent in Honduras; and 7 per cent in Nicaragua (*International Financial Statistics*, October 1991). Using the relationship $20,000 of investment per job, these calculations imply a need for external resources of some $2 billion a year, a figure similar to that of the Kissinger and Sanford Commissions. This is a most conservative figure of need for foreign resources. We doubt that the gross investment per job is as low as $20,000.

Current (1989) flows of external resources to Central America are $1.3 billion a year and would therefore have to be increased to provide the basis for employment for those entering the labour market or now under- or unemployed. The amount of aid needed would not be constant over 20 to 40 years. It would rise as increases in the EAP grew larger, but could also decline gradually as the backlog of under- and unemployed persons dissipates and as internal policies in the five countries serve to augment savings and investment ratios and attract private capital inflows. In any event, aid to Central America would have to increase substantially – our calculations indicate that it would have to double from the current level and remain at this high level for several decades. A modest amount of this requirement could come from debt relief, although once forgiven, debts cannot be forgiven again.

We wish to stress once more that we have little confidence in any calculation of the exact amount of aid needed. Apart from assumptions that are certain to contain simplifications, we, like the World Bank economists, put greater stress on policy measures taken by the country than we do on precise levels of capital flows to stimulate development. Capital flows without adequate policy measures will accomplish little to stifle emigration pressures. An important purpose of the external resource flows is to stimulate the proper policy response.

---

[18] One other estimate worth citing is that of Espenshade, 1989. He calculated that in Central America, it took $19,000 of investment to create each new job based on 1982 data for each of the countries. The ratio is low, significantly lower than for other countries in the Caribbean Basin. The figure of Mexico, for example, was almost $49,000 and for Panama $64,000. If the ratio is $20,000 of investment per job, this implies an annual investment need of $7 billion to create 350,000 new jobs; if the ratio is instead $30,000 of investment per job, based on the need to invest in non-traditional activities, this implies an annual investment need of $10.5 billion. For the five countries taken together, GDP is now about $25 billion in current United States dollars (World Bank, 1990b) which means that at the ratio of $30,000 investment per new job, gross investment must be more than 40 per cent of GDP. Some of this could come from internal sources and some from external assistance.

Policy recommendations

Foreign aid could work through two mechanisms to reduce emigration pressure. One is directly on population, to provide assistance in family planning to reduce birth rates. The second is to increase economic opportunities and job creation in Central America. Birth rates should decline as incomes rise, which means that the two mechanisms are not fully separable. The suggestions that follow are designed with these two mechanisms in mind. However, two limitations of this strategy should be noted. A number of observers have provided evidence that the very process of development stimulates migration, such as from rural areas to cities, and this disruption also increases migration out of the country (Massey, 1991, pp. 14-15;[19] and Gregory, 1991, p. 56). Díaz-Briquets and Weintraub concluded after a review of the relevant literature that a modest increase in income in a low-income country leads to increased emigration in the short term. They said they found no study contradicting this conclusion (Díaz-Briquets and Weintraub, 1991a, p. xvii).[20] Their conclusion is that the increase in income to reduce emigration pressure has to continue year after year for some time. The same conclusion can be reached with respect to foreign aid. It will work to staunch emigration only if the aid is sustained over many years, such as over the one or two generations specified in the terms of reference for this study.

The second limitation that must be kept in mind is that if the key determinant of emigration is the income disparity between the sending and receiving country, it could take up to 150 years for this to be erased. The weighted average per capita GDP in Central America is about $1,000 a year. If this increased by 3 per cent a year, per capita GDP would be $1,806 in 20 years and $2,427 in 30 years. If United States per capita GDP increased by only 1 per cent a year from its current level of roughly $20,000, it would be $24,404 in 20 years and $26,957 in 30 years. In other words, even at three times the rate of per capita GDP increase in Central America, the absolute income disparity between the region and the United States would grow for decades before it started to narrow. This, too, points to the need for consistency of policy over long periods before practical results can emerge.

This phenomenon of compound interest starting from disparate initial points highlights one other issue that can be crucial in the goal of reducing emigration pressure. This is that emigration is motivated not just by absolute income differences, or even relative disparity within the sending country, but by perceptions of opportunity at home for oneself and one's family. The direction of change can be as important as the absolute change. The conviction that opportunities at home are improving may be the key incentive for staying home rather than completely disrupting one's

---

[19] Massey (1991) provides data that the European development process from 1846 to 1924 led to just such an increase in emigration. He argues that the current levels of emigration from Latin American and Caribbean countries to the United States are precisely what one would expect based on the European experience.

[20] One possible explanation for this phenomenon is that for a low-income country, the absolute income increase in any one year, even at a high rate of growth, is quite modest. Thus, a 3 per cent increase in, say, El Salvador, would raise per capita GDP from $820 to $845 a year, hardly enough to alter life styles, but perhaps useful in helping to finance a trip out of the country.

life and moving to an alien society.[21] Table 5.3 above shows the sharp decline in apprehensions of undocumented Nicaraguans seeking entry into the United States in fiscal years 1990 and 1991 after the election of Violeta Chamorro as president and the cessation of hostilities. This is another piece of evidence that income disparities by themselves do not explain migration.

Our suggestions for the use of foreign aid to reduce emigration pressure can be divided under two broad headings: assistance given to areas from which there is significant out-migration; and that which deals more broadly with national economic development in Central America.

Assistance to out-migration areas within countries

There is extensive literature, plus considerable experience in Asian countries, on the development of regional centres in rural areas from which many migrants come (see essays in Díaz-Briquets and Weintraub, 1991b). The development of these regional centres is not based on increased agricultural employment, but rather on establishing small and medium-sized enterprises to permit migrants to move to relatively familiar areas not far from their original homes.

Because of its limited land area suitable for cultivation, the prospects for increasing agricultural output in Central America by expanding the cultivable area do not exist to any significant extent. Despite the fact that all of the countries are becoming increasingly urban, the rural population in Central America is still large, typically between 40 per cent and 60 per cent of the total. Thus, while there is no significant scope for keeping them down on the farm, there is still much pressure for people in Central America to move from farms to other places, particularly to urban areas; and it is precisely this movement that may trigger a later exodus out of the country.

Our recommendation to aid donors is to stress the development of small and medium-sized businesses in or near the rural areas from which there is now substantial out-migration. Our reasoning is based on a number of considerations. The first is as stated above, namely that intraregional migration is apt to be more congenial and less disruptive than forcing further overcrowding in large cities. The second is that half the jobs in Central America are now generated by businesses with 50 employees or less (Leguizamùn, 1991, p. 14). Finally, if relative deprivation in rural villages is an important determinant of emigration (Stark and Taylor, 1991) providing work opportunities nearby can provide some scope to facilitate equalization of incomes without migration out of the country.

The issue that must be addressed is how best to provide employment opportunities away from overcrowded capitals in Central America for persons who will inevitably leave agriculture. There may also be urban residents who would prefer to live in less crowded, less polluted places. The occupations into which these internal

---

[21] Gregory (1991, p. 53) points out that income disparities much lower than between Mexico and the United States led to large migration flows from Colombia to Venezuela, and from Greece and Portugal to the EC during the 1970s. Until the 1980s, larger income disparities between Central American countries and the United States than between Mexico and the United States did not lead to large-scale emigration out of Central America. This did not occur until the disruption of the unstable political situation and the civil wars there.

migrants would enter would most likely be small and medium-sized enterprises, such as workshops (*talleres* in Spanish), manufacturing and assembly plants, and service establishments. These can be located in essentially rural areas or in medium-sized regional centres from which rural areas can be serviced. Because the evidence is that emigrants who leave Central America tend to be above the average in education and socioeconomic status, it is necessary to consider medium-sized regional centres and not just rural areas. Our belief is that both possibilities should be examined.

The recommendation is straightforward, but its implementation is complex. Assisting the formation of viable businesses in rural areas and in small and medium-sized cities involves development of necessary skills, having in place the necessary physical infrastructure, providing credit for business establishments, giving technical assistance in production and marketing, teaching accounting skills, and instilling entrepreneurial motivation (see Leguizamùn, 1991, for a discussion of these issues). Social services dealing with education, health, and family planning must be provided to these rural regional centres (Gregory, 1991, pp. 57-59). Choosing the location of potentially viable regional centres is a delicate task. The centre must obviously be in a location that has the necessary natural base, such as water, and which would be relatively convenient for migrants from the surrounding area. The choice is important because this then determines where investment will be made in infrastructure development. Mexico, a few years ago, undertook a comprehensive study of the regional resource and population configuration of the nation with the objective of determining the desirability of different locations for development, but there is little evidence that the findings were fully exploited. The tendency in Mexico, as in Central America, has been to devote most central government attention to overall macroeconomic policy and give little heed to the microeconomic and microsocial details of regional development (Tamayo and Lozano, 1991a, 1991b).

We recommend that aid donors cooperate with the authorities in the Central American countries to undertake a comprehensive study of the viability of different regional locations for development and the receipt of migrants from their surrounding areas. These studies would have to be comprehensive in laying out the resources available in the regional centres and the investment that would be required to make them suitable as development sites. The experiences of Asian countries such as Taiwan (China) and of Mexico, can be drawn on in carrying out these examinations.

Appraisals of past foreign assistance to Central America have provided much insight on actions to avoid. One of the "don'ts" implicit in the previous recommendations is a development strategy that places great reliance on extensive agriculture in most of Central America. Another don't is to rely almost exclusively on overall macroeconomic policy at the expense of regional development. This was a common failing of past Latin American development strategies. This emphasis was accompanied by the centralization of tax collection, expenditure and administration, giving little authority to state and local authorities. The current focus in Latin America in favour of export-led development carries the danger of fostering large industrial complexes and ignoring the role that smaller enterprises can play, particularly in regional locations. *Our recommendation to donors is to encourage administrative decentralization in Central America and to insist on support to small and medium-sized businesses and not just to larger enterprises more able to directly generate exports.*

A corollary to this recommendation is the need to reorder priorities in development policy to avoid a common practice of the past in Latin America, which was to stress industrialization under import-substitution programmes at the expense of agricultural, and hence, rural, development (see Arroyo Alejandre et al., 1991, pp. 71-3). This took many forms, such as low producer prices, subsidies to residents in urban areas, the import of food on concessional terms at the expense of national production because of the budget support the imported food provided,[22] and the failure to provide adequate assistance to the small farmer. This is both a regional and a macroeconomic issue. The failures of past policy of favouring industrial and urban development over agricultural and rural development are now well known, but the old habits have not yet disappeared. *Our recommendation is that aid donors insist on national policies that do not penalize agricultural production and rural development generally.*

Using foreign aid to reduce emigration pressure

Before making the positive recommendations, we believe it useful to list some policies that experience teaches us to avoid in future aid programmes in Central America. Some of these have already been noted: excessive centralization of decision-making and administration; penalizing agriculture for the benefit of manufacturing; subsidizing the consumption of urban residents on the backs of agricultural producers; starving small and medium-sized businesses in credit allocation; placing almost exclusive reliance on macroeconomic policies and ignoring the more microeconomic needs of regions; and more generally, to operate regional development programmes without adequate study of the options for location and expenditures.

Other shortcomings of past aid and development policy have been identified in this study and in the literature on Central America. Agricultural programmes of the past have given little heed to their environmental consequences, particularly of soil erosion. Raising cattle for the purpose of increasing beef exports has often used lands more suitable for the production of crops. Beyond that, the stress on export agriculture, while understandable in terms of generating foreign exchange, has often taken place at the expense of production of staple products for local consumption.[23] In theory, if export agriculture provided a higher return than production for local needs, the increased resource generation could be used to finance food and fibre imports for domestic needs. However, because of income inequalities, the ability of large segments of the population to obtain foods not produced in the immediate region is more theoretical than practical. Much foreign aid in the past resulted in programmes that survived only as long as they were supported by the donors (see Bulmer-Thomas, 1987). We now know that projects endure only if they are supported by the host country. Thus, donors must avoid providing all the local currency financing or setting up projects that operate as enclaves divorced from the total development programme of the recipient country.

---

[22] United States programmes under Public Law 480, popularly referred to as the Food for Peace programme, often had this effect.

[23] A discussion on these issues can be found in Leonard, 1987.

It is clear, both from what to avoid and what to support, that foreign aid programmes require conditionality. In a sense, much of the discussion in this study is designed to set forth what conditions aid donors should insist on as the price of their support of development programmes that can have the desired objective of reducing emigration pressure. Some conditions are best set collectively by the donors, while others will presumably be set bilaterally. In Central America, many aid donors will not put a high priority on the migration objective because they do not receive many immigrants from this region. This is true of donors in Europe and Japan. Multilateral donors are not likely to put the same priority on emigration reduction from Central America as is the United States.

We recommend the establishment of a strong consultative or coordinating group to guide this division of labour. The collective group would be best positioned to establish macroeconomic conditions and those related to relative prices – interest rates, the exchange rate, producer prices for commodities – and bilateral donors the conditions in those areas and functions they wish to emphasize. The latter could include small and medium-sized business stimulation, regional polices, the fostering of off-farm regional centres, education, health care, and family planning.

We wish particularly to single out family planning services because this is the one mechanism that can work directly to reduce the immense demographic problem faced by Central American countries. The United States has programmes in Central America to foster democracy and improve the administration of justice. Conditions under these programmes are probably best set bilaterally. The division between bilateral and collective setting of conditions may overlap. We stress only that, as long as the two types of condition-setting take place, a mechanism is needed to avoid inconsistencies.

The development objective will obviously fail in the absence of basic structural reforms and valid macroeconomic policy. This is not the place to elaborate on the details of such policies, but they are the stuff of the deliberations in the coordinating mechanism.[24] *In addition to economic measures, a greater degree of social justice will be necessary in Central America if emigration pressures are to be reduced; aid donors should not neglect this.* Providing greater educational opportunities, and health care and family planning facilities can be considered both economic and social, as can attention to the more equal distribution of the benefits from future economic growth. Better administration of justice and the insistence by donors of free democratic choice are both social and political issues. The determinants of emigration from Central America are a mixture of many variables – economic, social and political.[25]

---

[24] Williamson (1990, pp. 358-380) sets forth areas of policy reform considered important by a group of economists. The areas stressed in this discussion are fiscal discipline, giving priorities in public expenditures to capital items and health and education, tax reform, liberalization of financial institutions, maintaining the correct exchange rate, liberalizing trade, encouraging foreign direct investment, removing burdensome regulations, and securing property rights. In assessing Central American performance under this structure, relatively high grades were given to Costa Rica, middle-range grades to Guatemala, and low grades to El Salvador, Honduras, and Nicaragua (pp. 395-397).

[25] Goering (1991) analyses two studies that used econometric techniques to determine what variables had most relevance in stimulating undocumented immigration into the United States. One of the studies focused on Latin American migration and found that social variables, such as education, were significant in explaining emigration. The second study, which looked at undocumented immigration into the United States from all sources, found that regional differences in sending countries were significant.

Donors should insist on a proper division of labour between the public and private sectors in Central America. Governments, both at the central level and regionally, have large roles in setting policies and managing programmes to reduce the attractiveness of emigration. At the central level, this includes undertaking the required structural reforms, establishing a stable macroeconomic environment, investing in the needed infrastructure, and fostering social justice. At the regional level, assuming greater decentralization of administration, the tasks of governments include encouragement to producers and small and medium-sized businesses, and facilitating marketing of products. However, there is enough accumulated evidence by now from experience around the world, that government encroachment into activities better handled by the private sector can stifle development.

We recommend that the donor countries, working in cooperation with the Central American countries, devote much effort to working out programmes to optimize the use of migrant remittances and to using return migrants to greater advantage than in the past (Díaz-Briquets and Weintraub, 1991d). Migrant remittances provide much foreign exchange for the Central American countries, but are used primarily for consumption. They can be made more productive if incentives are put in place for their use in fostering the development of small and medium-sized businesses in rural areas. This would require the cooperation of the Central American governments. In addition, return migrants should be able to play a greater role in the stimulation of off-farm rural development, but the evidence from other places where such programmes have been tried is that this requires cooperation between donors and countries of out-migration (Rogers, 1991, p. 251).

Aid donors should condition their aid on steps by the Central Americans to reinvigorate the Central American Common Market. There is a natural disposition by the Central American countries themselves to do this, but considerable resistance remains among powerful groups in each of the countries. The reduction of high tariffs undertaken since 1986, even if hesitant, is evidence of the desire of the Central American countries to strengthen the economic integration process, but import protection remains high. The Economic Commission for Latin America and the Caribbean labelled the Central Americans "gradual reformers" on trade liberalization (ECLAC, 1991a). The integration movement is unlikely to succeed if it is essentially protectionist, as it was in its first incarnation, but it may if it encourages competition in internal markets.

8. Final comments

We wish to stress several points made earlier:

- While this study has focused on the use of aid to reduce pressures to emigrate from Central America, aid is only as effective as the use to which the resources are put. Thus, while it is possible for purposes of presentation to separate aid from other aspects of the Central American economies and political structures, these matters are not separable in practice.

- The main precondition for aid to foster development and inhibit emigration from Central America is the restoration and maintenance of political order in the region. Large infusions of foreign resources during the 1980s did not serve to staunch emigration from those countries in Central America in which civil war was raging. Despite the dismal current state of the economy of Nicaragua, the evidence based on United States apprehensions of undocumented immigrants is that emigration from that country has slowed.

■ The economic incentive to emigrate from the sending countries in Central America cannot be eliminated in the short term. The evidence is that it takes years of consistent economic growth and job creation – it takes the creation of hope among the population that opportunities at home are growing – for emigration to slow down. This, in turn, requires foreign aid programmes to be devised for the long term, for decades, even for generations, to have the desired effect.

Bibliography

Arroyo Alejandre, Jesus; Adrian de Leon Arias; Basilia Valenzuela Varela. 1991. "Patterns of migration and regional development in the State of Jaliso, Mexico", in Sergio Díaz-Briquets and Sidney Weintraub (eds.): *Regional and sectoral developments in Mexico as alternatives to migration* (Boulder, Colorado, Westview Press), pp. 47-87.

Ascher, William; Ann Hubbard (eds.). 1989. *Central American recovery and development*, Task Force Report to the International Commission for Central American Recovery and Development (Durham, North Carolina, Duke University Press).

Bradford, Colin I., Jr. 1989. "Industrial prospects for Central America: A macroeconomic policy approach for Central America and the international community for the future (1987-92)", in William Ascher and Ann Hubbard (eds.): *Central American recovery and development* (Durham, North Carolina, Duke University Press), pp.154-180.

Bulmer-Thomas, Victor. 1987. *The political economy of Central America since 1920* (Cambridge, Cambridge University Press).

Comisión Económica para América Latina y el Caribe (CEPAL, or ECLAC). 1990. *Estudio Económico de América Latina y el Caribe: Guatemala* (Mexico City, doc. LC/L.560/Add.13, Nov.).

Crosby, Benjamin L. 1990. "Central America", in Anthony Lake (ed.): *After the wars* (New Brunswick, New Jersey, Transaction Publishers for the Overseas Development Council), pp. 103-138.

Díaz-Briquets, Sergio; Sidney Weintraub (eds.). 1991a. *Determinants of emigration from Mexico, Central America, and the Caribbean* (Boulder, Colorado, Westview Press).

—;—. (eds.). 1991b. *Regional and sectoral developments in Mexico as alternatives to migration* (Boulder, Colorado, Westview Press).

—;—. (eds.). 1991c. *Migration impacts of trade and foreign investment: Mexico and Caribbean Basin countries* (Boulder, Colorado, Westview Press).

—;—. (eds.). 1991d. *Migration, remittances, and small business development: Mexico and Caribbean Basin countries* (Boulder, Colorado, Westview Press).

—;—. (eds.). 1991e. *The effects of receiving country policies on migration flows* (Boulder, Colorado, Westview Press).

Durham, William H. 1979. *Scarcity and survival in Central America* (Stanford, Stanford University Press).

Economic Commission for Latin America and the Caribbean (ECLAC). 1991a. *Latin American and Caribbean trade and investment relations with the United States in the 1980s* (doc. LC/WAS/L.13).

—. 1991b. *Preliminary overview of the economy of Latin America and the Caribbean 1991* (doc. LC/G, 1696).

Espenshade, Thomas J. 1989. "Growing imbalances between labor supply and labor demand in the Caribbean Basin", in Frank D. Bean, Jurgen Schmandt, and Sidney Weintraub (eds.): *Mexican and Central American population and immigration policy* (Austin, Center for Mexican American Studies, University of Texas at Austin), pp. 113-160.

Feinberg, Richard E.; Robert A. Pastor. 1984. "Far from hopeless: An economic program for post-war Central America", in Robert S. Leiken (ed.): *Central America: Anatomy of a conflict* (New York, Pergamon Press).

Foreign Broadcast Information Service (FBIS). 1992a. Latin America, "Ambassador comments on debt with USSR", 6 Jan., p. 39.

—. 1992b. Latin America, "Russian embassy explains Nicaraguan debt figures", 21 Jan., p. 25.

Gendell, Murray. 1986. "Population growth and labor absorption in Latin America, 1970-2000", in John Saunders (ed.): *Population growth in Latin America and US national security* (Boston, Allen and Unwin), pp. 49-78.

Goering, John M. 1991. "The determinants of undocumented migration to the United States: A research note", in Sergio Díaz-Briquets and Sidney Weintraub (eds.): *Determinants of emigration from Mexico, Central America, and the Caribbean* (Boulder, Colorado, Westview Press), pp. 190-213.

Gregory, Peter. 1991. "The determinants of international migration and policy options for influencing the size of population flows", in Sergio Díaz-Briquets and Sidney Weintraub (eds.): *Determinants of emigration from Mexico, Central America, and the Caribbean* (Boulder, Colorado, Westview Press), pp. 49-73.

Grimmett, Richard F. 1991. *Conventional arms transfers to the Third World, 1983-1990* (Washington, DC, Congressional Research Service, Library of Congress).

Hayes, Margaret Daly. 1991. "Strategies for economic development", in Bruce L.R. Smith (ed.): *The next steps in Central America* (Washington, DC, The Brookings Institution), 43-53.

Hewitt, Daniel P. 1991. "Military expenditures in the developing world", in *Finance and Development*, Vol. 28, No. 3, pp. 22-25.

IDB. 1991a. *Annual Report 1990* (Washington, DC).

—. 1991b. *Economic and Social Progress in Latin America: 1991 Report* (Washington, DC).

ILO. 1986. *Economically active population: Estimates 1950-1980 and projections 1985-2025*, Vol. 3, Latin America (Geneva).

IMF. 1991. *International Financial Statistics* (Washington, DC, IMF), October.

Lake, Anthony (ed.). 1990. *After the wars* (New Brunswick, New Jersey, Transaction Publishers for the Overseas Development Council).

Leguizamùn, Francisco A. 1991. "The small business sector in Central America: A Diagnosis", in Sergio Díaz-Briquets and Sidney Weintraub (eds.): *Migration, remittances, and small business development: Mexico and Caribbean Basin countries* (Boulder, Colorado, Westview Press), pp. 11-44.

Leonard, H. Jeffrey. 1987. *Natural resources and economic development in Central America: A regional environmental profile* (New Brunswick, New Jersey, Transaction Books for the International Institute for Environment and Development).

Martin, Philip L. 1991. *The unfinished story: Turkish labour migration to Western Europe* (Geneva, ILO).

Massey, Douglas S. 1991. "Economic development and international migration in comparative perspective", in Sergio Díaz-Briquets and Sidney Weintraub (eds.): *Determinants of emigration from Mexico, Central America, and the Caribbean* (Boulder, Colorado, Westview Press), pp. 13-47.

Millett, Richard L. 1991. "Unequal partners: Relations between the Government and the military", in Bruce L.R. Smith (ed.): *The next steps in Central America* (Washington, DC, The Brookings Institution), pp. 64-84.

Montes Mozo, Segundo; Juan Jose Garcia Vasquez. 1988. *Salvadoran migration to the United States: An exploratory study*, Hemispheric Migration Project, Center for Immigration Policy and Refugee Assistance (Washington, DC, Georgetown University).

New York Times. 1991. "Germany to cut aid to countries that spend heavily on weapons", 3 Aug., p. 3.

—. 1991. "Europeans look for ways to bar door to immigrants", 29 Dec., p. 1.

Nuccio, Richard A. 1991. *A sign of the times: The decline of US preoccupation with Central America*, paper prepared for International Institute of Strategic Studies conference on political and economic reconstruction in Central America, San José, Costa Rica.

OECD. Various years. *Geographic Distribution of Financial Flows to Developing Countries* (Paris).

Programa Regional de Empleo para América Latina y el Caribe (PREALC). 1982. *Mercado de Trabajo en Cifras, 1950-1980* (Santiago, Chile).

Report of the International Commission for Central American Recovery and Development: Poverty, conflict, and hope: A turning point in Central America. 1989. (Durham, North Carolina, Duke University Press) (the Sanford Commission).

Report of the President's National Bipartisan Commission on Central America. 1984. (New York, Macmillan) (the Kissinger Commission).

Rogers, Rosemarie. 1991. "Return migration, migrants' savings, and sending countries' economic development: Lessons from Europe", in Sergio Díaz-Briquets and Sidney Weintraub (eds.): *The effects of receiving country policies on migration flows* (Boulder, Colorado, Westview Press), pp. 233-257.

Saborio, Sylvia. 1990. "Central America", in John Williamson (ed.): *Latin American adjustment: How much has happened?* (Washington, DC, Institute for International Economics), pp. 279-305.

Sanford, Jonathan E. 1989. *Central America: Major trends in US foreign assistance: Fiscal 1978 to fiscal 1990* (Washington, DC, Congressional Research Service, Library of Congress).

Smith, Bruce L.R. (ed.). 1991. *The next steps in Central America* (Washington, DC, The Brookings Institution).

Stanley, William D. 1987. "Economic migrants or refugees from violence? A time series analysis of Salvadoran migration to the United States", in *Latin American Research Review*, 21:1, pp. 132-152.

Stark, Oded; J. Edward Taylor. 1991. "Relative deprivation and migration: Theory, evidence, and policy implications", in Sergio Díaz-Briquets and Sidney Weintraub (eds.): *Determinants of emigration from Mexico, Central America, and the Caribbean* (Boulder, Colorado, Westview Press), pp. 121-144.

Storrs, K. Larry; Dianne E. Rennack. 1987. *US bilateral and economic and military assistance to Latin America and the Caribbean, fiscal years 1946 to 1987* (Washington, DC, Congressional Research Service, Library of Congress).

Summers, Lawrence. 1991. "Research challenges for development economists", in *Finance and Development*, Vol. 28, No. 3, pp. 2-5.

Tamayo, Jesus; Fernando Lozano. 1991a. "The economic and social development of high emigration areas in the State of Zacatecas: Antecedents and policy alternatives", in Sergio Díaz-Briquets and Sidney Weintraub (eds.): *Regional and sectoral developments in Mexico as alternatives to migration* (Boulder, Colorado, Westview Press), pp. 15-46.

—. 1991b. "Mexican perceptions on rural development and migration of workers to the United States and actions taken, 1970-1988", in Sergio Díaz-Briquets and Sidney

Weintraub (eds.): *Regional and sectoral developments in Mexico as alternatives to migration* (Boulder, Colorado, Westview Press), pp. 363-387.
Tapinos, Georges P. 1991a. "Development assistance strategies and emigration pressure in Europe and Africa", in Sergio Díaz-Briquets and Sidney Weintraub (eds.): *The effects of receiving country policies on migration flows* (Boulder, Colorado, Westview Press), pp. 259-274.
—. 1991b. *Can international cooperation be an alternative to the emigration of workers?*, paper prepared for an international conference on migration in Rome sponsored by the OECD.
Thomas, Vinod. 1991. "Lessons from economic development", in *Finance and Development*, Vol. 28, No. 3, pp. 6-9.
Tucker, Stuart K. 1991. "The potential of trade expansion as a generator of added employment in the Caribbean Basin", in Sergio Díaz-Briquets and Sidney Weintraub (eds.): *Migration impacts of trade and foreign investment: Mexico and Caribbean Basin Countries* (Boulder, Colorado, Westview Press), pp. 91-112.
Unauthorized migration: An economic development response. 1990. Report of the Commission for the Study of International Migration and Cooperative Economic Development (Washington, DC, US Government Printing Office).
UN. 1991. Department of International Economic and Social Affairs, *World Population Prospects 1990*, Population Studies No. 120 (New York, doc. ST/ESA/SER.A/120).
Wallace, Steven P. 1986. "Central American and Mexican immigrant characteristics and economic incorporation in California" in *International Migration Review*, No. 20 (Fall), pp. 657-671.
Washington Post. 1992. "Salvadorans agree to end civil war", 1 Jan., p. 1.
—. 1992. "US warns Salvadorans of deportations", 1 Jan., p. A12.
Washington Institute Task Force Report. 1984. *Central America in crisis* (Washington, DC, Washington Institute for Values in Public Policy).
Washington Report on the Hemisphere. 1991. *Tegucigalpa's forestry pact in doubt* (Washington, DC.), 18 Dec.
Weeks, John. 1985. *The economies of Central America* (New York, Holmes and Meier).
Weintraub, Sidney. 1983. "US foreign economic policy and illegal immigration", in *Population Research and Policy Review*, pp. 211-231.
—. 1991. "Policy-based assistance: A historical perspective", in Sergio Díaz-Briquets and Sidney Weintraub (eds.): *The effects of receiving country policies on migration flows* (Boulder, Colorado, Westview Press), pp. 13-38.
Williams, Robert G. 1986. *Export agriculture and the crisis in Central America* (Chapel Hill, University of North Carolina Press).
Williamson, John (ed.). 1990. *Latin American adjustment: How much has happened?* (Washington, DC, Institute for International Economics).
World Bank. 1990a. *World Debt Tables: 1990-1991*, Vol. 2, Country Tables, (Washington, DC).
—. 1990b. *World Development Report 1990* (New York and Oxford, Oxford University Press).
—. 1991. *World Development Report 1991* (New York and Oxford, Oxford University Press).

6

International aid to reduce the need for emigration: The Tunisian case

M. Bel Hadj Amor

1. Introduction

The most recent population and employment survey conducted in Tunisia in 1989[1] revealed the following:

- a population of 7.9 million compared with 7.0 million as recorded in the 1984 census. This denoted an average annual growth rate of 2.4 per cent over the period;
- an economically active population of 2.35 million, with an average variation of 2.0 per cent over the period;
- an employed population of 1.979 million, an increase of 2.2 per cent over the period;
- an unemployed population of 381,800, representing an unemployment rate of 16.2 per cent.

The unemployment rate can be lowered to 15.3 per cent if the term unemployed applies only to the active population unemployed aged between 18 and 59 years. This figure of 15.3 per cent compares with 13.1 per cent in 1984 and 12.9 per cent in 1975. This increase in unemployment over the years reflects the central problems of the Tunisian economy.

Economic, social and cultural development has, however, made considerable progress since independence in March 1956. Today, in 1992, Tunisia is in the process of finalizing its Eighth Plan 1992-96; the Ninth Plan takes the country up to the beginning of the third millennium.

Since 1960, Tunisia's development has been conducted through seven medium-term, 3- to 5-year plans: 1962-64, 1965-68, 1969-72, 1973-76, 1977-81, 1982-86 and 1987-91. (Reference is also made to three decades, the first 1962-71, the second 1972-81, and the third 1982-91.) Its achievements have been impressive, although the constraints have also been numerous.

The employment issue, in particular, has been a heavy burden. For a time, it was somewhat alleviated by emigration, mainly to EC countries. Emigration was

---

[1] 1 July 1989 is the median date of the survey period.

regarded as a temporary remedy to unemployment: Tunisians emigrated in search of work, and were encouraged to do so by their own Government as well by those of the host countries. Emigration was thus essentially the result of unemployment: it was regarded as a palliative until national growth and investment could generate the additional jobs and perhaps even create conditions for the reintegration of returning emigrants. These views prevailed until the early 1970s.

Today's national development strategies centre on the employment issue, but they are unable to come up with a durable solution (section 2). The employment problem, in fact, can be stated primarily in demographic terms: successive waves of jobseekers appear on the market as a result of demographic pressures, while the road to emigration is now blocked (section 3). Other solutions must be explored. In particular, a new concept of international cooperation must be created, so that foreign aid can help reduce the need for Tunisians to look for work on the European markets (section 4).

2. Tunisian economic strategy: Growth and development

The strategy's objectives and results

From the outset in 1957, the Tunisian authorities set themselves three ambitious development objectives: growth, self-development and human progress.

The first task was to promote a relatively high level of production of goods and services, without which there could be no credible prospect of human progress. The next imperative was independent development to reduce the country's commercial and financial dependence to an acceptable level. Finally, economic performance needed to be reflected in higher living standards, satisfying the basic needs of the population in respect of universal education and health services, improved living and housing conditions, employment creation and increased earnings.

These objectives underlying Tunisian planning in the first development decade continued into the succeeding decades, modified by experience from the field, as well as by the discovery of new issues or a better insight into existing problems. Thus, in the 1970s, while production growth remained the essential requirement for the promotion of higher living standards and earnings, it was also necessary to set new objectives concerning the quantitative and qualitative control of investment and the consolidation of the country's financial situation. Employment assumed its true dimension as a major development problem. At the same time, concern for social equilibrium was accentuating the need to remedy regional disparities, which had been aggravated by accelerated growth.

The 1980s confirmed employment as the primary development objective. However, an acceleration in production growth remained important. This required a rationalization of policies to ensure the smooth running of all economic aggregates – investment and financing, consumption and saving, imports and exports, external deficit and debt. Finally, the ultimate purpose of economic growth being human development, increased attention was paid to the fairer distribution of the fruits of this growth.

The polices for the 1990s are nearing completion. This decade will see greater use of market forces to strengthen the economy. The Tunisian planning authorities are talking of a watershed in the consolidation of economic reforms and in the "profound changes advocated in economic and social management methods, which should affect all areas and sectors of economic activity".[2] The expected outlook, in this context, concerns acceleration of growth and job creation, stimulation of private investment, readjustment of external trade and control of budget balances.

The performance of the Tunisian economy during the past 30 years bears witness to the effort expended. In the first place, as regards investment, the overall budget – in billions of dinars – came to 1.323 in the decade 1962-71, rising to 6.406 in the decade 1972-81 and reaching 19.515 for the decade 1982-91. Investment represented 22.8 per cent of GDP in 1962-71, 28.4 per cent in 1972-81, and 24.4 per cent in 1982-91.

Investment was strongly supported by national savings, which grew from 873.4 million dinars to 5,207.9 million dinars and then to 15,211.0 million dinars over the three periods. The national savings rate as a proportion of GDP stood at 15.0 per cent, 22.9 per cent and 19.9 per cent for the three periods; it covered 66.0 per cent, 81.3 per cent and 81.6 per cent of investment financing in the three periods. Recourse to external resources, amounting to one-third of the investment volume for 1967-71 and one-fifth for 1972-81 and 1982-91, none the less required new methods to find, mobilize and use the necessary capital.

This resulted in a real growth rate of 4.6 per cent and 7.1 per cent for the first two decades, with a downswing to 2.9 per cent in 1982-86 and 4.2 per cent in 1987-91 caused by unstable climatic conditions and a deteriorating international economic situation.

The investment effort and the growth generated by it made it possible, from the decade 1962-71 onwards, to lay the foundations of continued development, in both human capacity and the country's infrastructure and amenities.

Economic production has undergone profound changes: new sectors are emerging in the production of goods and services and in the creation of additional sources of foreign currency. As a result of rapid development, the industrial sector represented 27.7 per cent of GDP in 1991, compared with 15.8 per cent in 1961; manufacturing industry doubled its share of GDP from 7.2 per cent to 15.3 per cent over the same period. Tourism, with a mere 0.3 per cent at the beginning of the period, accounted for 3.9 per cent of GDP in 1991.

Agriculture fell from 22.9 per cent of GDP in 1961 to 16 per cent in 1991 – though climatic factors were partly responsible for these variations. Increased irrigation, stock-breeding and fishing have to a large extent mitigated the effects of the variable climate. The diversification of the Tunisian economy makes it possible today to limit the effect of "lean years" in agriculture. The 4.6 per cent growth rate achieved in 1962-71, by sectors other than agriculture, can be considered remarkable in light of the drought throughout that period which reduced agricultural production by an average annual rate of 1.8 per cent. The sector continued to develop at a negative rate of 1.8 per cent, at constant prices, during the Fifth Plan (1977-81), but the

---

[2] *Economic Budget Report, 1992,* December 1991.

overall economic growth rate was positive at 5.6 per cent. After three decades of development, Tunisia can therefore claim to have a sound industrial basis.

There has also been diversification in the sources of foreign currency. In 1961, 38.6 per cent was earned by agricultural production and mineral resources. Five new or established sectors generated over the three decades 41.6 per cent, 71.2 per cent and 68.9 per cent of current earnings. The sectors with their respective average earnings per decade are: textiles with 1 per cent, 8.9 per cent, and 17.6 per cent; tourism with 13.6 per cent, 17.0 per cent and 17.0 per cent; oil with 8.2 per cent, 26.8 per cent and 14.1 per cent; chemicals with 13.1 per cent, 9.4 per cent and 10.1 per cent; and earnings of emigrant workers with 5.7 per cent, 9.1 per cent and 10.1 per cent.

Social matters have not been eclipsed by economic growth. Growth is the means and precondition of development. In this respect, development has affected the lives of the population in all aspects, chief among them being employment and earnings. Investment in the first two decades led to the creation of some 535,000 jobs, while 400,000 will have been created in the decade from 1982 to 1991; performance has fallen short of needs, but it has meant that overcrowding on the labour market could, to a certain extent, be absorbed. Average per capita income went up by an annual 1.8 per cent in real terms in 1962-71, 4 per cent in 1972-81 and slightly less than that in 1982-91. Although with the increased level of household expenditure the improvement may not noticeable, in objective terms it is. A household budget and consumption survey, conducted by the Tunisian National Statistics Institute, and covering the period from June 1990 to June 1991, has revealed a marked improvement in the condition of Tunisians:

- per capita expenditure rose at an average annual rate of 11 per cent between 1975 and 1980, 13.7 per cent between 1980 and 1985, and 8.3 per cent between 1985 and 1990; this improvement was more pronounced in rural than urban areas;
- the Gini coefficient of income concentration dropped by 4 points, from 44 per cent in 1975 to 43 per cent in 1980, 43.4 per cent in 1985 and 40.1 per cent in 1990;
- the population subsisting on the poverty line fell from 48 per cent of the total population in 1966 to 22 per cent in 1975, 12.9 per cent in 1980, 7.7 per cent in 1985 and 6.7 per cent in 1990.

Education absorbed nearly 9 per cent of GDP. The goal of this development priority is to provide elementary schooling for virtually the entire population, to establish secondary and higher educational systems, to organize vocational training and, in general, to produce the qualified personnel necessary to the Tunisian economic and social system.

Health also accounted for some 9 per cent of GDP, for the provision of medical care through a broad network of national, regional and local structures and increasingly diversified amenities. The training of medical and para-medical personnel kept pace with these developments, producing large numbers of doctors and nurses each year.

The housing sector has created 700,000 new homes and becomes more dynamic with each decade. The population and employment survey referred to above found that an average of 38,000 new housing units were built each year during 1984-89.

The strategy's limitations

The achievements of the three decades of development bear witness to an overall progress, which, despite its many positive aspects, has not always provided the hoped-for solutions to the country's problems. Results rarely matched forecasts, leading to a questioning of economic policies and the need for a change of strategy.

As Table 6.1 shows, the results have been limited, in the face of constraints in terms of growth, employment and the country's solvency.

Admittedly, forecasts can always be contradicted by events. Thus it was that a series of endogenous and exogenous factors, such as drought years, the vagaries of political relations, reversals in the international economic situation, external price fluctuations and the instability of exchange rates, undermined the planners' estimates.

Apart from these concrete aspects, however, the Tunisian economy reveals its weakness in that the results expected for a given investment are not always achieved, especially in terms of growth, employment and balance of payments or, occasionally, in one or other of these aggregates. The lesson to be drawn from this situation is that Tunisia's problem lies in economic policy orientation and the nature of investment, rather than the actual investment volume or mobilization of funds.

It is an increasingly widespread view that the problems of the Tunisian economy are caused primarily by the nature of its investment, stemming from its policy of industrialization as an import substitution strategy. This has led it to overprotect the local market instead of effectively encouraging an export trade.

Capital-intensive investment is the underlying cause of the high marginal capital coefficient. Exemption from customs duty on capital goods involved in these investments creates distortions in the relative costs of capital and labour, and encourages the use of capital instead of labour. Similarly, these investments qualify for considerable advantages in connection with the number, rather than the cost, of the jobs created. Finally, the increase in the cost of the labour as a result of higher wages and social security contributions adds yet another disadvantage for labour-intensive industries.

Capital-intensive investment is inherent in the policy of industrialization through import substitution pursued by Tunisia for many years. Tunisia's industrialization started with the manufacture of products previously imported in quantities that made it unprofitable to manufacture them at home. At this early stage in the process, these were usually everyday consumer goods. Subsequently, increased national income led to increased imports of other consumer goods to an extent that it became profitable to manufacture them in Tunisia. As the process evolved, imports consisted increasingly of intermediate products and capital goods.

The advantage of this process is that it sets in motion the initial stage of industrialization for a traditional rural society. It also enables businessmen and workers to become familiar with mechanization and an industrial environment. Advocates of this strategy also believe that it should serve three sets of objectives: job creation, progress towards manufacturing intermediate products and capital goods, and foreign currency savings. Logically, it should lead to a reduction in the current deficit and in foreign dependence.

However, industrialization through import substitution presupposes the existence of a large domestic market and high income levels. Without these two conditions, the quantities imported will be too low for profitable local production. For this reason, governments that opt for this industrialization strategy are obliged – as was the case with Tunisia – to resort to strict protection of the local market by applying a wide range of measures, including prohibition, quotas, exorbitant customs duties, subsidies, and domestic tax rebates.

Such protection and the resultant economic characteristics can have serious disadvantages. First, protection, by increasing the price of imports, allows local industrialists to fix domestic prices at a level approaching those of the imported goods. No matter what form of price control the government imposes to counter this abuse, they fail, especially as domestic prices include account charges to cover the cost of underutilization of production capacity, a proportion of unnatural waste, and low productivity. Tunisian industry is not subject to any established standards. The public is thus paying higher prices for locally manufactured, and often inferior, goods. In this way, protection generates high profits, which attract new investors to the same segment of the market, without prices being affected by the extra competition. Thus protected, an industrialist is often free to increase his prices without having to improve his firm's productivity, and this creates demands for higher wages, which in turn encourages the inflationary spiral.

Second, as regards the distribution of investment, protection, by generating quick and easy profits, deflects the bulk of resources and initiative from more worthwhile sectors and activities, such as agriculture, in which profitability is considered to be remote and erratic. Moreover, the substitution process seldom leads to genuine industrialization, or to the manufacture of profitable intermediate or capital goods, as these generally require heavier investment and more advanced technology.

With regard to external finances, import substitution does not save foreign currency, but leads to a deterioration of these finances owing to the increase in imports of intermediate and capital goods to keep the consumer industries going.

Employment, the Achilles' heel of the Tunisian economy, is depressed by import substitution, as protection encourages capital-intensive, rather than labour-intensive, investments. Moreover, the import-substitution industry does not allow production to expand, owing to the restricted size of the market and the limited nature of the substituted products. This can explain why Tunisia has for several years had difficulty in identifying projects. Besides, it took 30 years – from 1961 to 1991 – for the manufacturing industries to increase their share of GDP from 7.2 per cent to 15.3 per cent, having stagnated at 10.5 per cent from 1976 until 1981. It was only during the third decade that, with a rise in textile exports, the manufacturing industries improved their share of GDP.

In fact, while protection may be justified in the case of countries such as Tunisia that are still in the early stages of industrialization, it should be moderated, then removed once the sector concerned has become competitive.

It is apparent that insufficient growth, the capitalist nature of investment, the current balance of payments deficit and unemployment are closely interrelated ills. The only possible approach to a solution of the unemployment problem lies in the development of labour-intensive activities. These activities cannot be expanded, nor can growth be sustained, within the limits of the local market: they require far greater access to the international market, and this raises the issue of re-examining national economic orientation.

From the earliest development plans, the Tunisian planning authorities realized the shortcomings of the strategy: pressure had to be brought to bear on investments to make them consistent with growth and employment objectives; the prescriptive nature of the earlier plans needed to be amended by supporting the investment effort with appropriate economic policies. At the end of the first decade, various adjustment measures were applied to development strategy.

The need for large-scale investment had been established; it was therefore essential to improve the country's capacity to exploit it, above all:

- to adjust the distribution of investment by category, two-thirds to be allocated to directly productive sectors, and the remaining one-third to *long-term* productive sectors;
- to adjust the distribution of investment by sector, with greater responsibility for the private sector. This sector was beginning to become significant, as a result of many incentives; it was to provide 40 per cent of investment with the public sector supplying 60 per cent;
- to consolidate national financial structures to enable the country to finance 80 per cent of investments with an external contribution of 20 per cent, a level regarded as acceptable to allow "the country to secure a generous international contribution without jeopardizing its solvency or its independence".[3]

These new policy objectives were backed by important reforms in project identification and promotion, acceleration and simplification of project authorization procedures, easing of exchange controls, modification of the tax system, export incentives, and improved vocational training. They were subsequently enhanced by an endeavour to increase the return on investment, both in terms of production by bringing pressure to bear on the marginal capital coefficient, and of employment by reducing labour costs.

Faced with deteriorating terms of trade, the new policy orientation also emphasized control of the domestic market with respect to consumption, and the need to increase exports of other goods besides oil, and to reduce food imports.

Since the mid-1980s (especially since the Gulf War) and the change in the international economic situation, the option for a less timid advance towards a free market economy has been offered: market mechanisms are slowly being established.

[3] *Report on the Second Decade of Development and the Fourth Plan.*

Table 6.1. Tunisia: Economic and demographic statistics, actual and forecast, 1961-96

Aggregates/Plan	1st Decade 1961-71	4th Plan 1973-76	5th Plan 1977-81	6th Plan 1982-86	7th Plan 1987-91	8th Plan 1992-96
Population (000s)	4 533	5 588	6 647	6 986	7 909	8 100
Overall factor productivity (%)	...	-1.1	-	-2.6	2.2	2.5
Marginal capital coefficient	...	5.4	5.3	9.1	5.1	4.3
Growth (%)						
forecast	6.0	6.6	7.5	6.0	4.0	6.0
achieved	4.6	4.4	5.6	2.9	4.2	
Investment (millions of dinars)						
forecast	1 310	1 194	4 200	8 200	11 200	22 870
achieved	1 245	1 568	4 539	8 885	10 650	
Investment rate (%)	23.0	24.9	30.2	29	23.1	28.0
Investment rate by type (%)						
Directly productive	50	62.8	60.3	60	53.5	57.5
Long-term productive	50	37.2	39.7	40	46.5	42.5
Investment (%) by						
Public sector	72	54.3	68	55.1	50.5	47.5
Private sector	28	45.7	32	44.9	49.5	52.5
Investment by sector (%)						
Agriculture and fishing	18.8	12.5	12.9	16.4	16.4	17.3
Manufacturing	11.9	18.0	18.0	18.1	16.7	17.5
Non-manuf. ind.	17.4	23.9	22.5	21.3	13.0	11.9
Non-admin. services	50.8	35.1	37.5	36.2	40.9	36.5
of which:						
Transport	11.8	16.5	17.6	...	12.8	12.4
Tourism	8.0	3.5	2.6	...	4.8	4.6
Housing	12.3	14.5	16.7	18.2	19.7	14.7
Community facilities	17.2	10.6	9.2	8.0	10.6	11.6
Savings rate/GDP (%)	17.0	22.3	23.3	19.8	19.0	25.6
Savings/Investment (%)	55.3	80.5	71.2	67.0	66.4	71.5
External aid/Investments (%)	44.7	19.5	28.8	33.0	33.6	28.5
Debt rate (%)	49.5	32	38.0	58.7	52.5	42.4
Debt servicing/Current revenues (%)	...	10.2	13.6	20.1	21.8	16.0
Jobs (000s)						
Extra demand	537	198	275	324	300	313
Jobs created	132	164	209	200	204	320
Emigration (000s)	140	...	97	...	50	0
Unemployment rate (%)	...	13	11.4	13.1	15.3	...

... = data not available.

Source: Population and employment surveys, and development plans, various years.

The state's management of the economy is disappearing, leading to a liberalization of prices on a range of products, the abolition of licences for certain imports, and a flexible trade policy.

Results are improving, as can be seen from Table 6.1 above, though admittedly they are still insufficient in the face of imponderable external factors – especially fluctuating prices and exchange rates, and protectionism – but also endogenous factors which economic policy measures have not yet effectively eliminated.

Meanwhile, the policy objectives of the Seventh Plan in October 1989 analysed the internal difficulties that beset steady development. The problem lies with productivity and competitiveness of the economy. There has been only a very slight improvement in productivity. Production capacity is not fully utilized, either in agriculture – 70 per cent of the irrigated areas are being farmed, compared with 50.1 per cent in 1981 and only 41.5 per cent during the Sixth Plan – or in the manufacturing industries – where capacity utilization varies between 50 per cent and 60 per cent.

The country's competitiveness does not appear to have been stimulated by liberalization. Protectionist unwieldiness remains, and national producers, apart from those in a few joint ventures with foreign partners, continue to prefer the local market to the hazards of the foreign market. The internal system still offers protectionist advantages in areas such as taxation, foreign trading, and price regulation. Such protection of the domestic market was highly prevalent in 1983.

As a result of external constraints and internal rigidity, employment and the balance of payments continue to be worrying aspects in the country's development.

An economy freed from administrative and bureaucratic shackles, with the role of the state reduced to that of regulator and counsellor, should be the objective. Economic policies must be regularly reassessed to expand job-creation capacity in labour-intensive sectors.

Investment must therefore double in the next ten years (it more than doubled at constant prices over the previous 30 years). However, perseverance in this endeavour will not be practicable unless basic equilibrium is maintained in the matter of savings, public finances, balance of payments and foreign debt. Furthermore, as the report on the Sixth Economic and Social Development Plan 1982-86 remarked in June 1982 "while the investments to be undertaken must contribute to the creation of the necessary jobs, they must also lead to the creation of new wealth by increasing production, so that Tunisians and Tunisian enterprises can improve their earnings and maintain their living standards by a moderate growth in consumption ... [because] to invest for the sole purpose of creating jobs without increasing production would be to reduce Tunisia to a mere work camp to combat unemployment." The employment problem is compounded, in fact, by the need to distribute more broadly the benefits of growth among the whole population and all regions. It implies a balance between the generations, in terms of sharing austerity measures and the immediate and future costs of investment.

3. The employment problem

The employment problem falls within the scope of economic and social development and its capacity to absorb an increasing population into the national productive system. In fact, the scale of the increase reminds us that the problem takes on a demographic aspect with natural population growth. For many years, emigration was presented as a partial and temporary solution to mitigate the gravity of the problem.

Demographic aspects of employment: Sustained pressure

The Tunisian population has increased at a rapid pace in recent decades, with annual average rates of 2.3 per cent, 2.5 per cent and 2.4 per cent respectively for the periods 1966-75, 1975-84, and 1984-89. This increase is the result of a high birth rate and a falling death rate. Births increased between the Fifth Plan (1977-81) and the Sixth Plan (1982-86) from annual averages of 218,000 to 224,000. In 1987 the number fell to 223,000, to 214,700 in 1988, and to 199,100 in 1989.[4] A certain levelling-off is therefore apparent; it is as yet insufficient, as it is characterized by the effects of age structures. Women of child-bearing age – from 15 to 49 years – represented 22.5 per cent of the population at the 1975 census; this proportion had risen to 23.6 per cent by 1984.

Between 1969 and 1980, the death rate fell steadily from 7.8 per thousand to 6.8 per thousand both in terms of infant mortality and deaths in childbirth. Over the entire period, the female death rate fell sharply for all age bands among women of child-bearing age, especially those aged 20-24 years (2.1 per thousand to 1.4 per thousand) 25-29 years (2.1 per thousand to 1.8 per thousand), and 30-34 years (3.6 per thousand to 2.2 per thousand).

However, the total fertility rate is at present declining. From 7.1 in 1966, it decreased to 5.2 in 1981, 4.5 in 1986 and 3.48 at the time of the last national census in 1989. This is a distinct improvement, bearing in mind that it had been estimated, on the basis of previous trends, that the fertility index would not go down to 3.9 until the year 2001. This falling trend indicates that Tunisia is well advanced in the process of demographic transition compared with the rest of the developing world.

It is clear that Tunisia has made remarkable progress in its demographic policy. A number of measures have led to a relative improvement in this field: health policy, the spread of universal education, increased urbanization and an overall improvement in living standards. Moreover, Tunisia has a vigorous family planning programme.

It is noteworthy that women, through their status in society and their recently acquired ease of access to education and employment, are the determining factors in demographic control. Whereas in 1975, only 30 per cent the female population aged between 15 and 49 years had received any education, by 1989, 56 per cent

---

[4] These figures are taken from the 1989 national population and employment survey, earlier surveys and censuses, or documents relating to the successive development plans.

had been through primary school and beyond. The proportion of women having received secondary education went up from 8.9 per cent to 21.4 per cent during the same period. The percentage of women among the economically active population, according to the general population census, increased from 6.1 per cent in 1966 to 18.7 per cent in 1975, to 21.3 per cent in 1984 (a level maintained in 1989). This promotion of women may well help to ease population pressures.

However, the improvement in the total fertility rate is still insufficient, in comparison with the countries of southern Europe that have completed their demographic transition: Spain with 2, Greece with 1.8 and Portugal with 1.6.

The relative decrease in the fertility rate, in conjunction with a steadily falling death rate, has led to a smaller proportion of young children, and a larger adult population, especially of working age.

The population structure in 1989 revealed a crude activity rate (in relation to total population) of 19.8 per cent, and a global activity rate (in relation to the population of working age) of 48 per cent. It also shows the distribution of the employed population: 79.1 per cent were men and 20.9 per cent women. The change in this active population, as seen from the censuses and surveys conducted between 1975 and 1989, shows an overall increase of 739,000 in 14 years, equivalent to an average annual demand for 53,000 jobs. For the 1980s alone, there was a 2.7 per cent average annual increase in the active population, for a total of 550,000 people. There were two distinct phases to this period: the first phase from 1980 to 1984 when the rate of increase was 4.2 per cent; and a second phase from 1984 to 1989 with a 2 per cent rate.

Throughout the period 1975-89, the number of jobs created was in the region of 40,000 per year, leading to a progressively wider gap between labour supply and demand and to greater numbers of unemployed. On 1 July 1989, according to the latest population and employment survey, the number of unemployed among the active population was 381,800 – 14.4 per cent for men, 21.9 per cent for women, and 54 per cent for young people under the age of 25 (among whom unemployment is increasing). The duration of unemployment is also getting longer: the proportion of people out of work for two years and more was 40.9 per cent in 1989 compared with 18.6 per cent in 1984. Finally, if the findings of the 1975 and 1984 censuses are compared with the 1989 survey, unemployment occurs increasingly among the more highly educated: respectively 10.5 per cent, 19.2 per cent and 29 per cent among those with secondary education; and 0.2 per cent, 0.7 per cent and 2 per cent among those with higher education.

The extra demand for jobs is caused by population growth. From early days, the Tunisian planning authorities relied on emigration to provide work for all or part of the excess labour supply that economic development was unable to absorb.

Emigration of unemployed people

Emigration was foreseen, and long regarded, as a temporary expedient both by the labour-exporting and host countries, and by the emigrants themselves. The host countries needed to fill jobs created by the development of industries and for which no national manpower could be found. As the jobs in question tended to be unskilled, poorly paid and unattractive, they were available to the unemployed and generally unskilled workers from the labour-exporting countries. These countries thus had the possibility of finding employment for their surplus manpower until such time as national growth restored the balance of labour supply and demand. Finally, from the workers' point of view, emigration opened the way to gainful employment and the possibility of building up enough savings for a respectable social and occupational reintegration into their country of origin. However, emigration as a solution to the employment problem has become a persistent phenomenon.

In the first development decade (1962-71), emigration improved the employment situation, especially for male workers: it is estimated that 140,000 people of working age left the country. A further 97,000 emigrated during the second decade (1972-81); a figure of 50,000 is expected for the decade 1982-91.

Initial emigration to France (and the rest of Europe) took place in the 1960s, owing to the shortage of jobs in Tunisia, and the demand for labour in France. At the time, most European countries were liberal in their immigration policies. The total number of immigrants admitted into the Federal Republic of Germany rose from 80,000 in 1955 to 2.6 million in 1973.

Manpower agreements were quickly concluded between the job-providing countries and Tunisia (and other developing countries). This was organized emigration, with a number of guarantees and advantages offered to the emigrant workers.

Tunisian emigration naturally flowed in the direction of Europe. For 1988,[5] round figures for the emigrant Tunisian population in EC countries are as shown in Table 6.2.

France hosts the largest number of North Africans – 1,416,400 out of a total of 1,805,500 in the EC, i.e. 78.4 per cent. North Africans account for 64.4 per cent of the 2,202,200 foreigners in France and 2.6 per cent of the total French population. Of the emigrant Tunisian population in Europe, 85.5 per cent are in France, compared with 97.8 per cent for Algerians and 55.9 per cent for Moroccans.

This emigrant Tunisian population accounts for 12.3 per cent of all North Africans in the EC, estimated at 1,805,500; 770,400 Moroccans (42.7 per cent) and 813,500 Algerians (45.0 per cent) make up the balance. North Africans also account for 23.0 per cent of all foreigners in the EC (a total of 7,860,000), and 0.6 per cent of the EC's total population of 320,525,700. Tunisians represent 2.8 per cent of all foreigners in the EC.

The worldwide economic recession following the 1973 oil shock led the EC countries to close the gates to migration; this raised the crucial problem of the emigrants' return to their country of origin. Repatriation incentives were introduced; stringent entry regulations imposed; frontier controls imposed and would-be immigrants turned away in France and, increasingly, other EC countries.

Officially, emigration to Europe was stopped in 1975. However, the Fifth Plan (1977-81) registered a net departure of 60,000 people; in 1982 and 1983, 5,900 and 9,000 net departures were recorded. This was because Tunisia had begun to

---

[5] According to data produced at the Symposium on emigrant Maghreb workers in the EEC, organized by the Union Syndicale des Travailleurs Maghrébins (Maghreb Workers' Union), the European Trade Union Confederation and the International Confederation of Free Trade Unions, and held in Tunis, 10-20 April 1991.

Table 6.2. Tunisians legally resident in EC countries, 1988

	Tunisian residents	Per cent
France	189 400	85.5
Germany, Fed. Rep.	21 600	9.8
Belgium	5 600	2.5
Netherlands	2 600	1.2
Italy	1 800	0.8
Denmark	200	0.1
Greece	200	0.1
Other	100	0.1
Total	221 500	

Source: see note 5.

exploit the possibility of finding employment in certain Arab countries, especially the Libyan Arab Jamahiriya. The outlook appeared relatively promising in two respects. First, the Gulf States employed nearly 2 million foreign workers. Second, demand in those countries was for skilled workers and for supervisory personnel in such sectors as education, health, communications, hotel and catering work – demand that Tunisia could well satisfy.

However, jobs in the Arab countries did not materialize at the expected rate. The Libyan labour market, the largest in the region, soon registered an economic downturn. As for the labour market in the Gulf States, there were specific factors that deterred Tunisian labour from making a genuine breakthrough. In the first place, it is a market that has a long tradition of recruiting labour from Pakistan, the Republic of Korea, the Philippines and Egypt. Second, social conditions there do not always resemble those of a modern economy. Finally, wages, conditions of work, and residence facilities are not sufficiently attractive.

As a result of this combination of factors – the closing of the traditional European markets, uncertain relations with the Libyan Arab Jamahiriya, and aversion to the Arab labour markets – the migration balance for the five years of the Sixth Plan 1982-86 was positive for the first time: some 27,000 emigrant workers returned to the country. Emigration was no longer a supplementary – or even temporary – solution to the employment problem.

The national population and employment survey of July 1989 revealed that, for the five years 1984-89, Tunisia registered a net emigrant return of 41,000 persons, of whom 22,400 – 54.6 per cent – were males. Returns during the 1979-84 period came to 34,300, 53.2 per cent of whom were males. Table 6.3 shows figures for returns between 1984 and 1989.

Paradoxically, it would appear that it was from the Arab countries that the returning tide of emigrants was flowing: 48.5 per cent of returnees compared with 41.5 per cent from Europe. This can be explained by the large numbers of those returning from the Libyan Arab Jamahiriya in 1984-85 (though these were offset by fresh departures to that country in 1988-89, after the resumption of normal relations between the two countries).

Table 6.3. Number of Tunisian return migrants, 1984-89

Total	41 000	Per cent
France	14 800	36.1
Libyan Arab Jamahiriya	13 300	32.4
Germany, Fed. Rep.	1 900	4.7
Saudi Arabia	1 200	2.9
Italy	700	1.7
Other Arab countries	5 400	13.2
Other countries	3 700	9.0

The survey also established that the returnees included a considerable proportion of young couples aged between 25 and 49 years, representing 40 per cent of the total registered. Retired persons, aged 60 years or more, accounted for 2 per cent of returnees. This implies a tendency among young people to attempt reintegration in their country of origin, whereas the less young apparently try to settle permanently in the host country. However, such conclusions should be treated with caution, given the limited numbers of returns from Europe, which, according to this survey, accounted for no more than 9 per cent of all Tunisian emigrants.

Despite the halt to official emigration, repatriation incentives, stiffer frontier controls and an array of deterrents, the phenomenon of emigration has not been eliminated. It adapts itself and takes new forms. There is the legal form of family reunification; there is also straightforward illegal or clandestine emigration.

The family reunification procedure, authorized by France and other European countries, has continued to swell migration and achieved a dual outcome, which was perhaps not immediately obvious. On the one hand, the arrival of family members in the host country's market created new demands for jobs for the emigrants' wives and children, and provided a new source of cheap labour in the underground economy. On the other hand, family reunification helped the emigrant to settle and create a traditional environment, so that the idea of returning eventually became irrelevant.

Subsequently, clandestine emigration became the chief source of recruitment for the alternative labour market in Europe. Today, no matter how many procedures and entry formalities are imposed by the Governments of the region, illegal workers always manage to cross frontiers, though to a lesser extent than before.

This is especially true now that illegal workers have found new openings, first in Italy, then Spain, Greece and Portugal. These countries applied more liberal entry laws for longer than other European countries. The "illegals" enter as "tourists" and stay for as long as necessary to find an opportunity of joining the traditional immigration countries. But the countries of southern Europe are also becoming immigrant countries and the "illegals" are deciding to settle there permanently. This is the case in Italy in particular, where various Italian sources refer to a Tunisian migrant population of some 55,000 people, around 30 times the official figure, mainly engaged in the informal sector.

This brief review of emigration trends permits two arguments. On the one hand, the phenomenon can be deflected to a certain degree, but it cannot be eliminated, until the emigrant-producing countries have managed largely to restore their labour market equilibrium. On the other hand, the constant pressure of the labour supply is counterbalanced by an equally steady demand in the host countries. The demand may take different forms, but it is present all the time: jobs of a precarious or temporary nature are available on European markets – and elsewhere – in activities for which employers prefer to make use of the flexibility of a labour force that is not too demanding in the matter of wages and working conditions. Emigration has to be seen as a two-sided phenomenon. This fact must be borne in mind in any action undertaken: there is the need to help the labour-exporting countries to create the necessary jobs at home; and the requirement to enforce greater discipline in the labour markets of the host countries to track down illegal employment.

4. International cooperation as a factor in reducing migration pressure

A new concept of international cooperation will have to be created, so that the type and volume of external aid can become a factor in reducing the need to look for work on the European markets. The object is to enable labour-exporting countries to achieve a sufficient rate of economic growth to cope with their population growth and employment problems, and to promote improved living and earnings standards.

The structure of cooperation is already improving and new forms of aid emerging. Tunisia is doing its utmost to influence the form of the contributions, giving preference to long-term over medium-term loans and making a more intense effort to obtain contributions. It is none the less true that the situation with the EC and its member countries is deteriorating. If development scenarios are to be envisaged to help potential emigrant workers to stay at home, the conditions and flow of aid will have to be seriously reconsidered.

Innovations in the context of external cooperation

External cooperation is intended primarily to finance planned projects. It has progressively taken on the form of partnership promotion, by making credit lines administered by the banks available to foreign direct investment. It ensures that the current balance of payments deficit is covered.

Multilateral institutions are becoming increasingly important in financial cooperation, and the 1980s witnessed a remarkable increase in Arab funding. Bilateral cooperation, in its various forms, is still a source of contributions to the financing of Tunisian development plans, but is declining in importance and is usually accompanied by ever more stringent terms. Tunisia is increasingly being considered as a middle-income country no longer entitled to the concessionary conditions of financial aid. Considerable reductions have been made by France, Italy and the United States, while Sweden, the Netherlands, the United Kingdom and Canada are reorganizing their contributions to take the form of improved credits or subsidies.

Financial cooperation is also becoming more diversified:

- project aid is still the principal source of development project financing; it is increasingly assuming the form of a budget, especially in the case of the EC countries, e.g. France, Germany, Italy and Spain;
- credit lines are established with the development banks; they come from multilateral institutions such as the International Bank for Reconstruction and Development, the Arab Development Bank (ADB) and the European Investment Bank (EIB), or from countries such as Italy or Sweden, which allow credit lines to be entrusted to commercial banks. Credit lines are allocated to the financing of public or private enterprise projects;
- programme aid finances imports, and the counterpart funds that it produces are made available to the aid budget. This form of cooperation has increased sharply with the economic reforms under way in Tunisia and the structural adjustment programme supporting them; considerable funds have been placed at the disposal of Tunisia, in this context, by the World Bank, the ADB and the EC, as well as by Germany, Japan and Italy;
- food aid, which is decreasing in volume each year, is intended to facilitate the import of grain, milk and vegetable oils. It is provided by the United States, Italy, France, Canada and the EC, and produces counterpart funds which are allocated to budget projects such as water and soil conservation, regional and forestry projects. These projects provide some unemployed people with jobs on public utility works;
- partnership lines have been created to finance projects carried out by Tunisian promoters with foreign partners. This form of cooperation, which encourages combined private investment, may well reduce the need to resort to foreign borrowing; it also provides easier access to new technologies and opens new markets. Conclusive experiments have been conducted with the French in this field; similar projects are planned with Italy, Spain and Belgium. There are also possibilities of involving Sweden, the United States, Canada, Japan and Switzerland;
- new prospects have recently emerged in respect of recycling the debt into projects for environmental protection, vocational training and the establishment of industrial estates.

Obviously, unless the flow of foreign capital is accompanied by favourable interest rates and repayment schedules, it will lead to an even heavier debt burden. A study by the author has drawn attention to this aspect of Tunisia's relations with the EC.[6] The flow comes from the EC as an institution, and from its member States, and consists of generous development aid and loans under market conditions.

The capital flow from the EC is combined with that of the member States, and is provided through specific channels. Three financial protocols already con-

---

[6] Capital flow and the problems of financing. International business forum on the theme "Europe and the Maghreb – A common future", organized by the Arab Institute of Heads of Enterprises of Tunis, 3-5 December 1987 in Port El Kantaoui, Soussa.

cluded with the countries of the Maghreb show definite progress, but the EC (as an institution) accounts for only a modest proportion of capital from the member States, compared with other sources of financing.

Capital flows

The agreements of April 1976 provide the earliest example of an EC financial contribution to the development of the Maghreb countries. The agreements of March 1969, with Morocco and Tunisia, described at the time as association agreements, were limited to trade. Financial cooperation was declared a priority with the EC's new global Mediterranean approach.

The structure of EC financing has two aspects. The EC's budget grants comprise loans on special conditions, repayable over 40 years, with ten years' deferment, to be allocated to the financing of social infrastructure and development, as well as risk capital. They also consist of non-refundable aid to pay the discount rate of interest on loans granted by the EIB (2 per cent) offered to the Maghreb countries only, and to finance long-term investment projects and training schemes.

Second, the EIB lends at market rates subject to market conditions, but applies a discount rate of interest. It also finances economic infrastructure, agricultural development and SMEs, and administers the special loans on budget resources for projects.

Alongside the financial cooperation of the EC, bilateral relations between the member States and the Maghreb countries have been maintained according to traditional long- and medium-term capital structures, from public sources on favourable terms and from private sources under market conditions. There has also been an increase in non-concessionary capital flows in the form of private bank loans and export credits. Direct investments and grants have steadily declined, if not entirely ceased.

There are several aspects to official aid from the member States of the EC. It is budget aid, jointly determined within the framework of the development plan, and is accompanied by favourable conditions for the receiving country. However, it is generally tied to a guaranteed private loan, which diminishes its concessionary aspect. It also tends to be linked to specific projects and the importation of goods from the donor country. Finally, official aid only partly covers expenditure in local currency.

During 1979-83, net contributions of public capital from the EC and the member States totalled US$ 2.6 billion, representing 34.2 per cent of total net contributions of the same kind received by the Maghreb at that time.

As mentioned above, the EC concluded three financial protocols with the Maghreb countries: for 1978-81 covering 339 million ECUs; for 1982-86 covering 489 million ECUs; and for 1987-91 covering 787 million ECUs. Of this, 41 per cent went to Morocco, 31 per cent to Algeria and 28 per cent to Tunisia.

However, the proportion of budget resources on favourable terms, which stood at 48 per cent in the first protocol, went down to 44 per cent in the second and to 41 per cent in the third which has, in fact, converted this source of financing into non-refundable aid.

EC contributions are still modest, accounting for only 11 per cent of total net public contributions from the EC and member States combined, and no more than 3 per cent of the overall net contribution received by the Maghreb countries.

The EC and its member States were the major suppliers of public capital to the Maghreb during 1979-83, ahead of OPEC countries (which accounted for 22.6 per cent of the total received), multilateral institutions (17.3 per cent), the other OECD countries (15.8 per cent) and the United States (10.2 per cent). As a proportion of net public capital inflow, these contributions represented 27.1 per cent for Morocco, 35.2 per cent for Algeria and very nearly half – 47.7 per cent – for Tunisia. The financial commitments of the EC countries to the Sixth and Seventh Tunisian Plans were 590.2 million dinars and 122.9 million dinars respectively.

An assessment of the 1979-86 period shows the extent to which Tunisia's external payments situation vis-à-vis the EC has deteriorated. Total net capital inflows from external operations with the EC were positive in 1979, leaving a comfortable surplus of 95.2 million dinars (equivalent to 3.8 per cent of GDP). This fell by more than half the following year, turned into a deficit in 1981, and worsened to the equivalent of 5.6 per cent of GDP in 1983. Thus, over the period, the net total deficit with the EC came to 1.1 billion dinars, whereas the total deficit with the rest of the world over the same period amounted to only 231.9 million dinars. Tunisia has thus contributed to the EC a net annual amount of 130.7 million dinars. The year 1986 was typical, when, despite its stringent adjustment programme, Tunisia had a net deficit of 163 million dinars vis-à-vis the EC, greater than the general balance of payments deficit of 152.7 million dinars.

Admittedly, this situation is caused by the current balance of payments deficit. Like a number of other countries, Tunisia has had serious difficulties in this area. The fall in energy prices, the difficulty in marketing citrus fruits and phosphates and their derivatives, the recession in the industrialized economies, and their increasing recourse to protectionism – have all helped to reduce export earnings and freeze wages; higher interest rates on private loans have added to the cost of debt servicing.

Furthermore, current revenues have increased in value by an annual average of 12.2 per cent, while current expenditure has risen at the rate of 15.2 per cent. The current balance, which was positive in 1979, ran into deficit in 1980, a deficit accentuated in the following year, increasing to 250.9 million dinars in 1982 and reaching a peak of 374.1 million dinars in 1983. This was equivalent to: 90 per cent of the general balance of payments deficit; 33.8 per cent of the year's exports of goods and services to the EC; and 6.7 per cent of GDP.

During 1982 and 1983, the general deficit fluctuated at around 400 million dinars; the current deficit vis-à-vis the EC increased by 42 per cent between 1982 and 1983. These two years also imparted a new rhythm to the spiral of deficit in current account transactions.

This escalation can be explained by the trade deficit, as merchandise transactions accounted for 52.6 per cent of current earnings and 75.7 per cent of current expenditure. We must also take into account the heavy restrictions imposed on imports, which were cut back in 1984-86. Export earnings declined between 1980 and 1982, rose slightly again in 1983, continued to progress in 1984-85 and virtually stagnated between 1985 and 1986. The restrictions on imports meant that they usually increased in value by only 3 per cent to 7 per cent annually, but with peaks in 1980, 1981 and 1983. The year 1983 was typical in this respect: exports of goods increased by 43.9 per cent, imports by 29.7 per cent, and yet the current EC deficit went up by 49.1 per cent, whereas the current global deficit varied by no more than 1.5 per cent. This was because services, which generally covered a large part of the trade deficit, also deteriorated from 1979 onwards and, with a brief improvement in 1981, provided for only one-third of this deficit in 1983, two-fifths in 1984, and half in 1985. Tourism, the main service industry, had an average annual increase rate of 7 per cent (with some 216 million dinars in earnings), but this was largely offset by the losses sustained by transport and other services, particularly public works.

The combined effect of Tunisia's increased foreign borrowings, higher interest rates on the European markets and the rise in value of repayment currencies, lifted interest payments on loans and investments significantly during the early 1980s, to stabilize only later.

Earned incomes, having risen in 1980 (by 14.1 per cent) and 1981 (by 30.6 per cent) have remained fairly constant since that date at an average level of 130 million dinars, falling in 1983 but recovering between 1985 and 1986 as a result of exchange rate movements.

The situation has thus taken a worrying, if not an alarming, turn, as far as current transactions are concerned, with: a disparity between export and import growth (a disparity kept slightly in check by restrictions on imports harmful to the country's amenities and development); a decline in earned incomes and tourism; and soaring debt servicing charges. All these factors have combined to place financial relations with the EC in an impasse. Capital flows have not helped the situation. During the period, net capital flows amounted to 495.8 million dinars, or an annual average of 61.9 million dinars, against an accumulated current payments deficit of 1,535.5 million dinars (191.9 million dinars per year). At the same time, the period was marked by a serious deterioration in the structure of capital flows. In the first place, loan capital accounted for 69.1 per cent of capital inflow, whereas grants dwindled to 3.9 per cent; direct investments accounted for 26.6 per cent.

Second, the most significant growth was in private loans, which, at 630.2 million dinars for the period, were one-and-a-half times as large as the inflow of public capital and represented 30.9 per cent of total capital inflow. This proportion is even higher if short-term capital is included: total private credits of this type were equivalent to half of gross capital inflow. In fact, like all middle-income developing countries, Tunisia borrowed heavily on the financial markets, while external public borrowing scarcely exceeded 20 per cent of total capital inflow, representing an annual average of 4.5 per cent of imports of goods and services.

Direct investment amounted to a record 511.3 million dinars for the period, but this related mainly to the oil prospecting sector, which absorbed 90 per cent of this flow. On the other hand, European participation in investment projects in manufacturing and tourism registered a sharp decline during the period.

Capital outflow during the period was large: 1,543.2 million dinars for an inflow of 2,038.4 million dinars. Overall, repayment of loan capital accounted for 91.6 per cent of capital outflow. Short-term debt outflow was twice as large as inflow: 701.9 million dinars against 355.1 million dinars.

Such a structure explains the heavy burden of Tunisian debt, both to the EC and elsewhere. In the five years 1982-86, debt servicing with the EC increased at an average annual rate of 18 per cent. In 1986 this reduced by 14.1 per cent current revenues from the EC, while the outstanding principal of the debt had multiplied by 2.6 in 6 years, to represent 20.6 per cent of GDP. The explanation is to be found in the worsening conditions of the debt: on average, for the first and second decades, and the 1982-84 period, interest rates were 3.4 per cent, 6.7 per cent and 8.04 per cent; repayment terms were 22, 14 and 12 years; while deferments were 7, 5.5 and 4.5 years.

Lastly, it should be borne in mind that, according to World Bank statistics for 1985, the outstanding debt per head of population was $ 567.9 for Tunisia, $ 621 for Algeria, and $ 669.8 for Brazil, the world's most heavily indebted country.

It is indeed a striking picture, over 20 years after the first association agreement of March 1969. The situation has compelled Tunisia to reduce its imports, slowing down economic activity, causing a fall in public revenues, a decline in investments and a consequent reduction in growth and cutbacks in jobs and incomes. Admittedly, the country is responsible for certain elements: the rigid structure of exports from enterprises and the lack of competitiveness in some products, the need to create a favourable trading climate, the concern to control budget deficits and increase the money supply and, finally, the necessity of establishing a realistic exchange rate for the national currency.

The structural adjustment programme adopted in 1986 takes these issues into account, urging economic realism based on a gradual but serious liberalization process, aimed at removing protection and deregulating the economy, and opening the country to external markets. Tunisia has enacted detailed and diversified legislation to encourage national and foreign investment; improvements are continually introduced to take into account the difficulties encountered in practice. The Government broadened these stimuli in 1987, exempting investment in export industries from all taxes and duties.

A framework such as this contains the conditions necessary for a cautious and sound recovery, and has been in place since the Seventh Plan targeted a current balance of payments deficit of 4.5 per cent of GDP (compared with 8.7 per cent for the Sixth Plan). However, consumption had to be severely reduced and investment cut – the latter was frozen at the same level as the Sixth Plan. The result was slower growth, which is precisely what job creation and borrowing capacity depend on.

Risks of full employment strategies

Tunisian planners have repeatedly devised scenarios for full employment, but on each occasion the targets have proved unachievable, mainly because of the reality of the economic and financial relations existing between Tunisia and the EC countries (as described above).

The Sixth Plan 1982-86 stated that a development pattern to ensure that the total additional demand for jobs – 324,000 – could be met without upsetting the financial balance, would require:

- double the volume of investment – 10 billion dinars – in relation to the preceding Plan, i.e. 30 per cent of GDP, with a strict orientation of investment towards labour-intensive productive sectors;
- an average annual GDP growth of 7.3 per cent, at constant prices;
- consumption maintained at a level well below that of production growth;
- increased export volume at an average annual rate of 8.3 per cent (14 per cent excluding oil).

The Seventh Plan devised a new scenario to provide employment for the 345,000 additional jobseekers expected, with:

- investment of 14 billion dinars, equivalent to 28 per cent of GDP;
- a GDP growth twice as high as that actually achieved under the preceding Plan (6 per cent instead of 3 per cent), with an annual 8 per cent increase in agricultural production at constant prices;
- severe cutbacks in consumer spending;
- exports to be increased by 9 per cent at constant prices (11.2 per cent for products other than oil).

If these targets are compared with the results achieved throughout the planning period, it becomes clear that they were beyond the country's reach. Moreover, they would have increased the current balance of payments deficit, recourse to external financing and the external debt. In both cases, the estimates were eventually reduced to more realistic levels.

The Eighth Plan 1992-96 will be the first Tunisian plan to be based on the idea of full employment of the additional workforce, estimated at 313,000 persons, through the creation of 320,000 new jobs.

In fact, bearing in mind the population growth of the past three decades and the findings of the 1989 population and employment survey, the additional demand for employment will go up to 645,000 for the decade from 1992 to 2001, i.e. an average of 65,000 per year, 63,000 per year for 1992-96 and 66,000 per year for 1997-2001. This extra demand will be marked by an increased proportion of people having received education or training – 70 per cent compared with 65 per cent under the Seventh Plan.

This Plan presupposes that 71 per cent of these new jobs will be in manufacturing and services. The steady growth of the manufacturing industries – as a result of incentives, the development of the partnership system, the satisfactory performance of textiles, leather and footwear and food industries – may well ensure the creation of 120,000 of the 210,000 jobs. The non-administrative services should provide 107,500 jobs in the tourism sector, in the wholesale and retail trade revitalized by greater liberalization, and in the small business and craft sector stimulated by investment incentives.

The rehabilitation of the fishing sector should result in the creation of some 10,000 jobs. Agriculture – which employed 25.8 per cent of the active population in

1989, compared with 37.2 per cent in 1975 and 48 per cent in 1966 – will continue to improve income levels for its population.

Investment will double during the Eighth Plan to 22,870 million dinars (equivalent to 26.1 per cent of GDP) compared with the Seventh Plan (10,650 million dinars, or 21.5 per cent of GDP). The investment structure will place greater emphasis on directly productive investment – 57.5 per cent of the total – and rely for the greater part on the private sector – 52.5 per cent.

Funding for these investments is scheduled as follows:

- increased national savings, equivalent to 25.7 per cent of GDP as against 19 per cent under the previous Plan;
- this will lead to reduced public and private spending, which will rise at an average annual rate of 4.2 per cent compared with 6 per cent for GDP;
- national savings would therefore finance 71.5 per cent of investments instead of the previous 66.4 per cent; external financing would cover 28.5 per cent instead of 33.7 per cent;
- exports of goods and services would grow, in volume, at an average annual rate of 10.9 per cent, excluding oil, with goods from industry, especially the mechanical and electrical engineering industries (14.9 per cent), and services from tourism (18.9 per cent). Imports, on the other hand, would increase only by 7.5 per cent in volume, owing to the progressive improvement of national industrial integration. The current balance of payments deficit would be kept at 2.9 per cent of GDP.

External financing is to assume the structure indicated in Table 6.4.

Table 6.4. Composition of external aid (per cent)

Sources/Plan	1962-71	4th Plan	5th Plan	6th Plan	7th Plan	8th Plan
Grants	21.7	14.1	4.9	2.8	5.0	3.4
Participation	11.3	18.8	25.0	25.9	19.0	18.3
Long-term loans	40.8	44.6	32.6	31.7	53.3	47.6
Medium-term loans	25.5	22.5	37.5	39.6	22.7	30.7

Although investments appear to be the same proportionally in the Eighth Plan as previously, this source of external financing is expected to involve more direct investment – other than in the field of energy prospecting – owing to such forms of cooperation as partnerships and subcontracting in activities with export possibilities. They are also the result of the opening up of the Tunisian financial market to the outside world and the scheduled privatization of public sector enterprises.

Long-term loans account for a considerable sum – 3.9 billion dinars. About half of this has yet to be raised, in the form of programme or project loans, and should be used mainly to finance the private sector.

Medium-term loans will increase proportionally, though that should not seriously affect Tunisia's foreign debt structure, which will still be dominated by long-term loans at the end of the period – 74.6 per cent compared with 77.5 per cent in 1991.

Is this projection realizable? The situation in the field over the past three decades compels prudence, despite the gains from the effort expended and the profound changes that have taken place in the Tunisian economy.

The debt problem is still overwhelming. Since 1986 the balance of net external borrowing for debt repayments and interest charges has been negative, and is likely to remain so throughout the entire Eighth Plan, and probably longer unless something fairly drastic is done.

In addition, demographic trends, though optimistic, indicate that severe pressure will be maintained on the labour market for at least two to three decades. If the total fertility rate continues to decline as recent figures suggest, it will go down to 2.61 in 2001 and 2.05 in 2026, the latter figure being the population replacement rate. If, on the other hand, these trends are accelerated through appropriate policy measures, the population replacement rate could be achieved at the beginning of the third millennium. However, current birth and death rates will lead to the following increases in the working-age population (persons 15-59 years as a percentage of the total population):

- 1991: 55.8 per cent;
- 1996: 58.4 per cent;
- 2001: 60.7 per cent;
- 2026: 64.8 per cent.

The coming decades: An ongoing challenge

The additional demand for jobs will continue to increase steadily and job-creating investment will have to be doubled for the next two decades at constant 1990 prices. On the basis of the demand identified for 1992-96, it is possible to assess the average demand for employment over the next two decades, allowing for existing unemployment at some 100,000 jobs per year. At $50,000 per job, this entails an annual investment of $5 billion.

Unemployment is the real challenge facing the Tunisian – and other Maghreb – economies. Emigration, self-sufficiency in food, balance of payments deficits, and foreign debt, all flow from this. The various countries will have to achieve the necessary efficiency to allocate their limited resources to the best possible ends.

An analysis of the progress of the Tunisian economy in section 2 of this paper shows that Tunisia has succeeded in altering its initial development strategies and is moving cautiously towards an economy freed from government management, with a redistribution of roles between the public and private sectors and a move to market practices of regulating the productive system. The procedure is as yet in its infancy, but progress is being made to a market economy based on free enterprise, realistic prices, enterprise as the driving force of growth, fair competition and, lastly, profit as a measure of performance.

In this setting, the country's economic problems can be clearly identified – and employment is the root cause. International cooperation is a necessary part of facing this challenge. The historic relations linking Tunisia and the Maghreb countries with Europe, especially the EC, are obvious. Yet the extent of the problems facing Tunisia and the Maghreb countries questions the reasoning behind and implementation of classic cooperation.

New forms of cooperation

The forms of international cooperation have already been examined. Innovations have been introduced. These should be enhanced in view of the specific problem of emigration. To start with, it would be helpful to drop the term "middle-income country" which has the effect of reducing international aid and of justifying the suspension of concessionary aid to such countries. While the term may reflect a certain level of income, it is not right that a country that has achieved some success should be penalized as a result.

In this context, official development assistance (ODA), with its high content of grants, programme aid and long-term loans on favourable terms, must be allowed to continue for a long time to come, at a sufficient level to cover investment in job creation to absorb potential emigrants.

When launching its vast economic reform programmes, Tunisia successfully managed to find the necessary bilateral and multilateral financial support. In particular, the World Bank, the ADB and the EC provided loans and grants in the form of programme aid to finance imports, and counterpart funds increased budget resources, intended mainly for training and employment. This support for recovery and reconstruction – the scope of which is to be widened to include new development objectives – must be sustained until the objectives have been achieved. Halting aid as soon as positive results appear would undoubtedly jeopardize the entire process.

This type of aid, however, still generates debt, at a time when the country's commitments are at their height. The aim should therefore be to try to expand foreign direct investment. As was pointed out earlier, Tunisia has introduced numerous incentives and guarantees in this respect. The partnership formula and the associated credit lines must be expanded, as they symbolize a joint commitment.

Finally, cooperation should take into account the size of the country's external debt. Tunisia is one of the few developing countries not to have applied to have its external debt rescheduled. The burden of these obligations was examined earlier. Tunisia has officially launched the idea of recycling this debt: this would involve using the interest payments and repayment of the principal to finance investment. It should be remembered that for the Seventh Plan 1987-91, the sum of interest and loan repayments made by Tunisia came to 5207.9 million dinars, which is very nearly the equivalent of the annual investment provided for in the Eighth Plan.

The 1991 World Bank annual report states that "Recent, more far-reaching understandings with Poland and Egypt through the Paris Club,[7] provide for reducing the net present value of future debt-service payments by 50 per cent. Over

---

[7] The term "Paris Club" refers to the ad hoc meetings of the creditor governments that organize the renegotiation of loan agreements between countries and private export credit agreements supported by official guarantees.

and above this relief, individual creditors may convert part of the debt into local currency obligations, through debt-for-equity, debt-for-environment and debt-for-development swaps."

Although the same report later specifies that such programmes "are considered as exceptional", the idea and techniques should be borne in mind for job-creating investment programmes. The idea was put into practice for the first time in Tunisia, with Germany granting an environment protection project for two-thirds of the annual debt service. Sweden later followed this example. Such a policy is worth developing.

Tunisia has also officially launched the idea of a regional development bank. This initiative has so far had less success than the European Bank for Reconstruction and Development – EBRD – to aid the Eastern European countries. A Maghreb Bank for Reconstruction and Development – MBRD – could be founded on the basis of funds deriving from debt repayments, consolidated by direct investment by the EC and the member States, as well as by capital from Maghreb and Arab States and financial institutions. The MBRD could initiate and finance Maghreb-Europe projects promoting job creation and consolidating trade relations between the two regions by opening up markets and facilitating the free movement of goods.

A certain degree of diversification is already apparent in existing cooperation. This must be further strengthened. International cooperation, already functioning in the field of training and family planning programmes, must be extended, as both of these sectors are directly linked to employment and emigration. Action must be further stepped up through the acquisition of new technologies and markets, through the consolidation of the national private sector and the opening up of new areas of intervention.

Job creation and the reduction of migration pressures require the range of cooperation to be broadened. Cooperation generally brings in new technology to adapt the country's production to the needs of consumer markets, and can expand export markets. The maintenance of agreements relating to Tunisia's exports of textiles – mainly garments, hosiery and knitted goods – is a case in point.

The economic reforms introduced in Tunisia, and the preceding structural adjustment programme, have limited the role of the state and, consequently, the mobilization of resources to finance the public sector; it would be realistic to open official aid credits to the private sector. Half the commitment of the ADB is geared towards private sector finance. The ADB and the International Finance Corporation (IFC) have shown willingness to support the private sector without requiring a state guarantee.

The restructuring and privatization of public sector enterprises begun by Tunisia is proceeding gently. The IFC and the World Bank have encouraged this process, especially when the necessary support is provided through EC cooperation.

Development, by its nature, generates new problems and needs. This applies in particular to the environment and the necessity of reconciling the imperative of growth with the need to protect the world in which we live. All multilateral cooperation schemes give broad support to research programmes and projects, technical assistance and investment in environment protection. Any reassessment of international cooperation must obviously retain this aspect.

Furthermore, the Tunisian economy, like many other developing country economies, suffers from regional disparities. Although successive development plans have brought about a better distribution of investment, the problem is still serious, especially as the regions have not benefited from development and they build up the pressure of migration, first to the capital and the major cities, then to other countries. It is therefore vital to target investment at regional integration. In terms of international cooperation, this is beginning to be developed by multilateral institutions – UNDP, ADB, and the Arab Economic and Social Development Fund. The EC has already advocated this course in its new Mediterranean policy. Admittedly, regional development is an arduous undertaking: well-designed regional projects are not always available. Rural development, and integrated rural development programmes, have been organized in Tunisia since the earliest development plans, but a greater level of effectiveness is required. International cooperation could offer positive initiatives.

In this context, the entire agricultural sector should be reviewed from the point of view of production, employment and earnings. Food self-sufficiency and improved agricultural employment are constant Tunisian agricultural policy objectives. However, the issues of land ownership, modernizing cultivation methods, investment options, and financing, etc., must be considered carefully.

5. Conclusion

An analysis of the problems associated with employment and emigration, from the point of view of economic strategy, brings out the major constraints confronting the Tunisian economy. These constraints, by their very nature, and by the volume of financing they call for, reflect the new dimension that international cooperation should assume, in its effort to help contain emigration. It must be said that international cooperation, in its present state as regards Tunisia and the Maghreb in general, lacks the capacity to cope with current problems. Can it acquire this capacity? It is hoped that this review of the various aspects of the problem in Tunisia suggests pointers to the ways in which it can.

7

International migration and foreign assistance: The case of the Philippines

G. Ranis

1. Introduction

One of the best known abstractions of economic theory is that there exists an underlying tendency towards international equalization of factor prices, partly achieved by the movement of people from poor to rich countries and of capital from rich to poor countries, but mainly by the movement of goods which assimilate both people and capital. Moreover, once we abandon the strict Heckscher-Ohlin assumptions about the equivalent state of technical knowledge everywhere, the transfer of technology between countries can become an additional important equalizing element.

Trade based on comparative advantage is undoubtedly the most important and powerful of the various forces leading to the equalization of factor prices, if not incomes, around the world. It has the capacity to absorb cheap labour in former colonies – the developing countries of today – and to ship it, in the form of labour-intensive goods, to the former mother country – the developed countries of today. The same principle applies in reverse for the flow of capital-intensive goods.

The main reason that the movement of factors – capital and labour – is only the second most important force is that it is subject to far greater restrictions than those relating to goods. Labour, especially, is restricted. The terms of reference for this paper are deceptively straightforward, i.e. to concentrate on what one particular form of capital movement from rich to poor countries – Official Development Assistance (ODA) – can accomplish in stemming the effective demand of labour to move from poor to rich countries. ODA will, however, be broadly defined, i.e. to include contributions by the multilateral international financial institutions and government-backed private flows. We will not deal directly with international trade nor the movement of private capital, even though we recognize them to be potentially important contributors to reducing the pressure for migration. Nor will we separately address the movement of human capital, i.e. highly skilled labour, usually from rich to poor countries – but sometimes, like perverse movements of private capital or "capital flight", moving in the opposite direction under the "brain drain" label. We shall also leave to one side any direct analysis of the process of technology transfer, presumably from rich to poor countries, and its adaptation in the poor country.

The implications of international migration – and of restrictions on it – for the welfare of either the donor or the recipient country, or for the global economy as a whole, will not be of concern to us. Nor will we analyse the factors which determine national immigration barriers or those which hinder or facilitate illegal migration. What we intend to focus on are the factors that influence the effective demand for migration – though we fully recognize the potential relevance of the discouragement factor and that the excess of effective demand over legally permitted levels increases the pressure for illegal migration and is indeed the cause of current enhanced international tensions on the subject. The focus of this paper is therefore severely restricted: to examine the potential role of a broadly defined ODA in reducing the effective demand for labour migration from a typical labour-abundant developing country (in this case, the Philippines) to a typical capital-abundant developed country (in this case, the United States).

However, while concentrating on the possible role of ODA in reducing the pressure for migration, we will include its possible indirect impact, i.e. by working through the development process itself which is intimately associated with other flows between rich and poor countries. As Douglas Massey put it, "The way for developed countries ultimately to control migration is to promote economic development";[1] the potential promotion instrument to be examined here is ODA.

The actual effective demand for migration can, moreover, be usefully broken down further into individuals' desire to migrate and their *ability* to migrate. The desire to migrate in turn is a function, inter alia, of a) the objective size of current gaps in average incomes, public amenities, and status levels between countries; b) the extent of individual actors' knowledge (or lack of it) about these differences; c) the individual actors' information or assessment about the probability of achieving given income, amenity, and status levels in the potential countries of destination, all over time.

The ability to migrate is a function, inter alia, of a) the precise level and quality of barriers to immigration in potential destination countries, possibly affecting various potential migrant groups differently; b) the distance, transportation and initial set-up costs in various potential destination countries; c) the extended family's financial resources (in the country of origin and the potential countries of destination) and its willingness to support the individual actor's migration decision; d) the extent of perfection of official capital markets to finance the actor's migration decision; and finally, e) home government policies encouraging (or discouraging) the emigration decision.

In addressing our main theme, we will find it useful to restrict our scope yet further and explicitly exclude consideration of some of these dimensions, or to make some reasonable assumptions about them. For example, in the "desire to migrate" category, we shall accept the fact that very large differences (approximately 20 times) in average wage levels exist between Filipino and United States workers and that we can assume no sizeable information gap, i.e. that the poorest peasants in relatively isolated parts of the Philippines know, via the media and, more important, via relatives and friends abroad, about the average current conditions of life in the United

---

[1] Massey, 1988.

States. Similarly, in the "ability to migrate" category, we shall take the current immigration policy of the rich countries, in this case that of the United States, as given, though this does not imply any judgement as to its optimality from either a national or global welfare point of view. The same holds for the distance, cost of migration and the possibilities and risks attached to illegal migration to the United States, all obviously very different for the individual Filipino than the individual Mexican.

Erasing some of these potentially very interesting issues from our canvas on pragmatic grounds still leaves us with a number of important dimensions to consider. Accordingly, section 2 will examine the pattern of postwar Philippine development in relation to international migration as well as the quantity and quality of various types of foreign aid. Our basic purpose in this section will be to document the marked absence of balance in the Philippine development path during the postwar era, which substantially increased people's desire for international migration, if also somewhat suppressing their *ability* to migrate.

Section 3 will look towards the future and focus on the potential for redressing the historical record by restructuring the way ODA is allocated and negotiated to reduce the effective demand for international migration from the Philippines. The emphasis will be mainly on how to diminish the desire to migrate while preventing the ability to migrate from improving substantially. Finally, section 4 will briefly summarize and attempt to generalize the argument.

2. The Philippines: Past development patterns, migration and the role of ODA

Past development patterns

If, as we assume, it is individual actors' perceptions of their present and prospective well-being in their home country relative to that in the potential destination country which is the crucial ingredient in the desire to migrate, it is important to understand how the past pattern of Philippine development has served consistently to enhance that desire. In brief, in 1946 the newly independent Government inherited a dualistic colonial structure composed of a relatively neglected food-producing agricultural subsector, a relatively favoured cash crop-producing agricultural subsector and a still small, mainly urban, industrial-cum-services sector.

After political independence, the normal restructuring associated with import substitution took place, i.e. the proceeds from the cash-crop exports were redirected from further enclave expansion into the creation of urban industry, supported by the well-known syndrome of protectionist/interventionist policies. While this first postcolonial step is common practice in developing countries, import substitution in the Philippines proved more severe and prolonged than elsewhere: protection was heavier, interest rates more repressed, the currency persistently more overvalued, and fiscal and monetary excesses greater. This meant more discrimination against agriculture, more neglect of medium- and small-scale industrial development outside Manila, and more discrimination against non-traditional exports.

Indeed, once the early, consumer goods type of import substitution regime had run out of steam in the early 1960s, policy-makers continued to pursue an increasingly narrow, unusually urban and capital-intensive industry-oriented development path, focused more now on durables, capital goods and the processing of raw materials, with necessarily increased domestic distortions and protection from the rest of the world. With respect to the majority of the population, concentrated in the rural areas and in the urban informal sector, this meant a continuously slower expansion of employment opportunities, increased underemployment and unemployment, a worsening distribution of income, and increased levels of poverty.

In summary, the premature shift to capital-intensive output mixes and technologies and the wholly inadequate participation of medium- and small-scale, especially rural, industrial activity led to the continuing slow expansion of demand for unskilled and semi-skilled labour. The rural economy, where approximately 50 per cent of people still reside, remained basically an afterthought, with mainly the cash crops, e.g. bananas, copra, and sugar, receiving some policy and research attention, at least relative to the food crops, e.g. rice, maize and the pulses. As a consequence, instead of balanced growth between an increasingly productive food-producing agricultural sector, on the one hand, and rural as well as urban non-agricultural activities, on the other, what happened in the Philippines was rural-urban migration without the simultaneous release of agricultural surpluses (food) and without the requisite creation of additional productive jobs, rural or urban. Such unbalanced growth in turn led to the rapid expansion of the so-called urban informal sector which is responsible for 60 per cent to 70 per cent of total non-agricultural employment and which contains a large proportion of those in disguised and open unemployment. It is estimated that over 90 per cent of past migrants were drawn from the urban population, fully one-third of which is made up of informal sector squatters.[2] Moreover, as population and labour force growth have added more to the pool of unemployed and underemployed people than could be absorbed into productive employment, rural or urban, this situation has become worse over time.

Given the Philippines' good natural resource base and the relatively plentiful inflow of foreign capital throughout the 1960s and 1970s, overall growth rates in income nevertheless remained quite respectable by international standards (approximately 6 per cent annually during 1965-80). How that growth was generated in the context of high and increasing levels of open and disguised unemployment was, however, crucial in persuading a large number of individuals to move to the urban areas, and a considerable number of these to want to leave the Philippines.

In brief, unlike the east Asian countries in the 1960s, and unlike some of the south-east Asian countries more recently, the Philippines has so far refused fundamentally to restructure its economy towards mobilizing its rural sector in a balanced growth context, and towards the full exploitation of its potential for labour-intensive industrial exports. The system's ability to continue on this inefficient path for several decades has been based in part on the financing made possible by the country's

---

[2] Alonzo, 1991, p. 67.

diversified natural resource export base, and in part by the willingness of foreigners, in particular the commercial banks in the 1970s, and official donors throughout, to continue to support it.

The Philippines' relatively easy access to foreign exchange has meant that this narrowly based, élitist growth path, with little rate of return justification required to direct the allocation of either domestic or foreign capital, could continue until the early 1980s. Whenever efforts were made, tentative though they might have been, to move away from the highly intervened or tightly controlled economy syndrome and towards substantial policy reform, as in the mid-1970s under Marcos and again in the early 1980s under Aquino, the heat was taken off by the ready availability of foreign capital, including ODA. There is little doubt that some of the gathering momentum for the Marcos reforms was reversed by the ready availability of low-interest commercial bank loans; and that some of the momentum for reform in the early Aquino days was again reversed by the eagerness of the United States, Japan and the multilateral donors to assist the new "people power" Government without really insisting on a fundamental change in the growth pattern. This has been the case despite the fact that donor negotiations have frequently emphasized aid instruments and carried promising structural adjustment-related titles for almost two decades.

Overall unemployment, poverty, and income distribution levels, initially already bad by international standards, continued to worsen throughout the 1970s and early 1980s. Expectations that substantial improvements are close at hand will have to overcome the massive disappointment over the failure of Marcos' "new society" and Aquino's "people power" to effect fundamental change. The distribution of the so-called social expenditures – health, education, etc. – has been heavily urban-biased. Individual Filipinos are frustrated with both the current and prospective distribution of public goods, as well as employment and income opportunities; to this frustration must be added a persistent feature which is as potent as expected lifetime earning and amenity gaps in generating a desire for migration. This is related to the less well-defined, and difficult to measure, idea of *status*. Simon Kuznets has called our attention to the importance of a spirit of nationalism providing hope for the eventual improvement of conditions through nation-building. For the individual this means that, even though one's own present status may be unsatisfactory – and likely to remain so in relative income terms – all may be forgiven if one can count on an improvement in relative status as the nation itself moves forward confidently and begins to assert itself. The point is that an individual may well prefer to be in a dynamic international "catch-up" situation to which he or she can expect to make a contribution than to be just another emigrant Filipino in the United States, possibly lower in relative income as well as social status, even if commanding a higher absolute level of income there.

The notion that the desire to emigrate is based more on expected relative status and relative income in the two situations, rather than simply current income gaps, is illustrated by the fact that the largest movement of people from Europe to the New World in the nineteenth century came from the United Kingdom, then the richest country in the world.[3] This has been a noted feature of the Philippines, traced

---

[3] See Thomas, 1954.

back, according to some observers, to the peculiarly unhappy combination of Spanish and United States colonial experience, which destroyed the national pride and cohesiveness so essential for nation-building and consequently contributed substantially to the desire to migrate.

Certainly there is hardly another society in the world where the gap between the potential, and achieved, participatory growth path is as large as in the Philippines. Governments' increasing lack of credibility has led to surprisingly good-natured cynicism and apathy which have allowed this gap to continue to widen and which have encouraged individuals to opt out of the system altogether. The implied absence of organic nationalism is also well demonstrated by the continued readiness of Filipinos – in spite of so many past disappointments – to continue to expect a "saviour" within an ostensibly open democratic system. This is well illustrated by the early Marcos and early Aquino days, which were soon followed by disappointment, and by the continuing apparent ability of the élites to continue to rule. The fact that Imelda Marcos could be seriously considered a presidential candidate in 1992 is a case in point. The consequence of such a perpetual cycle of naivety and disenchantment has, over the years, created a mounting desire among many urban skilled and unskilled workers to migrate, and has led to the well-recognized twin phenomena of capital flight and brain drain.

It is undoubtedly instructive in this context to compare the performance of the Philippines with Taiwan (China) and the Republic of Korea – early success stories – and with Thailand – a more recent success story. It should be emphasized that all these countries or areas were subjected to the shock of a deteriorating international environment. The Philippine performance in crucial aspects, e.g. per capita income growth (Table 7.1), income distribution (Table 7.2), and employment generation (Table 7.3) is comparatively bad and has continued to deteriorate even though the country's own aggregate performance has not been continuously disastrous. Comparing only Taiwan (China) and the Philippines (for data reasons) we may also note the remarkably greater success in Taiwan (China) in retaining workers in the rural areas engaged in non-agricultural activities.

In sum, it is the narrow, compartmentalized *nature* of the growth path, not its overall performance, which has been and remains the problem for many Filipinos' expectations and which has made them ever less ready to remain in the country. Even the "recovery" of the last few years is merely the country getting up off the floor as a consequence of a temporary respite in exogenous shocks, including an improvement in some key cash-crop export prices. As important, the Philippines continues to enjoy a strong geopolitical standing with donors, including the United States, Japan and the multilateral institutions.

Unfortunately, therefore, the current recovery from deep crisis does not constitute a change of direction for the economy. It is unlikely to redress the structural problems mentioned above, including the lack of participatory, especially rural, growth, the continued high incidence of poverty in both the rural and urban informal sectors, and continued overall regional imbalance. Indeed, if, in macroeconomic terms, nothing happens but a return to the higher growth rates of the 1970s, rather than a different direction for the economy, the pressure for international migration will not abate. In fact, disappointed yet again, this time with the failure of Aquino's

Table 7.1. Average real per capita GDP growth rates, selected countries or areas (per cent)

Country/Year	1950-59	1960-69	1970-79	1980-86
Philippines	3.2	2.1	3.3	-1.5
Thailand	2.8	5.0	5.0	3.1
Korea (Rep. of)	1.3[1]	4.9	7.5	4.3
Taiwan (China)	4.7[2]	5.9	8.1	5.6

[1] 1952-59.
[2] 1953-59.

Sources: United Nations, *Statistical Yearbook*, various years; United Nations, *National Income Statistics: Analysis of Main Aggregates*, 1983; Summers and Heston, 1984, pp. 207-262; *Statistical Yearbook of the Republic of China* [Taiwan], various years.

Table 7.2. Income distribution (Gini coefficients), selected countries or areas

Philippines	.49 (1956)	.50 (1961)	.49 (1971)	.50 (1977)	.45 (1985)
Thailand	...	.41 (1962)	.44 (1968)	.45 (1981)	...
Korea (Rep. of)	...	...	.37 (1971)	.38 (1976)	.36 (1982)
Taiwan (China)	.56 (1950)	.44 (1959)	.29 (1970)	.29 (1978)	.27 (1985)

... = figures not available.

Sources: Jain, 1975; Fei, Ranis and Kuo, 1979; Fields, 1989; *Philippine Statistical Yearbook*, various years.

Table 7.3. Annual growth of employment in manufacturing, selected countries or areas

Philippines		Thailand	
1956-65	1.51	1973-80	7.49
1965-75	4.13	1984-88	4.39
1975-83	1.32		

Korea, Rep. of		Taiwan (China)	
1965-70	10.76	1954-61	3.10
1970-75	11.33	1961-70	8.87
1975-80	6.21	1970-80	8.31
1980-88	5.81	1980-87	4.75

Sources: National Statistical Office, the Philippines, *Labour Force Survey*, various years; Shih, 1983; *Report of the Labour Force Survey*, Thailand, 1984-1988; The Bank of Korea, *Economic Statistics Yearbook*, various years; *Yearbook of Labour Statistics*, Taiwan, China; Ho, 1978.

"people power" to change things, average Filipinos' assessments of prospective incomes, amenities, and social status at home and in the United States are not likely to change markedly.

Past aid patterns

The contribution of bilateral and multilateral foreign assistance to economic development in the past has been less than optimal. In this context it is essential to focus on actual lending activities, rather than the economic analysis and rhetoric of the various donors. This is because, while the analytical system dominated by economists has usually done well in focusing on the shortcomings of the Philippine development path and in proposing improvements to it, the actual lending system, dominated by political considerations, has continued to reflect the institutional priority to keep the money flowing and maintain good relations with the Government. This has been the case even if it meant eventual major departures from the policy conditions mutually agreed to in negotiations. The latest evidence is the October cancellation of the February 1992 MAI (Multilateral Assistance Initiative) pledging session, only to be rescheduled for later in the year – once the IMF has given its inevitable, if delayed, green light.

Whether one uses a broad or narrow definition of foreign aid, the Philippines has consistently experienced substantial disbursements of assistance flows from abroad, both bilateral and multilateral (see Table 7.4). In fact, the approximately US$ 2 billion annual flow represents the highest per capita aid level in Asia, with the United States giving the country 75 per cent of its regional economic assistance. It should also be recalled that, especially before the debt crisis of the mid-1980s, most of the lending to the Philippines was of the project variety (see Table 7.5). While we do not suggest that such aid was wasted – much rural development was financed with many schools and roads built – relatively little of this investment can be said to have affected the structure of the economy.

Project assistance over the decades can be characterized, not too unkindly, as largely responsive to Filipino requests, marginally incorporating project-related policy improvements but largely staying away from macroeconomic or even sectoral policy issues which – if tackled at all – were left to the international financial institutions. The United States felt itself particularly handicapped by the presence of the United States bases, the controversy over whether aid related to the use of these bases really constituted rent or could carry conditions, plus the inevitable spillover of its "special relationship" with the Philippines onto that of other donors.

Balance of payments support, accompanied by policy discourse, did, of course, become the norm in the 1980s – along with World Bank structural adjustment loans and IMF standby and Extended Fund Facilities. But if one looks dispassionately at the record of achievement over several decades, it must be admitted that it has been at best, halting and incomplete, with one step backwards for every one-and-a-half steps forward. As already noted, the real difficulty has been that the lenders have been altogether too anxious to continue to help the Philippines by smothering it in foreign assistance, instead of recognizing that the best way to proceed may be by being less eager, and by engaging in major aid packages only when it is clear that local decision-makers have, in fact, designed their own programmes and credible reform packages. Unfortunately, the intrinsic donor unwillingness to take such a posture – incidentally not unique to the Philippines – has been exacerbated by the presence of the United States bases, as well as by Japan's, the ADB's and other donors' own reluctance to insist on policy reforms.

Table 7.4. Public and publicly guaranteed disbursements to the Philippines (millions of US dollars)

Year	1970	1980	1983	1984	1985	1986	1987	1988	1989	1990
Total	141	1 382	2 344	1 415	1 460	1 430	1 252	1 248	1 356	2 155
Official creditors	74	461	1 184	997	717	759	1 126	1 081	1 234	1 486
Multilateral	17	321	795	496	391	341	405	424	654	853
Concessional	6	61	130	94	62	73	69	75	82	139
IDA	0	2	13	10	13	8	8	3	1	0
Non-concessional	11	260	665	402	329	268	335	349	572	714
IBRD	16	229	600	291	263	189	262	258	463	506
Bilateral	57	140	389	502	326	418	721	658	580	633
Concessional	15	102	174	194	184	280	640	653	379	575
Private creditors	66	920	1 161	418	743	671	126	167	123	669
Bonds	0	96	75	0	0	0	0	0	0	424
Commercial banks	50	657	754	103	412	530	9	8	0	167
Other private	16	167	332	314	330	140	117	159	122	79

Source: World Bank, *World Debt Tables*, 1991.

Table 7.5. Sectoral allocation of United States aid disbursements to the Philippines (percentage distribution)

Sector/Year	1970	1980	1983	1984	1985	1986	1987	1988	1989	1990
Agriculture	4.9	3.4	2.1	13.3	10.6	11.0	8.1	28.0	4.2	10.6
Balance of payments support	22.4	8.0	3.4	14.3	39.9	47.6	41.1	15.9	33.9	39.3
Communication	1.4	0.1	0.4	0.6	0.5	0.5	1.2	3.4	7.2	0.6
Education	1.4	1.3	0.8	0.8	1.5	1.7	3.0	1.8	1.5	0.6
Energy	13.3	20.4	24.0	25.6	18.8	16.1	16.5	14.0	14.2	16.7
Industry and trade	2.1	1.6	0.0	0.0	0.5	0.8	0.0	0.0	0.0	0.5
Manufacturing	31.5	2.4	11.0	9.2	6.6	5.0	2.1	0.6	0.9	4.0
Social services	8.4	30.0	30.2	18.3	11.4	8.2	9.1	11.7	28.0	17.1
Transport	14.7	32.9	14.9	13.5	7.6	4.0	4.8	5.0	4.5	6.2
Other	0.0	0.0	13.2	4.3	2.5	5.1	14.2	19.6	5.5	4.4
Total	143	1 382	2 344	1 417	1 461	1 430	1 254	1 248	1 356	2 158

Source: World Bank, *World Debt Tables*, 1991.

Past migration patterns

Given the past conditions of economic growth and the role of ODA, it is small wonder that the Philippines has been one of a relatively small number of developing countries in which the demand for international migration has constituted a significant social and demographic phenomenon. With respect to the particular issue of Filipino migration to the United States, this phenomenon has a long history, going back to the early twentieth century agricultural labour needs of California and Hawaii. After an interwar hiatus, an increasing number of Filipinos wanted to emigrate to the United States after the Second World War, partly as a result of contact with American servicemen and partly as a result of changes in United States legislation. Amendments to the Immigration and Nationality Act of 1965 sharply increased Filipino immigration such that the Philippines soon took second place, after Mexico, as the main source of United States immigrants and became the leading exporter of Asian migrants to the United States, outdistancing others by substantial margins. The continued relative deterioration of the economy and the continuing political turmoil since have presumably only served to further fuel the desire for migration.

The pattern of just who is able to come, of course, is very much a function of United States immigration laws, e.g. the family reunification and occupational preference provisions of the code clearly provide the major explanation of the changing composition of Philippine arrivals in the United States. These provisions of United States law, plus the presence of the United States bases in the Philippines, have thus interacted to largely determine the sex and age composition of past legal immigrants. One notes the preponderance of females and of the relatively young among the migrants, even though the powerful family reunion provisions of United States law do not explicitly discriminate against either sex or any age group. But none of this vitiates the point about what basically influences the desire to move. What we maintain is that, everything else being equal, the desire of individuals to leave the Philippines, including those associated with United States personnel and those with links to previously migrated Filipinos, would have been substantially reduced had there been a different trend in Philippine economic conditions over time.

Turning briefly to the *ability* of Filipinos to migrate, it is clearly more difficult for the poor and those without reliably good prospects to move, especially when distances are substantial and costs not insignificant. Much would then depend on the extent of access to family resources or official capital markets by those keen to migrate. Those at the lower end of the income scale, urban slum dwellers, small landowners, tenants and landless rural workers, can be assumed to have virtually no access to official credit – especially given the rather repressed financial markets still in vogue in the Philippines, in spite of the repeal of the laws on usury some years ago. While there is no direct statistical evidence available on this subject, it is safe to surmise that the majority of would-be Philippine migrants to the United States have access mainly to the network of informal markets, specifically by receiving support from their relatives and friends already abroad. The formation of these networks also causes the information and transport costs of migration to fall over time, enhancing the ability to migrate.

It should also be noted here that the Philippine Government has historically actively promoted migration, especially to the Middle East. The Labour Code, for example, was amended in 1976 to explicitly support the Overseas Migrant Worker Programme which provides information and assistance to potential and actual migrants – though mainly focused on the guest worker phenomenon. Aware of the persistently serious unemployment and underemployment problem left in the wake of the failure of both macro- and microeconomic policies – as well as the occasional balance of payments crisis – the Government has positively encouraged the outflow of labour and the related inflow of remittances through the services of its Overseas Employment Administration. Remittances from migrant workers, whether voluntary or mandatory (as in the Philippines) have played an inordinately large role in the total foreign exchange earnings of many labour surplus developing countries, including the Philippines.[4] It is, moreover, interesting to note (see Tables 7.6 and 7.7) how drastically the composition of contract worker migration has shifted, from labourers going to the Middle East to professional and service workers going to Asia. While this effort of the Philippine Government – information, training, legal advice and emergency financial support – was initially focused heavily on the Middle East after the first and second oil shocks, it has undoubtedly also been reflected in an enhanced ability to migrate worldwide.[5]

There are, of course, other interactions between the desire to migrate and the ability to do so, either resulting from supply-side factors or from destination country limitations on entry. What is most relevant for our purposes is the size of the effective (or excess) demand for migration, i.e. the gap between the desire to migrate on the one hand, and the legal ceiling or the ability to migrate, whichever is lower, on the other. If the legal ceiling is the limiting factor, as is likely, this gap causes increased pressure for illegal migration and international tension.

Projecting a society's growth performance forward, we can, moreover, usefully distinguish between the case of an "unsuccessful", non-participatory, growth path (the Philippines) and a "successful", participatory, growth path (east Asia); these are illustrated heuristically in Figures 7.1a and 7.1b. On the assumption that the legal immigration ceiling is exogenously given – though it may be gradually rising over time in both cases – we focus our attention on the contrast in the changing patterns over time of the desire and ability to migrate.

Taking the Philippine historical case first, we may note the sharply rising volume of those keen to emigrate as their frustration continues to grow. Individual actors' ability to migrate probably also rises somewhat but rather more gently as a function of income growth, even if the pattern is non-participatory and poorly distributed. These trends are reflected in an ever increasing gap between the desire to migrate and the limiting factor – the excess demand.

In contrast, if we examine the east Asian case, we note that, while the desire to migrate may also rise for a time, it will ultimately decline, presumably once labour

---

[4] The dependence on remittance earnings, especially from the Middle East, was even more pronounced for Muslim countries such as Pakistan where they accounted for more than 90 per cent of export earnings in the early 1980s.

[5] It undoubtedly also raised people's awareness of the migration option – thus further stimulating the demand side.

Figure 7.1a Non-participatory growth path: The Phillipine case

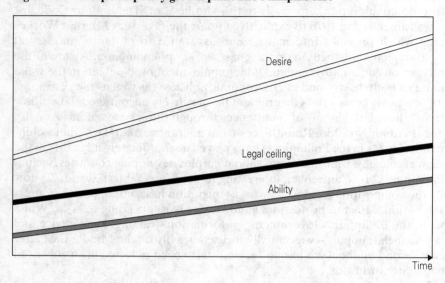

Figure 7.1b Participatory Growth path: The East Asian case

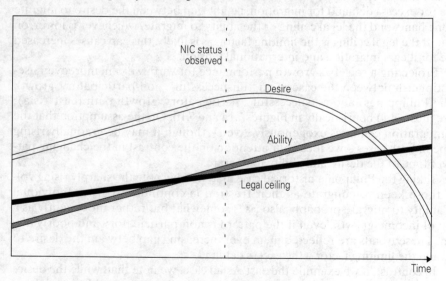

Table 7.6. Processed land-based Philippine contract workers by major occupation group, 1975-86

Year	1975	1976	1977	1978	1979	1980	1981	1982	1983	1984	1985	1986
Total	12 501	19 221	36 676	50 961	92 519	157 394	210 936	250 115	380 263	371 065	371 754	357 687
Group no.												
1	6 685	6 796	4 707	11 335	17 964	24 361	26 680	28 435	52 931	65 401	75 959	87 569
2	71	82	210	331	1 441	740	1 804	1 462	1 870	1 222	1 202	1 317
3	225	370	944	1 516	2 896	5 383	2 585	8 519	14 189	15 117	15 141	15 261
4	53	16	30	69	265	451	466	1 394	2 259	2 295	2 780	3 562
5	2 747	3 893	4 576	7 910	14 089	23 442	33 109	43 248	58 151	77 564	91 381	117 127
6	118	74	123	37	186	1 581	1 322	1 158	1 641	1 578	1 217	1 557
7	2 602	7 990	26 086	29 763	55 678	101 436	144 970	165 899	249 222	207 888	150 074	131 294

Group no. 1: Professionals, technical and related workers.
Group no. 2: Managerial, executive and administrative workers.
Group no. 3: Clerical workers.
Group no. 4: Sales workers.
Group no. 5: Service workers.
Group no. 6: Agricultural, animal husbandry and forestry workers, and fishermen.
Group no. 7: Production process workers, transport equipment operators, and labourers.

Source: Philippine Overseas Employment Administration.

Table 7.7. Processed land-based Philippine contract workers by major destination, 1975-86

Year	1975	1976	1977	1978	1979	1980	1981	1982	1983	1984	1985	1986
Total	12 501	19 221	36 676	50 961	92 519	157 394	210 936	250 115	380 263	371 065	371 754	357 687
Destination												
Africa	342	473	515	1 305	1 134	1 611	2 144	1 098	2 353	2 146	2 053	2 072
Asia	4 217	5 399	5 290	9 994	12 604	17 708	20 322	31 011	40 814	43 385	54 411	76 650
Europe	3 160	2 902	2 482	1 268	673	846	1 126	1 465	2 878	3 724	3 679	4 225
Middle East	1 552	7 813	25 721	34 441	73 210	132 044	183 582	210 972	323 414	311 517	266 617	262 758
Oceania	551	133	139	80	312	165	223	714	2 072	1 027	845	1 129
The Americas	2 286	2 168	2 266	3 371	3 744	3 534	2 101	3 707	5 646	5 905	6 897	6 692
Trust Territories	393	333	263	502	842	1 486	1 438	1 148	3 086	3 361	3 252	4 161

Source: Philippine Overseas Employment Administration.

surplus is exhausted and the status of newly industrialized country is reached. In fact, there is likely to be a net return of migrants at some point, as is now being witnessed in Taiwan (China).[6] Moreover, the ability to migrate will undoubtedly rise over time in this case as participatory, well-distributed income growth occurs and more people have access to liberalized credit markets. What is of crucial importance is that the gap between the desire to migrate and the supply-side limiting factor – the excess demand for migration – closes and ultimately disappears.

Let us now turn to an examination of how the pattern of Figure 7.1b might be approached in the case of the Philippines as the result of ODA-assisted domestic policy change.

3. Potential for change in the role of ODA, the development pattern and the size of the excess demand for migration

ODA and a rural block grant programme

While neither the past record of Philippine development nor the role of foreign assistance in that context has been particularly encouraging, there now clearly exists an opportunity for change. This is based not so much on the forthcoming Philippine election as on the likelihood of a healthier, slightly more distant, relationship between the United States and the other donors, and the Philippines in the wake of the termination of the United States bases agreement, the end of the Cold War, a diminished threat from the New People's Army as well as some signs of increased independence and assertiveness on the part of the other major bilateral donor, Japan. It must be hoped that the multilateral agencies, including the World Bank and the ADB, can also be persuaded that, to be really helpful, they may have to reconstitute the modalities of the MAI so that the initiative for putting together and "owning" serious restructuring agreements indeed shifts to the Philippine side.

This is perhaps not the place to detail our views on the precise package and sequencing of unfinished policy reforms relevant to the Philippine economy; but it is important to recognize that the potential future role of foreign assistance in reducing the demand for migration can only be realized if placed in the context of real, not merely rhetorical, links with the policy choices open to the Philippine authorities. We therefore intend to suggest some specific project and technical assistance actions under ODA financing over the next several decades which can be expected to help generate a more successful, labour-intensive development path. Moreover, it is our contention that the single most important contribution ODA can make in the future is to ensure that a process is securely put in place which links any major ballooning of assistance with a mutually agreed change at both the macro- and microeconomic levels. The current five-year MAI has just about reached its half-way point. There is an opportunity here, now that dimensions of the "special" relationship with the United

---

[6] Kindleberger (1967, p. 205) similarly notes that Italian worker migration to Germany in the postwar era was reversed by the initiation of Italian growth – not by a reversal in relative income levels.

States can be set aside, to use everyone's ODA to help the Philippines adjust to a new development path, rather than remain on the old, unchanging path.

Both future project and structural adjustment lending must focus on strengthening the twin blades of the developmental scissors: a) balanced growth in the rural areas of the Philippines, and b) the related expansion of competitive labour-intensive exports. Both are concentrated on generating substantial increases in the demand for the underemployed and the unemployed. Additional jobs and dependable increases in family incomes, accompanied by an improved distribution of income, can be expected to substantially change individual actors' expectations and thus reduce their desire to migrate.

The full mobilization of the rural economy, with the maximum efficient retention of labour there, must be the major aim. If rural-urban migration is substantially reduced, the demand for international migration, largely a function of the size of the pool of the urban disaffected, unemployed and underemployed, will be cut in turn. Foreign capital can be useful, both directly and indirectly, in ensuring that the necessary policy measures and institutional changes are facilitated.

Turning to details, the *sine qua non* of successful rural development is convincing the Philippine Government that substantial public sector decentralization is needed. This is tantamount to Manila "letting go", all the way from the determination of what should be this five-year plan's overall infrastructural priorities to precisely where mini-irrigation projects are to be placed. Such decisions have to be increasingly devolved to local governments, probably largely at the *municipio* level, and in some cases the provinces (but hardly ever the regions which are much too large and are artificial entities). Recent changes in local government legislation may be helpful, but current practice is still one of the delegation of central powers, not their devolution; moreover, implementation has usually lagged way behind legislation in the Philippines – especially in this context. The traditional lack of confidence by Manila in local governments because of their alleged inability to wisely allocate restricted resources remains a serious obstacle to the kind of balanced rural growth of which the Philippines is undoubtedly capable.

If a fundamental change in attitude could be achieved on this front, an additional bonus would be that the overall poor fiscal performance of the Philippine economy could be substantially improved by linking greater decentralization of public sector decision-making to expanded local financing on an incentive basis. The initiation of block grants to each municipality, for example, possibly associating foreign aid resources with those of the Philippine Government, would be one way of relieving that particular bottleneck. Such block grants should have the following features: automaticity, i.e. no prior approval at the centre but a dependable flow of resources, with priorities set by local bodies; universality, i.e. an across-the-board national programme, with all municipalities receiving certain, non-politically determined allocations, with differences based only on population and possibly a poverty level-related formula; and continuity, i.e. the local community can assume that it will receive the same amount every year. For example, given the approximately 1,400 *municipios* in the Philippines, a modest average annual infrastructural block grant allocation of $100,000 per municipio would constitute an annual programme of less than $150 million, a minor budgetary allocation for either foreign donors or the Philippine Government, but one with relatively significant potential economic and political consequences, including an impact on rural development and consequently, migration.

In other words, a block grant programme, supported from the outside both in terms of advice and matching financial resources, would provide much-needed transparency, enhancing both allocable efficiency today plus the quality of decision-making tomorrow. Moreover, it would provide one of the most undertaxed developing countries a chance to raise additional resources from taxes that are already under local government purview but that are not being collected. At present, less than 10 per cent of the estimated potential value of such local levies is being realized. It is not a dream, therefore, to assume that a dependable block grant programme would lead not only to a more efficient allocation of scarce resources but also to the generation of additional funds, locally collected for local purposes.

The past tendency to define public sector decentralization by deconcentration or delegation, i.e. either the spatial relocation of offices or assigning the implementation of Manila's decisions to ministerial branches, provides for no real initiative and very little real feedback from below. Such a process may work reasonably well for large-scale infrastructural and other promotional activities, as well as possibly for expenditures to advance major central government-determined macroeconomic objectives in the areas of health, education and other social services. But it has precious little to commend itself if prioritization at the local level, both with respect to the preferred type of rural infrastructure and the preferred type of education and health expenditure, is considered important on static efficiency as well as dynamic participation grounds. There is indeed a great difference between irrigation expenditure on the unsilting of channels and on dam construction – as there is between expenditure on primary and on university education, and between hospital construction and the expansion of preventive health care. The Municipal Development Councils, which today are largely "paper" bodies, should be strengthened and become the focus for decision-making with respect to both the "where" and the "what" of infrastructural and social sector expenditure allocations; line ministry technical expertise at the provincial level should continue to assist in questions of "how to". ODA can also assist local bodies through training programmes, including foreign technical assistance where needed. However, the alleged "lack of preparedness" of local government personnel is, we believe, consistently exaggerated; it is reminiscent of the "lack of preparedness" attributed to peasants in the days of agricultural neglect of the 1960s and early 1970s.

ODA and rural development: Projects and policies

Rural non-agricultural activity is distinctly absent in the Philippines in comparative Asian terms. Vigorous growth of rural industry and services would not only provide for an active interplay with agriculture in the static input-output sense but also offer additional investment incentives encouraging agricultural productivity change, and subcontracting arrangements with urban industry.

The support of balanced rural growth, of course, not only requires infrastructure but also access to rural credit at reasonable rates. Philippine policy has moved away from its historical subsidized credit approach for specific agricultural crops, often using credit lines supported by foreign aid. There remains, however, a need to shift from the segregated agriculture- and industry-oriented credit and lending quotas of the past towards broadly defined rural credit, with the possibility of a guarantee fund for all such activities rather than a loan fund for agriculture along the CALF lines. It is probably also necessary to reduce the percentage guaranteed to below 50 per cent.

A more serious problem may be one of physical bank presence. With many of the rural banks having become bankrupt in the final years of the Marcos regime, and their "sanitation" process under Aquino only partially successful, so-called "over-banking" in metro-Manila has consistently been associated with "under-banking" in the rural areas. Even if 600 rural banks remain in place, augmented by branches of the Development Bank of the Philippines, the Philippines National Bank and the Land Bank, to serve as the dispersed agents of the banking system in the rural areas, there is likely to be a continued severe segmentation of credit markets. Commercial and cooperative branch banking needs to be encouraged.

With respect not only to agricultural activities, but perhaps especially to non-agricultural rural activities, much additional work is required in information and technology diffusion. Worldwide evidence suggests that the adoption and adaptation of appropriate labour-intensive technologies are more critical for "growth with equity" outcomes than the enhanced availability of domestic or foreign capital. Even if the capacity of individual rural decision-makers in the Philippines is as good as is generally perceived, they are nevertheless likely to require information on alternative ways of producing agricultural commodities adapted to local conditions, and on specifications for alternative industrial goods for either domestic or international markets. Such information can be highly useful for small producers to subcontract for larger urban units and to service generic international or domestic niche markets effectively. The access of rural decision-makers to credit and infrastructure must therefore be supplemented by enhanced information flows and new technology, whether this be new varieties of rice or new ways of making shoes. On the agricultural side, this has been in large part resolved internationally through the foreign aid-assisted CIGYAR family represented by the International Rice Research Institute (IRRI), customarily supplemented by local adaptive research institutions. In the Philippines, however, this has been a controversial issue as the Government has, in fact, neglected adaptive rice research under the mistaken assumption that, by virtue of its location, IRRI was handling it adequately. A more serious, still largely unrecognized, problem exists on the rural, non-agricultural side. Substantial human and financial resources have traditionally been allocated to a sizeable network of science and technology centres, which have however been of only modest use to the economy. Very little has happened by way of integrating these various research units into the productive system, e.g. by changing the internal incentive structure within these institutes and shifting them from full government funding to a range of private sector contracts. In addition, most of these centres are located near Manila and insufficiently focused on dealing with widely disparate local environments.

Given the well-established fact that the "routinization" of science and technology is virtually synonymous with the successful transition to modern growth, and given the importance of adaptive technology in generating additional efficient employment opportunities, this represents an area of serious neglect which urgently needs to be corrected, possibly with the assistance of foreign donors at the project level. Efforts to establish branches of the Philippine Department of Trade and Industry, People's Industrial Enterprises and Regional Industrial Centres, among others, have thus far proved incapable of providing the necessary market and technology information network for potential, small rural industrialists. Information on variations in product specification, technologies, etc., in both the process and product senses, might be better handled through designated channels of a decentralized banking system, and possibly even through branches of commercial banks. Such information capacity as part of a broadly defined technology diffusion network might generate some initial support if linked to a supervised credit scheme on the Grameen Bank model, possibly linked up with private NGO activities (though kept separate from the credit function proper, which should not be subsidized).

One additional observation on the potential use of foreign capital at the project or sectoral level may be in order. It is by now fairly well accepted that the Comprehensive Agricultural Reform Programme of the Aquino Government, which started inauspiciously by letting the landlord-dominated Senate determine the critical details, has failed to make much progress on land reform; it has also probably had a net disruptive effect on agricultural productivity growth owing to the additional uncertainties it created. Replacing a progressive land tax by acreage ceilings for the present patchwork of provisions for handling non-government land would remove government from the business of giving out titles and yet permit it to exert effective pressure for smaller holdings. Foreign donor attention to the possibilities of technical assistance in this general area would probably be highly productive.

Of course, terms of trade and discrimination in resource allocation against the rural economy, both in its agricultural and non-agricultural components, has to be reduced at the macroeconomic level. There is little need to reiterate the need to reduce the gap in effective protection which, in spite of the many years of negotiated import liberalization, still favours urban industry. The exchange rate's continued overvaluation, low real interest rates, persisting anti-rural interventions in the domestic terms of trade, and remaining restrictions on competitive access in urban industry settings, all constitute evidence that macroeconomic policy reform still has a long way to go. It is vital to eliminate these distortions within a considered and credible reform package, supported by future foreign assistance.

ODA and enhanced export performance: Projects and policies

Turning to the second blade of the developmental scissors, namely support for the expansion of competitive labour-intensive exports, one would want to ensure that the Omnibus Investment Code, which has been amended several times, definitively eliminates the residual provisions that adversely affect the prospects for appropriate microeconomic technology choices. For example, accelerated depreciation allowances should be removed, incentives based on actual value-added performance created (rather than those based on installed capital capacity) and other features which have consistently discriminated against employment in the choice of both product and process mixes, eliminated. The provision of fiscal incentives via the Board of Investments – where only 2,000 or more firms are currently registered, few below a capital value of $ 50,000 – is indicative of the continued urban, large-scale and capital-intensive bias. What investors, foreign and domestic alike, need is the eradication of the past pattern of whimsical *ad hominem* treatment, of policy instability, and of unequal access to credit.

In addition to the influence of foreign assistance on such dimensions of the policy setting, additional specific ODA activities could include assisting in the construction of additional export processing zones and bonded factories, not modelled on the Bataan but rather on the Cebu precedent, i.e. zones located near labour surplus areas, thus providing employment, export and income growth opportunities. Similarly, the Philippines continues to suffer from power shortages, especially since the mothballing of the Westinghouse nuclear energy plant. Alleviating selective bottlenecks of this kind – especially if accompanied by power pricing reforms that eliminate preferential treatment for Manila – could contribute substantially to the expansion of dispersed non-agricultural and export activity, and would be an appropriate high priority project for foreign assistance.

Such ODA allocations to specific projects to facilitate exports, and balance of payments or structural adjustment funds to support policy change which encourages competitive exports, not only provide the opportunity to employ additional workers but also to "export" them through trade. Thus, while we are restricting ourselves to the impact of ODA on the desire and ability to migrate, it should also be clear that one of the most important consequences of any successful development effort must be to enhance, within a dynamic setting, the continuing ability of a country to penetrate international markets. Foreign assistance projects and programmes can be of extreme importance in facilitating the changes required.

It also goes without saying that the more successful a country's development effort, the more likely that private investment will flow in from abroad, and that financial and human capital which fled abroad earlier will return. Thus ODA should be viewed as an important catalyst for facilitating the growing contribution of substitute solutions for migration. The east Asian experience of recent decades provides an excellent example of such a process, with well-allocated foreign aid helping to make it possible for follow-on flows of trade, private investment and human capital to solve substantially the migration problem.

A special word on educational investments may be in order. Partly under the influence of the United States, the Philippines has in the past focused too much on traditional academic activities. As a consequence, secondary education, for instance, neglects vocational careers and contributes, along with an excessively liberal arts-oriented higher education structure, to many unemployed people's overeducated embitterment. ODA, especially from the United States, could be of great help in effecting a correction.

ODA and reducing the demand for migration: Other suggestions

In the final analysis, the major contribution of bilateral and multilateral ODA to reducing the demand for migration must be located in the policy arena, both macro- and microeconomic, rather than in the search for an expanding number of "magic bullet" projects. For this purpose, structural adjustment or programme lending, accompanied by discourse on the specific set of required policy changes is, of course, the key instrument. Such assistance is useful not only because it is free-flowing and quick to disburse, thus providing additional leverage opportunities, but, more important, because it is able to address immediate points of real or imagined "pain" during a proposed policy change process. Examples include a run on the reserves as import liberalization takes place, or a loss in tariff revenue as protection is reduced, or the provision of a temporary safety net as short-term unemployment increases with privatization.

On this subject it is well to recall that the contribution of Filipino academics to the assessment of the country's economic problems and to the required policy reforms has been substantial. The so-called Yellow and Green Books prepared by economists at the University of the Philippines in the early days of the Aquino regime laid the groundwork for anticipated wholesale policy reforms which never came. Unfortunately, however, the Philippines does not yet have the equivalent of a Thailand Development Research Institute (TDRI) – a relatively independent, interdisciplinary think-tank – which could be helpful in generating such socioeconomic analysis and policy advice away from the daily crisis-dominated activities of government. A small amount of foreign assistance in building such an institution could have significant long-term compensation. The relevant fact is that the human capital of the Philippines is substantial in comparison with that of several of its economically more successful neighbours. However, there is less institutional capacity to enable economists (and others) to convince policy-makers of how to put the economy on a different set of tracks.

The real obstacle, however, to fundamental change in the Philippines is within political economics rather than technical economics. Having been left behind, once in the 1970s by the east Asian "Tigers" and, once again, in more recent years, by the south-east Asian "Tigers", it is clear that what is required is a fundamental change in the process of providing foreign assistance. Such a change must ensure, via careful prior negotiation, that additional resources render policy change politically feasible by easing the pains of adjustment, rather than once again becoming the medium by which the Philippines is able to avoid such change, as has happened so frequently in the past.

If foreign assistance is, in fact, going to make a substantial impact on the participatory nature of the development process, any continuation of the MAI requires a significant change in approach. Experience in the Philippines, as well as in such places as Egypt and Turkey, provides enough examples of the dangers of combining the strategic and geopolitical objectives of the donor community with economic aims. There exists an excellent opportunity at the moment to shift the policy dialogue away from symbolic gestures. Real liberalization and structural change require agreements worked out locally, rather than conditions imposed by the IMF or World Bank, in a package of assistance committed over a five- to ten-year period. This would be consonant with the kind of longer-term perspective specifically tailored to the needs of the country, with the timing, sequence and necessary escape clauses worked out multilaterally.

Recent Latin American experience, for example in Mexico, indicates that governments are finding it much easier to win domestic acceptance of painful policy change packages if they, rather than foreigners, are seen to be taking the initiative and if relevant decision-making groups are indeed fully convinced of the merits of the case. The "consultative group" mechanism, originally intended for the discussion of such resource-cum-policy packages, has become too much of a ritual, even though it may now be cloaked with the MAI. The donors must make it clear that their need to lend is less important than the need to initiate credible quality change associated with additional resources.

Realistically, a given annual level of ODA allocation to the Philippines following the previous system will undoubtedly be maintained, regardless of what happens in policy-focused negotiations. But for any major expansion along MAI lines, both the commitments of the Philippines and those of the creditors/donors must be sufficiently firm, long-term and credible. The occasional delay in IMF or World Bank disbursements, inevitably followed by a "full-steam ahead" resumption of the resource flows – without a significant departure in policy – has undermined donor credibility and contributed to cynicism on all sides, including potential migrants. Initiating a departure from the past via a focused review of the fundamental ailments the Philippine economy would, of course, include the issues currently under debate with the IMF and the World Bank.

If all the parties begin to think about the fashioning of such a credible multilateral framework for assessing the situation and helping to effect longer-term change, an ODA package, endorsed in advance by all the major international donors, could do much to change individual Philippine actors' perspectives on the prospects of the economy. This is the only credible way in which we can reduce the demand for migration from a country like the Philippines.

An additional suggestion for the allocation of migration-stemming foreign assistance would challenge one of the assumptions made above, i.e. that the resistance to migrants and implicitly also the resistance to imports from labour surplus countries are invariable and not subject to policy change. The average textile worker in the United States is not really concerned whether his job is being threatened by textile imports from the Philippines or by immigrants from the Philippines, even though the immigrants may provide an easier target for protest. In both instances, he is very likely to lobby his Representative in Congress for protection, especially if he feels trapped in his present job.

Thus, the problem of adjustment to the ever changing development of comparative advantage around the world, including some levels of migration, must be seen as part of a much larger issue, that of our inability thus far to find a reasonable solution to the difficulties of domestic adjustment and retraining. These difficulties are exemplified in the missing safety nets for privatization efforts in Eastern Europe and in collecting the elusive peace dividend through reduced defence budgets in the United States. In brief, while adjustment assistance programmes have been implemented in many developed countries for some time, the overall experience has been uncertain at best, and never fully examined. Perhaps the Japanese have been more successful by ensuring guaranteed employment through the extended "family-of-firms" system, which permits people to be re-employed in sunrise activities of the same organization as sunset activities fade away. The same industrial organization structure does not, of course, obtain elsewhere, but it is likely that other devices can be more carefully examined. There has been too little effort to learn from the few successes and many failures of past developed country efforts at adjustment assistance and worker retraining, in order to construct an international system capable of accommodating required output changes in the future.

Most observers agree that globalization will continue, that international trade and investment flows are likely to rise in absolute terms and probably relative to GNP, and that both consumers' and producers' interests will continue to be threatened by powerful rearguard actions of relatively small groups concentrated in declining industries. Economic nationalism and protectionism threaten to proliferate, to the detriment of national and global welfare.

The willingness of rich countries and thus the capacity of international agencies to provide substantial levels of aid is becoming increasingly suspect. A more narrowly self-interested set of policies is likely. In such a context, it might be possible, nevertheless, to allocate additional resources to what might be called "foreign aid spent at home", either in the form of a domestic adjustment assistance programme which works, or as part of an international system working through a global adjustment assistance fund. In either case, the rules should focus on shifting and retraining workers threatened by immigrants or imports rather than on providing unemployment insurance to keep them where they are, often termed "burial assistance", and on providing low-interest loans to capitalists for the same purpose, i.e. enhancing the capacity to shift their output mix. We do not underestimate the possible short-term pain that can be inflicted on workers and employers during the implementation of any structural adjustment package; but what is clearly needed is more ingenuity in rendering all our productive systems more flexible in the era of instant knowledge diffusion and drastically lower communication and transport costs.

It should be clear by now that a successful shift to a more employment-oriented participatory development track can be expected to reduce substantially individual actors' desires to migrate out of the system. International experience suggests that our best hope lies in bringing about a reversal of the intense desire to migrate; past significant pressures for migration out of Taiwan (China), for example, have now reversed themselves, culminating in a net return of migrants as domestic economic opportunities have improved. But successful growth is also likely to enhance people's ability to migrate. Once an economy begins to move in a participatory fashion – incomes rise, distribution improves, and poverty levels are reduced – we can expect the ability to migrate to improve. This might mean that, for a time, only the excess demand for migration is reduced, but that is the critical magnitude. Moreover, if we then think in terms of a 30- to 40-year perspective, we can ultimately expect not only the demand for migration to fall but to reverse itself. Migration patterns similar to those governing capital flight will obtain over time.

It might also be possible, in the context of a multilateral programme of lending, to persuade or add some additional resources, with the express purpose of "inducing" the Philippine Government to desist from further direct or indirect assistance to prospective migrants. As was pointed out earlier, the Philippine Government's overseas employment effort not only encourages unskilled labour migration but also broadens awareness of the migration option. It is based on the twin objectives of reducing the labour surplus while easing balance of payments pressures through increased remittances. While aid-related efforts to persuade the Turkish Government to plant fewer poppies or the Bolivian Government to eliminate coca production have not been signal successes, it would be much easier to monitor the simple cessation of emigration promotion activities by the Philippine Government. This though is a relatively minor matter. It should be clear that the emphasis in any negotiations on policy change and greater ODA to relieve short-term pain should focus on a better functioning economy and the consequent reduction in migration demand in as short a time as possible.

4. Conclusions

We have focused on a particular developing country, the Philippines, and the excess demand to migrate, in particular to the United States. Our main conclusions can be stated here as propositions, with the hope of more general applicability:

- The main variable that ODA must address is a reduction of people's desire to migrate. This desire is a function of relative life-time expectations concerning income and status levels in the home and potential receiving countries. It is likely to be substantially above the constraints to migration represented by barriers to legal immigration or people's capacity to migrate. It is this excess demand to migrate which causes increased pressures for illegal migration and raises international tensions.

- The desire to migrate internationally is most effectively reduced via a reduction in the desire for domestic rural-urban migration, i.e. by policies and ODA allocations which serve to retain actors productively engaged in agriculture and in rural non-agricultural activities.

- ODA can also be helpful directly, as well as indirectly, by enhancing the developing economy's capacity to export labour-intensive products and attract private financial capital: these replace the pressure to emigrate on the part of unskilled and semi-skilled workers.

- ODA efforts to reduce the demand for migration can, of course, only be effective if the recipient country itself is fully convinced of the merits of shifting to a more participatory, egalitarian strategy of balanced rural growth combined with labour-intensive industrial exports.

- At the project level, ODA should consider supporting block grants which enhance the allocable decision-making powers of local governments with respect to rural infrastructure as well as social sector expenditures, the expansion of a rural banking presence, alternative technology information and diffusion networks, the creation and expansion of export processing zones and the elimination of other bottlenecks, e.g. power and transport, which restrict an expansion of output. ODA can also be helpful in supporting primary and vocational education at the secondary level as opposed to current higher and classical education alternatives.

- At the programme or structural adjustment level, multilateral ODA efforts should support the package of macroeconomic stabilization accompanied by market liberalization policies, customarily supported by the IMF and the World Bank, but should also supplement it by a strong emphasis on reducing the anti-rural bias in both macro- and microeconomic policies.

- The method of providing multilateral assistance should be re-examined to ensure a) that there is full prior agreement with the recipient country on just what needs to be done over the course of an extended period to move the system onto a more participatory growth path; and b) that required policy self-conditionality is established to give real credibility to both the provision and possible cessation of resource inflows over time.

- Consideration should be given to establishing substantial effective adjustment assistance programmes within each of the major industrial countries – possibly following multilaterally agreed rules – but clearly focused on inducing sunset industry workers and entrepreneurs, directly affected by migration or imports from developing countries, to be retrained for sunrise activities.

- Possibly in return for additional ODA programme support, developing countries should be asked to refrain from policies which provide financial or other support enhancing their citizens' ability to migrate. Instead, a strong public policy effort to provide citizens with greater equality of opportunity and status, as part of a more egalitarian, participatory growth path must constitute the essential component of any multilateral agreement between donors/creditors and developing country governments.

Bibliography

Alonzo, Ruperto P. 1991. "The informal sector in the Philippines", in A. Lawrence Chickering and Mohamed Salahdine (eds.): *The silent revolution: The informal sector in five Asian and Near Eastern countries* (San Francisco, The International Center for Economic Growth).

Anand, Sudhir; Ravi Kanbur. 1991. *International poverty projections*, Policy, Research and External Affairs Working Paper No. 617 (Washington, DC, World Bank).

Appleyard, Reginald. 1989. "Migration and development: Myths and reality", in *International Migration Review*, Vol. 23, No. 3.

Arnold, F.; N.M. Shah (eds.). 1986. *Asian labor migration: Pipeline to the Middle East* (Boulder, Colorado, Westview Press).

Fawcett, James T.; Benjamin V. Carino (eds.). 1987. *Pacific bridges: The new immigration from Asia and the Pacific Islands* (Staten Island, New York, Center for Migration Studies).

Fei, J.C.H.; G. Ranis; S.W.Y. Kuo. 1979. *Growth with equity: The Taiwan case* (New York, Oxford University Press).

Fields, Gary S. 1989. *A comparison of data on inequality and poverty for the developing world* (Ithaca, New York, Cornell University, mimeo).

Ho, Samuel P.S. 1978. *Economic development of Taiwan, 1860-1970* (New Haven, Connecticut, Yale University Press).

Jain, Shail. 1975. *Size distribution of income* (Washington, DC, World Bank).

Jasso, Guillermina; Mark R. Rosenzweig. 1990. *The new chosen people: Immigrants in the United States* (New York, Russell Sage Foundation).

Kindleberger, Charles. 1967. *Europe's postwar growth: The role of labor supply* (Cambridge, Massachusetts, Harvard University Press).

Massey, Douglas. 1988. "Economic development and international migration in comparative perspective", in *Population and Development Review*, Vol. 14, No. 3.

Shih, J.T. 1983. "Decentralized industrialization and rural nonfarm employment in Taiwan", in *Industry of Free China* (Taipei, Taiwan, China), Vol. 60, No. 2, August, pp. 1-20.

Summers, R.; Heston, A. 1984. "Improved international comparisons of real product and its composition", in *Review of Income and Wealth*, No. 30, June, pp. 207-262.

Thomas, Brinley. 1954. *Migration and economic growth: A study of Great Britain and the Atlantic economy* (Cambridge, Cambridge University Press).

8

Reducing emigration pressure in Turkey: Analysis and suggestions for external aid

G. Schiller

1. Introduction

The political events of the last two years provide an unambiguous, but distressing, empirical test of the success of development strategies. With the economic collapse of the former USSR, the concept of a planned industrial breakthrough was definitively shown to be erroneous. This approach, however, served for many decades as a model of a successful escape from the underdevelopment trap and in the variant of import-substituting industrialization guided many countries' development efforts. Capital-intensive industrialization headed by state economic enterprises formed an important dimension of those policies, which tried to enforce development by concepts of planned sectoral growth. In one way or another a "modern" sector was to be created, which for some time existed along with a traditional sector, until the latter was soaked up by the former. The analytical "dual economy" models of Lewis or Ranis/Fei belonged to this group, as did Mahalanobis' planning approach for India (Mellor and Johnston, 1984, pp. 550 ff.).

Turkey was well advised to dismiss this strategy a decade ago. However, the policy of export orientation (EO) only constitutes a halfway change. EO policies do not aim at "development" as such but at including all countries in the international division of labour on the basis of comparative advantage. Special support is not given to consumer or capital goods industries, but to competitive export industries. EO strategies bear the structural risk of expanding industries where forceful competition among developing countries keeps prices and wages at a minimum.

There exists no standard formula yet how to proceed from "comparative advantage specialization" to "export-led growth" (for a comprehensive study see Porter, 1990). It has to be noted, however, that the interests of industrialized countries are severely affected by the difference. Although it is inconvenient for developed countries to allow the decline of certain branches of their economy, "comparative advantage specialization" exerts a healthy pressure on them to modernize their economic structure and to keep abreast of technical progress. In contrast, "export-led growth" means changing the rules of accumulation and redistributing the benefits of world trade because not all countries can realize an export surplus at the same time. The test whether the industrialized world supports such a fundamental change of economic relations with increasing financial aid has yet to come (see Riese, 1986).

Economic assistance gains full effectiveness only in combination with a favourable domestic environment. Among the aspects contributing to it, the following may be mentioned.

- While a moderate growth of population stimulates economic prosperity, because it provides a smoothing flexibility for the labour market, a high population growth rate may be detrimental. A strong rise in the population overstrains the expanding social infrastructure and outpaces the creation of jobs.
- Phases of rapid industrialization are introduced by a push of productivity in agriculture (Mellor and Johnston, 1984, pp. 556 ff.). The importance of agriculture lies in the fact that, first, agricultural products form the essential wage goods at low incomes, and second, agricultural incomes, especially of peasant farmers, are spent largely on local consumer and capital goods produced with labour-intensive technologies. Support of agriculture on the basis of family farming and a balanced income distribution are favourable preconditions for rapid and regionally balanced industrial growth.
- The availability of investment capital as a development factor is easy to overemphasize. The past experience of many countries has been characterized by huge misallocations of physical investments. The educational level of the population and favourable institutional conditions have been underemphasized. Investments in human capital will be the most important prerequisite of rapid growth and change.
- Among the institutional factors, prime importance must be given to the internal competitive climate. The discrediting of the "infant-industry argument" does not result from its theoretical invalidity but from its fusion with monopolistic rent collection in oligopolistic domestic markets.
- Economic policy has to adopt a sensitive middle course between outdated concepts of centralized macro-planning and a well-considered industrial policy concentrating support on clearly defined priority areas, while thwarting "free ride" behaviour. Reliance on free market forces alone will fail, too, as long as internal competition is not sufficiently developed and external competitiveness is lacking. (In this respect, the experience of the former German Democratic Republic is illustrative.)

2. The economic framework of migration between Turkey and Germany

Economic development and Turkish policy since 1950

Since the foundation of the Turkish Republic in 1923, the country's economic strategies have oscillated between extremes. State-driven industrialization was in 1950 followed by a period of outward-oriented and liberal market policies until the end of the decade. From 1961 to 1980 a strongly inward-looking development policy was pursued, based on five-year development plans and a growing sector of state economic enterprises. From 1980 onwards, the strengthening of market forces and an export or outward orientation have been the guiding principles of economic policy. Traditional state economic planning has been abolished.

In more detailed terms for 1961 to 1980, the economy performed quite satisfactorily until 1978. Growth rates of manufacturing output reached about 9 per cent, and GDP per capita increased by 3.9 per cent annually. Under pressure of newly established trade unions, real wages were pushed up and income distribution showed tendencies of becoming more equal, at least outside agriculture. Shares of investment in national expenditure – private and public – climbed from 15 per cent in 1961-63 to 22 per cent in 1977-79 (Hansen, 1989a, pp. 12-30). With import protection, foreign exchange rationing, and priority for state economic enterprises, Turkey managed successfully to create a substantial industrial sector, especially in consumer goods and in basic industries.

The strategy followed the theoretical approach of unbalanced growth and Harrod-Domar-Keynesianism. Economic growth was seen as dependent on the investment (and savings) rate. According to this theory, capital-intensive modes of production should copy the structure of industrialized countries, starting from consumer goods and then proceeding to capital goods and basic industries. High savings rates were a by-product of market protection and a policy of keeping production costs low. Investment in agriculture was neglected. The policy aimed at enforcing a structural breakthrough and disregarded considerations of comparative advantage and factor endowments.

The principal defect of import substitution (IS) strategies turned out to be the impossibility of reducing the foreign exchange constraint. In fact, extending substitution efforts to intermediate and capital goods boosted import requirements to unexpectedly high levels.

Policy mistakes added to the dismantling of IS strategies in Turkey. After 1973 the Turkish Government did not react to the changed terms of trade enforced by OPEC. Instead of forcing through energy savings by higher prices, the cost effects of the bigger oil bill were internally cushioned by elevated subsidies.

Of course, there were a number of interlinked factors in the crisis years of 1978-80. Some of them will be examined later. Whether a more sensitive policy would have changed the results fundamentally must be doubted. Somehow IS strategies started from the wrong assumption of an isolated economy and an omnipotent government, views which can also be traced back to Keynes. Even analytically, they lack any means to reintegrate the domestic economy into the world market, after industrialization has been accomplished. Thus they disregard the internationalization of the economic process.

Although quite impressive in retrospect, employment creation in Turkey did not satisfy the need for jobs. Turkey had a rapidly growing population, but too few employment opportunities outside agriculture.

Until 1950 Turkey was a thinly settled country with a population of 21 million. During the 1950s population growth rates climbed to 2.8 per cent per year, and were about 2 per cent per year in 1980. Since 1960 a growing agrarian surplus population, pushed out of agriculture by mechanization, has led to massive rural-urban migration movements. High rates of urbanization and a regional reallocation of population towards the western and southern provinces created the phenomenon of large circles of *Geçecondu* settlements around the big cities.

Massive emigration to European countries was one of the new features of Turkish society in this period. The discussion on the economic effects of this movement will probably never be settled definitely (for a recent assessment see Martin, 1991). At any rate, European labour mobility brought Turkey and Western Europe closer together.

With hindsight, the shortcomings of import-substitution policies become clearer. A policy of separation from the world economy leads to neglect of market signals. A preference for capital-intensive investments instead of labour-intensive industrialization was in contrast to factor scarcities and worsened the allocation of resources. A determined policy of agricultural modernization and measures to enhance productivity increases in agriculture might have reduced labour surpluses and migration pressure, at the same time maintaining a more balanced regional distribution of population.

However, past achievements must not be undervalued. By 1980 Turkey possessed a substantial industrial sector flexible enough to change quickly to the new strategy of export orientation. By 1980 also, the private business sector, still embryonic in 1960, had grown. In addition, over the period 1960-80 Turkey managed to remain self-sufficient in food despite a growing population.

After two years' consideration, in January 1980 the Government introduced a radical change of economic philosophy: import substitution, comprehensive planning, and state industrialization policies were abandoned. This revolutionary turn was regarded as necessary owing to an inflation rate of more than 100 per cent, a negative growth rate of GDP, and a continuing balance of payment crisis.

The measures announced in the reform programme included (see OECD, 1981, *Economic Survey: Turkey*, p. 25):

- institutional changes to improve formulation and implementation of economic policy;
- a devaluation of the Turkish lira against the US dollar of 33 per cent;
- liberalization of foreign trade and payment regimes;

- reduction of subsidies to and privatization of state economic enterprises (SEEs);
- promotion of exports and of foreign investment;
- price increases of state-traded goods and the abolition of price controls;
- tax reforms;
- reforms of capital and credit markets.

After the military takeover in September 1980, massive stabilization measures were added to the package. They included interventions in the labour market, especially new restrictions on collective bargaining and the right to strike (which were relaxed gradually after 1983). This line of economic philosophy is still practised although the individual items have followed their own course. On the whole the impression is that during the early years a more determined policy prevailed while, from 1984 onwards, the pace of reforms slowed down.

A policy of continuous currency devaluation has been pursued for most of the period, but since 1988 there has been currency appreciation. Budget deficits came down to 4.5 per cent of GNP in 1986, but rose to about 9 per cent in 1990. Inflation rates dropped to 27 per cent in 1982; they have since climbed back to 60 per cent to 70 per cent. Real wages shrank drastically during the early years, but since 1988 large wage increases have overtaken the trend of productivity change again, thus adding to inflationary pressure. Deposit interest rates have changed their sign several times during the decade; most recent data show that they are negative again, as in the 1970s. The foreign debt increased steadily from US$ 18 billion in 1980 to US$ 49 billion in 1990, putting a burden of US$ 3 billion for interest payments alone on the balance of payments.

The most impressive success has been the rapid expansion of manufactured exports, from $ 1 billion in 1980 to $ 9 billion in 1989. Unfortunately, imports have risen proportionately. Thus the economy still struggles with a trade deficit, indicating a high dependence on intermediate imports and a correspondingly low degree of interindustrial linkages.

Since 1988 exports have stagnated, apparently because of a slightly appreciating currency. The reshaping of incentive schemes may have reduced exports which were stimulated by excessive subsidies. Hansen mentions the case of cement, which was exported during the first half of the 1980s in considerable volumes, although the country certainly has no comparative advantage in cement production. Since then cement has disappeared completely from export statistics (see Hansen, 1989a, pp. 208 f.). On the whole, exports react very sensitively to the level of subsidies, indicating the competitiveness of these markets.

Despite trade deficits of about $ 9 billion in 1990 and 1991 (*Yapi Kredi Economic Review*, 1991, p. 73) Turkey does not face short-term problems of international creditworthiness. On the one hand, tourism has become a source of substantial foreign exchange receipts with high growth potential for the future. Furthermore, migrant remittances still contribute considerably to foreign exchange revenues. However, high interest rates are necessary to attract foreign capital, while the term structure of the foreign debt is worsening.

Despite the intended freeing of market forces and substantial real wage decreases during most of the 1980s, investment in manufacturing remained sluggish during the decade. This is a matter of serious concern, as investments are a necessary precondition of long-term growth and modernization. In recent years only have total (public and private) investments recovered to 1977 levels. Most private investments, however, have gone into housing and service sectors such as trade, transportation and, most recently, tourism. Housing alone received more than twice as much investment as manufacturing, while public investment in manufacturing became negligible as a consequence of policy changes. Even inadequate data (see Table 8.1) reveal the surprising fact that profits did not create new manufacturing capacity.

Consequently, growth rates have been moderate, on average, while oscillating sharply, and employment in manufacturing rose at a rate of 2.8 per cent between 1980 and 1988 (cf. Table 8.1 and Figures 8.1 and 8.2). In fact, employment in agriculture increased more than in manufacturing, which may be suggestive of a swelling labour surplus in rural regions.

The initial success of increased exports has probably been overrated. By means of severe demand curtailment it has been possible to move resources quickly into export production on the basis of existing technologies. In the medium term, the problem of import dependency was only eased to a limited degree.

Macroeconomic policy, perhaps, did not resist resolutely enough the downward slide with respect to fiscal deficits, inflation and foreign debt. Laxity in these fields, prompted by, for example, impending elections, may set off a vicious circle of wrong signals to the private sector and increased public compensation measures. The strong credit demand of the Government and ensuing high lending rates have apparently formed an attractive alternative to physical investment, except in speculative fields such as housing (OECD, 1991a, p. 19).

The optimal sequencing of reform measures can also be questioned. Liberalization of capital and foreign exchange markets, which react quickly, was introduced before economic stabilization and changes in the economic structure had been accomplished. In the meantime even the policy of real undervaluation of the currency is counteracted by market forces, which stimulate short-term capital imports because of high interest rates (Boeri, 1991).

The results have to be weighed against a difficult regional economic environment. While world economic conditions stabilized during the period, the economic relations in the region were marked by extreme disruptions. As a consequence of the second oil price shock the terms of trade deteriorated strongly at the beginning of the 1980s; later the war between the Islamic Republic of Iran and Iraq and its aftermath caused strong fluctuations in Middle East trade relations; recently the Gulf War inflicted heavy damage on the balance of payments; and the hopes of booming business relations with the former USSR have to be set aside during a period of uncertainty.

Owing to the lack of private investments, an adjustment of the economic structure, a change of the product mix and an enlargement of the range of comparative advantage have not yet occurred on a broad scale. Hence, no scope exists for growth-stimulating or demand-side policies. This restriction has been painfully felt during the past decade, as any attempt to step up growth and employment became

Table 8.1. Performance of the Turkish economy, 1961-89

Year	Growth GNP (%) Manu	Growth GNP (%) Total	Growth of private investment (%) Manu	Growth of private investment (%) Total	Growth of public investment (%) Manu	Growth of public investment (%) Total	Growth of total investment (%) Manu	Growth of total investment (%) Total	Growth of employment (%) Manu	Growth of employment (%) Total	Growth of labour productivity (%) Manu	Growth of labour productivity (%) Total
1961	14.53	1.71	...	...	...	...	...	...	6.61	1.15	7.43	0.56
1962	2.88	5.29	...	...	...	...	...	...	0.74	1.00	2.13	4.25
1963	14.46	10.09	...	...	...	...	...	...	1.95	1.11	12.27	8.88
1964	8.13	4.11	-28.29	-7.87	26.79	9.37	-18.12	0.02	12.17	1.59	-3.60	2.49
1965	9.51	2.97	-11.93	5.45	-4.58	5.17	-9.83	5.31	4.86	1.39	4.44	1.56
1966	15.30	12.16	17.32	16.41	42.56	21.26	24.96	18.84	5.36	1.89	9.43	10.08
1967	10.62	3.52	27.70	9.76	25.31	5.96	26.88	7.82	6.30	1.25	4.06	2.24
1968	15.05	7.52	19.92	13.42	32.41	20.50	24.18	16.97	4.87	1.58	9.71	5.85
1969	9.92	5.77	14.56	14.50	29.88	8.39	20.13	11.34	3.06	1.01	6.66	4.71
1970	2.92	6.24	11.69	10.45	7.18	5.90	9.92	8.16	8.49	1.61	-5.13	4.56
1971	8.47	10.19	-1.54	-0.38	1.93	-8.55	-0.21	-4.40	2.86	1.76	5.45	8.29
1972	10.70	7.01	23.17	11.85	43.31	8.26	31.05	10.16	10.40	2.72	0.28	4.17
1973	11.99	5.21	7.51	12.91	-10.73	13.14	-0.30	13.02	7.15	1.80	4.52	3.35
1974	6.97	7.49	9.83	1.63	5.49	17.01	8.17	8.76	8.65	2.00	-1.55	5.38
1975	8.04	7.86	17.26	15.91	76.47	33.99	39.39	24.92	1.03	1.18	6.94	6.60
1976	9.71	8.02	15.30	21.01	3.77	19.15	9.84	20.02	2.39	1.33	7.16	6.59
1977	7.42	4.43	0.79	-1.11	4.63	8.16	2.50	3.81	9.40	3.13	-1.81	1.26
1978	3.62	4.34	-9.71	-6.18	-23.04	-14.93	-15.79	-11.02	0.57	1.31	3.03	2.99
1979	-4.99	-0.07	-31.81	-13.90	21.60	4.82	-9.54	-4.00	1.24	1.44	-6.15	-1.49
1980	-6.11	-0.87	-14.06	-17.01	2.93	-4.43	-4.53	-9.75	1.07	1.21	-7.10	-2.06
1981	9.18	3.40	-2.00	-8.62	-11.56	6.38	-7.78	0.55	0.64	0.80	8.49	2.58
1982	5.26	4.03	2.32	6.69	-13.31	2.21	-6.74	3.79	3.01	-0.55	2.18	4.60
1983	8.40	3.46	-1.47	2.37	-24.69	-6.97	-13.98	-3.58	3.37	0.93	4.86	2.50
1984	9.99	6.24	5.92	8.43	-17.13	-4.71	-4.95	0.36	2.26	1.43	7.56	4.75
1985	5.46	4.20	6.11	8.18	7.26	23.10	6.58	16.89	3.55	1.58	1.84	2.58
1986	9.39	7.08	13.89	16.41	-19.79	7.53	-0.05	10.96	1.52	1.72	7.75	5.27
1987	9.72	6.59	-4.16	18.57	-40.27	-3.39	-16.15	5.49	3.03	2.12	6.49	4.37
1988	-1.92	-4.36	0.73	13.34	-25.95	-14.07	-5.58	-1.61	4.77	2.39	-2.72	1.92
1989	3.10	1.21	-4.88	2.74	-17.40	-10.23	-7.20	-3.44				

... = figures not available
Manu = Manufacturing

Source: Uygur, 1990.

embroiled in mounting inflation rates and trade deficits, forcing economic policy into an uneasy "stop-go" pattern.

The difference between industrialized and industrializing countries relates to the fact that the former possess "scarce" resources, consisting of technology, organizational capacity and human capital, while the latter, besides natural resources, have only unqualified labour, of which there is an unlimited supply globally. An international division of labour under such conditions places the developing countries permanently at a disadvantage. They are invited to sell their labour-intensive products under the rules of cut-throat competition on the world market, while the indus-

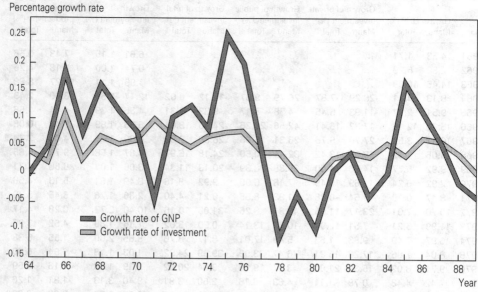

Figure 8.1. Growth rate of GNP and investment, Turkey, 1964-88

Source: Uygur, 1990.

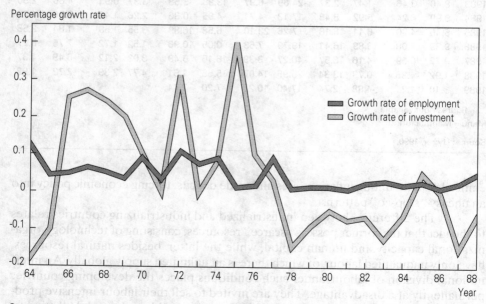

Figure 8.2. Growth rate of employment and investment (in manufacturing), Turkey, 1964-88

Source: Uygur, 1990.

trialized countries pay with their sophisticated products, for which they have monopolies. While the industrial countries could produce all the goods they import, the developing countries cannot. Hence the industrial countries can demand prices which allow them to pay high wages to their workers and to finance social costs; in addition they can afford to allocate huge resources to science, education and training. For the developing countries the situation of the classical political economy has reappeared. The prices they obtain for their products on the world market permit them to pay only the "natural price of labour", i. e. subsistence wages. There is no margin left to finance social welfare measures or investments in human capital. In other words, the Prebisch-Singer problem of continuously worsening terms of trade for the products of developing countries re-emerges.

To spur economic development, it is imperative to break the vicious circle of unlimited supply of labour and world market integration on the basis of comparative advantage. Import substitution was such an attempt to escape from the underdevelopment trap by copying the industrial structures of developed countries under an umbrella of massive protection. It turned out that, in spite of considerable success in terms of growth rates and employment creation, this strategy ultimately failed: an unfounded confidence in the economic competence of governments and state bureaucracies, the formation of domestic monopolies and proliferation of rent-seeking behaviour rendered the approach inefficient.

Viewed from a dynamic perspective, IS and EO are not mutually exclusive alternatives, but are related to each other as sequential stages or as complements. In implementing IS policies, developing countries frequently overlooked the instrumental character of protection. Shielding the new industries from world competition was a means and an end at the same time, holding out a prospect of reaping immediately the fruits of industrialization in the form of elevated incomes, government services and public welfare programmes.

The question as to whether an initial phase of import substitution policies can gradually be relaxed towards world market integration is more empirical than theoretical. The answer depends on how much economic spirit could be mobilized during this period, on the state of entrepreneurship, human resource development and bureaucratic efficiency. Most countries failed to create a stringent internal competitive climate, in which entrepreneurship could grow to competence. But an outward-oriented strategy does not provide an automatic remedy to these crucial problems. There is no certainty that managerial and entrepreneurial spirits exist everywhere and only have to be awakened by resetting some economic parameters. It may just be that rents and subsidies are collected under new labels.

The structural implications of an outward-oriented strategy have to be considered carefully as well. Specialization in industries with existing comparative advantage leads to a concentration on a narrow range of products in which world market conditions deteriorate because of increasing competition of exporting countries and protection measures of importing countries. For Turkey these branches are textiles, clothes, leather, and iron and steel. More than half of Turkey's industrial exports consist of these products. By stressing the criterion of exportability the structural aspect of strengthening the interindustrial linkages is neglected. In the end a pattern of "exporting domestic production and importing domestic consumption" may be formed.

Summarizing, export promotion or import substitution strategies have centred on the problem of balance of payments constraints. Import substitution policies have achieved a satisfactory growth record but have failed on the balance of payments issue. Export orientation has performed better with respect to the balance of payments but has not fulfilled the high expectations of employment growth and structural adjustment to technological progress.

Among the structural deficiencies impeding a quick modernization of the Turkish economy, the following should be mentioned:

- a regional and sectoral segmentation of the economy;
- a fragmentation within the economic sectors of agriculture, industry and services;
- a backlog with respect to science, education and vocational training in comparison with industrialized countries.

It is in these fields that further progress has to be accomplished to put the economy firmly on a path of sustained growth, prosperity and competitiveness.

Complementing the strategy of export promotion hitherto followed, more mixed policies might be added in future. While it is certainly necessary to build up a strong and competitive export sector, the promotion of a more domestically or locally oriented sector of small and medium-sized businesses and crafts could broaden the productive base of the economy. As demand stimulation raises dangers of inflation, supply-side policies should be preferred, aimed at improving productive capacity for large-scale final and intermediate consumption.

Labour supply and surplus

Emigration pressure cannot be quantified exactly. One way to approach the subject is to look for suitable indicators of major push factors. For an economist, the employment situation and the level of incomes will be of prime importance. In Turkey, the haziness of statistics with respect to employment arises from the informal nature of the labour market. Therefore, the precise determination of labour market and employment status is even more intricate. Only a minority of dependent workers, those working in government institutions including state enterprises and in medium-sized and large private enterprises, are covered by strictly formalized labour contracts. Beyond these segments much remains vague.

Two segments are of primary importance: the agricultural sector with a high seasonal variation of labour demand, and the large range of informal activities in urban areas, i.e. the multifaceted forms of self-employment and of variable and unregulated work in small craft shops and businesses. Additional ambiguities arise as employment statistics, whether census or survey data, are essentially based on self-declaration and therefore may contain a bias, probably in the direction of embellishing employment status. One reaction to this situation is to look not only at the actual state of the labour market but to interpret it as part of long-term trends.

For several years, regular household surveys have provided labour market participation and employment data. The latest available figures are presented in Table 8.2. Rural and urban areas are distinguished according to size of place of living: towns of more than 20,000 inhabitants are defined as urban areas.

Statistics on rural and urban areas cannot be easily compared. Although the areas have equal shares of the population, the labour force is distributed 60 per cent to 40 per cent. In rural districts for most inhabitants the employment situation is determined by belonging to a farm family; 72 per cent of the labour force or 76 per cent of employment consists of self-employed farmers and unpaid family workers. For women the farmer household is practically the only place of work: only 4.7 per cent of women employed in rural areas (230,000) declare a job outside agriculture, mainly manufacturing (108,000) and social and communal services (80,000). Obviously, participation and unemployment statistics lose their significance under such circumstances, because the employment situation is no longer defined by labour market categories but by socioeconomic status. For the analysis of productive employment in rural areas other concepts such as labour surplus, which indicate labour demand on the basis of technical estimates, have to be applied (see Table 8.3).

Table 8.2.   Labour supply and employment in Turkey, 1990

	Men Rural	Urban	Women Rural	Urban
Population 12 years and over (million)	9 114	10 048	9 801	9 633
Labour force (million)	7 105	7 060	5 021	1 466
Participation rate (%)	78.0	70.3	51.2	15.2
% of labour force				
Fully employed	86.1	82.1	95.1	70.0
Underemployed	8.0	7.1	1.0	3.9
Unemployed	6.0	10.8	3.9	26.1

Source: State Institute of Statistics (SIS), 1991, Household Labour Force Survey Results, April 1991, Ankara.

Table 8.3.   Labour surplus in the Turkish economy, 1975-87

	1975	1980	1985	1986	1987
Registered unemployment	1.4	1.5	5.3	5.8	6.4
Discouraged workers	6.2	9.2	7.4	6.5	5.6
Disguised unemployment in agriculture[1]	5.7	4.1	3.6	3.5	3.2
Domestic labour surplus rate	13.3	14.8	16.3	15.8	15.2

[1] Defined as labour surplus in peak seasons.

Source: State Planning Organization.

The urban employment statistics reveal some puzzling features of their own. Most striking is the low employment rate of women. The declared rate of labour market availability of women is only 15.2 per cent to which an unemployment rate of 26.1 per cent has to be added. Women declaring themselves as full-time workers constitute only 10.7 per cent of the population 12 years old and over in urban places, while two-thirds (67.7 per cent) declare themselves to be housewives, and 11 per cent pupils and students. Even if younger age groups are excluded for better comparability, this low participation rate in working life contrasts with developments in post-industrial countries, where participation rates of women generally surpass 50 per cent.

Declared unemployment is markedly different for men (10.8 per cent) and women (26.1 per cent) and is mostly an entry phenomenon: 50 per cent of unemployed men and 57 per cent of unemployed women are under 25 years of age, and 77 per cent of the young women and 44 per cent of the men are seeking a job for the first time. Their difficulty in finding first-time employment is generally not caused by a lack of formal education: one-third of the men and half of the women have more than primary education; one-quarter of unemployed women have completed secondary education.

These figures highlight some aspects of labour market reality in Turkey. Open unemployment is very much a problem of modernization and aspiration. It is the good jobs which are missing, and it takes a long time to find a suitable workplace or to lower one's personal ambitions. Women especially face difficulties of finding an occupation corresponding to their qualifications.

Intermittent unemployment resulting from dismissal, lack of qualifications and old age, so typical of the industrial countries, is not reflected in the data. Indeed, shedding of labour in slack business periods does not occur as frequently as in industrial countries. Employment is increasing even during recessions, with resulting falling labour productivity. Consequently, the risk of unemployment is transferred to the younger generation and is reflected in problems of entry into the employment system.

The job-creating capacity of the Turkish economy has diminished during the past decades, especially in manufacturing. Growth rates of employment were, in per cent:

	Manufacturing	Total
1960s	5.7	1.5
1970s	4.1	1.6
1980-88	2.8	1.3

In 1990 employment in agriculture still amounted to 50 per cent of the total, while only 13 per cent of employed people worked in manufacturing.

It seems evident that substantial labour redundancy exists in the Turkish economy. Calculations of the State Planning Organization can be regarded as minimum estimates.

Another economic push factor of migration may be formed by an unsatisfying income situation. The question of growth and distribution of incomes in Turkey has aroused controversy in recent years. There is no doubt that real wages and agricultural incomes shrank considerably during the first half of the 1980s and that income distribution worsened. More recently some counter-movements have taken place. A comprehensive survey by the State Institute of Statistics based on 1987 data finds that personal income distribution changed very little after 1973, and even shows certain improvements in Gini coefficients. These results, however, are not corroborated by a study of TÜSIAD for 1986. In functional distribution, wage shares have remained practically unchanged according to the SIS survey (29.3 per cent in 1987 versus 28.3 per cent in 1973). As the ratio of wage earners in total employment increased, their collective position worsened slightly. Agricultural incomes contracted sharply, to 23.2 per cent in 1987 from 39.9 per cent in 1973. In personal distribution these shifts were compensated by the fact that most households receive incomes from different sources. Only a minority receive only wage or only agricultural incomes.

How can these employment- and income-related figures be related to migration propensities? It is certain that the overall employment situation has not improved since the 1970s. If younger and more educated people are the most mobile, a readiness to exploit opportunities in other countries can be assumed. In addition, decelerating employment growth in the cities may have prevented part of the population in rural areas from leaving the countryside. The experience of stepwise migration might well repeat itself, if the borders were opened again (see Martin, 1991, on what might happen if borders were open).

In economic terms, the existence of push factors cannot be denied. Migration decisions, however, are the result of multifaceted considerations, in which economic calculations are only one factor. As history does not repeat itself, it would be questionable to derive definite answers from such a narrow information base.

3. Economic cooperation and assistance

General remarks

For decades Turkey has been a prominent partner of economic cooperation with the industrialized countries. Turkey was included in the Marshall Plan in return for joining the Western alliance against the Communist bloc. From the Federal Republic of Germany alone Turkey received more than 100 million DM per year on average in the 1960s. From the 1970s the volume of assistance rose to about 200 million DM (see Table 8.4). Outstanding credits amounted to 4.6 billion DM in 1991. While other countries (especially Japan, the United States, and France) contributed as well, the World Bank was by far the largest source of credits for Turkey. In 1991, pledges amounted to about $10 billion. World Bank credits are usually given on nonconcessional terms. The European Community granted credits of 770 million ECU in the framework of the Association Treaty, while another tranche of 600 million ECU has been blocked since 1980 (figures communicated by the Ministry of Economic Cooperation, Bonn).

The term "development assistance" or "development aid" needs some clarification. Principally, grants must be distinguished from credits. The "aid" compo-

Table 8.4. Development assistance from Germany to Turkey, 1961-90 (million DM)

Year	Financial cooperation		Technical cooperation	Total payments	Net transfers	Ratio (6):(5)
	Agreements	Payments				
(1)	(2)	(3)	(4)	(5)	(6)	(7)
1961	347.0		3.5			
1971	158.0		5.8			
1981	460.0		17.5			
1985	130.0	125.3	18.3	143.6	26.7	18.6%
1986	130.0	144.9	13.9	158.8	-82.3	-51.8%
1987	130.0	226.3	17.2	243.5	135.1	55.5%
1988	280.0	178.1	29.1	207.2	15.0	7.2%
1989	135.0	168.0	36.4	204.4	1.9	0.9%
1990	240.0	394.6	15.9	410.5	76.0	18.5%

Source: Ministry of Economic Cooperation, Bonn.

nent of credits is only partially expressed under preferential conditions compared with commercial loans, "IDA" conditions being a kind of standard for "pure" aid (30 years' duration, 2 per cent interest and 10 years' grace). If access to credits in foreign exchange is limited for a country, loans at world market conditions can contain an aid element as well. In 1989, 85 per cent of multilateral credits, most of them World Bank loans, were on non-concessional terms (OECD, 1991b, p. 193). Interest rates for loans from multilateral agencies can rise to as much as 14 per cent, as has been the case for certain IMF credits.

In the case of Turkey, more than 90 per cent of foreign assistance takes the form of loans. The net advantage for the country depends on the difference between new allocations and repayments. If allocations have a constant monetary volume, the net inflow levels off in the course of time, and foreign assistance takes the form of a constant volume of credit in foreign currency under more or less preferential conditions. Even in this case interest payments can lead to a net transfer of resources from the receiving to the donor country. As the following analysis shows, Turkey is reaching the phase where only increasing amounts of allocations can prevent net return flows.

The economic implications of foreign debts are completely different for Turkey than a country such as the United States. In order to service loans, the United States has only to tax its citizens. Turkey, however, as her currency has no contract quality in international financial markets, has to procure foreign exchange to pay for her foreign debts. This may be a costly undertaking, as high additional budget expenditures or opportunity costs in the form of subsidies and/or tax exemptions etc. have to be incurred to procure sufficient foreign exchange revenues. Any tapping of foreign capital sources thus implies high costs for countries with weak currencies.

Furthermore, in the case of the United States, the creditors bear the risk of currency devaluation (and of revaluation), if debts are expressed in US dollars. In other words, the United States can reduce its foreign debt by inflation, if it regards it as advantageous. For Turkey this escape route is closed. Inflation leaves the value of the foreign debt unchanged, and devaluation of the Turkish lira permanently increases the value of foreign debts in national currency.

Countries with weak currencies – and economies – operate from a generally disadvantaged position in the world market. This fact also suggests a new assessment of the beneficial effects of foreign credits for industrializing countries even if they are given at preferential terms (see Riese, 1986; Spahn, 1991). An enterprise takes up credits if the expected returns – the Keynesian "marginal efficiency of capital" – exceed the interest rate. If this does not materialize, the credit cuts into the economic substance of the enterprise. By analogy, only those foreign credits which reproduce – directly or indirectly – their means of repayment in international liquidity are really "sound". Applying this rule would definitely scale down the range of projects suitable for foreign credit financing.

In terms of the effective transfer of resources, the balance of development assistance looks much less impressive. For World Bank credits the relation between gross payments and net transfers in the 1980s is shown in Table 8.5.

Conventionally in economic cooperation, the two branches of financial assistance and technical cooperation are distinguished. The first concerns provision of finance in the form of grants and credits, the latter makes available professional expertise to the receiving country.

Financial assistance

In the early 1980s financial assistance to Turkey reached its peak. In a coordinated effort the IMF, the World Bank and the OECD countries arranged a package of measures comprising short-term balance of payment credits, medium-term adjustment loans, rescheduling of commercial credits, and new public credits to overcome an insolvency crisis and to cushion the change of economic strategy from import substitution to export orientation (see Wolff, 1987).

Most of the special agreements have now been repaid. Turkey has repaid the stand-by credits of the IMF and serviced all her debts regularly. In fact, Turkey is presented as a prominent example of successful restoration of international solvency achieved through coordinated international assistance in combination with a deter-

Table 8.5. Financial assistance of the World Bank, 1980-84 (million US$)

Year	Gross payments	Net transfers	Ratio %
1980	312.6	179.2	57
1981	454.0	290.3	64
1982	500.2	290.9	58
1983	486.3	212.4	44
1984	628.5	288.4	46

Source: IBRD, *World Debt Tables*, Washington, DC.

mined change of domestic economic policy. This result, however, has been accompanied by a steadily rising weight of foreign debt which amounted to $ 49 billion in mid-1991. This level of international indebtedness is not regarded as another impending crisis, but it compares unfavourably with a foreign debt of $ 16 billion in 1980 (Wolff, 1987, p. 64). In 1989 interest servicing burdened the balance of payments with more than $ 3 billion (OECD, 1991b, p. 193).

German financial assistance normally takes the form of credits on IDA terms and is administered by the Kreditanstalt für Wiederaufbau, Frankfurt. Since the mid-1980s, yearly pledges have amounted to about 130 million DM, which may be topped up by special programmes. Payments vary between years with the speed of implementation of projects. Large grants have been given recently to compensate for the effects of the Gulf War. In 1988 a grant of 40 million DM for environmental projects in poor regions was given.

Net flows from Germany have become very modest. Owing to the long period of cooperation, allocations and repayments (including interest) balance each other out, despite the fact that interest rates are low (see Table 8.4).

If one looks for the impact of foreign assistance on the economic development of Turkey, the small effective volume of resource transfers has to be taken into account. The allocation of regular loans – whether bilateral or multilateral – follow fairly established patterns. Most of the credits are used for investments in the physical infrastructure such as energy, communications, transport and community services etc. (For World Bank loans see Wolff, 1987, p. 88.) There are, indeed, critical shortcomings in all these fields in Turkey and hence the contribution of foreign financial assistance to the national welfare both with respect to the quality of life and economic growth cannot be disputed.

The changing concerns of donor countries leave their imprint in the allocations. Germany, for example, puts a stronger emphasis on questions of environmental protection. Subjects which rank low among Turkish and foreign priorities tend to get neglected, such as large-scale reforestation or modernization of the railway system, both of which would yield tremendous economic and ecological benefits to the country.

Until now the reduction of emigration pressure has not been explicitly placed on the agenda of economic cooperation. Of course, speeding up economic development also helps to keep the population at home. However, new fields of cooperation are being explored. One such project has been the Industrialization Fund set up in 1989 for the purpose of improving credit to small and medium-sized enterprises. The fund received a first loan of 150 million DM. Half of the individual credits can be used for working capital. The project, aiming at establishing a revolving fund, is administered in Turkey by selected banks, among them Halk Bankasi, a public bank serving small entrepreneurs. The crucial variable is that inflation does not consume the real value of credits, because, if real interest rates become negative, credit demand may be influenced by rent-seeking behaviour.

Technical cooperation

Technical cooperation takes the form of offering professional expertise in various forms such as long- and short-term consultancy; training (on-the-job, seminars, workshops and fellowships); and procurement of equipment.

In Germany it was organized by the *Deutsche Gesellschaft für technische Zusammenarbeit*, Eschborn (GTZ). Yearly allocations have varied between 15 million and 30 million DM in recent years. GTZ extended cooperation in the fields of agriculture, vocational training, tax administration and support for establishing enterprises. (Since 1990 its role has been performed by the *Deutsche Ausgleichsbank*.) In the context of this paper, those activities which are related to the industrial development of Turkey merit special interest.

One project operates in the field of vocational training schools. Turkey is at present engaged in transforming the existing scheme of vocational education into a "dual system" that transfers the practical training to private enterprises. Actual cooperation embraces design and practical performance of two vocational training courses, one relating to electrical and automotive engineering, the other to the garment industry. The project includes the provision of technical equipment and the preparation of teaching material. Both courses are models for potential nationwide replication.

The reform of the vocational training system has high priority for the Turkish Government. Utilizing the technical equipment of private enterprises, the capacity for training technicians – a crucial bottleneck to industrial progress – can be increased. The scope of application, however, will be limited by the requirement that enterprises with modern technological equipment participate in sufficient number. As these are concentrated in the more developed parts of the country, regional imbalances may be accentuated. Second, the vocational training schools are a branch of the secondary education level. They only take in pupils who have finished middle school. Until compulsory education up to middle school level is implemented nationwide, a large proportion of teenagers will be excluded from the system. Third, the expansion of this vocational training system depends crucially on budget allocations and administrative capacity.

Since 1985 returning Turkish migrants who want to set up their own small or medium-sized enterprise can draw on a "special credit fund", which is financed by the Turkish and German Governments with an equal input of 11 million DM annually; it is administered in Turkey by Halk Bankasi. The fund provides credits to returning migrants up to an amount of 1 million DM and up to 50 per cent of total required capital. The credits, with an interest rate of 26 per cent, are very attractive, as they contain a considerable grant component (owing to much higher inflation rates). In addition, migrants participate in seminars in Germany prior to their departure, and in Turkey receive help through an extension service of Halk Bankasi.

A recent evaluation for the period 1985 to 1990 indicates successful performance by the programme. During this period, 900 enterprises received a total credit of about 100 million DM. Average credit amounts, about 100,000 DM, were comparatively low. Nevertheless, 17,000 jobs were created; credits per job amounted to less than 6,000 DM.

Of course, this programme appeals only to a small fraction of returning migrants; most are not interested in setting up a new enterprise. However, motivated returning migrants – and people returning to developing countries – can have a substantial stimulating economic effect through the transfer of modern technologies and management practices to home countries. For this reason the programme deserves further consideration.

In the framework of cooperation there exist a number of other activities which are channelled through churches, foundations and private organizations. One of these projects concerns the promotion of vocational training in the form of an apprenticeship scheme. As a cooperating body, the Foundation for the Promotion of Vocational Training and Small Industry, Ankara (MEKSA) was established in 1985. Its objective is to support the introduction of a "dual" apprenticeship scheme in small enterprises. One of the primary tasks consists in organizing and running supra-enterprise training workshops, as most craft shops cannot conduct the technical training themselves. MEKSA is one of the few organizations in Turkey having practical experience in this field. At present, financial assistance is used for maintaining training units and for compensating entrepreneurs for the cost of participating in training programmes. As enterprises are obliged now to provide vocational training, such incentives are no longer necessary or possible if the system is to be introduced nationwide. Instead, other functions of consultancy, training of trainers, of making available foreign experience and of promoting activities in peripheral regions might be given higher priority.

Evaluation

Cooperation has the important side-effect of leading to discussion on priorities between countries, and of starting pilot undertakings which otherwise might not have materialized.

To reduce emigration pressure in the medium term, it will be important to add new dimensions to socioeconomic development. Preference has to be given to labour-intensive industrialization, to stepping up human capital formation and to the promotion of entrepreneurial initiative. Economic cooperation tackling these objectives will have to reassess established practice in various respects.

One question concerns the volume of assistance. During the next few years a substantial enhancement of allocations will be necessary to maintain a notable net effect and to avoid return flows of resources. Another question concerns the shares of technical cooperation and financial assistance. If priority is given to the transfer of expertise and know-how, technical cooperation might be increased relative to financial assistance. In fact, Turkey has demonstrated that it can mobilize financial funds for projects of supreme national interest in various other ways. Some pertinent examples are the Bosphorus bridges, the Ankara metro or the spectacular south-east Anatolian (GAP) project.

In the past, financial assistance had been mainly spent on physical investments in technical infrastructure, especially for covering import shares. The Industrialization Fund for Small and Medium-sized Enterprises constitutes an interesting example which includes socioeconomic objectives in the scope of cooperation.

Financial assistance combines the provision of foreign exchange and of credit potential. Both may be allocated to different purposes. Such a splitting would permit supporting projects which require resources in domestic currency, while at the same time foreign exchange constraints can be eased in other fields.

4. Sectoral focus of measures

Selection of priority areas

To reduce emigration pressure in the medium term, the employment- and income-creating capacity of the economy has to be substantially enlarged. To this end current trends have to be reversed. During the 1980s the growth of labour demand diminished considerably in Turkey – and in large parts of the world. Especially in manufacturing, manpower input was cut back because of rapid technological progress, pushed by burgeoning factor costs (i.e. wages, energy and capital). Countries with a high birth rate faced additional difficulties in satisfying the welfare aspirations of the population (see e.g. Bruni and Venturini, 1991).

In looking for additional employment potential, the broad economic sectors of agriculture, services (primarily tourism), and manufacturing form a convenient starting-point.

Certainly, in both agriculture and tourism, Turkey still has a strong development and employment potential. The expansion of labour-intensive cultivation in irrigation agriculture as envisaged in the GAP project, and the establishment of agriculture-based industries and intensive cattle raising, will enhance productive labour absorption in this sector. Promotion of agriculture has the favourable effect of retaining the population in rural regions and of slowing down urban sprawl. Nevertheless, agriculture, already suffering from concealed unemployment, cannot absorb additional labour but has to release part of the manpower to other occupations.

Tourism can improve the employment balance, especially in coastal regions, and would be an important generator of foreign exchange.

However, the solution to the employment problem in the medium term under conditions of high population growth, necessitates the full mobilization of the goods-producing sector of the economy. Two fields are especially promising for enhancing the productive capacity of the country, increasing employment rapidly and narrowing regional development gaps, namely, the promotion of small and medium-sized enterprises (SMEs), and the extension of vocational training.

SMEs and the crafts already provide a high share of employment in manufacturing in Turkey. As they have a high income-employment elasticity, the rate of additional employment with increasing income is much greater than in large enterprises. As they are located mainly in rural districts their expansion reduces the propensity to migrate internally. In moderating the rate of urbanization external migration pressure is eased as well.

Small enterprises are bound into a dense network of neighbourhood relations and induce imitating behaviour; they emit strong local and regional multiplier effects, which increase their income-generating ability. There also exist close forward and backward linkages with the agricultural sector.

The promotion of SMEs and the extension of vocational training are closely interlinked. Vocational qualifications greatly improve the productive capacity of SMEs, while raising the educational standard for a large part of the younger generation. Institutionally, SMEs and their organizations will in future bear the main responsibilities for one branch of vocational training.

The promotion of SMEs and of vocational training is one field suitable for intensive economic cooperation. The Federal Republic of Germany has a long history of the "dual system of vocational training", which in essence has been adopted in the recently enacted Turkish scheme. Other countries could offer their experience with different institutional characteristics.

The promotion of SMEs is a fairly new topic for bilateral economic cooperation. It has a longer tradition in multilateral activities, e.g. of UNIDO and the World Bank. Ambiguities still exist as to the most efficient forms of support. Industrialized countries' experience cannot be directly transferred to industrializing countries, given the very different conditions of resource availability. A screening of methods applied in industrialized countries and an evaluation of their effectiveness are necessary to select the most appropriate schemes. Nevertheless, given the crucial importance of this issue, new efforts should be undertaken to intensify cooperation.

Structure and performance of small-scale industry

Analysing statistics always raises arguments as to the adequate subdivision of size classes and to the selection of meaningful indicators. Here these questions will be decided pragmatically using the statistical sources at hand. Turkish statistics take employment as an indicator of enterprise size, distinguishing principally between three groups: small enterprises (SEs – also known as micro or artisan enterprises) with up to nine people engaged; medium-sized enterprises (MEs) of 10 to 25 people; and large enterprises with more than 25 people.

Frequently, medium-sized and large enterprises (MLEs) are lumped together, thus suppressing specific information on structure and performance. Furthermore, "persons employed" are distinguished from "persons engaged", the latter category including the owner and others working without payment. "Employment" means "wage employment".

In the rhetoric of development policy, SMEs take a prominent place. For example: "In recent years it has been typically recognized in many developing countries that small and medium-scale industries play a decisive role in expanding and diversifying industrial production as well as in attaining the basic objectives of development. ... There is growing disappointment and disillusionment with the results of development strategies focusing on large-scale, capital-intensive and highly import-dependent industrial projects, which more often than not failed to increase the rate of

Table 8.6. Performance of enterprises according to size, 1985

Enterprises	Small (Percentages)	Medium	Large	Absolute totals[1]
Number of establishments	94.50	2.98	2.52	193 638
Persons engaged	35.96	6.19	57.84	1 462 840
Output	10.88	4.31	84.82	19 984
Value added	12.50	3.14	84.37	6 460
Gross investments	2.66	1.94	95.41	1 145

[1] investments, value added and output in billion Turkish lira.
Source: SIS, 1991a, p. 154 f.

labour absorption in the industrial sector and to generate self-sustaining growth" (UNIDO, 1987, pp. 1 f.).[1]

While the above quotation may be appealing, it is only vaguely supported by factual evidence. The actual importance of SMEs, as revealed by statistics, seems to be rather limited in Turkey.

The industrial census of 1985 counted 193,638 enterprises in manufacturing industry. Table 8.6 compiles some performance indicators for size classes.

On the whole, statistically declared employment in manufacturing industry is comparatively low (1.5 million people in 1985) and has grown only moderately. Comparing the periods 1970-80 and 1980-85, annual employment growth slowed from 4.5 per cent to 3.3 per cent in MLEs, and from 4.2 per cent to 1.3 per cent in SEs. With the exception of employment, the figures in Table 8.6 indicate a limited contribution of SMEs to the national economy. Of enterprises with up to 25 people engaged, 97.5 per cent contributed only 15 per cent to output and value added, and a mere 4.6 per cent of investments. Of the 4,870 "large" enterprises, 392 belong to the public sector, employing about one-third of 850,000 people engaged in this size class and producing 37.6 per cent of output. For industrial employment, however, SEs have considerable importance, the more so as underreporting may occur frequently.

The number of people that individual small enterprises engage is very low: from 1970 to 1985 it increased from 1.9 to 2.9. Most of them are owners or unpaid family members, and less than half work for payment (44 per cent in 1980, 49 per cent in 1985). In MLEs nearly all those engaged are wage or salary earners.

Table 8.8 suggests that small and large enterprises operate in different economic worlds. Wages paid in MLEs are six to ten times as high as those in SEs. Labour productivity (value added per person engaged) is four to five times as high in MLEs, and the share of wages in value added, extremely low compared to industrial countries, differs markedly between MLEs and SEs. (In the Federal Republic of Germany the share of wages in value added amounted to 70 per cent for manufacturing in 1989). It would be completely misleading, however, to infer a higher profitability of SEs from the lower wage share. Some of the difference is due to depreciation, which has some relevance for MLEs, but is negligible for SEs: 95 per cent of all investments

---

[1] For an assessment of the importance of small-scale enterprises for the prosperity of industrial countries, see Piore and Sabel, 1984.

are in large enterprises (see Table 8.6). Most of the difference, however, is caused by the high level of employment of owners and unpaid family members in SEs. Calculating a normal remuneration for this group, profitability turns out to be much lower than for MLEs (SESRTCIC, 1987, pp. 71 f.). A lower efficiency among SEs is confirmed by the large difference in labour productivity.

The large payment differences between SEs and MLEs point to the existence of pronounced labour market segmentation. SEs especially employ young people and others who do not find work in more attractive sectors of the labour market. Small-scale enterprises recruit school-leavers; they pass through a traditional form of apprenticeship until they start their army service and receive only a small payment (one-third of minimum wages).

Owing to factors such as capital shortage and lack of skills, SEs show high failure rates. For the period 1963-70 a survival rate of 53 per cent has been calculated (see SESRTCIC, 1987, p. 67). From UNIDO (1987, p. 45) it can be inferred that SEs were hit most severely by the depression of 1978-80.

In Turkey as well as in other industrializing countries, SEs typically cluster in industries using relatively simple, labour-intensive production techniques (leather, footwear, furniture, metal products) and industries using spatially dispersed raw material (food processing and wood processing). In fact, nearly three-quarters of employment in SEs is concentrated in six branches (see Table 8.7). Some of them are still strong relative to MLEs.

Surprisingly, the structural relations of the economy did not change fundamentally between 1970 and 1985. On closer inspection one finds, however, that economic policies had quite different impacts for small and large enterprises. While during the 1970s the profit situation of MLEs worsened slightly compared to that of SEs, it improved substantially after 1980. The ratio of wage levels between SEs and MLEs increased from 9.3 per cent in 1980 to 16.6 per cent in 1985; in MLEs wage shares of value added increased from 25.9 per cent to 30.7 per cent. Between 1980 and 1985 MLEs reduced the wage share by one-third to 21.2 per cent of value added. For SEs the wage share scarcely changed: 15.3 per cent in 1970; 13.7 per cent in 1980; 14.3 per

Table 8.7. Employment in selected branches, 1985

	Employment Small enterprises	Medium-sized and large enterprises (MLEs)
Food manufacturing	71 714	137 807
Textiles	44 974	185 062
Wearing apparel	71 620	37 020
Wood and cork production	53 235	15 559
Furniture and fixtures	49 160	6 118
Fabricated metal products	84 743	45 242
Total	375 446	426 808
Share of employment in respective size class	71	46

Source: SIS, 1990, *Statistical Yearbook of Turkey.*

Table 8.8. Wages and labour productivity in small and large enterprises, 1970-85

	1970	1980	1985
Ratio of wage levels of SEs to MLEs (%)	12.7	9.3	16.6
Share of wages in value added for SEs (%)	15.3	13.7	14.3
Share of wages in value added for MLEs (%)	25.9	30.7	21.3
Labour productivity (SEs in % of MLEs)	20.7	21.0	26.5

Source: SIS, *Statistical Yearbook of Turkey*, various issues.

cent in 1985 (see Table 8.8). Obviously, any movement in real wages is felt much more by large than by small enterprises.

The effects of policy changes on employment can be seen in Table 8.9. Under the umbrella of import protection and a favourable investment climate, small enterprises expanded strongly in capital goods industries. In contrast, some branches of the consumer goods sector, such as clothes and leather in which SEs faced more competition, reduced employment during the 1970s: the number of establishments fell from 56,000 to 38,000. Under the EO regime both these trends reversed.

In capital goods industries during 1980-85, as a result of import competition and higher quality demands of customers, employment contracted by a rate of 15.9 per cent per year. In the manufacture of transport equipment the number of enterprises shrank from 21,000 to 3,300, and employment from 58,000 to 12,000 people. At the same time SEs expanded in the consumer goods sector, supplying the lower strata of the domestic market. In 1985, 61.8 per cent of SE employment was concentrated in this sector (see Table 8.9).

Although not directly supported during the phase of import substitution, SEs benefited from the generally protective climate, from rising wages in the formal sector and expanding demand. After 1980, stabilization policy measures – real-wage reduction, tight money policy and demand restraint – were felt by SEs especially. As SEs are oriented towards local markets, they suffered from shrinking agricultural and wage incomes which have a high demand elasticity for their products.

The analysis so far suggests that the performance of SEs did not meet the planners' high expectations (Hiç, 1986). Casual empirical evidence and available statistics confirm this. (For recent case studies see, e.g. Hummen, 1989; Orak, 1991; Wolff, 1984.) Stronger market orientation of economic policy after 1980 improved allocative efficiency, but sluggish growth, a decreasing share in production, and shrinking profits resulting from low productivity and rising wages, all added to the financial vulnerability of many small ventures.

The position of the small enterprise sector in the Turkish economy is reflected in weak structural integration. No reliable information is available about their participation in exports, but it is substantially lower than their share of production. In principle, they could contribute considerably to foreign trade, because they operate in the major export industries. At present, this potential is not exploited because of poor technological standards of production and low product quality.

Market segmentation also prevails in the domestic economy. For the booming tourist industry it has been found that luxury hotels pursue an outward-looking

Table 8.9. Growth of employment in small and large enterprises, 1970-85

Industry	Growth rate of employment					
	Large enterprises			Small enterprises		
	1970 to 1980	1980 to 1985	Engagement 85 (%)	1970 to 1980	1980 to 1985	Engagement 85 (%)
Food manufacturing industries	4.7	2.2	14.7	2.5	5.7	13.6
Beverage industries	1.7	0.7	1.3	-7.8	0.9	0.2
Tobacco industries	4.3	-3.9	-4.6	/	/	/
Manufacture of textiles	2.4	2.2	19.7	7.1	4.5	8.5
Manufacture of clothes and footwear	10.8	23.0	4.7	-0.5	5.1	18.7
Fur and leather industries	4.4	10.1	0.7	-4.1	9.0	1.4
Manufacture of wood and cork products	4.3	2.5	1.7	4.2	1.3	10.1
Manufacture of furniture and fixtures	2.0	12.4	0.7	10.2	6.5	9.3
Consumer goods industries	3.7	2.9	48.1	2.8	4.7	61.8
Manufacture of paper products	3.9	4.4	2.4	5.6	-2.5	0.4
Printing and publishing	0.8	6.0	1.5	5.8	3.9	2.5
Manufacture of industrial chemicals	3.6	5.3	6.0	8.1	12.5	1.5
Petroleum, coal derivates	16.6	4.3	0.9	/	/	/
Plastic products and rubber	9.5	2.1	2.6	22.6	0.8	3.4
Manufacture of pottery, glass and non-metallic mineral products	4.9	3.8	7.6	5.5	1.9	3.5
Basic metal industries	9.2	1.6	8.6	32.1	30.9	1.6
Manufacture of metal products	0.8	4.3	4.8	3.1	4.8	16.1
Intermediate goods industries	5.2	3.3	34.4	5.4	4.7	29.0
Manufacture of machinery	8.6	3.4	6.0	13.3	-17.0	2.6
Manufacture of electrical machinery, etc.	11.9	5.6	4.3	6.6	-8.9	1.7
Manufacture of transport equipment	3.8	4.4	6.3	6.7	-27.2	2.2
Misc. manufacturing industries	-6.2	13.0	0.9	-3.8	12.0	2.6
Investment goods industries	6.1	4.7	17.5	6.8	-15.9	9.1
Average	4.5	3.3	100.0	4.2	1.3	100.0

Source: SIS, 1990, *Statistical Yearbook of Turkey*, 1989.

sourcing policy and have a national network of suppliers. Only *pensions* and small hotels use SEs located in the neighbourhood (Hummen, 1989).

Subcontracting, which plays an important role in other countries such as Italy or Japan, is relatively undeveloped in Turkey; its impact decreased further in the 1980s. Large enterprises prefer to cooperate with other MLEs because they can give better guarantees for product quality, timely delivery and adequate volumes. Here, too, the typical handicaps such as lack of modern equipment and technical qualification prevent more intensive cooperation.

"Symbiosis by segmentation" instead of "symbiosis through cooperation" seems to be the rule. In the first variant, SEs serve functions derived from MLEs as they take over repair, maintenance and adaptation of products to special uses (SES-RTCIC, 1987, p. 73). In the second variant they are linked to the production process of MLEs, supplying components, tools etc., which the contractors find uneconomic to produce themselves. Generally, such cooperation requires strict specialization so as to attain high quality standards at low cost. Although not without risks of dependence or even exploitation, subcontracting may offer opportunities of diversification and upgrading of production for SMEs.

What are the reasons for such an apparent lack of prosperity? Analytically, they might be placed under the headings "traditions", "qualifications", "scale factors" and "economic policy".

Outside artisan production, Turkey does not have a strong tradition of entrepreneurial activity. Rather, agriculture and trade have determined the economic history of the country. The industrialization of Turkey was based on two pillars: state economic activity from the 1930s to 1980 and, after 1945, large private enterprises, the most important of which have become powerful holdings.

Another constraint is the low standard of managerial and technical qualifications, which impedes the absorption of modern techniques of production and the improvement of product quality (Wolff, 1984). A widening technological gap between small and large enterprises runs the risk of further divergence between them. While large enterprises have switched to national or even international sourcing, preferring to import state-of-the-art capital goods, small producers have to resort to technically more modest domestically produced machinery. There is consequently the possibility of a chasm appearing between small enterprises, crowding in shrinking markets for traditional products, and a modern large enterprise sector in which production standards are set by imported technologies. The current gap is widening as large enterprises attract the graduates of vocational training schools. Hedged in a production segment of low-quality, cheap and labour-intensive products, SEs cannot expand into the important markets of intermediate products, of production-oriented services and of meeting the specialized demands of the urban population, where economies of scale are unimportant.

Such economies of scale are a major source of large enterprises' comparative advantage. They operate not only in industrial production, but also in transactions such as credit negotiations.

All studies confirm that the most serious handicap of SEs concerns the difficulty of obtaining credit for investments or working capital through the regular banking system. The banks' conservative credit policy, which demands physical collateral rather than looking at the dynamic aspects of profitability, worsens the SEs' position. In addition, the generally deficient credit supply and high interest rates – boosted by inflation and the banks' own profit requirements – work to their detriment.

Some of the handicaps of SEs, such as factors of scale, are in the nature of things and shape the frontiers of competitive advantage for different size classes of enterprise. Others though are created by economic policy. Under import substitution, special preference was given to state economic enterprises; their low productivity determined the degree of protection against external competition. Big private enterprises profited from this policy by collecting super-profits. In addition, because of their stronger lobbying position in dealing with the planning authorities, large enterprises had better access to foreign exchange assignments and preferential credits etc., than SEs. Under the EO strategy SEs suffered from the stabilization measures and were disadvantaged by the incentive system.

Even today the contribution of SEs to economic and social development should not be underrated. First, the employment and training function must be mentioned. Youth unemployment would be much higher without the absorbing role of SEs. Furthermore, successful entrepreneurs have often acquired their managerial and technical experience in artisan enterprises (see e.g. Kirim and Ates, 1989). Thus SEs form a reservoir of manpower resources which is tapped by larger enterprises, while historically, the accumulated production knowledge in traditional enterprises was an important asset in the change to export orientation.

The informal sector in Turkey: A black box

Since the ILO report on employment and development in Kenya (ILO, 1972) the employment absorption capacity of the informal sector has been emphasized. The question arises whether this concept is helpful for the analysis of the Turkish labour market and for labour market policy. Can the informal sector generate attractive employment opportunities and strengthen the individual's determination to stay at home, or does it only offer marginal jobs which are abandoned at the first opportunity? The motivational implications are ambiguous. On the one hand, informal employment can raise personal satisfaction, if it yields sufficient income and gives a feeling of social integration. On the other, greater awareness and increased self-confidence can sharpen the view of economic deprivation and arouse a feeling of hopelessness.

Unfortunately, intensive international discussion since the 1970s has led to deadlock. As clear-cut operational criteria for separating formal and informal activities could not be formulated, the specification of welfare effects was impossible. Informal activities could neither be classified in terms of modern or traditional, nor could they be analytically separated from phenomena such as the underground economy and concealed employment, etc. Informal sectors have since been "discovered" in industrialized countries, e.g. Italy, where they are said to have contributed considerably to national wealth (see Piore and Sabel, 1984).

Hönekopp and Yalman recently reviewed the information on the informal sector in Turkey. One finding is that comprehensive studies on informal employment do not exist. Even the topological qualities of the concept are widely doubted, reducing its significance to a "general descriptive term to refer to the rich variety of small-scale activities" (Hönekopp and Yalman, 1990, p. 20). As for entrepreneurial activities, Ayata distinguishes between different forms of market integration of factors: artisans "acquire some of their means of production outside the market", while petty commodity producers "are totally dependent on the market". In contrast to small-scale capitalists, who employ wage labour, the former rely mainly on self-employment and unpaid labour (see Hönekopp and Yalman, 1990, p. 20 ff.). Because the available studies, usually branch-specific, are in Turkish, it was impossible to evaluate them for this paper. It seems, however, that they are more interested in the problems of social evolution than of economic performance. The analytical distinction of artisan production, petty commodity production and small-scale capitalist production would merit special interest for economic policy if it also referred to systematic differences in profitability, economic viability and structural change.

So far, ambiguities and inferences pervade the discussion. Among the questions impossible to answer are the following:

- To what degree do official statistics include activities that might be regarded as informal? It appears that petty commodity production in the above sense is largely covered by the census data of small industrial establishments.

- What impact do business cycles and development strategies have on informal or small-scale activities? Prevailing opinion assumes that export-oriented industrialization has "given new impetus to the rise of petty commodity production, unlike the preceding strategy of import substitution" (Ayata, quoted in Hönekopp and Yalman, 1990, p. 23). Even a process of "informalizing the entire economy to some degree" (Keyder, quoted in Hönekopp and Yalman, 1990, p. 23) has been supposed.

Such conclusions seem to flow from the assumption that the export boom has induced enterprises to resort to subcontracting on a large scale. However, they are not corroborated by certain other sources. Higher demands of product quality and technical standards set limits to these alternatives. As far as self-employment is concerned, strict informality seems to be the exception in Turkey. There exists for example a rather comprehensive affiliation of independent activities such as taxi driving or retailing within the crafts. Informal employment is more frequent for wage labour that is not registered for social security purposes, etc.

Discussions on the informal sector to date stress its country-specific characteristics. It can therefore be misleading to fill in for a lack of knowledge by drawing analogies from other countries. As a matter of fact, the Turkish employment system still has many features of a "black box". Of course, if formal employment shrinks during recessions, rising self-employment is a logical reaction. The same happens if growth in dependent employment lags behind for other reasons (but in these cases, only marginal jobs are generated which disappear when the economy improves again).

State support of small enterprises

From the foregoing analysis it is clear that the potential contribution of small-scale enterprises to the development of the country cannot be assessed properly from past performance. The course of economic development in Turkey has been shaped by large – state and private – enterprises. Private enterprises also relied strongly on state aid. "The state support is an absolute necessity. Those who are unable to obtain such support find it impossible to stay afloat" (Ilkin, 1991, p. 24). Small-scale entrepreneurs have never been in such a privileged position. Hence, there was never competition on equal terms.

Another interesting feature is a rigid segmentation of Turkish business society. Ilkin finds that "virtually no [big] industrialist [came] from the background of small-scale production" (ibid., p. 24); many had a bureaucratic background.

Investigating the Turkish textile industry, Kirim and Ates (1989), present a more differentiated picture. The authors stress the interrelations between the "traditional" and the "modern" sector which have to be distinguished from "big industry". According to them the traditional sector forms a very important learning base with respect to qualities of materials and details of production processes. "A large number of firms in the modern sector have been founded by people who, in the past, had their own enterprises in the traditional sector" (Kirim and Ates, 1989, p. 6) or at least had working experience there.

Support measures for small and medium-sized industry have from the beginning been an important topic in the economic development plans. In the first Five-year Economic Development Plan (1963-67) the following measures were proposed:

- expand sources of "controlled credit";
- concentrate small establishments in industrial estates;
- establish a small-scale industry development centre;
- encourage cooperation;
- reorganize the apprenticeship system (SESRTCIC, 1987, p. 87).

In fact, this list can still be taken as valid for present priorities. Today, the lack of access to commercial credit forms the most crucial obstacle to expansion. Besides informal sources of credit, small enterprises are dependent on concessional credits provided by public banks, the principal agent being Halk Bankasi. Most of the credits are channelled through 3,200 credit cooperatives (with about 2 million members). As the bank runs about 600 branch offices throughout the country and offers technical assistance at the same time, it is in principle a competent institution for that purpose. It is evident, however, that a single institution disposing of limited funds and depending on government allocations cannot meet nationwide demand. Funds are lacking, especially with respect to long-term credit, with the consequence that credit periods are simply extended repeatedly. By this practice funds for short-term credits are quickly exhausted.

A public consulting organization, KUSGET, has been founded to offer technical assistance to small enterprises, building on the experience of an earlier institution, KUSGEM. KUSGET pursues an integrated approach "to stimulate the availability of service programmes, training consultancies, and financial assistance geared to the needs of small and medium enterprises..." (World Bank, quoted in SESRTCIC, 1987, p. 91). In this instance as well it would seem difficult to serve the needs of such a scattered and heterogeneous clientele by a single agency. As KUSGET is bound to the salary structure of the public service, finding qualified staff is a major problem (ibid., p. 91). In fact, KUSGET, which receives support from UNDP/UNIDO, concentrates much of its efforts on the reorganization of one branch, the foundry industry.

Great efforts have been made to solve location problems for small and medium-sized enterprises. In large cities such endeavours have become imperative for ecological reasons, because outdated shops and factories in crowded central areas cause problems ranging from inaccessibility to environmental pollution and ineffective town planning.

Two programmes are oriented towards enterprises of different size classes, namely organized industrial estates, and small industrial districts.

In the framework of the first programme, plots of land fully integrated into the public infrastructure are offered to medium-sized enterprises. Administrative assistance is provided; the buildings are constructed by the owners themselves. Until 1986 only nine out of a total of 42 projects had been completed, most of them in the western part of the country (ibid., p.98; Hummen, 1989, p. 36, quotes a figure of 34 completed projects in 1988). SESRTCIC (1987) appraises the scheme somewhat sceptically, pointing to slow progress in completion, uneven regional distribution and inadequate utilization. Some of the projects owe their existence to local political ambitions; sometimes the plots, which are highly subsidized, are held for speculation rather than production.

In contrast, small industrial districts have become quite successful. They are usually situated outside towns on newly reclaimed land, and they serve to relocate old artisan enterprises or craft shops, as well as attract new ones. Constructed and operated by cooperatives, small industrial districts offer ribbon-development turnkey workshops without existing connection to the public infrastructure. In 1987 a total of 303 government-assisted projects had been registered, about half of them already completed, in which 230,000 workers were employed.

Some of the reasons for the success of these small industrial districts are, first, the fact that they cater to the real needs of the clientele of artisans and small entrepreneurs; second, their modest design keeps construction costs low, and consequently, much lower subsidies enable the programme to be conducted on a larger scale, extending it to rural areas and peripheral regions. For the owners of expensive land in urban areas, relocation offers the opportunity to realize this fortune and invest the proceeds, in other words to "plough parts of urban rents back into production" (SESRTCIC, 1987, p. 103). After finishing construction, the programme benefits from a low level of public interference. Finally, a concentration of craft shops and enterprises in organized districts facilitates the organization of vocational training and the installation of training workshops.

Despite the general success of the programme, its mobilizing effects must not be overestimated. Providing workshops does not suffice to spur business-mindedness, and in the smaller towns most of the shops are occupied by car repair and maintenance services.

Summary and conclusions

In spite of various programmes, effective support to small and medium-sized enterprises has been limited. This is true also for the present phase of export-oriented policies. Of course, small economic units are much more difficult to reach by administrative measures than are large enterprises. Subsidies are normally allocated directly by bureaucratic decisions on the basis of applications and documented performance. Small entrepreneurs are always handicapped in doing paper work and have difficulties in furnishing evidence. Administrators prefer to handle large applications. Petty producers, craftsmen and small industrialists are at a disadvantage in organizing and defending their interests in dealings with the civil service.

In view of this adverse situation, general indirect measures may reach a greater number of people more effectively than sophisticated specialized services and programmes. A sound policy of economic stabilization and low inflation, and a determined competition policy to curb oligopolies, can improve the economic position of small enterprises by eliminating distortions. A reduction of the general level of subsidies may have the same effect.

On the positive side in Turkey, craftsmen and SME business people are strengthening their organizational status. Besides corporate institutions such as TESK – the Confederation of Craftsmen and Small Businessmen, which is currently stepping up its activities – private associations such as TOSYÖF, a foundation supporting small and medium-sized entrepreneurs, have emerged to deal with the special needs of their members. Such developments can bring about new starting-points for public support and foreign assistance. Research and information on the performance and the structure of this sector, largely lacking at present, may be forthcoming, thereby helping to design appropriate support policies. Dialogue with, and the active cooperation of, competent partners will enable policy measures to be more precisely focused and their effectiveness improved.

5. Selected fields of cooperation

General remarks

Potential assistance programmes should focus on basic human resource development. Preferably, the partners involved should have experience cooperating in the respective fields and agree in principle on procedures and objectives to implement programmes quickly.

Further, institutional settings to reach and to mobilize the target groups should exist. An important factor in institutional effectiveness refers to the degree of decentralization and self-administration. In a country with a centralized structure such as Turkey, a transfer of competence to non-governmental institutions is essential to tap initiative, to lift administrative blockages and to overcome budgetary constraints.

In view of these criteria the promotion of small and medium-sized enterprises, including the crafts, is proposed as the most promising field of intensive cooperation. The economic position of this sector can be strengthened through improvements in the availability of human and physical capital by introducing a comprehensive vocational training scheme, and by improving the credit supply.

Expansion of vocational training

Informality is not the critical issue in reaching small enterprises through administrative measures in Turkey. Among craftsmen, small entrepreneurs and even among the self-employed, vocational or craft bodies are prevalent (if street vendors, shoe shiners and the like are disregarded). The establishment of voluntary organizations, usually as foundations, indicates an increasing demand for professional support and representation of interests.

While industrial and commercial entrepreneurs are affiliated to "chambers of industry and commerce", which form regional federations and a national confederation (TOBB), craftsmen, small entrepreneurs and the self-employed, such as traders and restaurant or taxi owners, are organized into "chambers of trade and small-scale business" at the district level with a subdivision into guilds. At provincial and national levels, the chambers are represented by associations (at the provincial level), federations (trade-specific at the national level) and TESK. At the national level there exist ten trade-specific federations, comprising 3,700 guilds with altogether more than 4 million members.

The vocational training system is regulated in the Law of Trade and Small-scale Business of 1964, amended in 1985 and, most recently, in May 1991. In the context of this paper it is of special importance that in the amendment of 1991 the "principal task" to accomplish the practical part of vocational training in a "speedy, efficient, comprehensive and systematic manner" (amended paragraph 15) was given to these corporate institutions. In this way the Turkish Government has assigned the critical function of vocational training in crafts to the self-administration of a non-governmental corporate institution. The various bodies have been granted extensive authorization power. TESK has general competence for practical vocational training (amended paragraph 16), and bodies at various levels are permitted to establish vocational training centres (amended paragraph 17).

In addition, significant financial provisions are anticipated, including:

- at all levels of organization, 20 per cent of gross revenues must be spent on vocational training measures;
- at the confederation level, a Fund for the Promotion and Support of Vocational Training in Crafts and Small Businesses has been set up; it is funded by various sources (amended paragraph 18).

The chambers keep apprenticeship registers, and are responsible for organizing examinations.

The legal framework is complemented by Law No. 3308 of 1986 on vocational training, by which a vocational training levy is imposed on enterprises. (Until now this levy has formed a kind of tax collected by the Ministry of Education.)

With this scheme, influenced by the German experience, the Turkish Government has opted for a "dual system" of vocational training in which the practical training takes place in the enterprises themselves, in the form of "learning by doing" while theoretical subjects are taught in public "apprenticeship training centres".

Major institutional responsibility rests with the crafts organizations. The new scheme, introduced under Law No. 3308 of 1986 and detailed with Law No. 3741 of 1991, aims to reorganize and improve the largely informal traditional apprenticeship system which is practised mainly in small enterprises (see Annex). These employ teenagers between the end of compulsory schooling and military service, and give them an elementary vocational knowledge.

To appreciate its importance, it has to be related to other features of the Turkish educational system (see Lauterbach, 1986; OECD, 1989). While this dual apprenticeship system is to come after the present five years of compulsory basic education, there exists a different scheme of vocational education which starts after middle school (eight years of education). It is organized in the form of full-time schooling in vocational training secondary schools, and offers technical and theoretical education.

At present, education in these "vocational lycées" is being remodelled into a dual form as well, where practical training will take place in enterprises in block release form. Enterprises with more than 50 employees will be obliged to take in apprentices at a rate of 5 per cent to 10 per cent of personnel, otherwise they have to pay a levy. Graduates of such reformed "vocational lycées" will lose direct access to higher education entrance examinations which they have now. To reach these exams, they will have to complete another year's course at a "technical lycée".

Compulsory education is to be extended to eight years, i. e. to include present middle school, by the year 2005. Two competing systems of vocational training would then exist for the same age group with obviously very different qualification levels.

The pace of implementation of these three very ambitious reforms – reorganization of the dual apprenticeship system, reform of vocational lycées and introduction of compulsory middle school – is still uncertain. Both vocational training systems require the cooperation of the private sector, which is especially demanding in the case of vocational lycées. Enterprises have to offer training places for practical instruction in block periods. In parts of the country it will be difficult to find a sufficient number of such training places. At present, the reform is still in an experimental stage. In 1985/86 the industrial, vocational and commercial lycées were attended by 320,000 students compared to 630,000 students in "general lycées" and 6.7 million students in primary schools (OECD, 1989, p. 42). Taking into account these proportions, it seems obvious that vocational lycées will not for a long time come close to meeting the demand for vocational training in Turkey.

Under these perspectives the reform of the dual apprenticeship scheme is a remarkable step to modernizing and upgrading the standards of vocational qualifications and to preparing the young generation for work in modern industry. If implemented successfully, it will provide the country with a wealth of qualified manpower, trained in modern technologies.

Among the positive aspects of the apprenticeship system, the following are especially noteworthy:

- it can be introduced quickly throughout the country and can be operated on a large scale;
- the costs are moderate because the Government finances only the element of theoretical education while enterprises carry out the technical training;

- it acts as a model for responsibility-sharing among Government, corporate bodies and the private sector;
- it enhances the social level of crafts and small enterprises.

The extension in compulsory basic education, desirable to improve apprentices' general knowledge, will not cause organizational complications.

At present this project is at an early stage of implementation. Most craft shops and small enterprises do not have the modern technical equipment for adequate practical training. In most cases "supra-company training units" have to be established for this purpose. Three parties will need to cooperate: workshops and enterprises for practical work experience; supra-enterprise training units for technical training; and government-employed teachers for theoretical subjects.

Establishing and running such a vocational training system on a national scale forms a major challenge for both the Government and the private sector.

The basic responsibility for running supra-enterprise training units rests with the various trade chambers, associations and federations. They can also be organized by other bodies such as societies or foundations. Prior to 1988, 40 training units had been set up, enrolling 12,000 to 15,000 apprentices per year. Even if plans to increase this number to 100,000 are realized, only a minority of an estimated 800,000 apprentices will be adequately served.

Enterprises and training centres lack qualified training instructors. In the medium term, graduates from apprenticeship lycées, and vocational or technical lycées, having obtained additional teacher training will form the resource base from which trainers can be recruited. Craftsmen, after three years of vocational practice and additional schooling, can obtain the licence of a trainer. In the meantime, training personnel for in-firm training will have to use crash courses.

Provision of capital for small enterprises

In addition to the promotion of vocational qualifications, there are other essential fields of support for crafts and small enterprises. The unavailability of credit is by far the greatest obstacle for expansion and diversification of this sector. The regular banking system frequently adds to the problem of regional imbalance instead of reducing it, as it collects savings in the countryside and channels them to the core regions where operating conditions are easier.

In the framework of economic assistance, funds financed by the donor country or by both countries are established for credits. Two forms can be distinguished: regular credit funds, and credit guarantee funds.

Turkey and Germany have gained some experience in the management of credit funds for SMEs, through the Programme for the Promotion of the Foundation of Enterprises by Returning Migrants, and the Industrialization Fund.

Special attention should be given to a proposal from Turkish crafts and SME organizations to create a credit guarantee fund. The fund would guarantee repayment in the event of default on a debt. Thus the problem of a lack of physical collateral among SMEs, especially severe for new enterprises, is alleviated. The credits themselves have to be procured from other sources.

Credit guarantee schemes are useful for a number of reasons:

- they permit the mobilization of larger volumes of credit than do regular credit funds;
- they strengthen the negotiating position of SMEs with commercial banks;
- they consolidate the organizational network of SMEs;
- they open access to other sources of credit;
- they reduce dependence on government support and strengthen the vitality of the private sector.

The activities of such schemes should include the guaranteeing of medium-term credits to boost working capital. Although a national organization is necessary, decentralized units would be required to check applications and supervise borrowers' performance, best conducted by experienced administrators in the regions. Credit guarantee funds are a novelty for Turkey, and as such need an initial input of technical and financial assistance. The potential social and economic mobilization effects strongly suggest that this initiative should be supported.

Another constraint for SMEs and craft enterprises is the shortage of managerial skills. Consultancy services, and accounting, marketing or organization training courses could be offered to owners, linked with credit or credit guarantee schemes.

6. Concluding remarks

A broadening of the resource base in terms of human and physical capital, together with the strengthening of an enterprising, self-reliant middle class, form the pillars of a successful development strategy. Decentralization and self-administration deserve consideration. The participation of non-government institutions and of voluntary associations greatly enhances commitment, initiative and responsibility. A prospering sector of small and medium-sized enterprises will substantially improve the rate of self-sustained growth in Turkey.

The success of such a strategy depends critically on the macroeconomic environment, as well as on political priorities. High, fluctuating levels of inflation, high real interest rates and a restrictive demand situation have a significant negative impact on the small-scale industrial sector. The budget allocations for education, which have fallen disproportionately in recent years (see Böhmer, 1990), must be adjusted upwards.

The industrial countries have to play their part as well. A crucial issue will be the volumes of allocations. For the projects suggested above, a great deal of financial assistance is needed in domestic currency to increase internal allocations. Assistance for expenditure in foreign currency is not required. Besides increasing the volumes of assistance and the share of grants, foreign exchange (and the domestic equivalents) of loans and grants could be used for different purposes. While the foreign exchange serves to meet urgent import demand, the recipients have to pay in domestic currency which could be used in the various programmes. Put another way, the country's debt burden and budgetary constraints could be greatly relieved if the creditor countries would accept repayments of loans in Turkish currency and channel them into the respective funds.

Assistance alone will not suffice to change the economic hierarchy of nations. The industrial countries have to abstain from restrictive practices in world trade and from setting the parameters of economic exchange according to their own interests.

Economic cooperation does not yet focus on the areas suggested in this paper – but a certain experience can be drawn on. There exist a number of pilot programmes which can be evaluated as to feasibility and effectiveness. Commitment from both sides might render emigration pressure obsolete within about two decades. With such achievements Turkey would form a model of development for many countries in Eastern Europe and the Middle East which are looking for a new orientation of their economic orders and policies.

Bibliography

Boeri, Tito. 1991. *Problems in implementing structural reforms in developing countries: The experience of Turkey in the 1980s*, Centro Studi Lucca D'Agliano, Development Studies Working Papers, No. 35, Feb.
Böhmer, Jochen. 1990. *Zwischen Exportboom und Re-Islamisierung: Stabilisierungs- und Strukturanpassungspolitik 1980-1987* (Münster, Lit. Münster).
Böhning, W. R. 1984. *Studies in international labour migration* (London, Macmillan).
Bruni, Michele; Venturini, Alessandra. 1991. *The Mediterranean Basin: Human Resources and Economic Development*, paper for an international conference on migration, Rome, 13-15 March 1991, mimeo.
Deutsche Gesellschaft für technische Zusammenarbeit. 1991. *Bericht über das Programm zur Förderung türkischer Einzelexistenzgründer durch den Kreditsonderfond I 1985-1990* (Eschborn).
Gordon, Jan; Thirlwall, A. P. (eds.). 1989. *European factor mobility* (London, Macmillan).
Hansen, Bent. 1989a. *The political economy of poverty, equity and growth: Turkey*, mimeo.
—. 1989b. *Unemployment, migration and wages in Turkey 1962-85: Policy, planning, and research* (Washington, DC, World Bank, working paper WPS 230).
Hiç, Müccerem. 1986. "Industry, handicraft and tourism" in Klaus D. Grothusen: *Südost-Europa Handbuch, Band 4 – Türkei* (Göttingen, Vandenhoeck & Ruprecht).
Hönekopp, Elmar; Yalman, Galip. 1990. *Employment aspects of the "informal sector" in Turkey* (Nuremburg, mimeo).
Hummen, Wilhelm, et al. 1989. *Economic links between tourism and small and medium industry*, case study of Antalya, Turkey (Berlin, German Development Institute, mimeo).
Ilkin, Selim. 1991. *Businessmen: Democratic stability* (Ankara, mimeo).
ILO. 1972. *Employment, incomes, and equality: A strategy for increasing productive employment in Kenya* (Geneva).
Jesske-Müller, B.; Over, A.; Reichert, Ch. 1991. *Existenzgründungen in Entwicklungsländern*, Werkstattberichte 31, Wissenschaftliches Zentrum für Berufs- und Hochschulforschung der Gesamthochschule Kassel.

Katseli, Louka T.; Glytsos, Nicholas P. 1989. "Theoretical and empirical determinants of international labour mobility: A Greek-German perspective", in Gordon, Jan and Thirlwall, A. P. (eds.): *European factor mobility* (London, Macmillan), pp. 95-115.
Kirim, Arman; Ates, Hüseyin. 1989. *Technical change and technological capability in the Turkish textile sector*, METU studies in development, No. 1-2, (Ankara), pp. 1-30.
Lauterbach, Uwe. *1986. Berufliche Bildung des Auslands: Türkei*, Schriftenreihe der Carl-Duisberg-Gesellschaft (Baden-Baden).
Livi Bacci, Massimo. 1991. *South/North migration: A comparative approach to North American and European experience*, paper for an international conference on migration, Rome, 13-15 March 1991, mimeo.
Martin, Philip L. 1991. *The unfinished story: Turkish labour migration to Western Europe* (Geneva, ILO).
—; Hönekopp, Elmar; Ullmann, Hans. 1990. "Europe 1992: Effects on labour migration", in *International Migration Review*, Vol. XXIV, pp. 591-603.
Mellor, John F.; Johnston, Bruce F. 1984. "The world food equation", in *Journal of Economic Literature*, Vol. 22, pp. 531-574.
Molle, Willem; van Mourik, Aad. 1989. "A static explanatory model of international labour migration to and in Western Europe", in Gordon and Thirlwall (eds.), 1989, pp. 30-52.
Olson, Mancur. 1982. *The rise and decline of nations* (New Haven, Yale).
Orak, Kemal. 1991. *Die Automobilindustrie in der Türkei und der EG-Binnenmarkt* (Munich, Hieronymus Buchreproduktion).
OECD. 1989. *Reviews of national policies for education: Turkey* (Paris).
—. 1991a. *Economic surveys 1990/91: Turkey* (Paris).
—. 1991b. *Financing and external debt of developing countries: 1990 survey* (Paris).
Piore, Michael J.; Sabel, Charles F. 1984. *The second industrial divide: Possibilities for prosperity* (New York, Basic Books).
Porter, Michael E. 1990. *The competitive advantage of nations* (London, Macmillan).
Riese, Hajo. 1986. "Entwicklungsstrategie und ökonomische Theorie – Anmerkungen zu einem vernachlässigten Thema", in *Ökonomie und Gesellschaft, Jahrbuch 4*: Entwicklungsländer und Weltmarkt (Frankfurt and New York).
—. 1989. "Schuldenkrise und ökonomische Theorie", in Riese, H.; Spahn, H. P., (eds.): *Internationale Geldwirtschaft, Studien zur monetären Ökonomie* (Regensburg, Transfer), pp. 187-216.
Small Industry Development Organization (SIDO). 1987. "Institutional support for small and medium-sized enterprises in Turkey", in *Journal of Economic Cooperation among Islamic Countries*, pp. 115-124.
Spahn, Heinz-Peter. 1991. "Sparmangel, Akkumulationsfinanzierung und Außenhandel", in *Zeitschrift für Wirtschafts- und Sozialwissenschaften*, Vol. 111, No. 4, pp. 601-607.
State Institute of Statistics (SIS). 1990. *Income distribution, household income and consumption expenditures: Survey results* (Ankara).
—. Various issues. *Statistical Yearbook of Turkey* (Ankara).
—. Various issues. *Household Labour Force Survey* (Ankara).
Statistical, Economic, and Social Research and Training Centre for Islamic Countries (SESRTCIC). 1987. "Small and medium-sized manufacturing enterprises in Turkey", in *Journal of Economic Cooperation among Islamic Countries*, pp. 55-114.
Straubhaar, Thomas. 1988. *On the economics of international labor migration* (Bern, Haupt).
Tapinos, Georges. 1991. *Can international cooperation be an alternative to the emigration of workers?*, paper for an international conference on migration, Rome, 13-15 March 1991 (Paris, OECD, mimeo).
Thomas, Brinley. 1961. *International migration and economic development* (Paris, OECD).

UNIDO. 1987. "The role of small and medium-scale industries in OIC member States", in *Journal of Economic Cooperation among Islamic Countries*, pp. 1-54.
Uygur, Ercan. 1990. "Policy, productivity, growth and employment in Turkey, 1960-1989 and prospects for the 1990s". *Mediterranean Information Exchange System on International Migration and Employment* (MIES) 90/4, Special Study Topic (Geneva, ILO).
Werner, Heinz. 1991. *Migration movements in the perspective of the Single European Market*, paper for an international conference on migration, Rome 13-15 March 1991 (Paris, OECD).
Wolff, Peter. 1984. *Entwicklungsperspektiven und Förderbedarf von Handwerk und Kleinindustrie in Izmir/Türkei* (Berlin, Deutsches Institut für Entwicklungspolitik, mimeo).
—. 1987. *Stabilisierungspolitik und Strukturanpassung in der Türkei 1980-1985* (Berlin, Deutsches Institut für Entwicklungspolitik).
World Bank. Various issues. *World Debt Tables* (Washington, DC).
Yapi Kredi Economic Review. 1991. Vol. 5, pp. 51-98 (editorial).

Annex

Funds for promotion of vocational training and apprenticeship

Financial sources of the Fund for the Development and Extension of Apprenticeship, Vocational and Technical Training at the ministry of education:

- an additional levy (one per cent to three per cent) on income and corporation tax;
- a levy to be paid by those firms which do not meet their legal obligation to offer part-time training to vocational school students;
- contributions from chambers of industry and commerce, and from unions;
- an allowance allocated in the annual ministerial budget.

Sources: OECD, 1989, p. 36; Lauterbach, 1986, pp. 127-131.

Financial sources of the Fund for the Promotion and Support of Vocational Training in Crafts and Small Businesses:

- the respective allocations in the budget of the Confederation;
- 25 per cent of revenues of institutions affiliated to the Confederation and run on a profit basis;
- 25 per cent of the share which has to be paid from the "Fund of Promotion and Support to the Confederation";
- 25 per cent of the shares to be paid by institutions affiliated to the Confederation which do not spend their educational budget in this field;
- a contribution of the Fund established by Law No. 3308 (Fund for the Promotion and Support of Vocational Training in Crafts and Small Businesses);
- the share (50 per cent) of vocational training levies not reimbursed from the Fund established in Law No. 3308 to those craft shops and small businesses which perform vocational training;
- contributions from other funds;
- revenues of this fund;
- revenues for issuing certificates of apprenticeship and for printing materials of all kinds;
- other revenues of any kind, and donations.

Source: Law No. 3741 (1991) on Crafts and Small Businesses, amended paragraph 18, (from an unofficial German translation).

Epilogue
Reducing emigration pressure:
What role can foreign aid play?

P.L. Martin

Some 80 million to 100 million immigrants, refugees or asylum-seekers and migrant workers are outside their country of citizenship. If assembled in one nation, they would be the world's tenth largest country. Despite generally closed or closing doors to the rich industrial nations that many of these migrants want to enter, their number is increasing by 2 per cent to 3 per cent annually, making this "nation of migrants" one of the world's fastest growing nations.

Much of today's migration is unwanted by the migrants as well as by the countries they seek to enter. Refugees are driven from their homes by persecution, and many economically motivated migrants would remain at home if they could find jobs there. About half the world's migrants are in industrialized nations, and these nations have been grappling with the difficult trade-offs involved in tightening their immigration controls and preserving open doors for humanitarian or needed economic migrants while, on the other hand, accelerating the development of conditions in emigration countries that do not force or encourage people there to leave.

There are many ways in which industrialized countries could induce migrants to stay at home, ranging from the draconian – such as using military forces to police borders – to financial encouragement. But force and financial incentives are not long-term solutions to unwanted migration: durable solutions require political freedom and economic growth in emigration nations. Achieving freedom and growth was not easy for today's rich industrialized nations, and it is a daunting challenge for the developing nations from which most migrants come.

The industrialized nations interact with developing nations in a variety of ways. Most nations belong to the international organizations that establish rules for promoting trade and investment, protecting the environment, and avoiding domestic and international conflicts. Industrialized nations also have bilateral and multilateral arrangements with developing nations, some of which condition economic assistance or trade preferences on policies of the developing nation that range from economics to human rights.

The papers in this volume focus on the promises and pitfalls of using Official Development Assistance (ODA) to reduce emigration pressures. ODA is one of the four primary means through which industrialized countries individually and collectively influence economic and political developments in emigration countries. Governments can influence the volume and type of *trade* between emigration and immigration nations, and thus indirectly affect the level of economic activity, jobs and wages, and emigration pressures in developing nations. Democratic governments can encourage *foreign direct investment* in emigration nations, so that the jobs created by such investments reduce the incentive to emigrate for economic reasons. Industrialized country governments can also directly and indirectly affect *political freedom* in emigration nations, with instruments that range from military intervention to moral suasion. But only *ODA* is a universally recognized tool that is under the direct control of industrialized country governments and can theoretically be tailored to influence emigration pressures in other nations.

The premise of this book is that if aid-giving governments understood more about how their aid influenced refugee and economic emigration, the volume, form, and aims of their aid policies could be modified to achieve desired migration-reducing goals. For this reason, the contributors to the ILO-UNHCR meeting of May 1992 were asked to review the role that aid had played in the various countries and regions which sent large numbers of economic migrants and political refugees across national borders in the 1970s and 1980s. The contributors were then asked to consider the level and type of aid that would be necessary to virtually eliminate economically and politically motivated migration within a generation or two, perhaps by the year 2030. This volume comprises a selection of the documents submitted in working paper form in May 1992.

All authors assumed that the rich industrialized countries would continue to provide financial grants, loans, and technical assistance to developing nations. However, the contributors recognized that the world of the 1990s is quite different from the previous era which spawned most of the literature on aid and development. In particular, authors noted that, with the end of the Cold War, there would be fewer refugee-producing conflicts sustained by superpower rivalry. This means that there may be fewer refugees in areas where the East and West armed and funded opposing local factions, such as in many African conflicts and in Central America, but there may be more refugee-producing conflicts in areas that were previously under the control of one of the two superpowers, such as the former Yugoslavia and the former USSR.

Most aid is intended to accelerate economic growth and job creation, and to fuel hope for the residents in developing nations that their lives will improve. The willingness of the industrialized countries to provide foreign aid is declining, and there is an apparent consensus that many past aid policies were not always altruistic in economic terms. The authors in this volume endorse the general tendency to change the focus of aid from funding needed for projects, to supporting growth policies. Instead of building a dam to provide poor farmers with irrigation water, donor countries are beginning to realize that their aid will do more to accelerate stay-at-home development if it is used to help a developing country to get its agricultural policies right. Changing the focus of aid from projects and institution-building to policy reform also encourages coordination among aid donors and imposes on them a longer-run commitment to maintain policies that promote economic growth.

Can a reformed aid policy eliminate emigration pressures within one or two generations? The papers reach different conclusions. Most of the contributors who focused on refugees recognized that humanitarian relief in the 1990s must expand from the "two Rs" to "four Rs": in addition to *relief* and *resettlement*, refugee policies must be expanded to reconstruct areas to encourage *repatriation*, and a new emphasis must be placed on policies that can reduce the *root causes* of refugee-producing conflicts. Aid is necessary for these additional tasks.

The papers dealing with the role that aid can play to reduce economically motivated emigration were more explicit about the need for larger sums, for economic policy reforms in recipient countries, and for donor countries to recognize that their choice is not aid *or* trade but aid *and* trade. Perhaps the single most important "aid" that industrialized countries can provide to emigration nations is to remain open to their goods, which are often produced in labour-intensive or job-creating ways. Contributors emphasized that industrialized countries are often hypocritical on the aid and trade issue: they wonder why aid has so few effects, even as they restrict imports of farm and textile products. The developing nations must share the blame: in too many cases, aid has been a crutch that permitted them to maintain import-substitution economic strategies under which politically favoured monopolies produced low-quality and expensive goods for the country.

Definitions

What is emigration pressure, and what does it mean to reduce emigration pressure? *Schaeffer* defined emigration pressure as the number or proportion of people wishing to leave a country and stay in another during a given time period.[1] Beginning from a situation in equilibrium, internal (marriage, etc.) or external (economic or political) changes in conditions can encourage migration. Schaeffer argues that changes in external conditions are most likely to stimulate mass migrations. *Straubhaar* distinguishes between migration potential and pressure, and emphasizes that restrictions on immigration create migration pressure.[2]

Regardless of its precise definition, one can accept *Böhning*'s notion[3] that emigration pressure refers to a situation where more people want to leave a country than the countries that they wish to enter willingly accept. The determinants of migration pressure are familiar – economic inequality and conflicts push migrants out; jobs that pay relatively high wages, and safe havens pull migrants in; and communication and network factors link migrants and destinations.

Reducing migration pressure entails affecting these push and pull factors, or the network that motivates migration (or all these elements). Industrialized countries do not want to reduce the pull factors of high wage jobs or safe havens; they want to maintain peace and prosperity. Similarly, industrialized countries cannot overturn the communications and transportation revolutions that make it easier for migrants to learn about opportunities abroad, nor do these countries wish to abandon their tradition of permitting families to unify on their soil. This leaves reducing push forces as the morally acceptable durable remedy for unwanted migration.

The focus of this book is on the role aid can play in reducing migration push factors. The aid that industrialized countries provide to developing nations can take many forms, from loans that require the recipient to buy donor country goods to "no strings attached" gifts. Once received, aid funds can be spent according to the priori-

---

[1] Schaeffer, 1991, pp. 10-34.
[2] Th. Straubhaar: "Migration pressure", in Böhning, Schaeffer and Straubhaar, pp. 35-62.
[3] W.R. Böhning: "International aid as a means to reduce the need for emigration", ibid., p. 4.

ties of the recipient, the donor, or both. Aid funds can be dispersed throughout the country, or concentrated in one area or on one group in order to achieve a narrow goal, such as satisfying basic human needs or minimizing emigration pressures.

There is a vast literature on aid and development, but relatively little has been written on the relationship between aid and migration. The contributions in this volume help to begin to fill this void.

Aid and refugees

ODA and the international refugee regime was a product of the Cold War. ODA was meant to keep developing nations aligned with the capitalist West or the communist East. The refugee regime adopted in 1950 envisioned temporary asylum for those fleeing political persecution, and then resettlement in a third country.

Aid and refugee policies have changed. With the collapse of communism, aid is no longer used to carry political favours. The refugee regime has also changed. New conflicts produced refugees where there had been none before, as in the former Yugoslavia, former USSR, and Eastern Europe; the large numbers of refugees made traditional responses obsolete, as in south-east Asia and Afghanistan; and multilateral efforts were made to prevent persons from becoming refugees in Iraq, Africa and Central America.

How can ODA reduce the number of refugees, or prevent their formation, in the 1990s? The conclusion of most authors is that conflict and refugees will continue to be prominent features of the 1990s.

Suhrke[4] notes that the social conflicts which produce refugees arise in both the formation of nation states and during the resolution of conflicts within them. The conventional wisdom is that instead of generating refugees by creating new nation states, existing national borders should be respected, but the international community should work cooperatively with nations in which there are social conflicts to prevent refugee movements.

It is not clear how this conventional wisdom can be implemented universally, nor is it clear how aid can be used to resolve internal social conflicts. The main conclusions of those who study conflict as a cause of refugees are that aid during the Cold War often intensified and prolonged conflicts, thus increasing refugee flows. The end of the Cold War thus requires a new refugee regime.

The refugee regime established in the 1951 Geneva Convention emphasized the "two Rs" response: *relief* and *resettlement*. Relief meant that persons fleeing political persecution needed a temporary safe haven, and resettlement was a recognition that those fleeing, for example, communist regimes would be unlikely to return. The end of the Cold War requires an expansion to the "four Rs": the refugee regime must also deal with *repatriation* and *root causes*. In order to encourage voluntary repatriation after conflicts end, there must be reconstruction assistance; peace must be accompanied by development assistance to encourage the repatriation of refugees.

[4] Zolberg, Suhrke and Aguayo, 1989.

Preventing refugees is preferable to relief, resettlement, and repatriation. But how can aid reduce the root causes of the conflicts that generate refugees? *Suhrke* argues that the social conflicts that produce refugees cannot be extirpated. She distinguishes two types of refugee-producing conflicts: state formation (e.g. Bangladesh) and internal struggles (e.g. peasant revolts in Central America).

According to *Suhrke*, "good aid" can at best help to stabilize democratic regimes, but aid cannot, and should not, try to eliminate all refugee-producing conflict, since such conflict seems inevitable in desirable social change. Thus, industrialized countries must remain open to be safe havens for refugees.

Instead of developing general policies for general refugee problems, countries can (and do) develop specific policies for specific groups. Some Western European governments have sorted potential migrants from Eastern Europe and the former USSR into various groups, and then adopted policies for each group. For example, Germany hopes to encourage diaspora ethnic Germans in the former USSR to stay there by offering development and other assistance to them in their current "homeland" areas. To discourage the migration of Gypsies, attempts are being made to reduce discrimination and accelerate development where they now are. While developing a taxonomy of the various actual and potential migrant groups, and describing policies that have been or are being tried to keep them at home, *Blaschke* notes that there are as yet few general and few specific development policies that have been seen to reduce the emigration of specific groups.

Zolberg and Callamard argue that the coexistence of refugees and large infusions of aid in the Horn of Africa are the result of an attempt to create a modern state in a very poor and ethnically diverse region where the superpowers jockeyed for position. Ethiopia, Somalia, and Sudan received substantial development assistance – about 16 per cent of Ethiopia's GDP was ODA in the late 1980s, as was almost half of Somalia's GDP and 10 per cent of Sudan's GDP. In addition, all three countries received emergency food, refugee, and military assistance.

This outpouring of aid failed to eliminate or reduce significantly the root causes of refugees. There are several competing explanations: local recipients were not involved, or only local élites were involved; aid given to national governments was sometimes used to reinforce the non-democratic regimes that produce refugees; and even massive assistance could not undo the biases against developing nations in the international economic order.

Zolberg and Callamard propose reforms in the local, national and international organizations that receive and disperse aid, not in aid flows or their purposes. For example, they advocate determining, in a democratic process, whether local communities wish to be helped when the intention is to move them to a more promising location. At the national level, majority national governments should be encouraged to respect minority rights, especially if they have centralized and powerful government apparatus. At the international level, there should be a reconsideration of the doctrine that national borders are inviolate and, when UN agencies go into the field, they should have the power to deal comprehensively with problems there.

Aid and economic migration

Industrialized nations have been trying to accelerate economic growth in developing nations since the end of the Second World War. There are three primary means through which industrialized countries can modify their policies to accelerate economic growth and thus reduce emigration pressures. First, industrialized countries can permit the products produced in emigration countries to enter on a preferential basis; trade theory and common sense suggest that if it is made easier to export Mexican tomatoes, then fewer Mexican tomato pickers will seek jobs in a tomato-growing country such as the United States. Second, industrialized countries can encourage private and pubic investment in emigration countries. These developing economies typically have plenty of labour and not enough capital, so that promoting investment can lead to faster job and wage growth. Third, industrialized countries can provide aid to spur stay-at-home development.

The papers in this volume agree that massive amounts of aid would be needed to achieve the economic growth necessary to keep economically motivated migrants at home. In the case of Central America, it is estimated that aid would have to be almost US$ 100 per person per year alive today for the next 20 or 30 years to eliminate economic incentives to emigrate.

It is very difficult to determine how much aid would be needed to reduce economically motivated East-to-West migration in Europe. Per capita income differences today range from 20 to 1 (the Swiss to Albanian ratio), but are more typically in the 10-15 to 1 range. If Western Europe were to grow by just 2 per cent annually, and Eastern Europe by 5 per cent annually, the per capita income gap might be closed to 3-4 to 1 by 2020.

What level and type of aid would be needed to keep Eastern Europe growing 3 per cent faster than Western Europe over 30 years? *Molle et al.* believe that $ 20 billion to $ 40 billion annually would be needed to achieve such fast growth in Eastern Europe, and that this aid should be used to increase the capacity of these countries to produce goods for export markets.

There are various types of East to West migrants, ranging from privileged citizens returning to their homelands to asylum-seekers to legal and illegal workers, yet they play remarkably similar roles in Western European labour markets – most tend to be "gap fillers" in often lower-wage, seasonal, and low-status construction, agricultural and services jobs.[5] As with guest workers in the 1960s, it appears that few of these migrants are acquiring the skills necessary to accelerate development at home, and the remittances they send home tend to be spent on current consumption and housing rather than investment in factories.

Even if the legal and illegal employment of Eastern Europeans in Western Europe generates fewer real development benefits than are sometimes imagined, *Molle et al.* argue that emigration pressures are likely to rise during the next two decades. Unemployment in Poland, for example, increased by almost 20 times to 2 million between 1989 and 1991, and the Polish unemployment rate was projected to

---

[5] For the notion of gap fillers, see Böhning, 1991, pp. 445-458.

rise to 3.5 million, or almost 20 per cent of the labour force, 12 months later. The prognosis is for more unemployment and thus more reasons to emigrate – factories continue to shed workers and, in single-industry areas, there is no alternative but to move; agricultural restructuring will displace older workers who are not entitled to unemployment benefits; and government deficits will make it hard to employ newly graduated teachers, nurses and people with similar skills.

Will the workers who want to leave Eastern Europe find jobs in Western Europe? There are relatively few opportunities to work legally, but a growing number of employers and labour intermediaries are willing to assemble crews of illegal workers. In this manner, young Eastern Europeans are being absorbed into the underground economies of agriculture, construction, and some manufacturing and services. *Molle et al.* speculate that 2 million Poles might emigrate in the 1990s, including 1.4 million to Western Europe. Most of them will presumably seek jobs there.

What can be done? The authors argue that only Poles can transform Poland into a country that keeps potential migrants at home. Foreign aid can be used, for example, to launch needed infrastructure projects that can temporarily employ the unemployed, but only the Polish Government can reduce generous unemployment benefits, discourage labour hoarding in state-owned factories, and let the labour market function.

Weintraub and Díaz-Briquets note that the Central American economies experienced rapid economic growth during the 1960s (GDP increased at a 5 per cent to 6 per cent average annual rate), uneven but generally rapid growth in the 1970s, and slow or negative growth during the 1980s. During the 1980s, foreign aid poured into the region, and refugees poured out, suggesting an inverse relationship between aid and emigration.

Aid flowed into Central America during the 1980s as the superpowers supported opposing sides in Nicaragua and El Salvador. Conflicts in the region were rooted in slow growth and economic inequality, which the fighting and aid aggravated. The trickle of economic migrants and political refugees from the region to the United States and Mexico widened as networks with anchor families in the United States became established, and as United States decisions allowed some Central Americans to stay.

The five Central American countries in 1990 had a population of 27 million, a labour force of 9 million, and a weighted per capita GDP of $1,000. Population momentum is expected to give the region a population of almost 60 million by 2025, and a labour force of 25 million. How can aid create 350,000 to 550,000 jobs per year, and close the roughly 20 to 1 per capita GDP gap between the United States and the Central American economies? *Weintraub and Díaz-Briquets* estimate that if a $20,000 investment is needed to create each new job in Central America, then $2 billion per year in aid would be necessary to prevent unemployment and underemployment rates from worsening; today they are in the 30 per cent range. Since the region received $1.6 billion in aid in the mid-1980s and $1.3 billion in 1989, such an increase in aid might seem feasible. But the authors warn that the end of the Cold War has reduced the interest of the major donor – the United States – in the region, and they caution that it may be difficult to persuade the United States to increase aid to the region to reduce emigration pressures.

The lessons from Central America are sobering. Economic policies that seemed to work during the 1960s began to fail in the 1970s, when problems such as inequality inherent in that style of growth became apparent. Aid flowed to the region in response to conflict, almost reaching levels that, it is now estimated, might be sufficient to accelerate economic growth to reduce emigration pressures. However, the aid flowing to the region included military assistance, and the economic aid that accompanied it rarely produced "take-off" development in the conflict-ridden region. Now that peace would permit aid to stimulate economic development, interest in aid flows, and the flows themselves, to the region have declined.

The Tunisian case illustrates the truism that the nature of economic growth affects migration. In Tunisia's case, a capital-intensive import-substitution development model created neither enough manufactured goods to export nor enough jobs. Despite changes in its economic policies, there is still a gap between jobs created and new workforce entrants: during the 1980s, there were an additional 53,000 workers each year, but only 40,000 new jobs.

Until the mid-1970s, Tunisia exported workers to Europe. Tunisia hoped to export workers to the Libyan Arab Jamahiriya and the Gulf, but its workers found relatively few jobs there. Throughout the 1980s, there was a net return migration to Tunisia.

Bel Hadj Amor states that Tunisia now faces a development dilemma. It needs foreign capital, but it is considered too rich to receive large amounts of concessional aid. Loans, however, add to the country's debt and interest burdens. Tunisia plans to create slightly more than the 50,000 new jobs needed annually to employ additional workers, largely in textile manufacturing and tourism services. However, at a cost in investment of $50,000 per new job created, Tunisia must have foreign capital. *Bel Hadj Amor* argues that the international community should write off some of Tunisia's external debt, so that foreign investors would be more inclined to invest in Tunisia. According to the author, Tunisia could obtain the external help it needs through a new regional bank for Northern Africa that would channel additional foreign aid to the country in a way that encourages such capital inflows.

Ranis argues that aid can be used in ways that increase emigration pressures. The Philippines, he observes, traditionally received the highest per capita levels of aid in Asia, but geopolitical and historical factors prevented donors from forcing the Philippines to adopt what the author regards as the sound macro- and microeconomic policies necessary for stay-at-home development. *Ranis* argues that aid helped to cause the Philippines to miss out on the revolution in economic growth that produced the first generation of "Asian Tigers" – Taiwan (China), the Republic of Korea, Hong Kong, and Singapore – and aid may leave the Philippines further behind such second stage "Tigers" as Thailand and Malaysia.

The Philippines had a segmented dual economy at independence in 1946. The agricultural sector had two distinct subsectors: the farming of cash export crops such as bananas and sugar, and (often) subsistence farming of food crops such as rice and beans. There was also an urban economy, dominated by capital-intensive manufacturing and a large informal services sector. According to *Ranis*, the agricultural sector provides neither enough jobs, food, nor export earnings. As a result, rural people migrate to the cities where, by one estimate, one-third of the labour force is in the informal economy. However, this growing unemployment and underemployment was disguised during the 1960s and 1970s by capital inflows, aid, and other factors which also cloaked rising income inequality and increased poverty.

As in many other countries, aid donors and international organizations in the 1970s began to press aid recipients to adopt macroeconomic policies that fostered non-inflationary growth and microeconomic policies that fostered competition. *Ranis* argues that if the Philippines had been forced to adopt such policies, economic growth could have accelerated, and emigration pressures would have been reduced. But the United States, the provider of three-quarters of the Philippines' $2 billion annual aid package, did not want to push too hard to force the country to adopt painful economic policies when the primary purpose of the aid was to secure concessions on military bases. *Ranis* faults the Philippine Government for not adopting economic policies that lead to long-term economic growth, and aid donors for not requiring the Philippines to take such steps.

If the Philippines were to adopt promising economic policies, *Ranis* believes that emigration pressures would eventually decrease as economic growth accelerates. He notes that the ability to emigrate often rises over time, so that the only way to avoid increased emigration is to reduce the desire to emigrate. The desire to emigrate fell as the economies of the "Asian Tigers" boomed, while emigration pressures rose in the floundering Philippines.

Schiller reviews Turkey's economic and emigration record and concludes that aid could help to reduce emigration pressures there. Turkey followed many other developing nations down the import-substitution road during the 1960s and 1970s, and this strategy seemed to produce rapid growth. However, as in Tunisia and the Philippines, rapid increases in manufacturing output and GDP masked Turkey's failure to create enough jobs. As wage gaps between the protected manufacturing sector and rural areas widened, the stage was set for rural-urban migration. When there was an opportunity to migrate abroad, many of these previously internal migrants became migrant workers in Western Europe.

Turkey changed to an export-oriented economic policy in 1980. This too produced a decade of rapid economic growth, but also high inflation, falling real wages, and once again not enough jobs. *Schiller* explains that Turkey has very low labour force participation rates, especially for urban women. The 1990 labour force of 20 million in a population of 58 million suggests that only one-third of the population is in the labour force, compared with 50 per cent in most industrialized countries (the United States, for example, has a population of 250 million and a labour force of 125 million). However, even the figure of one-third is deceptive in Turkey, because virtually all adults in rural areas are assumed to be self-employed farmers. As a result, rural areas have about 40 per cent of Turkey's population, but 60 per cent of Turkey's labour force.

What is the emigration pressure in a country in which a low percentage of the population is in the labour force? As *Schiller* explains, official measures of unemployment and underemployment vastly understate the number of workers who would be available for good jobs if they were available. Furthermore, joblessness is most severe for the young people most likely to emigrate. It is for these reasons that the author concludes that Turkey's adoption of the "correct" export-oriented economic strategy, which accelerated economic growth, nevertheless did little to reduce emigration pressures.

Like the Philippines, Egypt, and several other emigration nations, Turkey used its location to extract high levels of aid from industrialized countries during the Cold War. Most of Turkey's aid in recent years has come in the form of World Bank loans, which Turkey must repay in the same foreign currency (dollars and deutsche marks) in which the funds arrived. Turkey had a foreign debt of $49 billion in mid-1991, which required $3 billion in foreign currency earnings to service. Germany and the EC provide additional assistance to Turkey, usually in the form of grants.

Turkey may be unique in the level of technical assistance it receives, especially from Germany. Technical assistance has a cost that is just 5 per cent of the cost of German financial assistance to Turkey, but its effects may be longer-lasting. Among the many projects undertaken in the form of technical assistance, two stand out. Germany is helping Turkey to introduce its dual apprenticeship training system, which involves classroom learning as well as paid work and training in a workplace. Germany is also providing credit and training for returning Turkish migrant workers who wish to start businesses in Turkey.

Schiller concludes that jobs are the answer to emigration pressure in Turkey. His sector-by-sector review of the options for job creation suggests that there are opportunities in agriculture, tourism, and manufacturing, especially if efforts are made to support enterprises that employ fewer than 25 workers and that can provide or benefit from vocational training. However, small enterprises did not fare particularly well in Turkey during the export-oriented 1980s. Even though 90 per cent of the almost 200,000 manufacturing operations in the country in 1985 had less than 25 employees, they contributed just 5 per cent of all investment and 15 per cent of manufacturing output.

Can the smallest manufacturing firms (nine or fewer workers) raise their wages and productivity in a manner that reduces emigration pressure? They employed over one-third of the 1.5 million manufacturing employees in the mid-1980s, but they paid far lower wages and had much lower labour productivity than larger firms. Since small firms are most likely to be started by returning migrants, and to employ the young people most likely to emigrate, what can be done to improve their ability to create jobs that keep potential migrants in Turkey? Small firms risk becoming vulnerable subcontractors to larger firms in Turkey's segmented economy and labour market, a trend that *Schiller* would like to see reversed so that those employed in small firms can grow with the firm rather that treat the job there as a possible bridge to a job elsewhere in Turkey or abroad. However, until Turkey can more readily make credit available to small firms and end their vulnerable status as buffers for larger firms, the author believes that it will be difficult to make the small firms that easily create additional jobs long-term anchors for potential migrants.

Schiller hopes that the 1991 revisions to Turkey's vocational training system can increase the number of trained workers and thus accelerate economic growth. Under the law, non-governmental bodies are responsible for administering the training system, which is to be financed by the requirement that 20 per cent of each firm's gross revenues are to be spent on vocational training. These vocational training reforms are being combined with an extension of compulsory schooling from five to eight years, but *Schiller* notes that, in the mid-1980s, there were training slots for fewer than 10 per cent of the young people who may have wanted to be trained.

A plan for action

How can these lessons and experiences be translated into action? The Canadian International Development Agency (CIDA) is a bilateral assistance organization which recognizes that, in a world of fewer resources, there is a need to coordinate aid better, to target aid efforts in a way that produces demonstrable results, and to make the long-term commitment necessary to permit aid to achieve its goals. CIDA is one of the first national development agencies to try to bring together its short-term-oriented refugee relief programmes with long-term-oriented development aid. Although CIDA may be blazing the trail by reorganizing its assistance efforts, the results are not yet known.[6]

The UNHCR and the ILO have also begun to implement these recommendations. The UNHCR recognizes that attitudes towards refugees are changing, and that new governmental actors and NGOs must be involved in seeking durable solutions to refugee problems. The UNHCR has evolved from an agency that provided mainly humanitarian assistance to refugees after they were displaced into a more complex action agency that is cognizant of the fact that humanitarian relief cannot be separated from political initiatives to resolve the conflicts that produce refugees.

UNHCR also wants to take the lead in finding policies that prevent unwanted migration. As is well known, the establishment by the international community of safe havens for potential refugees inside Iraq set one precedent for preventing refugees from flowing across borders. UNHCR also recognizes that ODA can be used in a manner that encourages repatriation and reintegration – it is one thing to stop the conflict that produced refugees, and another to make the areas from which the refugees fled, economically attractive to those who return.

The ILO has embarked on an initiative in North African emigration countries designed to concentrate the ODA that is aimed at them on more rapid employment creation. Instead of donors unilaterally selecting the projects to be supported, the donor and recipient countries are jointly to determine how ODA will be used in the Maghreb countries to reduce the economic incentive to emigrate. Including the emigration factor in the assistance equation helps donor countries to comprehend some hard facts. For example, if the training provided by ODA is most useful in the donor country, or the product produced with ODA cannot be sold in the donor country, then the donor country's ODA may be increasing rather than reducing emigration pressures.

[6] Brem and Rawkins, 1992.

The view from 2030

If the recommendations made here – expansion of the refugee regime from "two Rs" to "four Rs", and use of increased development aid to make economic policies right in both immigration and emigration countries – were adopted, what types of migration pressure would probably exist in two generations from now?

The refugee specialists are unanimous in their conviction that there will continue to be refugees in need of help. The reasons for conflicts that generate refugees may change, but these commentators do not foresee a world without refugees. However, there may be fewer refugees if the world pays more attention to extirpating the root causes of conflict that generate them, and it may be easier to repatriate refugees if homes devastated by conflict are reconstructed with international assistance.

The economic development specialists are both more optimistic and more pessimistic. They are more optimistic in the sense that there are economic development scenarios that produce the growth needed to keep migrants at home – it has been done in southern Europe and east Asia, and aid can accelerate the process. However, the economists are pessimistic that such a development process will in fact be launched in the 1990s. There are many obstacles: not enough industrialized country aid; the aid available dispersed over too many areas or projects; or the aid makes it unnecessary for the recipient country to modify economic policies that slow down growth.

Reducing economically and politically motivated migration pressures will take money – large amounts of it. Compassion-fatigued publics in the industrialized countries have generally been more willing to provide short-term refugee relief than the longer-term assistance necessary to deal with the root causes of emigration. Making the case for more aid will not be easy. For example, if the argument for more aid is made by saying that, without aid, immigrants will arrive, the aid meant to curb illegal entries might also become an argument to close the legal door to immigrants.

The industrialized world appears to be breaking into three trading blocs, each of which has a different policy towards the aid and migration dilemma. In the EC, the policy seems to be aid not trade, or, in more memorable words, Polish workers seem to be preferred to Polish pork. In North America, the policy seems to be trade, not aid. The United States has historically granted little aid to Mexico, and it hopes to use NAFTA as a means eventually to reduce emigration pressures from there. In Asia, the policy has been investment, not aid or trade. Japan has traditionally moved labour-intensive operations overseas rather than import migrant workers, but it may have reached the limits of this strategy.

Observers in the year 2030 may note the recommendations made in the early 1990s for more aid as a means to reduce emigration pressure. They may also note that the industrialized countries seemed to look inward as economic growth slowed, and to focus on migration pressures only in their own backyards. As a result, as migration pressures rose, industrialized countries were forced to take ever more draconian steps to reduce unwanted entries. The world can avoid this fate if it is bold enough to act today.

Bibliography

Böhning, W.R. 1991. "Migration and immigration pressures in Western Europe", in *International Labour Review* (Geneva, ILO), Vol. 130, No. 4, pp. 445-458.
—; P.V. Schaeffer; Th. Straubhaar. 1991. *Migration pressure: What is it? What can one do about it?* (Geneva, ILO, WEP working paper), pp. 10-34.
Brem, M.; Ph. Rawkins. 1992. *Development assistance, migration and the Canadian agency: Linking policy, programmes and actions* (Geneva, ILO, WEP working paper).
Schaeffer, P.V. 1991. "A definition of migration pressure based on demand theory", in Böhning, Schaeffer and Straubhaar, 1991.
Zolberg, Aristide R.; Astri Suhrke; Sergio Aguayo. 1989. *Escape from violence: Conflict and the refugee crisis in the developing world* (New York, Oxford University Press).